FREE DVD   FREE DVD

Essential Test Tips DVD from Trivium Test Prep

Dear Customer,

Thank you for purchasing from Cirrus Test Prep! Whether you're looking to join the military, get into college, or advance your career, we're honored to be a part of your journey.

To show our appreciation (and to help you relieve a little of that test-prep stress), we're offering a **FREE** *Praxis Essential Test Tips DVD** by Cirrus Test Prep. Our DVD includes 35 test preparation strategies that will help keep you calm and collected before and during your big exam. All we ask is that you email us your feedback and describe your experience with our product. Amazing, awful, or just so-so: we want to hear what you have to say!

To receive your **FREE** *Praxis Essential Test Tips DVD*, please email us at 5star@cirrustestprep.com. Include "Free 5 Star" in the subject line and the following information in your email:

1. The title of the product you purchased.
2. Your rating from 1 – 5 (with 5 being the best).
3. Your feedback about the product, including how our materials helped you meet your goals and ways in which we can improve our products.
4. Your full name and shipping address so we can send your **FREE** *Praxis Essential Test Tips DVD*.

If you have any questions or concerns please feel free to contact us directly at 5star@cirrustestprep.com.

Thank you, and good luck with your studies!

* Please note that the free DVD is <u>not included</u> with this book. To receive the free DVD, please follow the instructions above.

CSET Social Science Test Prep:

800+ Practice Questions and Study Guide for the California Subject Examinations for Teachers

J.G. Cox

About the Authors

Alicia Chipman has taught history and social sciences in Chicago, Illinois, since 2003. Having worked with both high school and junior high school students, Alicia has developed curricula to prepare students for AP exams and entrance into the International Baccalaureate diploma program. She is now Student Teacher Supervisor at the Chicago Center for Urban Life and Culture. She obtained her master's degree in Educational Policy at the University of Illinois Urbana-Champaign in 2013.

Caroline Brennan spent several years on the front lines of multilateral diplomacy at the United Nations, working with the International Committee of the Red Cross (ICRC) in humanitarian affairs from 2007 – 2012. Previously, she studied international development, postcolonial theory, and history in Canada, Europe, and North Africa; she obtained her master's degree from the University of Pennsylvania in 2007, specializing in Middle Eastern history.

Sandy Thomson is currently an instructor at Wright Career College and at Park University. She previously worked as a social studies teacher in Tulsa, Oklahoma, in the Union Public Schools from 1997 – 2014, both online and in the traditional education program. She served as the Department Chair from 2009 – 2011.

Tom Brennan is adjunct faculty at Drexel University's Antoinette Westphal College of Media Arts and Design in Philadelphia, Pennsylvania, and an educator with 826NYC, a nonprofit writing center in Brooklyn, New York. He has a decade of editorial experience for print, digital, and web content.

Table of Contents

ONLINE RESOURCES   I

INTRODUCTION   III

ONE: US HISTORY   1

North America Before European
Contact 1

Colonial North America 7

Revolution and the Early
United States 17

Civil War, Expansion, and Industry ... 30

The Gilded Age and the
Progressive Era 39

The United States Becomes a
Global Power.. 46

The United States and
World War II 52

Postwar and Contemporary
United States 55

Political Conservatism, Social
Liberalism, and the Twenty-First
Century.. 61

Practice Questions Answer Key.......... 68

Check Your Understanding
Answer Key.. 71

TWO: WORLD HISTORY   73

Early Civilizations and the Great
Empires.. 73

World Religions.................................... 90

Feudalism through the Era of
Expansion.. 92

Armed Conflicts 121

Global Conflicts................................... 146

Post-Cold War World 175

Practice Questions Answer Key........ 183

Check Your Understanding
Answer Key.. 185

THREE: PRINCIPLES OF AMERICAN DEMOCRACY (CIVICS)   187

Political Theory 187

Constitutional Underpinnings
of the US Government 195

The Legislative Branch....................... 204

The Executive Branch 217

The Judicial Branch 225

Civil Liberties and Rights.................. 230

American Political Systems 234

Comparative Politics and
International Relations..................... 241

Practice Questions Answer Key........ 253

Check Your Understanding
Answer Key.. 258

FOUR: Principles of Geography 261

What is Geography?............................261
Human Characteristics of Place........279
Economic Patterns............................290
Political Geography..........................300
Human-Environment Interaction....308
Movement.......................................320
Practice Questions Answer Key........328
Check Your Understanding
Answer Key.....................................332

FIVE: Principles of Economics 333

Fundamental Economic Concepts...333
Supply and Demand 342
Elasticity...348
Factors of Production......................350
Behavior of Firms............................354
Types of Markets..............................360
Government Intervention 362
Macroeconomics..............................365
Practice Questions Answer Key........376
Check Your Understanding
Answer Key.....................................378

SIX: California History 381

California Geography 381
Pre-Columbian Period
Through the End of
Mexican Rule 382
From the Gold Rush to the
Present......................................389
Answer Key...404

SEVEN: CSET Practice Test 1 405

Answer Key...435

Online Resources

Cirrus Test Prep includes online resources with the purchase of this study guide to help you fully prepare for your CSET Social Science exam.

PRACTICE TEST

In addition to the practice test included in this book, we also offer an online exam. Since many exams today are computer based, practicing your test-taking skills on the computer is a great way to prepare.

REVIEW QUESTIONS

Need more practice? Our review questions use a variety of formats to help you memorize key terms and concepts.

FLASH CARDS

Cirrus Test Prep's flash cards allow you to review important terms easily on your computer or smartphone.

FROM STRESS TO SUCCESS

Watch "From Stress to Success," a brief but insightful YouTube video that offers the tips, tricks, and secrets experts use to score higher on the exam.

REVIEWS

Leave a review, send us helpful feedback, or sign up for Cirrus Test Prep promotions—including free books!

Access these materials at:
www.cirrustestprep.com/cset-social-science

Introduction

Congratulations on choosing to take the California Subject Examinations for Teachers (CSET) Social Science exam! By purchasing this book, you've taken the first step toward becoming a social studies teacher.

This guide will provide you with a detailed overview of the CSET, so you know exactly what to expect on test day. We'll take you through all the concepts covered on the test and give you the opportunity to test your knowledge with practice questions. Even if it's been a while since you last took a major test, don't worry; we'll make sure you're more than ready!

WHAT IS THE CSET?

CSET Series tests are designed by the California Commission on Teacher Credentialing (CTC) as a part of teaching licensure in California. Along with basic skills requirements and other certification tests, passing the CSET is a part of a prospective teacher's application for licensure. These tests are criterion referenced, standardized to measure your skills and knowledge in social sciences. For more information about credentialing in California, refer to http://www.ctcexams.nesinc.com/.

The social studies tests are interdisciplinary; they test your ability to understand relationships among fields in social studies. These include world history and geography, U.S. history and geography, civics, economics, and California history. You'll integrate your knowledge of all of these subjects in order to answer the questions correctly.

What's on the CSET?

The content in this guide will prepare you for the CSET: Social Science exam. CSET tests are divided into subtests, which you may choose to take one at a time or all at once. Each subtest is comprised of multiple-choice and constructed-response questions. For the constructed-response questions, you will typically be given a resource, such as a text, map, or graph, to discuss. This question type is intended to exercise your critical thinking skills and gauge your ability to interpret social science materials. Some constructed-response questions are extended and will require deeper and lengthier analysis, while others are focused and will demand a more concise answer.

Each subtest has a time limit that is indicated in the following table. If you choose to take all three subtests in one sitting, expect it to take 6 hours and 15 minutes. You are allowed to allocate your time within each subtest as you see fit. Be sure to allow yourself time to write answers to the constructed-response questions.

What's on the California Subject Examinations for Teachers (CSET) Social Science Exam?

Subtest	Domain	Number of multiple-choice questions	Number of constructed-response questions	Time Allotted
I	World History	35	2	
	World Geography	4	1	2 hours and 15 minutes
		39	3	
II	U.S. History	35	2	
	U.S. Geography	4	1	2 hours and 15 minutes
		39	3	
III	Civics	18	1	
	Economics	15	1	1 hour and 45 minutes
	California History	7	1	
		40	3	
Total		**118**	**9**	**6 hours and 15 minutes**

How is the CSET Scored?

On the CSET, the number of correctly answered questions are used to create your scaled score. The multiple-choice questions consist of seventy percent of your overall score, while the constructed-response essays comprise the other thirty percent.

Scores are scaled to a number in the range of 100–300. A passing score is 220 on each subtest. Each subtest is scored separately.

There is no penalty for guessing on the CSET, so be sure to eliminate answer choices and answer every question. If you still do not know the answer, guess; you may get it right! Keep in mind that some multiple-choice questions are experimental questions for the purpose of the CSET test-makers and will not count toward your overall score. However, since those questions are not indicated on the test, you must respond to every question.

Scores are reported within seven weeks of testing. You and any institution you designated at your registration will receive your passing status and scaled scores. For more information about scoring, refer to http://www.ctcexams.nesinc.com/.

How is the CSET Administered?

The CSET is administered as a computerized test. The CSET is available at testing centers across California.

On the day of your test, be sure to bring your admission ticket (which is provided when you register) and photo ID. At your testing center, your palm will be scanned and your picture will be taken. The testing facility will provide a locker outside of the testing room to store your personal belongings. You are allowed no personal effects in the testing area. Cell phones and other electronic, photographic, recording, or listening devices are not permitted in the testing center, and bringing those items may be cause for dismissal, forfeiture of your testing fees, and cancellation of your scores. For details on what to expect at your testing center, refer to the Pearson web site.

About Cirrus Test Prep

Cirrus Test Prep study guides are designed by current and former educators and are tailored to meet your needs as an incoming educator. Our guides offer all of the resources necessary to help you pass teacher certification tests across the nation.

Cirrus clouds are graceful, wispy clouds characterized by their high altitude. Just like cirrus clouds, Cirrus Test Prep's goal is to help educators "aim high" when it comes to obtaining their teacher certification and entering the classroom.

About This Guide

This guide will help you master the most important test topics and also develop critical test-taking skills. We have built features into our books to prepare you for your tests and increase your score. Along with a detailed summary of the test's format, content, and scoring, we offer an in-depth overview of the content knowledge required to pass the test. Our sidebars provide interesting information, highlight key concepts, and review content so that you can solidify your understanding of the exam's concepts. Test your knowledge with sample questions and detailed answer explanations in the text that help you think through the problems on the exam and two full-length practice tests that reflect the content and format of the CSET. We're pleased you've chosen Cirrus to be a part of your professional journey!

US History

North America Before European Contact

Before European colonization, diverse Native American societies controlled the continent. They would later come into economic and diplomatic contact—and military conflict—with European and US colonizers, forces, and settlers.

Civilizations of the Northeast, Midwest, Southeast, Great Plains, Southwest, and Pacific Northwest have played an important and ongoing role in North American history.

The Northeast

The **Iroquois** and **Algonquin** comprised the major Native American societies in the Northeast. Both would become important allies of the English and French, respectively, in future conflicts.

The Iroquois consisted of five tribes, or the Five Nations:

▶ Mohawk

▶ Seneca

▶ Cayuga

▶ Oneida

▶ Onondaga

According to tradition, the Five Nations made peace under the leadership of **Hiawatha**. They organized into the regionally powerful Iroquois Confederacy, bringing stability to the eastern Great Lakes region. The Tuscarora tribe eventually joined, and the union became known as the **Six Nations**.

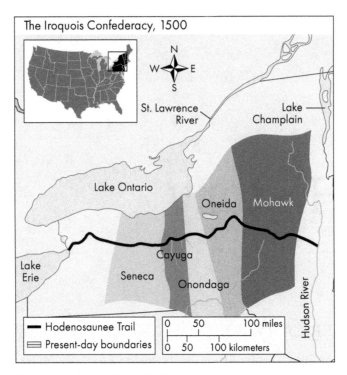

Figure 1.1. Iroquois Confederacy

The Iroquois were known for innovative agricultural and architectural techniques:

▶ farming maize

▶ constructing longhouses

▶ the three sisters tradition of farming, which became used throughout North America

In the three sisters system, maize, beans, and squash, are planted together. These crops complement each other, providing natural protection from pests and the elements, and increasing the availability of nitrogen necessary for growth.

While many Native American, or First Nations, people speak variants of the Algonquian language family, the **Algonquin** people themselves are distinct Indigenous peoples. They have historically been a majority in what is today Quebec and the Great Lakes region.

Active in the fur trade, the Algonquin developed important relationships with French colonizers and a rivalry with the Iroquois. Many Algonquin in French-controlled North America converted to Christianity.

THE MIDWEST

During early western expansion, the young United States would come into conflict with the Shawnee, Lenape, Kickapoo, Miami, and other tribes in present-day Ohio, Illinois, Indiana, and Michigan.

These Algonquin-speaking peoples eventually formed the Northwest Confederacy to fight the United States (see "Revolution and the Early United States," page 17).

▶ The **Shawnee** were based in the Ohio Valley. However, their presence extended as far as the present-day Carolinas and Georgia.

▷ While socially organized under a matrilineal system, the Shawnee had male kings and only men could inherit property.

▶ The **Lenape**, also a matrilineal society, originally lived in what is today New York, New Jersey, and the Delaware Valley.

▶ The **Kickapoo** were originally from the Great Lakes region but would move throughout present-day Indiana and Wisconsin.

HELPFUL HINT

The Lenape were eventually forced farther west by European colonization. The Lenape were respected by the Shawnee as their "grandfathers."

▶ The **Miami** tribe moved from Wisconsin to the Ohio Valley region, forming settled societies and farming maize. They also took part in the fur trade as it developed during European colonial times.

THE SOUTHEAST

Many major Indigenous peoples of southeastern North America descended from the **Mississippi Mound Builders,** or Mississippian cultures. These societies constructed mounds from around 2,100 to 1,800 years ago. It is thought that these mounds are the remains of burial tombs or the bases for temples.

Figure 1.2. Mississippi Mounds

The Chickasaw were a settled tribe originally based in what is today northern Mississippi and Alabama and western Kentucky and Tennessee. Like the Iroquois, the Chickasaw farmed in the sustainable three sisters tradition.

HELPFUL HINT

The Chickasaw and Choctaw would later form alliances with the British and French, fighting proxy wars on their behalf.

The Choctaw, whose origins trace to Mississippi, Louisiana, Alabama, and Florida, spoke a similar language to the Chickasaw. The Choctaw operated as a matriarchal society. Women were responsible for farming, gathering, and caring for the family. Men were primarily responsible for hunting and defense.

The **Creek**, or **Muscogee**, also descended from the Mississippian peoples, originated in modern Alabama, Georgia, South Carolina, and Florida. Speaking a language similar to those of the Chickasaw and Choctaw, the Creek would later participate in an alliance with these and other tribes—the Muscogee Confederacy— to engage the United States, which threatened tribal sovereignty.

Unlike the Chickasaw, Choctaw, and Creek, the **Cherokee** spoke (and speak) a language of the Iroquoian family. It is thought that they migrated south to their homeland in present-day Georgia sometime long before European contact, where they remained until they were forcibly removed in 1832.

Organized into seven clans, the Cherokee were also hunters and farmers, like other tribes in the region. They too would come into contact—and conflict—with European colonizers and the United States of America.

GREAT PLAINS

Farther west, tribes of the Great Plains would later come into conflict with American settlers as westward expansion continued.

Major Great Plains peoples included:

▶ **Sioux**

▶ **Cheyenne**

▶ **Apache**

▶ **Comanche**

▶ **Arapaho**

These tribes depended on **buffalo** for food and materials to create clothing, tools, and domestic items. They were nomadic or seminomadic, following the herds. Before horses were introduced to North America, hunters surrounded buffalo or frightened them off cliffs.

SOUTHWEST

In the Southwest, the **Navajo** lived in present-day Arizona, New Mexico, and Utah. The Navajo were descendants of the **Ancestral Pueblo,** or **Anasazi**, who had settled in the Four Corners area and are still known today for stone construction, including cliff dwellings.

Figure 1.3. Ancestral Pueblo Cliff Palace at Mesa Verde

The Navajo also practiced pastoralism. They lived in semi-permanent wooden homes called *hogans*, the doors of which face eastward to the rising sun. The Navajo had a less hierarchical structure than other Native American societies and engaged in fewer raids than the Apache to the north.

PACIFIC NORTHWEST

In the Pacific Northwest, fishing was a major source of sustenance, and Native American peoples created and used canoes to engage in the practice. First Nations of the Pacific Northwest also created totem poles, which are hand-carved monuments that depict histories.

The **Coast Salish**, whose language was widely spoken throughout the region, dominated the Puget

Sound and Olympic Peninsula area. Farther south, the **Chinook** controlled the coast at the Columbia River.

Ultimately, through both violent conflict and political means, Indigenous civilizations lost control of most of their territories and were forced onto reservations by the United States. Negotiations continue today over rights to land, opportunities, and reparations for past injustices.

PRACTICE QUESTIONS

1) **Which of the following best describes the political landscape of the Northeast before European contact?**

   A. Many small, autonomous tribes scattered throughout the region fought over land and resources.

   B. Several organized tribes controlled the region, including a major confederation.

   C. A disorganized political landscape would facilitate European colonial domination.

   D. The land was largely uninhabited, allowing easy exploitation of resources.

2) **Which of the following BEST illustrates tribal interactions before European contact?**

   A. Having been pushed westward by the Iroquois, the Lenape are just one example of forced migration in early North American history.

   B. The migration of the Miami from Ontario to the Ohio Valley shows how the Algonquian language family diffused throughout the continent.

   C. Indigenous peoples of the Great Plains forced the Pueblo to move south by consuming resources like buffalo.

   D. Ongoing conflict between the Northwest Algonquin Confederacy and the Iroquois Confederacy resulted in instability that forced tribes to move throughout the region.

3) **When Europeans arrived in North America, who was living in what is today the southeastern United States?**

   A. the Mississippi Mound Builders

   B. settled tribes who spoke Muskogean and Iroquoian languages

   C. the Chinook and Coast Salish

   D. the Ancestral Pueblo cliff dwellers

4) Tribes living in the Great Plains region were dependent on which of the following for survival?

    A.   buffalo for nutrition and materials for daily necessities

    B.   domesticated horses for hunting and warfare

    C.   access to rivers to engage in the fur trade

    D.   three sisters agriculture

5) How were the Navajo influenced by the Ancestral Pueblo, or Anasazi?

    A.   The Navajo continued the practice of pastoralism, herding horses throughout the Southwest.

    B.   The Navajo expanded control over land originally settled by the Ancestral Pueblo.

    C.   The Navajo began building cliff dwellings, improving on the Anasazi practice of living in rounded homes built from wood.

    D.   The Navajo developed a strictly hierarchical society, abandoning the looser organization of the Ancestral Pueblo.

COLONIAL NORTH AMERICA

The Americas were quickly colonized by Europeans after Christopher Columbus arrived in 1492. Throughout the sixteenth, seventeenth, eighteenth, and nineteenth centuries, the British, French, and Spanish all controlled major territories in North America.

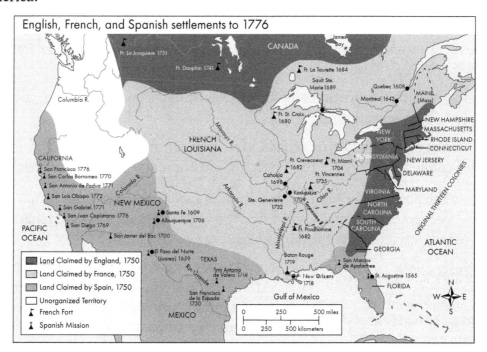

Figure 1.4. European Colonization of North America

SPAIN IN THE WEST AND SOUTHWEST

Spanish *conquistadors* explored what is today the southwestern United States. They claimed this land for Spain despite the presence of the Navajo and other civilizations. Prominent *conquistadors* included **Hernando de Soto** and **Francisco Vasquez de Coronado**.

Spanish colonization extended beyond controlling and settling land. Spain also intended to spread Christianity. **Missions** were established for this purpose in the West and Southwest, throughout Mexico, and parts of what are today Texas, New Mexico, Arizona, and California.

The Spanish government granted individual European settlers *encomiendas* to establish settlements regardless of the existing local population. Under the European legal system, encomiendas allowed the holder to ranch or mine the land. Colonists used encomiendas to demand tribute and forced labor from Indigenous peoples, essentially enslaving them.

Throughout the Southwest, Spanish colonizers encountered resistance. In 1680, the **Pueblo Revolt**, led by the leader **Popé**, resulted in a two-year loss of land for Spain. Sometimes referred to as part of the ongoing **Navajo Wars**, this revolt included several Native American tribes.

(In the literature and in some primary sources, *pueblo* is often used interchangeably with "Indian" to refer to Native Americans; here, the term refers to Navajo, Apache, and other tribes that came together to resist Spanish hegemony in the region.)

Spain eventually reconquered the territory, subjugating the peoples living in the region to colonial rule.

The conflict led to friction among Spanish thinkers over the means, and even the notion, of colonization.

▶ The priest **Bartolomé de las Casas**, appalled at the oppression of colonization, argued for the rights and humanity of Native Americans.

▶ The philosopher **Juan de Sepulveda** argued that Indigenous peoples needed the rule and "civilization" brought by Spain, justifying their cruel treatment at the hands of colonizers.

DID YOU KNOW?

De las Casas lived in the Americas and had firsthand experience with the brutal consequences of colonization. **Juan de Sepulveda** never left Spain.

Despite ongoing conflict between Native Americans and Spanish colonizers, there was social mixing among the people. Intermarriage and fraternization resulted in a stratified society based on race. These racial identities extended in North America and throughout Spanish and Portuguese holdings in the Americas.

According to the *casta* system, an individual's place in societal hierarchy was determined by their race. White people were considered the most privileged. The term *mestizo* referred to people with mixed white European and Indigenous American backgrounds. They, in turn, were more privileged than the Indigenous American peoples.

Indigenous people in Mexico and the Southwest suffered under colonization. Countless people were killed through forced labor and European diseases like **smallpox**, to which they had limited immunity. To exploit these resource-rich lands, Spain (and eventually, other European countries) turned to enslaving African people.

In the trans-Atlantic slave trade, people were kidnapped from Africa to be enslaved in the Western Hemisphere. Torn from their homes and families, they were forced to travel across the Atlantic Ocean in brutal conditions. Upon arriving in the Americas, African people were enslaved in mines and plantations. They were subject to horrific conditions and not compensated. They were considered property, not people.

French Hegemony in the Midwest and Northeast

French explorers such as **Samuel de Champlain** reached what is today Quebec, Vermont, upstate New York, and the eastern Great Lakes region as early as the seventeenth century. While the explorer **Jacques Cartier** had claimed New France (present-day Quebec) for France in the sixteenth century, Champlain founded Quebec City and consolidated control of France's colonies in North America in 1608.

Unlike Spain, which sought not only profit, but also to settle the land and convert Native Americans to Christianity, France prioritized trade.

Beaver pelts and fur from game plentiful in the Northeast were in great demand in Europe. Eventually, France would control much of the Great Lakes and the Mississippi region through Louisiana and New Orleans—valuable trade routes.

French colonists were more likely to establish agreements and intermarry with local Native Americans than other European powers. The term *métis* described mixed-race persons.

Civilizational Contributions of Enslaved Africans

The civilizational contributions of enslaved African people and their descendants to North American society were many and long-lasting. They included the introduction and production of important crops like rice and okra in the Gulf Coast area and American foods enjoyed today like peanut butter and gumbo.

Enslaved Africans and Black Americans also brought traditional music to North America that would evolve into blues music (and later, jazz, rock, and hip hop).

Some West African art and dances evolved into the festive practices seen today in New Orleans and Louisiana during Mardi Gras.

ENGLAND AND THE THIRTEEN COLONIES

In the sixteenth century, Sir Walter Raleigh established the Roanoke colony in present-day Virginia. Roanoke disappeared by 1590, but interest in colonization reemerged as **joint-stock companies** sought royal charters to privately develop colonies on the North American Atlantic coast. The first established colony, **Jamestown**, was also located in Virginia, which became so profitable that the Crown took it over as a colony in 1624.

The colonial leader **John Rolfe** introduced **tobacco** to Virginia farmers, which became the primary cash crop. Tobacco required plantation farming. At first, Virginia used **indentured servants**, who were freed from servitude after a period of work. Some of these indentured servants were from Africa, and in 1660 the **House of Burgesses**, which governed Virginia, declared that all Black people would be enslaved for life.

DID YOU KNOW?

Spanish and French settlers were usually single men looking to trade and were more likely to intermarry with local people. On the other hand, English colonists brought their families and settled in North America, with the goal of establishing agricultural settlements.

The South became increasingly socially stratified, with enslaved persons, indentured servants, landowners, and other classes. The Carolinas and Georgia would also become important sources of tobacco and rice.

South Carolina institutionalized slavery in North America for the next two centuries by adopting the slave codes from Barbados.

While Jamestown and Virginia were comprised of diverse populations of settlers, businessmen, indentured servants, and enslaved people, the demographics were different farther north. In New England, **Separatists**—members of the Church of England who believed it had strayed too far from its theological roots—arrived in North America seeking more religious freedom.

CHECK YOUR UNDERSTANDING #2

List some major exports from colonial North America.

The first group of Separatists, the Pilgrims, arrived on the *Mayflower* in 1620. They drew up the **Mayflower Compact**, guaranteeing government by the consent of the governed.

The Pilgrims were later joined by the **Puritans**, who had been persecuted in England. The colonial Puritan leader **John Winthrop** envisioned the Massachusetts Bay Colony in the model of the biblical *City upon a Hill*, rooted in unity, peace, and what would be a free, democratic spirit; its capital was Boston. These philosophies would later inform the American Revolution.

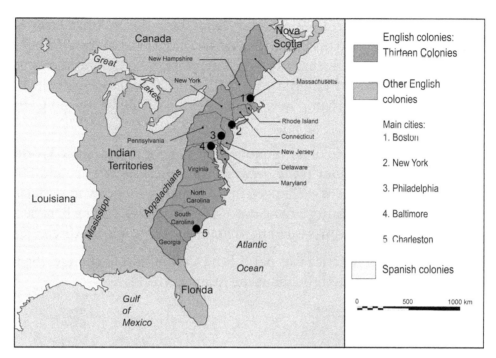

Figure 1.5. The Thirteen Colonies

Despite differences from the South, social stratification existed in New England as well. According to Puritan belief, wealth and success showed that one was a member of the **elect** (privileged by God). Poorer farmers were generally tenant farmers. They did not own land and rarely made a profit.

The mid-Atlantic region, with fertile lands and natural harbors, was well suited for agricultural crops and trade. It was also home to concepts of religious tolerance.

The Dutch settlement of New Amsterdam became an important port and trading post. In 1664, England took control of this settlement under terms of surrender from the Dutch that included religious toleration. The settlement was renamed New York.

In 1682, the Quaker **William Penn** founded the city of Philadelphia based on tolerance. Penn had been given the land—later called Pennsylvania—by the British Crown to settle a debt.

Pennsylvania, New Jersey, and Delaware were all founded in the Quaker spirit as part of Penn's **Holy Experiment** to develop settlements based on tolerance.

HELPFUL HINT

Slavery was practiced in the northern colonies but not as widely as in the southern colonies. The northern land and climate did not support plantation agriculture. This led to far less demand for slaves than in the south, where labor was needed to harvest tobacco and later, cotton.

DID YOU KNOW?

Quakerism promotes equality, community, nonviolence, conflict resolution, and tolerance. These tenets are at the root of the name of Philadelphia, the "City of Brotherly Love."

Earlier in the region, in 1649, the **Maryland Toleration Act** had ensured the political rights of all Christians there, the first law of its kind in the colonies. This was due, in part, to the influence of **Lord Baltimore**, who had been charged by Charles I to found a part of Virginia (to be called Maryland) as a Catholic haven. This helped the king maintain power in an England divided between Catholics and Protestants.

The North American colonial economy was part of the **Atlantic World** and participated in the **triangular trade** between the Americas, Africa, and Europe. Enslaved African people were exchanged in the Americas for raw materials. Raw materials were shipped to Europe to be processed into goods for the benefit of the colonial powers, and sometimes exchanged for enslaved people in Africa.

In this way, North America was part of the **Columbian Exchange**, the intersection of goods and people throughout the Atlantic World.

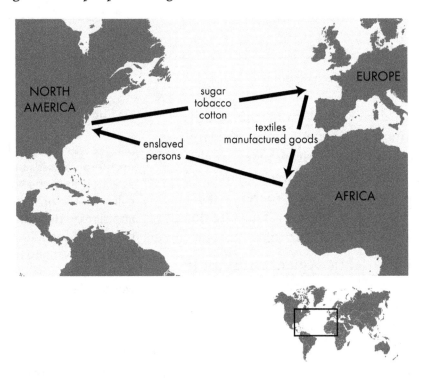

Figure 1.6. Triangular Trade

Exploitation of colonial resources and the dynamics of the Columbian Exchange supported **mercantilism**, the prevailing economic system: European powers controlled their economies to increase global power. Ensuring a beneficial **balance of trade** is essential; the country must export more than it imports.

An unlimited supply of desirable goods obtainable at a low cost made this possible, and the colonies offered just that. In this way,

HELPFUL HINT

Long-term consequences of mercantilism included the decline of feudalism and the rise of capitalism.

European powers would be able to maintain their reserves of gold and silver rather than spending them on imports.

Furthermore, countries with access to more gold and silver—notably, Spain, which gained control of mines in Central America and Mexico—exponentially increased their wealth. This dramatically changed the balance of economic power in Europe.

THE RISE OF COLONIAL DISCONTENT

Throughout the chaos in England during the **English Civil War**, policy toward the colonies had been one of **salutary neglect**, allowing them great autonomy. However, stability in England and an emerging culture of independence in the Thirteen Colonies caught the attention of the British Crown. To ensure that the British mercantilist system was not threatened, England passed the **Navigation Acts** in 1651 and 1660. These restricted colonial trade with any other countries.

An early sign of colonial discontent, **Bacon's Rebellion** in 1676 against Governor Berkeley of Virginia embodied the growing resentment of landowners, who wanted to increase their own profits rather than redirect revenue to Britain.

Following the 1688 Glorious Revolution in England, many colonists thought they might gain more autonomy. However, self-rule remained limited.

American colonists were also increasingly influenced by Enlightenment thought. John Locke's *Second Treatise* was published in 1689. Critical of absolute monarchy, it became popular in the colonies.

Locke argued for **republicanism**, the idea that the people must come together to create a government for the protection of themselves and their property, thereby giving up some of their natural rights. However, should the government overstep its bounds, the people have the right to overthrow it and replace it.

> **HELPFUL HINT**
>
> Locke's concepts of government by consent of the governed and the natural rights of persons eventually became the bedrock of US government.

FRENCH AND ENGLISH CONFLICTS IN NORTH AMERICA

Meanwhile, North America also served as a battleground for France and England. These countries were already in conflict in Europe and elsewhere.

In the mid-seventeenth century, the Algonquin (allied with the French and Dutch) and Iroquois (allied with the English), fought the **Beaver Wars** for control over the fur trade in the northeastern part of the continent.

Given the British alliance with the Iroquois, England would also refer to the

> **HELPFUL HINT**
>
> The Iroquois would ultimately push the Shawnee and other tribes associated with the Algonquin from the Northeast and Great Lakes area farther west to present-day Wisconsin.

Beaver Wars and Iroquois control over the Northeast (today, the Ohio Valley and Great Lakes region) to assert their own claim over this area, which was called the **Northwest Territories**.

Not only did France clash with Britain in the northern part of the continent, but the two colonial powers came into conflict in the South as well. France had come to control the vast **Louisiana Territory**, including the important port city of New Orleans. In 1736, French forces, allied with the Choctaw, attacked the English-allied Chickasaw as part of France's attempts to strengthen its hold on the southeastern part of North America in the **Chickasaw Wars**.

The Seven Years' War broke out in Europe in 1756; this conflict between the British and French in North America was known as the **French and Indian War**. War efforts in North America accelerated under the British leader **William Pitt the Elder**, who invested heavily in defeating the French beyond Europe (see "World History" for details).

Ultimately, Britain emerged as the dominant power in North America. France had allied with the Algonquin, traditional rivals of the British-allied Iroquois. However, following defeats by strong colonial military leaders like George Washington and despite its strong alliances and long-term presence on the continent, France eventually surrendered.

Britain gained control of French territories in North America—as well as Spanish Florida—in the 1763 **Treaty of Paris** which ended the Seven Years' War.

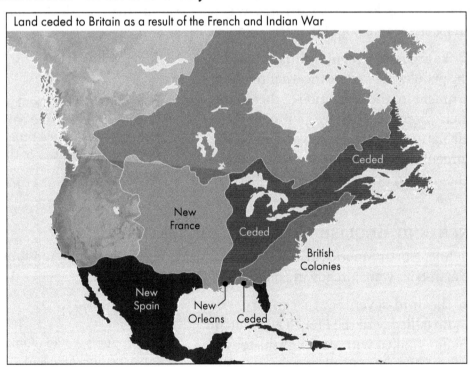

Figure 1.7. British Gains in the French and Indian War

Following another period of salutary neglect in the colonies, in 1754, French and English conflict exploded once again in North America as fighting broke out in the Ohio Valley. The British government organized with North American colonial leaders to meet at Albany. **Benjamin Franklin** helped organize the defensive Albany Plan of Union and argued for this plan in his newspaper, the *Pennsylvania Gazette*, using the famous illustration *Join, or Die*. However, the Crown worried that this plan allowed for too much colonial independence, adding to tensions between the Thirteen Colonies and England.

Figure 1.8. Join, or Die.

In the mid-eighteenth century, a sense of religious fervor called the **Great Awakening** spread throughout the colonies. People broke beyond the confines of traditional Christianity, attracted to traveling preachers and public pronouncements of religious fervor.

▶ The Great Awakening helped develop a more singularly North American religious culture.

▶ It also created a divide between traditional European Christianity and emerging North American faiths.

DID YOU KNOW?

Many universities, including some Ivy League schools, were founded during this time to train ministers.

PRACTICE QUESTIONS

6) **What were the differences between Spanish and French colonization in North America?**

A. Both intermarried with Native Americans; however, the Spanish took a more aggressive approach in spreading Christianity.

B. Spain sought accord and agreement with Native Americans, while France forced marriages as part of settling the land, resulting in the mixed-race métis class.

C. France colonized the Southwest; Spain colonized the Northeast and Midwest.

D. France imported enslaved Africans as part of the Triangular Trade in order to support New France, while Spain mainly exploited local Native American tribes, forcing them to perform labor and essentially enslaving them.

7)   **How did geography contribute to differences between northern and southern colonies on the Atlantic coast of North America?**

A.   Climate and terrain in the south supported plantation agriculture.

B.   Numerous natural ports in the southern colonies led to the development of major cities there.

C.   Mountainous terrain prevented major settlement in northern colonies.

D.   Small farmers in the north grew cotton and tobacco, thanks to the mild climate.

8)   **Which of the following was a factor in stirring up colonial discontent?**

A.   balance of trade

B.   mercantilism

C.   John Locke's *Second Treatise*

D.   the Columbian Exchange

9)   **Upon what premise were Mid-Atlantic colonies like Pennsylvania, Delaware, and New Jersey founded?**

A.   a beacon of unity and humanity, reminiscent of John Winthrop's *City Upon a Hill*

B.   tolerance, as part of William Penn's *Great Experiment*

C.   profit, in accordance with their roots in joint-stock companies seeking profit from the land through royal charters

D.   conquest and conversion, in order to take land from Native American tribes and convert those original inhabitants to Christianity

10)   **How did the British and French rivalry spill over into North America?**

A.   While Britain and France were often on opposite sides in European conflict, they found common ground against Native Americans in North America.

B.   European conflicts between Catholics and Protestants affected Catholic French and Protestant English settlers; related violence from the Hundred Years' War broke out between them as a result.

C.   These European powers engaged in proxy wars, supporting the Iroquois and Algonquin, respectively, as well as the Chickasaw and Choctaw, in jockeying for control of land in the Great Lakes and southeastern regions of North America.

D.   France and Britain formed an alliance to prevent Spain from moving eastward on the continent.

REVOLUTION AND THE EARLY UNITED STATES

THE AMERICAN REVOLUTION

Though victorious in the French and Indian War, Britain had gone into debt. Furthermore, there were concerns that the colonies required a stronger military presence following **Pontiac's Rebellion** in 1763. The leader of the **Ottawa** people, Pontiac, led a revolt that extended from the Great Lakes region through the Ohio Valley to Virginia. This land had been ceded to England from France, with no input from Indigenous residents.

The Ottawa people and other Native Americans resisted further British settlement and fought back against colonial oppression. To make peace, **King George III** signed the **Proclamation of 1763**, an agreement not to settle land west of the Appalachians. Still, much settlement continued in practice.

> **CHECK YOUR UNDERSTANDING #3**
>
> Why did Pontiac lead resistance? What was the consequence of Pontiac's Rebellion?

As a result of the war and subsequent unrest, Britain once again discarded its colonial policy of salutary neglect. In desperate need of cash, the Crown sought ways to increase its revenue from the colonies.

King George III enforced heavy taxes and restrictive acts in the colonies to generate income for the Crown and punish disobedience.

Table 1.1. Controversial Acts and Taxes

Act	Purpose	Consequences
Sugar Act of 1764 (expansion of the Molasses Act of 1733)	taxed sugar and molasses	• sugar, produced in the British West Indies, was widely consumed in the Thirteen Colonies • colonists were heavily impacted
Quartering Act of 1765	required colonists to provide shelter to British troops stationed in the region	• increased resentment among colonials forced to provide shelter to British troops • protests against this act led to the 1770 Boston Massacre
Stamp Act of 1765	taxed all documents by requiring a costly stamp	• first direct tax on the colonists • seen as a violation of rights because they were not represented in British parliament
Townshend Acts	empowered customs officers to search colonists' homes for forbidden goods with **writs of assistance**	• enacted in response to actions of the Sons and Daughters of Liberty • increased resentment • repealed in 1770

continued on next page

Table 1.1. Controversial Acts and Taxes (continued)

Act	Purpose	Consequences
Tea Act of 1773	taxed tea, a popular beverage	• led to Boston Tea Party, a protest when colonists tossed tea from ships into the harbor
Intolerable Acts of 1773	• closed Boston Harbor • put Massachusetts firmly under British control	• colonial leaders held First Continental Congress

Patrick Henry protested the Stamp Act in the Virginia House of Burgesses. In Britain, however, it was argued that the colonists had **virtual representation** and so the Act—and others to follow—were justified.

As a result, colonists began boycotting British goods and engaging in violent protest. **Samuel Adams** led the **Sons and Daughters of Liberty** in violent acts against tax collectors. He led the **Committees of Correspondence**, which distributed anti-British propaganda.

Protests against the Quartering Act in Boston led to the **Boston Massacre** in 1770, when British troops fired on a crowd of protesters. By 1773, in a climate of continued unrest driven by the Committees of Correspondence, colonists protested the latest taxes on tea levied by the **Tea Act** in the famous **Boston Tea Party** by dressing as Native Americans and tossing tea off a ship in Boston Harbor. In response, the government passed the **Intolerable Acts**, closing Boston Harbor and bringing Massachusetts back under direct royal control.

Subsequently, colonial leaders met in Philadelphia at the **First Continental Congress** in 1774. They issued the *Declaration of Rights and Grievances*, presenting colonial concerns to King George III, who ignored it.

Violent conflict began on April 19, 1775, at **Lexington and Concord**. American militiamen (**minutemen**) gathered to resist British efforts to seize weapons and arrest rebels in Concord. On June 17, 1775, Americans fought the British at the **Battle of Bunker Hill**. Despite American losses, the number of casualties the minutemen inflicted on the British

---

DID YOU KNOW?

The famous phrase "no taxation without representation" originated in John Dickinson's Letters from a Farmer in Pennsylvania and Samuel Adams's **Massachusetts Circular Letter**, which argued for the repeal of the Townshend Acts.

DID YOU KNOW?

King George III hired Hessian mercenaries from Germany to supplement British troops. The addition of foreign fighters only increased resentment in the colonies, creating a stronger sense of independence from Britain.

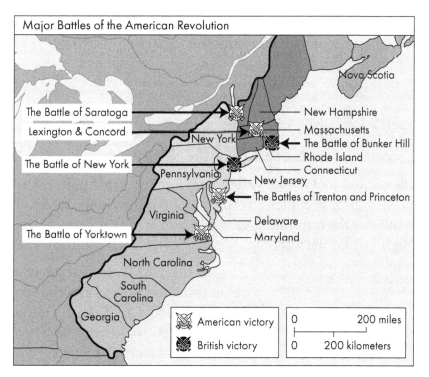

Figure 1.9. Major Battles of the American Revolution

caused the king to declare that the colonies were in rebellion. He deployed troops, and the Siege of Boston began.

In May 1775, the **Second Continental Congress** met at Philadelphia to debate the way forward. Debate between the wisdom of continued efforts at compromise and negotiations versus declaring independence continued.

The king ignored two pleas from the Second Continental Congress:

- *the Declaration of the Causes and Necessities of Taking Up Arms*, which asked him to again consider the colonies' objections

- the **Olive Branch Petition**, which sought compromise and an end to hostilities

> **HELPFUL HINT**
>
> In early 1776, **Thomas Paine** published his pamphlet *Common Sense*. Informed by Locke's concepts of natural rights and republicanism, it popularized the notion of rebellion against Britain.

By summer of 1776, the Continental Congress agreed on the need to break from Britain. On July 4 of that year, it declared the independence of the United States of America and issued the **Declaration of Independence**, drafted mainly by **Thomas Jefferson** and heavily influenced by Locke.

Still, Americans were divided over independence:

- **Patriots** were in favor of independence.

- Tories remained loyal to England.

General George Washington had been appointed head of the Continental Army. He led a largely unpaid and unprofessional body of troops. Despite early losses, Washington gained ground due to:

▶ strong leadership

▶ superior knowledge of the land

▶ support from France, Spain, and the Netherlands

The tide turned in 1777 at **Valley Forge**, when Washington and his army survived the bitterly cold winter to overcome British military forces. The British people did not favor the war, voting so in parliament. The incoming parliamentary majority sought to end the war.

HELPFUL HINT
The American Revolution would go on to inspire revolution around the world.

In the 1783 **Treaty of Paris**, the United States was recognized as a country. It agreed to repay debts to British merchants and provide safety to British loyalists who wished to remain in North America.

THE CREATION OF US GOVERNMENT

Joy in the victory over Great Britain was short-lived. Fearful of tyranny, the Second Continental Congress had provided for only a weak central government by adopting the **Articles of Confederation** to organize the Thirteen Colonies—now states—as a loosely united country.

▶ A unicameral central government had limited powers:

▷ wage war

▷ negotiate treaties

▷ borrow money

▶ States could be taxed, but not citizens.

▶ Westward expansion and the establishment of new states was planned.

HELPFUL HINT
The Northwest Ordinances effectively nullified King George III's Proclamation of 1763, which promised Native Americans that colonization would cease in the Ohio Valley region. Tensions would lead to the Northwest Indian Wars.

The **Northwest Ordinances** of 1787 prohibited slavery north of the Ohio River. Areas with at least 60,000 people could apply for statehood.

However, it soon became clear that the Articles of Confederation were not strong enough to keep the nation united.

The US was heavily in debt. Currency was weak and taxes were high. In Massachusetts,

Daniel Shays led a rebellion. During **Shays' Rebellion**, indebted farmers protested debtor's prisons and aimed to prevent courts from seizing their property.

Such debt and disorganization made the new country appear weak and vulnerable. Furthermore, if the United States were to remain one country, it needed a stronger federal government.

Alexander Hamilton and **James Madison** called for a **Constitutional Convention** to write a constitution as the foundation of a stronger federal government.

Federalists believed in the **separation of powers**, republicanism, and a strong federal government. Madison, Hamilton, and John Adams were important Federalists.

To determine the exact structure of the government, delegates at the convention settled on the **Great Compromise**, a **bicameral legislature**. Two plans had been presented:

▶ The **New Jersey Plan benefitted smaller states.** It proposed a legislature composed of an equal number of representatives from each state.

▶ The **Virginia Plan** benefitted larger states. It proposed a legislature composed of representatives proportional to the population of each state.

Enslaved Black Americans had no place in the political process. Still, they were represented in a state's population to determine that state's number of representatives in Congress. States with large enslaved populations accounted for those persons with the **Three-Fifths Compromise**, which counted an enslaved Black American as three-fifths of a person.

Both plans were adopted, and a bicameral legislature was created:

▶ The **House of Representatives** followed the Virginia Plan model.

▶ The **Senate** followed the New Jersey Plan model.

Anti-Federalists, like **Thomas Jefferson,** called for even more limitations on the power of the federal government. They were unsatisfied with the separation of powers provided for in the Constitution.

In response, Madison introduced a list of guarantees of American freedoms in the first ten amendments to the Constitution: The **Bill of Rights**. The Federalists considered this a concession to the Anti-Federalists.

To convince the states to ratify the Constitution, Hamilton, Madison, and John Jay wrote the *Federalist Papers*, articulating the benefits of federalism. Likewise, the Bill of Rights helped convince the hesitant.

HELPFUL HINT

The Anti-Federalists would later become the **Democratic-Republican Party** and eventually, the Democratic Party that exists today.

In 1791, the Constitution was ratified. **George Washington** was elected president, with John Adams serving as vice president. Washington appointed Alexander Hamilton as Secretary of the Treasury and Thomas Jefferson as Secretary of State.

EARLY AMERICAN DIPLOMACY AND LEGISLATION

Hamilton prioritized currency stabilization and the repayment of debts. He also believed in establishing a national bank—the **Bank of the United States (BUS)**. President Washington signed the BUS into law in 1791.

Hamilton also favored tariffs and excise (sales) taxes. However, **Democratic-Republicans (Anti-Federalists)** vehemently opposed these. In 1795, rebellion against the excise tax on whiskey broke out. The **Whiskey Rebellion** indicated unrest in the young country and was put down by militia.

Meanwhile, the French Revolution had begun in Europe. However, President Washington issued the **Neutrality Proclamation** in 1793. Despite this action, British and French ships accosted American ships in the Atlantic and forced American sailors into naval service (**impressment**). Several treaties and events marked this era.

Table 1.2. Early American Incidents in Foreign Relations

Major Diplomatic Event	Causes and Consequences
Neutrality Proclamation (1793)	• issued by President Washington • intended to avoid entanglement in the French Revolution and related conflict
Jay's Treaty (1794)	• failed attempt by John Jay to stop impressment of US soldiers in the Atlantic by France and Britain • unsuccessful and unpopular • removed British forts in the western frontier
Pinckney's Treaty (1795)	• treaty with Spain negotiated by Thomas Pinckney • secured US rights on the Mississippi River and Port of New Orleans • defined US border with Spanish Florida • diplomatic success • ratified by all thirteen states • also known as Treaty of San Lorenzo

Major Diplomatic Event	Causes and Consequences
XYZ Affair (1797)	• US diplomats traveled to Paris to negotiate an end to French seizures of US ships • France asked US diplomats for bribes to meet and treated them poorly • resulted in undeclared conflict in the Caribbean until the Convention of 1800
Embargo Act (1807)	• an effort to avoid conflict with European powers at war • only damaged the US economy
Non-Intercourse Act (1809)	• repealed Embargo Act • allowed trade with foreign countries besides Britain and France

The ongoing **Northwest Indian Wars** continued conflict with the Shawnee, Lenape, Kickapoo, Miami, and other tribes in the Ohio region. Following the defeat of allied tribes at the **Battle of Fallen Timbers** in 1794, the Americans gained more territory in Ohio and Indiana.

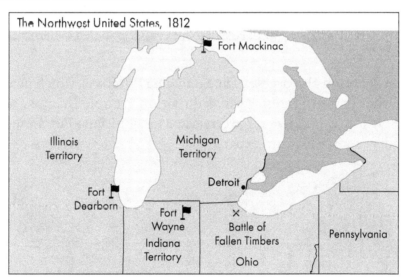

Figure 1.10. Battle of Fallen Timbers

In President Washington's **Farewell Address**, he recommended the United States follow a policy of neutrality in international affairs, setting a precedent for early American history. Vice President John Adams, a Federalist, became the second president.

During the Adams administration, the Federalists passed the harsh **Alien and Sedition Acts**.

Table 1.3. Alien and Sedition Acts

Alien Act	Sedition Act
• allowed the president to deport "enemy aliens"	
	• prohibited criticism of the president
• increased the residency requirements for citizenship	• prohibited criticism of Congress

Divisions between the Federalists and the Democratic-Republicans were deeper than ever. Nevertheless, Thomas Jefferson was elected to the presidency in 1801 in a nonviolent transfer of power.

FOUNDATIONS OF WESTWARD EXPANSION

President Jefferson took several actions pleasing Anti-Federalists:

▶ shrank the federal government

▶ repealed the Alien and Sedition Acts

▶ enacted economic policies that favored small farmers and landowners

This contrasted with his predecessors' Federalist policies, which supported big business and cities.

However, Jefferson also oversaw the **Louisiana Purchase**, which nearly doubled the size of the United States. This acquisition troubled some Democratic-Republicans, who saw it as federal overreach. The Louisiana Purchase would be a major step forward in westward expansion.

Spanish Territory

Louisiana Purchase

United States of America

Figure 1.11. Louisiana Purchase

Jefferson hoped to find an all-water route to the Pacific Ocean via the Missouri River. He dispatched **Meriwether Lewis** and **William Clark** to explore the western frontier of the territory. This route did not exist, but Lewis and Clark returned with a deeper knowledge of the territory the US had come to control.

WAR OF 1812

British provocation at sea and in the northwest led to the **War of 1812**. Congress declared war to:

▶ protect the US from chaotic trade practices

▶ end the impressment of American sailors

▶ expand US territory

Growing nationalism in the United States also pressured Madison into pushing for war after the **Battle of Tippecanoe**. In this Indiana battle, **General William Henry Harrison** fought the **Northwest Confederacy**, a group of tribes led by the Shawnee leader **Tecumseh**.

The Shawnee, Lenape, Miami, Kickapoo, and others had come together to form the Northwest Confederacy.

▶ They wanted to maintain independent territory at the northwest of the United States (present-day Indiana and region).

▶ They also followed Tecumseh's brother **Tenskwatawa**, who was considered a prophet.

Despite the Northwest Confederacy's alliance with Britain, the United States prevailed.

The War of 1812 resulted in no real gains or losses for either the Americans or the British. Still, the United States had successfully defended itself as a country and reaffirmed its independence. Patriotism ran high.

Figure 1.12. Tecumseh

THE ERA OF GOOD FEELINGS AND THE SECOND GREAT AWAKENING

During the presidency of **James Monroe, a** strong sense of public identity and nationalism grew. This was called the **Era of Good Feelings**. Religious revival became popular. People turned from Puritanism and predestination to Baptist and Methodist faiths, among others, following revolutionary preachers and movements. This period was called the **Second Great Awakening**. In art and culture, romanticism and reform movements elevated the "common man," a trend that would continue into the presidency of Andrew Jackson.

The country would again struggle economically. The **Tariff of 1816 was meant to boost domestic manufacturing**. But it divided northern industrialists from southern landowners. Industrialists believed in nurturing American industry, whereas southern landowners depended on exporting cotton and tobacco for profit.

Later, following the establishment of the **Second Bank of the United States (BUS)**, the **Panic of 1819** erupted when the government cut credit following overspeculation on western lands. The BUS wanted payment from state banks in hard currency, or **specie**. Western banks foreclosed on western farmers, and farmers lost their land.

MANIFEST DESTINY AND THE MONROE DOCTRINE

With the Louisiana Purchase, the country had almost doubled in size. The idea of **manifest destiny** prevailed. According to manifest destiny, it was the fate of the United States to expand westward and settle the continent.

Also in 1819, the United States purchased Florida from Spain in the **Adams-Onis Treaty**. The **Monroe Doctrine**, President James Monroe's policy that the Western Hemisphere was "closed" to further European colonization or exploration, asserted US hegemony in the region.

Westward expansion triggered questions about the expansion of slavery. Southern states depended on enslaving people to maintain the plantation economy. But slavery was increasingly condemned in the North. Furthermore, the Second Great Awakening had fueled the **abolitionist** movement, which sought to abolish slavery.

In debating the nature of westward expansion, Kentucky senator **Henry Clay** worked out a compromise. The **Missouri Compromise**, also known as the **Compromise of 1820**, allowed Missouri to join the union as a slave state, but provided that any other states north of the **thirty-sixth parallel (36°30')** would not permit slavery. Maine would also join the nation as a free state. However, more tension and compromises over the nature of slavery in new states were to come.

Demographics were changing throughout the early nineteenth century. Technological advances such as the **cotton gin** had allowed exponential increases in cotton production. The result: more persons were enslaved than ever before, bringing more urgency to the issue of slavery.

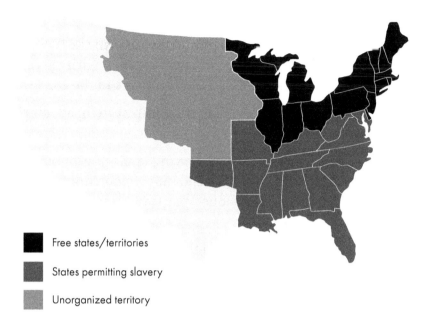

Free states/territories

States permitting slavery

Unorganized territory

Figure 1.13. Missouri Compromise

Other technological advances like the **railroads** and **steamships** were speeding up westward expansion and improving trade throughout the continent. A large-scale **market economy** was emerging.

With early industrialization and changing concepts following the Second Great Awakening, women were playing a larger role in society, even though they could not vote.

In addition, **immigration** from Europe to the United States was increasing—mainly Irish Catholic and German immigrants. Reactionary **nativist** movements like the **Know-Nothing Party** feared the influx of non-Anglo Europeans, particularly Catholics. Discrimination was widespread, especially against the Irish.

Most states had extended voting rights to white men who did not own land or substantial property: **universal manhood suffrage**. Elected officials would increasingly come to better reflect the electorate.

During the election of 1824, Andrew Jackson ran against **John Quincy Adams**, Henry Clay, and William Crawford. The candidates were all Republicans (from the Democratic-Republican party); John Quincy Adams won.

By 1828, divisions within the party had Jackson and his supporters, then known as Democrats, in favor of states' rights and supporting small farmers and the inhabitants of rural areas. Clay and his supporters became known as **National Republicans** and, later, **Whigs**, a splinter group of the Democratic-Republicans which supported business and urbanization; they also had federalist leanings. The **two-party system** had emerged.

JACKSONIAN DEMOCRACY

Considered a war hero, Andrew Jackson was popular with the "common man"—white, male farmers and workers who felt he identified with them. Thanks to universal manhood suffrage, Jackson had the advantage in the 1828 election.

Jackson rewarded his supporters using the **spoils system**, appointing them to important positions.

Socially and politically, white men of varying levels of economic success and education gained stronger political voices and more opportunities in civil society. Women, Black Americans, and Indigenous Americans remained oppressed.

Opposed to the Bank of the United States, Jackson issued the **Specie Circular**. This devalued paper money and instigated the financial **Panic of 1837**.

Despite his opposition to such deep federal economic control, Jackson was forced to contend with controversial tariffs.

▶   The **Tariff of 1828** (also known as the **Tariff of Abominations**) benefitted northern industry but heavily affected southern exports.

▷   Senator **John C. Calhoun** of South Carolina spoke out in favor of **nullification**, arguing that a state had the right to declare a law null and void if it was harmful to that state.

▶   The **Tariff of 1832** increased tensions: South Carolina threatened to secede if its economic interests were not protected, causing the **Nullification** Crisis.

Jackson managed the **Nullification Crisis** without resorting to violence. Paradoxically, he protected the federal government at the expense of states' rights by working out a compromise in 1833 that was more favorable to the South.

In the Supreme Court case *Cherokee Nation v. Georgia* (1831), the Cherokee argued for the right to their land —and lost. President Jackson enforced the 1830 **Indian Removal Act**, forcing Cherokee, Creek, Chickasaw, Choctaw, and others from their lands in the southeast.

Figure 1.14. The Trail of Tears

To make way for white settlers, thousands of people were forced to travel with all their belongings, mainly on foot, to Indian Territory (today, Oklahoma) on a route that came to be called the **Trail of Tears**. Brutal conditions killed many people.

Throughout the nineteenth century, violent conflicts would continue on the frontier farther west between US forces, white settlers, and the Apache, Comanche, Sioux, Arapaho, Cheyenne, and other tribes.

PRACTICE QUESTIONS

11) **How did the Quartering Act impact the colonists?**

   A. A tax was levied on all documents produced in the Thirteen Colonies, which caused resentment.

   B. Early Americans were forced to build quarters for British soldiers who were stationed locally.

   C. Landowners had to provide one-quarter of their earnings to support British soldiers stationed locally.

   D. Colonists were forced to take British soldiers into their homes, and protests led to the Boston Massacre.

12) **What was the impact of Shays' Rebellion?**

   A. It showed resistance to imposing excise taxes on whiskey and other consumer goods.

   B. It showed the tenuous nature of governmental control in the young United States and illustrated the need for a stronger federal government.

   C. Inspired by *Letters from a Farmer in Pennsylvania*, Daniel Shays and other farmers rose up to protest taxes and the fiscal policies engineered by Alexander Hamilton during the Washington administration.

   D. Shays, who was concerned about strengthened federal powers under the new Constitution, organized radical Democratic-Republicans to protest the fiscal measures espoused by Hamilton, particularly the Bank of the United States.

13) **The United States did not recognize the Proclamation of 1763. What was the impact of that diplomatic reversal?**

   A. Indigenous tribes organized into the Northwest Confederacy, fighting American westward expansion.

   B. The French and British formed the Northwest Confederacy, allying against the United States to control more land in North America.

   C. The British attacked the United States from Canada, starting the War of 1812.

   D. The Northwest Confederacy of British and American soldiers united to drive Indigenous tribes from what is today the Midwest region of the United States.

14) **How did demographics play a part in democratic change during the early and mid-nineteenth century, particularly in the context of Jacksonian Democracy?**

    A. The rising strength of industry in the Northeast, coupled with the beginnings of railroads, strengthened support for pro-business politicians and the business class.

    B. Wealthy European immigrants shifted the balance of power away from the "common man" to business owners and the elites, leading to the rise of the powerful Whig party.

    C. Universal manhood suffrage shifted the balance of political power away from the elites; immigration accelerated westward expansion and began to power early industry and urban development.

    D. Jackson's focus on strengthening the federal government dissatisfied the South, leading to the Nullification Crisis.

15) **Which of the following is true about the Missouri Compromise?**

    A. It illustrated a united approach to westward expansion.

    B. It showed the impact of the abolitionist movement on politics.

    C. It led to increased immigration to the United States.

    D. It eliminated slavery in all new states established in the west.

CIVIL WAR, EXPANSION, AND INDUSTRY

THE ROAD TO CONFLICT

The Civil War was rooted in ongoing conflict over slavery, states' rights, and the reach of the federal government. Reform movements of the mid-nineteenth century fueled the abolitionist movement. The Missouri Compromise and the Nullification Crisis foreshadowed worsening division to come.

Texas, where there were a great number of white settlers, declared independence from Mexico in 1836. One important reason was that Mexico had abolished slavery. In 1845, Texas joined the Union. This event, in addition to ongoing US hunger for land, triggered the **Mexican-American War.**

As a result of the **Treaty of Guadalupe Hidalgo**, which ended the war, the United States obtained territory in the Southwest: the Utah and New Mexico Territories, and gold-rich California.

The population of California would grow rapidly with the **gold rush** as prospectors in search of gold headed west to try their fortunes. However, Hispanic people who had lived in the region under Mexico lost their land and were denied many rights, despite a promise of US citizenship and equal rights under the treaty. They also endured racial and ethnic discrimination.

Meanwhile, social change in the Northeast and growing Midwest continued. The **middle class** began to develop with the market economy and early industrialization.

Social views on the role of **women** changed:

▶ extra income allowed them to stay at home

▶ the **Cult of Domesticity**, a popular cultural movement, encouraged women to become homemakers and focus on domestic skills

Figure 1.15. Seneca Falls Convention

At the same time, middle-class white women were freed up to engage in social activism and became active in reform movements. Activists like **Susan B. Anthony** and **Elizabeth Cady Stanton** worked for women's rights, including women's suffrage. This culminated in the 1848 **Seneca Falls Convention** led by the **American Woman Suffrage Association**.

Women were also active in the temperance movement. Organizations like the Woman's Christian Temperance Union advocated for the prohibition of alcohol. This was finally achieved with the Eighteenth Amendment, although it was later repealed with the Twenty-first.

Reform movements, which ranged from moderate to radical, continued to include abolitionism, which became a key social and political issue in the mid-nineteenth century.

> **HELPFUL HINT**
>
> All American women were denied their right to vote until the ratification of the Nineteenth Amendment in 1920. Black women and American women of color were restricted further until the Voting Rights Act of 1965.

The American Colonization Society wanted to end slavery and send former slaves to Africa.

The writer and publisher **Frederick Douglass**, who had himself been enslaved, also advocated for abolition. However, Douglass was strongly opposed to the American Colonization Society's idea of sending freed slaves—many of whom were born and raised in the US—to Africa.

An activist leader, Douglass publicized the abolitionist movement along with the American Anti-Slavery Society and publications like Harriet Beecher Stowe's *Uncle Tom's Cabin*. The radical abolitionist **John Brown** led violent protests against slavery.

Figure 1.16. Frederick Douglass

The industrial and demographic changes in the North did not extend to the South, which continued to rely on plantations and cotton exports. Differences among the regions grew, and disputes about extending slavery into new southwestern territories obtained from Mexico continued. Another compromise was needed.

Anti-slavery factions in Congress had attempted to halt the extension of slavery to the new territories obtained from Mexico in the 1846 **Wilmot Proviso**, but these efforts were unsuccessful.

The later **Compromise of 1850** admitted the populous California as a free state. Utah and New Mexico joined the Union with slavery to be decided by **popular sovereignty**, or by the residents.

This compromise also reaffirmed the **Fugitive Slave Act**, which allowed enslavers to pursue escaped slaves to free states and recapture them. It would now be a federal crime to assist people escaping slavery. This was unacceptable to many abolitionists.

Shortly thereafter, Congress passed the **Kansas-Nebraska Act of 1854**. This act allowed the Kansas and Nebraska territories to decide slavery by popular sovereignty as well, effectively repealing the Missouri Compromise.

As a result, a new party—the **Republican Party**—was formed by angered Democrats, Whigs, and others. Violence broke out in Kansas between pro- and anti-slavery factions in what became known as **Bleeding Kansas**.

In 1856, **Dred Scott**, a Black American who had escaped slavery, sued for freedom at the Supreme Court. Scott had escaped to the free state of Illinois and sought to stay there. Sandford, his enslaver, argued that Scott remained enslaved even though he had escaped to a free state.

The Court heard the case, *Scott v. Sandford*, and ruled in favor of Sandford. This ruling upheld the Fugitive Slave Act, the Kansas-Nebraska Act, and nullified the Missouri Compromise. The Court essentially decreed that Black Americans were not entitled to rights under US citizenship.

In 1858, a series of debates between Illinois Senate candidates, Republican **Abraham Lincoln** and Democrat **Stephen Douglas**, showed the deep divides in the nation over slavery and states' rights. During the **Lincoln-Douglas Debates**,

Lincoln spoke out against slavery, while Douglas supported the right of states to decide its legality on their own.

In 1860, Abraham Lincoln was elected to the presidency. Given his outspoken stance against slavery, South Carolina seceded immediately. Mississippi, Alabama, Florida, Louisiana, Georgia, and Texas soon followed. On February 1, 1861, they formed the Confederate States of America, or the **Confederacy**, under the leadership of **Jefferson Davis**, a senator from Mississippi.

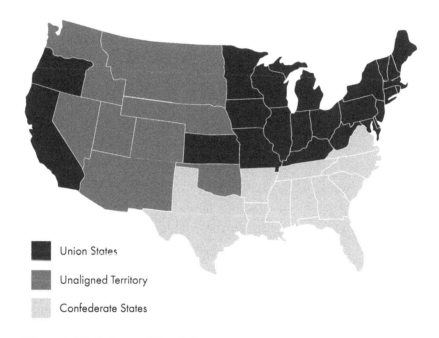

Figure 1.17. Union and Confederacy

THE CIVIL WAR BEGINS

Shortly after the South's secession, Confederate forces attacked Union troops in Charleston Harbor, South Carolina. The **Battle of Fort Sumter** sparked the Civil War. As a result, Virginia, Tennessee, North Carolina, and Arkansas joined the Confederacy.

Both sides believed the conflict would be short-lived. But it became clear that the war would not end quickly.

Realizing how difficult it would be to defeat the Confederacy, the Union developed the **Anaconda Plan**, designed to "squeeze" the Confederacy. The South depended on international trade in cotton for much of its

DID YOU KNOW?

West Virginia was formed when the western part of Virginia refused to join the Confederacy.

income, so a naval blockade would seriously harm the Confederate economy. The Anaconda Plan included:

▶ a naval blockade of the Confederacy

▶ Union control of the Mississippi River

Following the **Siege of Vicksburg**, Mississippi, Union forces led by **General Ulysses S. Grant** gained control over the Mississippi River. This completed the Anaconda Plan.

During the war, on January 1, 1863, President Lincoln decreed the end of slavery in the rebel states with the **Emancipation Proclamation**.

Table 1.4. Major Battles of the Civil War

Battle	Impact and Results
Battle of Fort Sumter (1861)	• Confederates attacked Union troops in Charleston, South Carolina • sparked the Civil War • Virginia, Tennessee, North Carolina, and Arkansas joined the Confederacy
First Battle of Bull Run (1861)	• Union failed to rout the Confederacy • showed Civil War would not end quickly
Second Battle of Bull Run (1862)	• Confederate victory • showed strength of Confederate leadership (Robert E. Lee and Stonewall Jackson) • blow to Union morale
Battle of Antietam (1862)	• first battle fought on Union soil • General McClellan prevented Confederate invasion of Maryland • Union did not defeat Confederate forces • Lincoln declared the Emancipation Proclamation
Battle of Gettysburg (1863)	• major Union victory • bloodiest battle in American history up to this point • Confederate army could not recover
Battle of Atlanta (1864)	• final major battle of the Civil War • Union forces penetrated the South • fall of Confederacy
Battle of Appomattox Court House (1865)	• Confederate loss • General Lee surrendered to General Grant, ending the war

The Confederacy had strong military leadership and a vast territory. But the Union prevailed thanks to:

▶ a larger population (strengthened by immigration)

▶ stronger industrial capacity (including weapons-making capabilities)

▶ the naval blockade of Southern trades

▶ superior leadership

> **DID YOU KNOW?**
>
> President Lincoln delivered the Gettysburg Address onsite at Gettysburg shortly after the battle. He framed the Civil War as a battle for human rights and equality.

AFTERMATH AND RECONSTRUCTION

Bitterness over the Union victory persisted. President Lincoln was assassinated on April 15, 1865. Post-war **Reconstruction** would continue without his leadership.

Before his death, Lincoln had crafted the **Ten Percent Plan**. If ten percent of a Southern state's population swore allegiance to the Union, that state would be readmitted into the Union. However Lincoln's vice president, Andrew Johnson, enforced Reconstruction weakly.

The white supremacist **Ku Klux Klan** emerged to intimidate and kill Black people in the South. Likewise, states developed the oppressive **Black Codes** to limit the rights of freed Black Americans.

As a result, Congress passed the **Civil Rights Act** in 1866, granting citizenship to freed Black Americans and guaranteeing Black American men the same rights as white men.

Eventually former Confederate states also had to ratify the following amendments:

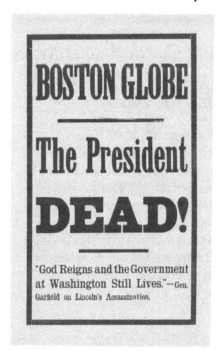

Figure 1.18. Lincoln's Assassination

▶ the **Thirteenth Amendment**, which abolished slavery

▶ the **Fourteenth Amendment**, which reaffirmed the Civil Rights Act (equality under the law)

▶ the **Fifteenth Amendment**, which in 1870 granted Black American men the right to vote

> **DID YOU KNOW?**
>
> Despite ratifying the amendments, Southern states instituted the Black Codes to continue oppression of freedmen, or freed African Americans, who faced ongoing violence.

Conflict over how harshly to treat the South persisted in Congress between Republicans and Democrats. In 1867, a Republican-led Congress passed the **Reconstruction Acts**. These put former Confederate states under the control of the US Army, effectively declaring martial law.

Resentment over the Reconstruction Acts never truly subsided. Military control of the South finally ended with the **Compromise of 1877**, in which:

▶ the disputed presidential election of 1876 was resolved

▶ Rutherford B. Hayes obtained the presidency

▶ troops were removed from the South

Tensions and bitterness existed between Union authorities and Southern leaders. But Reconstruction helped modernize Southern education systems, tax collection, and infrastructure. The **Freedmen's Bureau** was tasked with assisting formerly enslaved Americans and poor whites in the South.

JIM CROW, SEGREGATION, AND CIVIL RIGHTS

DID YOU KNOW?

On June 19, 1865, Union troops arrived in Galveston, Texas. They announced the end of slavery. Many enslaved people in the South had been unaware of the Emancipation Proclamation up to this point. Today the holiday Juneteenth is celebrated in honor of the end of slavery.

Enslaved Black Americans had technically been freed. But many freedmen were unaware of this. Still others remained working on plantations voluntarily—or involuntarily.

Eventually, all enslaved people were freed. But few had education or marketable skills. Furthermore, they could not thrive under oppressive social structures. The **Jim Crow laws** enforced **the separation of races** in the South. Black people's rights were regularly violated.

Black leaders like **Booker T. Washington** and **W.E.B. DuBois** sought solutions.

Table 1.5. Post–Civil War Perspectives on Civil Rights

Booker T. Washington believed in...	W.E.B. DuBois believed in...
• gradual desegregation	• immediate segregation
• vocational education for Black Americans	• higher education and social leadership positions for Black Americans
• the Tuskegee Institute, where he offered vocational education to Black men	• the **National Association for the Advancement of Colored People (NAACP)**, an advocacy group that supported his ideas

These differing views reflected diverse positions within and beyond the African American community over its future.

In 1896, the Supreme Court upheld segregation. Homer Plessy, a Black man, was forced off a whites-only train car. Plessy challenged the law in *Plessy v. Ferguson*, but the Court decided that segregation was constitutional. According to the Court, *separate but equal* still ensured equality under the law. This would remain the law until **Brown v. Board of Education** in 1954.

As part of a broader, ongoing movement known as the **Great Migration**, many Black Americans began leaving the South for better opportunities farther west and in the cities of the north.

Settlement of the West

Throughout the Civil War and the chaotic post-war Reconstruction period, settlement of the West continued. California had already grown in population due to the gold rush. By the mid-nineteenth century, **Chinese immigrants** began arriving in large numbers to California—also in search of gold—but were met instead with racial discrimination.

Meanwhile, the US was opening trade with East Asia, thanks to **clipper ships** that made journeys across the Pacific Ocean faster and easier. In 1853, **Commodore Matthew Perry** had used "gunboat diplomacy" to force trade agreements with Japan. Even earlier, the United States had signed the **Treaty of Wangxia**, a trade agreement, with Qing Dynasty China.

Figure 1.19. Clipper Ship

While Chinese immigrants faced racism, Americans of European descent were encouraged to settle the frontier. The **Homestead Act of 1862** granted 160 acres of land in the West to any pioneer who promised to settle and work it for a certain number of years. However, frontier life proved difficult because the land of the Great Plains was difficult to farm. Ranching and herding cattle became popular and profitable.

White settlers also hunted the buffalo. Mass killings of buffalo threatened Indigenous survival.

The Great Plains and Rocky Mountains were already populated with Sioux, Cheyenne, Apache, Comanche, Arapaho, Pawnee, and others. Conflict between Native American tribes and white settlers was ongoing.

In 1864, US troops ambushed Cheyenne and Arapaho people in Colorado in what became known as the **Sand Creek Massacre**, which triggered even more violence.

The United States came to an agreement with the Sioux in South Dakota, offering them land as part of the **reservation** system. However, by the late nineteenth century, gold was discovered in the Black Hills of South Dakota on the **Great Sioux Reservation**.

The US reneged on its promise, encouraging exploration and seeking control over that gold. The resulting **Sioux Wars** culminated in the 1876 **Battle of Little Big Horn** and General George Custer's "last stand." While the US was defeated in that battle, reinforcements would later defeat the Sioux and the reservation system continued.

Figure 1.20. Ogallala Sioux Ghost Dance at Pine Ridge, 1890

The **Ghost Dance Movement** united Plains tribes in a spiritual movement and in the belief that whites would eventually be driven from the land. In 1890, the military forced the Sioux to cease this ritual. The outcome was a massacre at **Wounded Knee** and the death of the Sioux chief, **Sitting Bull**.

In 1887, the **Dawes Act:**

▶ ended federal recognition of tribes

▶ withdrew tribal land rights

▶ forced the sale of reservations—tribal land

▶ harmed Indigenous families

Indigenous children were sent to boarding schools, where they were forced to abandon their cultures and languages, and speak English, not their native languages.

PRACTICE QUESTIONS

16) **Which of the following BEST describes the roots of the Civil War?**

   A. John C. Calhoun developed the doctrine of nullification to uphold slavery.

   B. Early nineteenth century immigration to the North represented a threat to the smaller South.

   C. Lincoln and Douglas provoked pro-war sentiment in their debates around the country.

   D. The country was divided over whether slavery should be permitted as the United States grew.

17) **How did the Dawes Act impact Indigenous Americans in the West?**

   A. It forced them to move from their ancestral lands to what is today Oklahoma.

   B. It revoked tribal rights to land and federal recognition of tribes, forcing assimilation.

   C. It granted them land on reservations.

   D. It provided 160 acres of land to any settler willing to farm land on the Great Plains.

The Gilded Age and the Progressive Era

Back in the Northeast, the market economy and industry were flourishing. Following the war, the **Industrial Revolution** accelerated in the United States.

The Industrial Revolution had begun on the global level with textile production in Great Britain, had been fueled in great part by supplies of Southern cotton, and was evolving in the United States with the development of heavy industry—what would come to be called the **Second Industrial Revolution**.

Though products from the US market economy were available in the United States; the country needed more markets abroad to continue to fuel economic growth.

New Imperialism described the US approach to nineteenth and early twentieth century European-style imperialism. Rather than controlling territory, the US sought economic connections with countries around the world.

INCOME INEQUALITY OF THE GILDED AGE

The **Gilded Age** saw an era of rapidly growing income inequality. Inequality was justified by theories like **Social Darwinism**. The **Gospel of Wealth** argued that the wealthy had been made rich by God and were, therefore, socially more deserving of it.

Much of this wealth was generated by heavy industry in what became known as the **Second Industrial Revolution**. Westward expansion required railroads, railroads required steel, and industrial production required oil. These commodities spurred the rise of powerful companies like John D. Rockefeller's Standard Oil and Andrew Carnegie's US Steel.

Figure 1.21. Perspectives on the Senate during the Gilded Age

The creation of **monopolies** and **trusts** helped industrial leaders consolidate their control over the entire economy. A few Americans began holding a huge percentage of income.

Monopolies let the same business leaders control the market for their own products. Business leaders organized into trusts. **Trusts** ensured their control over each other's industries, buying and selling from each other. The results: the economy was dominated by a select few.

These processes were made possible thanks to the vertical and horizontal integration of industries:

▶ **vertical integration**: One company dominates each step in manufacturing a good, from obtaining raw materials to shipping the finished product.

▶ **horizontal integration**: This describes the process of companies acquiring their competition, thereby monopolizing their markets.

With limited governmental controls or interference in the economy, American **capitalism**—the free market system—was becoming dominated by a small percentage of wealthy Americans.

CHECK YOUR UNDERSTANDING #5

What was the driving force behind the Second Industrial Revolution?

Government corruption led only to weak restrictive legislation:

▶ the **Interstate Commerce Act** (1887) was intended to regulate the railroad industry

▶ the **Sherman Antitrust Act** (1890) was intended to break up monopolies and trusts to create a fairer marketplace

These measures would remain largely toothless until President Theodore Roosevelt's "trust-busting" administration in 1901.

The free markets and trade of the **capitalist** economy spurred national economic and industrial growth. But the **working class**—comprised largely of poor immigrants working in factories and building infrastructure—suffered from dangerous working conditions and other abuses.

Figure 1.22. Triangle Shirtwaist Factory Fire

As the railroads expanded westward, white farmers lost their land to corporate interests. In addition, with limited (or nonexistent) regulations on land use, Mexican Americans and Indigenous Americans in the West were harmed and lost land.

> **DID YOU KNOW?**
>
> In New York City, the Triangle Shirtwaist factory caught fire in 1911, killing 146 employees. It exposed dangerous working conditions and inspired future legislation to protect workers.

Black Americans in the South were also struggling. Under **sharecropping**, many worked the same land for the same landowners who had enslaved them. Black sharecroppers were forced to lease land and equipment at unreasonable rates, essentially trapped in the same conditions they had lived in before.

These harmful consequences led to the development of reform movements, social ideals, and change.

POPULISM AND THE PROGRESSIVE ERA

The 1890 **Sherman Silver Purchase Act** allowed Treasury notes to be backed in both gold and silver. But political conflict, economic troubles, the silver standard, and the failure of a major railroad company led to the financial **Panic of 1893**. President **Grover Cleveland**, who had never been in favor of the silver standard, repealed the Sherman Silver Purchase Act as a result.

In response to corruption and industrialization, farmers, sharecroppers, and industrial workers formed several alliances to improve working conditions and level the economic playing field.

- **The People's (Populist) Party** was formed in response to corruption and industrialization injurious to farmers.

  - Later, it would also support reform in favor of the working class, women, and children.

- **The National Grange** advocated for farmers who were suffering from crushing debt in the face of westward expansion, which destroyed their lands; they were also competing (and losing) against industrialized and mechanized farming.

- **Las Gorras Blancas** was an extremist group that disrupted the construction of railroads to protect farmers and their land from corporate interests.

- **The Greenback-Labor Party** was formed to introduce a silver standard, which farmers believed would inflate crop prices by putting more money into national circulation.

- **The Colored Farmers' Alliance** was formed to support sharecroppers and other Black farmers in the South, who were harmed by Jim Crow laws.

Around the same time, **the labor movement** emerged to support mistreated industrial workers in urban areas.

▶ **The American Federation of Labor (AFL),** led by **Samuel Gompers**, used **strikes** and **collective bargaining** to gain protections for the workers who had come to cities seeking industrial jobs.

▶ **The Knights of Labor** empowered workers by integrating unskilled workers into actions.

▶ The activist Marry Harris Jones, better known as **Mother Jones**, revolutionized labor by including women, children, and African Americans in labor actions.

Figure 1.23. Mother Jones

With the continual rise of the **middle class**, women took a more active role in advocating for the poor and for themselves. Women activists also aligned with labor and the emerging **Progressive Movement**.

Poor conditions also inspired workers to consider philosophies of reform:

▶ **socialism**: the idea that workers should own the means of production and that wealth should be distributed equally, using economic planning

▶ **utopianism**: the concept of creating utopian settlements with egalitarian societies

▶ **the Social Gospel**: a religious movement believing in the notion that it was society's obligation to ensure better treatment for workers, immigrants, and society's most vulnerable

The Progressive **Theodore Roosevelt** became president in 1901 following the assassination of President William McKinley. The Progressive Era reached its apex.

Roosevelt became known as a *trust-buster*. He enforced the Sherman Antitrust Act and prosecuted the **Northern Securities** railroad monopoly under the Interstate Commerce Act, breaking up trusts and creating a fairer market.

> **DID YOU KNOW?**
>
> The **Sherman Antitrust Act**, despite its intended purpose—to prosecute and dissolve large trusts and create a fairer marketplace—had actually been used against unions and farmers' alliances.

Roosevelt also led government involvement in negotiations between unions and industrial powers, developing the *square deal* for fairer treatment of workers. The Progressive Era also saw a series of acts to protect workers, health, farmers, and children under Presidents Roosevelt and Taft.

THE SPANISH–AMERICAN WAR AND US IMPERIALISM

Spanish abuses in Cuba had concerned Americans. But many events were sensationalized and exaggerated in the media. This **yellow journalism** aroused popular concern and interest in intervention in Cuba.

Other causes of the Spanish-American War included the discovery of an insulting letter from the Spanish minister de Lôme, and the mysterious explosion of the United States battleship *USS Maine* in Havana.

DID YOU KNOW?

Sanford Dole led a takeover of the Hawai'i, an independent monarchy. He and other white landowners overthrew Queen Liliuokalani and created the Republic of Hawai'i before US annexation. Today, the Dole Food company still grows and sells fruit worldwide.

The Spanish-American War was the first time the United States had engaged in overseas military occupation and conquest beyond North America, entirely contrary to George Washington's recommendations in his Farewell Address. This **new imperialism** expanded US markets and increased US presence and prestige on the global stage.

The United States did not annex Hawai'i in the Spanish-American war. However, nationalism helped push Pacific imperialism and annexation. White plantation owners had been taking over Hawai'ian land to grow sugar and fruit. They supported annexation of this independent kingdom for economic reasons.

The Treaty of Paris ended the Spanish-American War, granting certain Caribbean and Pacific territories to the United States. At the same time, nationalist sentiment drove US imperialism in strategic areas in the Caribbean, Pacific, and Latin America.

Table. 1.6. United States Expansion in Latin America and the Pacific

Country or Region	Consequences	Legislation or Treaty
Cuba	• Cuba would revert to independence following the war.	**Teller Amendment**
	• The United States effectively took over Cuba (against the wishes of many Americans).	**Platt Amendment**
Panama Canal (Central American Colombia/ Panama)	• England ceded claims in Colombian Central America to the US. • Colombia refused to recognize the treaty. • President Roosevelt engineered a revolution, creating the new country of Panama. • Panama Canal construction began.	**Hay-Pauncefote Treaty**

Country or Region	Consequences	Legislation or Treaty
Philippines	• The United States retained control over the Philippines despite having promised it independence. • Guerilla war resulted as the Philippines resisted US occupation.	**Treaty of Paris (1898)**
Hawai'i	• Hawai'ian Queen Liliuokalani strengthened the monarchy in the face of US sugar and fruit interests. • Supporting US plantation owners, the US annexes Hawai'i in 1898. • Sanford Dole made first Hawai'ian governor under US annexation.	**Newlands Resolution**
Puerto Rico and Guam	• Some Puerto Ricans expected independence. • US had strong foothold in the Caribbean and Pacific.	**Treaty of Paris (1898)**

President Roosevelt continued overseas expansion following the **Spanish-American War.** The **Roosevelt Corollary** to the Monroe Doctrine promised US intervention in Latin America in case of European action there. This essentially gave the US total dominance over Latin America.

PRACTICE QUESTIONS

18) **How was a small elite group of wealthy businesspersons able to dominate the economy during the Gilded Age?**

   A.   The Sherman Antitrust Act put a few expert business leaders in charge of economic policy.

   B.   Monopolies and trusts, developed through horizontal and vertical integration, ensured that the same business leaders controlled the same markets.

   C.   Industrialization was encouraging the United States to shift to a planned economy in keeping with philosophical changes in Europe.

   D.   The silver standard allowed specific businesspeople holding large silver reserves to dominate the market.

19) **How did the Progressive Movement change the United States during the Second Industrial Revolution?**

   A.   Trade unions fought for workers' rights and safety; the Social Gospel, an early philosophy of charity and philanthropy, developed to support the poor and urban disadvantaged.

   B.   The Seneca Falls Convention drew attention to the question of women's suffrage.

   C.   Progressives argued to extend rights and protections to Native Americans, particularly those displaced by settlement on the Great Plains.

   D.   The Supreme Court ruled segregation unconstitutional in *Plessy v. Ferguson*.

20) **How did the Spanish-American War change perceptions of the United States?**

   A.   The United States lost its military, territorial, and economic aspirations as an imperial power.

   B.   The United States had begun to prove itself on the global stage as a military power.

   C.   United States citizens became dismissive of nationalism.

   D.   United States military extended into Europe and the Mediterranean.

THE UNITED STATES BECOMES A GLOBAL POWER

SOCIOECONOMIC CHANGE AND WORLD WAR I

Social change led by the Progressives in the early twentieth century resulted in better conditions for workers, increased attention toward child labor, and petitions for more livable cities.

Continuing economic instability also triggered top-down reform. Banks restricted credit and overspeculated on the value of land and other investments. There was also a conservative gold standard. These led to the **Panic of 1907**.

To stabilize the economy and rein in the banks, Congress passed the **Federal Reserve Act** in 1913 to protect the banking system. Federal Reserve banks were established to cover twelve regions of the country. Commercial banks had to take part in the system, allowing "the Fed" to control interest rates and avoid a similar crisis.

While the United States became increasingly prosperous and stable, Europe was becoming increasingly unstable. Americans were divided over how to respond.

DID YOU KNOW?

Jacob Riis' groundbreaking book and photo essay, *How the Other Half Lives*, revealed the squalor and poverty the poor urban classes—often impoverished immigrants—endured, leading to more public calls for reform.

Following the Spanish-American War, debate had arisen within the US between **interventionism** and **isolationism.** This debate became more pronounced with the outbreak of World War I in Europe.

▶ interventionism: the belief in spreading US-style democracy

▶ isolationism: the belief in focusing on development at home

Several inflammatory events triggered US intervention in WWI:

▶ German submarine warfare in the Atlantic Ocean

▶ the sinking of the *Lusitania*, which resulted in many American civilian deaths

▶ the embarrassing Zimmerman Telegram (in which Germany promised to help Mexico in an attack on the US)

▶ growing American nationalism

With victory in 1918, the US had proven itself a superior military and industrial power. Interventionist **President Woodrow Wilson** played an important role in negotiating the peace. His **Fourteen Points** laid out an idealistic international vision, including an international security organization. The Fourteen Points were not used after WWI, but they informed future international diplomacy.

Divisions between interventionists and isolationists continued.

▶ Following the Japanese invasion of Manchuria in 1932, the **Stimson Doctrine** determined US neutrality in Asia.

▶ Congress also passed the **Neutrality Acts** of 1930s in light of conflict in Asia and ongoing tensions in Europe.

> **HELPFUL HINT**
>
> The Neutrality Act of 1939 would allow some financial support to allies, like the United Kingdom. It was used before the United States entered WWII.

ISOLATION, XENOPHOBIA, AND RACISM

On the home front, fear of communists and anarchists, and xenophobia against immigrants led to the **Red Scare** in 1919 and a series of anti-immigration laws. Attorney-General Palmer authorized a series of raids—the **Palmer Raids**—on suspected radicals. This accelerated the hysteria of the Red Scare. Palmer was later discredited.

Xenophobia and isolationism were widespread following the First World War. Congress limited immigration from Asia, Eastern Europe, and Southern Europe with two major racist acts:

▶ **Emergency Quota Act** of 1921

▶ **National Origins Act** of 1924

The ongoing Great Migration of Black Americans to northern and western states led to differing views on Black empowerment. Leaders like **Marcus Garvey** believed in self-sufficiency for Black Americans, who were settling in urban areas and facing racial discrimination and isolation.

Garvey's **United Negro Improvement Association** would go on to inspire movements like the Black Panthers and the Nation of Islam. Those radical philosophies of separation were at odds with the NAACP, which believed in integration. Tensions increased with the 1919 race riots. Racist events like the Tulsa race massacre happened throughout the country.

The Ku Klux Klan was growing in power, especially in the South. Black Americans faced intimidation, violence, and death. Black Americans were kidnapped and killed in extrajudicial executions called lynchings. Some lynchings occurred publicly, terrorizing Americans.

> **DID YOU KNOW?**
>
> White residents attacked Black people and businesses on what was known as "Black Wall Street" in the Greenwood area of Tulsa, Oklahoma, on May 31 and June 1, 1931. In what became known as the Tulsa race massacre, a young Black man was accused of assaulting a young white woman. He was arrested, and Black and White residents confronted each other over rumors that he would be lynched. Days of mob violence followed. Black businesses were destroyed, and many people were killed.

THE HARLEM RENAISSANCE AND THE ROARING TWENTIES

Still, African American culture flourished and powered the growth of American popular culture. The **Harlem Renaissance** launched Black music (especially **jazz**), literature, and art into mainstream US culture. So did the evolution of early technology like radio, motion pictures, and automobiles—products that were available to the middle class through credit.

The women's rights movement was empowered by the heightened visibility of women in the public sphere. In 1920, the **Nineteenth Amendment** was ratified, giving all women the right to vote. However, the **Roaring Twenties**, a seemingly trouble-free period of isolation from chaotic world events, would come to an end.

THE GREAT DEPRESSION

Following WWI, the United States experienced an era of consumerism and corruption. The government sponsored **laissez-faire** policies and supported **manufactur-**

ing, flooding markets with cheap consumer goods. Union membership suffered. So did farmers, due to falling crop prices.

While mass production helped the emerging middle class afford more consumer goods and improve their living standards, many families resorted to **credit** to fuel consumer spending. These risky consumer

loans, **overspeculation** on crops and the value of farmland, and weak banking protections helped bring about the **Great Depression**, commonly dated from October 29, 1929, or Black Tuesday, when the stock market collapsed.

At the same time, a major drought occurred in the Great Plains. American farmers lost their crops in the dust bowl phenomenon and headed to cities. Millions of Americans faced unemployment and poverty.

Figure 1.24. Great Depression

Speculation, or margin-buying, meant that speculators borrowed money to buy stock. Then they sold it as soon as its price rose. Because the price of stocks fluctuated aggressively, buyers would lose confidence in the market and begin selling their shares. This caused the value of stocks to plummet. Borrowers could not repay their loans. As a result, banks failed.

FDR AND THE NEW DEAL

Following weak responses by the Hoover administration, **Franklin Delano Roosevelt** was elected to the presidency in 1932. FDR offered Americans a New Deal: a plan to bring the country out of the Depression.

During the *First Hundred Days* of FDR's administration, a series of emergency acts (known as an *"alphabet soup"* of acts due to their many acronyms) was passed for the immediate repair of the banking system. Notable acts included:

▶ **Glass-Steagall Act**: established the **Federal Deposit Insurance Corporation (FDIC)** to insure customer deposits in the wake of bank failures.

  ▷ the **Securities and Exchange Commission (SEC)** was later established to monitor stock trading. The SEC also has the power to punish violators of the law

▶ **Agricultural Adjustment Act (AAA)**: reduced farm prices by subsidizing farmers to limit production of certain commodities

▶ **Home Owners Loan Corporation (HOLC)**: refinanced mortgages to protect homeowners from losing their homes

▶ **Federal Housing Administration (FHA)**: insured low-cost mortgages

▶ **Tennessee Valley Authority (TVA)**: the first large-scale attempt at regional public planning and a long-term project despite being part of the First Hundred Days.

The New Deal addressed more than economic issues. Several acts provided relief to the poor and unemployed. The federal government allotted aid to states to be distributed directly to the poor through the **Federal Emergency Relief Act**. The New Deal especially included legislation designed to generate jobs:

▶ **Public Works Administration (PWA)**: used by the federal government to distribute funding to states for the purpose of developing infrastructure and to provide construction jobs for the unemployed.

▶ **Civilian Conservation Corps (CCC)**: created to offer employment in environmental conservation and management projects.

DID YOU KNOW?

The TVA was intended to create jobs and bring electricity to the Tennessee Valley area. But one of its true objectives was to accurately measure the cost of electric power, which had been supplied by private companies. The TVA was the first public power company and still operates today.

- **Works Progress Administration (WPA):** established during the **Second New Deal** and a long-term project that generated construction jobs and built infrastructure throughout the country.

- **Federal Writers' Project** and **Federal Art Project:** part of the WPA; created jobs for writers and artists, who wrote histories, created guidebooks, developed public art for public buildings, and made other contributions.

- **Wagner Act:** designed to address labor issues as well; ensured workers' right to unionize and established the **National Labor Relations Board (NLRB)**. Strengthening unions guaranteed collective bargaining rights and protected workers.

Despite the recovery afforded by acts passed during the First Hundred Days, millions of Americans, still unemployed, were critical of the New Deal. Fearing a third-party challenge in the 1936 election, FDR requested Congress to pass additional New Deal legislation, often referred to as the Second New Deal.

FDR was a Democrat in the Progressive tradition. The Progressive legacy of social improvement was apparent throughout the New Deal and his administration. The New Deal and its positive impact on the poor, the working class, unions, and immigrants led these groups to support the Democratic Party, a trend that continues to this day.

DID YOU KNOW?

The Federal Writers' Project enlisted unemployed writers to interview Black Americans who had been enslaved. The outcome was a compilation, *Born in Slavery: Slave Narratives from the Federal Writers' Project, 1936 – 1938* that is available at the Library of Congress. These narratives are some of the few recorded histories of Black Americans who had been enslaved, in their own words and from their perspective.

PRACTICE QUESTIONS

21) **Which of the following precipitated US entry into the First World War?**

   A.   the sinking of the *Lusitania*

   B.   the Great Depression

   C.   the attack on the *Maine*

   D.   the New Deal

22) **How did the New Deal repair the damage of the Great Depression and help the United States rebuild?**

A. Immediate economic reforms stabilized the economy during the First Hundred Days; later, longer-term public works programs provided jobs to relieve unemployment and develop infrastructure.

B. Social programs put into effect during the First Hundred Days provided jobs for Americans; measures to protect homeowners, landholders, and bank deposits followed to guarantee financial security.

C. Programs like the Tennessee Valley Authority helped the government determine proper pricing and institute price controls for important public goods.

D. FDR proposed supporting banks and big business with federal money to reinvigorate the market by limiting government intervention.

23) **How did the United States change in the 1920s?**

A. The Great Migration ceased.

B. African American culture became increasingly influential.

C. The Great Depression caused high unemployment.

D. Thanks to the New Deal, millions of Americans found jobs.

THE UNITED STATES AND WORLD WAR II

COOPERATION WITH EUROPE

The entire world suffered from the Great Depression, and Europe became increasingly unstable. With the rise of the radical Nazi Party in Germany, the Nazi leader, Adolf Hitler, became a threat to US allies after bombing Britain and leading German takeovers of several European countries.

However, the United States was weakened by the Great Depression and reluctant to engage in international affairs. Public and political support for isolationism continued and was reinforced by the Neutrality Acts. The US remained militarily uncommitted in the war.

CHECK YOUR UNDERSTANDING #7

List some reasons for US reluctance to enter WWII.

The Neutrality Act of 1939 did, however, allow cash-and-carry arms sales to combat participants. In this way, the United States could militarily support its allies (namely, the United Kingdom).

FDR was increasingly concerned about the rise of fascism in Europe, seeing it as a global threat. To ally with and support the United Kingdom without technically declaring war on Germany, FDR convinced Congress to enact the **Lend-Lease Act**. The Lend-Lease Act directly supplied Britain with military aid, in place of cash-and-carry.

FDR and the British Prime Minister **Winston Churchill** met in response to the nonaggression pact between Hitler and Stalin to sign the **Atlantic Charter**, which laid out the anti-fascist agenda of free trade and self-determination.

To garner support for his position, FDR spoke publicly about the **Four Freedoms**:

▶ freedom of speech

▶ freedom of religion

▶ freedom from want

▶ freedom from fear

THE US ENTERS WWII

After the Japanese attack on **Pearl Harbor** on December 7, 1941, the US entered the war. Even though the United States had been directly attacked by Japan, it focused first on the European theater. The US and other Allied powers (the United Kingdom and the Soviet Union) agreed that Hitler was the primary global threat.

The United States focused on eliminating the Nazi threat in the air and at sea, destroying Nazi U-boats (submarines) that threatened the Allies throughout the Atlantic. The US also engaged Germany in North Africa, defeating its troops to approach fascist Italy from the Mediterranean.

On June 6, 1944, or **D-Day**, the US led the invasion of Normandy, invading German-controlled Europe. After months of fighting, following the deadly and drawn-out **Battle of the Bulge** when the Allies faced fierce German resistance, the Allies were able to enter Germany and end the war in Europe.

Figure 1.25. Battle of the Bulge

The US was then able to focus more effectively on the war in the Pacific. The US had been able to break the Japanese code. But Japan had been unable to crack US code thanks to the **Navajo Code Talkers**, who used the Navajo language, which Japan was unable to decipher.

The US strategy of **island hopping** allowed it to take control of Japanese-held Pacific islands, proceeding closer to Japan itself despite **kamikaze** attacks, in which Japanese fighter pilots intentionally crashed their planes into US ships.

President **Harry Truman** took power following FDR's death in 1945. Rather than force a US invasion of Japan, which would have resulted in huge numbers of casualties, he authorized the bombings of **Hiroshima** and **Nagasaki**, the only times that **nuclear weapons** have been used in conflict. The war ended with Japanese surrender on September 2, 1945.

In the United States, Japanese Americans were forced to live in internment camps. Under FDR's Executive Order 9066, these Americans were forced to give up their belongings and businesses and live in harsh military camps scattered throughout the West until the end of the war. They were surrounded by barbed wire and armed guards.

> **DID YOU KNOW?**
>
> Executive Order 9066 targeted Americans of Japanese descent, but other Americans suspected of having ties to the enemy due to their ethnicity, like German Americans, Italian Americans, and even some Aleutian Americans, were also forced into internment during WWII.

Fred Korematsu argued that Executive Order 9066 was unconstitutional and fought to the Supreme Court for the rights of Japanese Americans. But the Court upheld FDR's order in *Korematsu v. United States*. Congress issued a formal apology to the survivors in 1988.

The Postwar World

The **United Nations** was formed in the wake of the Second World War, modeled after the failed League of Nations. Unlike the League, however, it included a **Security Council** comprised of major world powers, with the authority to militarily intervene for peacekeeping purposes in unstable global situations. Most of Europe had been destroyed, and the victorious US and the Soviet Union emerged as the two global **superpowers**.

In 1945, Stalin, Churchill, and Roosevelt met at the **Yalta Conference** to determine the future of Europe. The Allies had agreed on free elections for European countries following the fall of the fascist regimes.

After the war, however, the USSR occupied Eastern Europe, preventing free elections. The US saw this as a betrayal of the agreement at Yalta. Furthermore, while the US-led **Marshall Plan** began a program to rebuild Europe, the USSR consolidated its presence and power in eastern European countries, forcing them to reject aid from the Marshall Plan. This division would destroy the alliance between the Soviets and the West, leading to the **Cold War** between the two superpowers and the emergence of a **bipolar world**.

PRACTICE QUESTIONS

24) **Why did the United States and the Soviet Union turn against each other after the Second World War?**

A. Stalin felt that the Marshall Plan should have been extended to the Soviet Union.

B. Because of the fear of communism in the United States, the US had considered invading the USSR following the occupation of Nazi Germany.

C. Despite assurances to the contrary, the USSR occupied Eastern European countries, preventing free elections in those countries.

D. The Soviet Union was concerned that the United States would use the nuclear bomb again.

25) **What was the purpose of the United Nations Security Council?**

A. to provide a means for international military intervention in case of conflict that could threaten global safety, in order to avoid another world war

B. to provide a forum for the superpowers to maintain a dialogue

C. to provide a means for countries to counter the power of the US and USSR to limit the reach of the superpowers

D. to develop a plan to rebuild Europe and Japan

POSTWAR AND CONTEMPORARY UNITED STATES

COLD WAR AT HOME AND ABROAD

With the collapse of the relationship between the USSR and the US, distrust and fear of **communism** grew. Accusations of communist sympathies against public figures ran rampant during the **McCarthy Era** in the 1950s, reflecting domestic anxieties.

President Harry S Truman's **Truman Doctrine** stated that the US would support any country threatened by authoritarianism (communism). This led to the **Korean War** (1950 – 1953), a conflict between the US and Soviet-backed North Korean forces, which ended in a stalemate.

DID YOU KNOW?

Truman never requested an official declaration of war. Instead, fighting in the Korean War was backed by the United Nations. The US would drop more explosives on Korea during this conflict than throughout the entirety of those used in the Pacific during WWII.

US foreign policy was defined by two ideologies:

▶ **Containment**: the need to contain Soviet (communist) expansion

▶ **Domino theory**: once one country fell to communism, others would quickly follow

Other incidents continued under the administration of the popular President **John F. Kennedy**:

▶ the **Bay of Pigs** invasion in Cuba (1961), a failed effort to topple the communist government of Fidel Castro

▶ the **Cuban Missile Crisis** (1962), when Soviet missiles were discovered in Cuba and military crisis was narrowly averted

Meanwhile, in Southeast Asia, communist forces in North Vietnam were gaining power. Congress never formally declared war in Vietnam but gave the president authority to intervene militarily there through the **Gulf of Tonkin Resolution** (1964).

This protracted conflict—the **Vietnam War**—led to widespread domestic social unrest. Social unrest increased as US deaths rose, especially after the Vietnamese-led **Tet Offensive** (1968). The US ultimately withdrew from Vietnam. North Vietnamese forces, led by **Ho Chi Minh**, took over the entire country.

Figure 1.26. The Tet Offensive

CIVIL RIGHTS AND SOCIAL CHANGE

During the 1960s, the US experienced social and political change, starting with the election of the young and charismatic John F. Kennedy in 1960. Following JFK's assassination in 1963, President **Lyndon B. Johnson**'s administration saw the passage of liberal legislation in support of the poor and of civil rights.

The **Civil Rights Movement**, led by activists like the **Rev. Dr. Martin Luther King Jr.** and **Malcolm X**, fought for Black American rights, including the abolition of segregation in southern states and better living standards for Black people in northern cities.

In 1954, the Supreme Court heard the case ***Brown v. Board of Education***, against segregating schools. Under Chief Justice Earl Warren, the Court found segregation unconstitutional and overturned its decision in *Plessy v. Ferguson. Brown* occurred shortly after the desegregation of the armed forces. Public support for civil rights and racial equality was growing.

The **Southern Christian Leadership Conference (SCLC)** and Dr. King, a religious leader from Georgia, believed in civil disobedience, nonviolent protest. In Montgomery, Alabama, **Rosa Parks**, an African American woman, was arrested for refusing to give up her seat to a white man on a bus. Buses were segregated at the time, and leaders including Dr. King organized the **Montgomery Bus Boycott** to challenge segregation. The effort was ultimately successful.

Building on their success, civil rights activists, now including many students and the **Student Nonviolent Coordinating Committee (SNCC)**, led peaceful demonstrations and boycotts to protest segregation at lunch counters, in stores, and other public places.

The movement grew to include voter registration campaigns organized by CORE, the Congress of Racial Equality. White and Black students and activists from around the country supported CORE. These students and activists became known as the **Freedom Riders**, so-called because they rode buses from around the country to join the movement in the Deep South.

CHECK YOUR UNDERSTANDING #8

What was the initial goal of SCLC?

SNCC and activists organized to protest segregation at government and public facilities and on university campuses. The movement gained visibility as nonviolent protesters were met with violence by the police and state authorities, including attacks by water cannons and police dogs in Alabama. Undaunted, activists continued to fight against segregation and unfair voting restrictions on African Americans.

The Civil Rights Movement gained national public attention and had become a major domestic political issue. Civil rights workers organized the **March on Washington** in 1963, when Dr. King delivered his famous *I Have a Dream* speech.

Widespread public support for civil rights legislation was impossible for the government to ignore. In 1964, Congress passed the **Civil Rights Act**, which outlawed segregation.

Figure 1.27. March on Washington

Meanwhile, **Malcolm X** was an outspoken proponent of **Black empowerment**, particularly for African Americans in urban areas. Unlike Martin Luther King Jr., who supported integration, Malcolm X and other activists, including groups like the **Black Panthers**, believed that Black Americans should stay separate from White Americans to develop stronger communities.

THE VOTING RIGHTS ACT

Despite the successes of the Civil Rights Movement, African Americans' voting rights were still not sufficiently protected. According to the Fifteenth and the Nineteenth Amendments, all Black Americans—men and women—had the right to vote. But many southern states had voting restrictions in place, like literacy tests and poll taxes, which disproportionately affected African Americans.

To draw attention to this issue, Dr. King and civil rights workers organized a march from Selma to Montgomery, Alabama. Marchers were attacked by police. In 1965, led by President Lyndon B. Johnson, Congress passed the **Voting Rights Act**, which prohibited restrictions on voting, including literacy tests. Separately, the **Twenty-Fourth Amendment** made poll taxes unconstitutional.

DID YOU KNOW?

Today, some states have instituted voter identification laws that disproportionately affect minorities. Many Americans believe these laws are similar to literacy tests and poll taxes. Debate continues in Congress and in the public sphere over the constitutionality of voter ID laws.

CIVIL RIGHTS FOR MORE AMERICANS

The Civil Rights Movement extended beyond the Deep South. **Cesar Chavez** founded the **United Farm Workers (UFW)**, which organized Hispanic and migrant farm workers in California and the Southwest to advocate for unionizing and collective bargaining. Farm workers were underpaid and faced racial discrimination. The UFW used boycotts and nonviolent tactics similar to those used by civil rights activists in the South. Cesar Chavez also used hunger strikes to raise awareness of the problems faced by farm workers.

The Civil Rights Movement also included **feminist** activists who fought for fairer treatment of women in the workplace and for women's reproductive rights. The **National Organization for Women** and feminist leaders like **Gloria Steinem** led the movement for equal pay for women in the workplace. The landmark case of *Roe v. Wade* struck down federal restrictions on abortion.

The **American Indian Movement (AIM)** brought attention to injustices and discrimination suffered by Native Americans nationwide. Ultimately it was able to achieve more tribal autonomy and address problems facing Native American communities throughout the United States.

In New York City in 1969, the **Stonewall riots** occurred in response to police repression of the gay community. These riots and subsequent organized activism are seen as the beginning of the Lesbian, Gay, Bisexual, Transgender, and Queer (LGBTQ) rights movement.

THE WAR ON POVERTY

President Kennedy had envisioned a liberal United States in the tradition of the Progressives. His youth and charisma were inspiring to many Americans, and his assassination in 1963 was a shock.

Kennedy's vice president, Lyndon B. Johnson, continued the liberal vision with the **Great Society**. LBJ embraced **liberalism**, believing that government should fight poverty at home and play an interventionist role abroad (in this era, by fighting communism).

Johnson launched a **War on Poverty**, passing reform legislation designed to support the poor and vulnerable:

DID YOU KNOW?

In a commencement address delivered to University of Michigan graduates in 1964, LBJ outlined his vision of the Great Society and challenged the new graduates to join him in tackling issues in cities, the environment, and classrooms to advance the quality of life in America.

▶ **Medicare Act:** provided medical care to American senior citizens

▶ **Department of Housing and Urban Development:** increased the federal role in housing and urban issues

▶ **Head Start:** provided early intervention for disadvantaged children before elementary school

▶ **Elementary and Secondary Education Act:** increased funding for primary and secondary education

During LBJ's administration, the **Immigration Act of 1965** was also passed. It overturned the racist Emergency Quota Act.

While taking steps to combat poverty at home, LBJ's overseas agenda was becoming increasingly unpopular. Adhering to containment and domino theory, Johnson drew the United States deeper into conflict in Southeast Asia.

The **Vietnam War** became extremely unpopular in the US due to:

▶ high casualties

▶ the unpopular draft (which forced young American males to fight overseas)

▶ confusion over the purpose of the war

Student activists, organizing in the mold of the Civil Rights Movement, engaged in protest against the Vietnam War. The rise of a **counterculture** among the youth added to a sense of rebellion among Americans, usurping government authority and challenging traditional values. Aspects included:

▶ the development and popularity of **rock and roll music**

▶   the culture of **hippies**

▶   changing concepts of drug use and sexuality

PRACTICE QUESTIONS

26) **Why did the Civil Rights Movement continue to push for legislative change even after the passage of the 1964 Civil Rights Act?**

   A.   While the Civil Rights Act provided legal protections to African Americans and other groups, many believed it did not go far enough since it did not outlaw segregation.

   B.   Leaders like Malcolm X believed further legislative reform would ensure better living conditions for blacks in cities.

   C.   Civil rights leaders wanted legislation to punish white authorities in the South who had oppressed African Americans.

   D.   Legal restrictions like literacy tests, poll taxes, and voter registration issues inhibited African Americans from exercising their right to vote, especially in the South.

27) **Which of the following best describes liberalism under LBJ?**

   A.   Liberalism was the philosophy that the government should be deeply involved in improving society at home and committed to fighting communism abroad.

   B.   According to liberalism, the US should devote its resources to improving life at home for the disadvantaged but refrain from direct intervention in international conflict.

   C.   Liberals believed in moderate social programs with limited spending.

   D.   Liberalism frowns upon conflict intervention, as shown by the mass demonstrations against the Vietnam War in the 1960s.

POLITICAL CONSERVATISM, SOCIAL LIBERALISM, AND THE TWENTY–FIRST CENTURY

Radical social change in the 1960s, coupled with the toll of the Vietnam War on the American public—many of whom had lost loved ones in the war or themselves served in combat—led to backlash against liberalism.

Conservatism strengthened in response to several factors:

▶   the heavy role of government in public life throughout the 1960s

▶   high rates of government spending

▶   social challenges to traditional values

Due in great part to the escalation of the Vietnam War, LBJ announced his intention not to run for another term. The conservative **Richard Nixon** became president in 1970.

ECONOMIC AND INTERNATIONAL CRISES

During President Richard Nixon's administration, the conflict in Vietnam ended, and a diplomatic relationship with China began. Nixon also oversaw economic reforms. He lifted the gold standard in an effort to stop **stagflation**, a phenomenon when both unemployment and inflation are simultaneously high. Ending the gold standard reduced the value of the dollar in relation to other global currencies and foreign investment in the United States increased.

However, the Nixon administration was found to have engaged in corrupt practices. A burglary at the Democratic National Headquarters, based at the Watergate Hotel, was connected to the Oval Office. The **Watergate scandal** eventually forced Nixon to resign, and Vice President **Gerald Ford** took office for one term. Nixon's resignation further destroyed many Americans' faith in their government.

> CHECK YOUR UNDERSTANDING #9
>
> Define *stagflation*.

During the 1970s, the economy suffered due to US involvement in the Middle East. US support for Israel in the Six Day War and 1973 Yom Kippur War caused **OPEC** (the Organization of Petroleum Exporting Countries), led by Saudi Arabia and other allies of Arab foes of Israel, to boycott the US. As a result, oil prices sky-rocketed. In the 1979 Iranian Revolution and the resulting **hostage crisis**, when the US Embassy in Tehran was taken over by anti-American activists, the economy suffered from another oil shock.

While President Jimmy Carter had been able to negotiate peace between Israel and Egypt in the **Camp David Accords**, he was widely perceived as ineffective. Carter lost the presidency in 1980 to the conservative Republican **Ronald Reagan**.

Reagan championed domestic tax cuts and an aggressive foreign policy against the Soviet Union. The Reagan Revolution revamped the economic system, cutting taxes and government spending. According to supply-side economics (popularly known as *Reaganomics*), cutting taxes on the wealthy and providing investment incentives, would result in a "trickle down" of wealth to the middle and working classes and the poor. But tax cuts forced Congress to cut or eliminate social programs that benefitted millions of those same Americans. Later, the **Tax Reform Act** of 1986 ended progressive income taxation.

REAGAN AND THE ARMS RACE

Despite promises to lower government spending, the Reagan administration invested huge sums of money in the military. This investment in military technology—the **arms race** with the Soviet Union—helped bring about the end of the Cold War with the 1991 fall of the USSR and, later, a new era of globalization.

In addition to funding a general arms buildup and supporting measures to strengthen the military, the Reagan administration funded and developed advanced military technology to intimidate the Soviets, despite having signed the **Strategic Arms Limitation Treaties (SALT I and II)** limiting nuclear weapons and other strategic armaments in the 1970s. Ultimately, the US would outspend the USSR militarily, a precipitating factor to the fall of the Soviet Union.

The Reagan Revolution also ushered in an era of conservative values in the public sphere. After the Civil Rights Era, whose victories had occurred under the auspices of the Democratic Johnson administration, many southern Democrats switched loyalties to the Republican Party. At the same time, the Democrats gained the support of African Americans and other minority groups who benefitted from civil rights and liberal legislation.

During the Reagan Era, conservative Republicans espoused a return to "traditional" values. **Christian fundamentalism** became popular, particularly among white conservatives. Groups like **Focus on the Family** lobbied against civil rights reform for women and advocated for traditional, two-parent, heterosexual families.

THE END OF THE COLD WAR AND GLOBALIZATION

The administration of **George H.W. Bush** signed the **Strategic Arms Reduction Treaty (START),** with the Soviet Union in 1991, shortly before the dissolution of the USSR. Later, it would enter into force in 1994 between the US and the Russian Federation as an agreement to limit the large arsenals of strategic weapons possessed by both countries.

With the collapse of the Soviet Union, the balance of international power changed. The bipolar world became a unipolar world, and the United States was the sole superpower.

A major crisis occurred in the Middle East when Iraq, led by **Saddam Hussein**, invaded oil-rich Kuwait. This threatened international access to petroleum.

The US intervened with the blessing of the United Nations and the support of other countries. The resulting **Gulf War**, or **Operation Desert Storm** (1991), cemented US status as the world's sole superpower. Saddam's forces were driven from Kuwait, and Iraq was restrained by sanctions and no-fly zones.

With the election of President **Bill Clinton** in 1992, the US took an active role in international diplomacy, helping broker peace deals in the former Yugoslavia, Northern Ireland, and the Middle East.

Clinton's election also indicated a more socially liberal era in American society. While conservative elements remained a strong force in politics and sectors of society, changing attitudes toward minorities in the public sphere and increased global communication (especially with the advent of the internet) were a hallmark of the 1990s.

As part of **globalization**—the facilitation of global commerce and communication—the Clinton administration prioritized free trade. The United States signed the **North American Free Trade Agreement (NAFTA),** which removed trade restrictions with Mexico and Canada and created a free trade zone throughout North America.

The Clinton administration also eased financial restrictions in the US, rolling back some of the limitations provided for under Glass-Steagall. These changes were controversial: many American jobs went overseas, especially manufacturing jobs, where labor was cheaper.

Furthermore, globalization began facilitating the movement of people, including undocumented immigrants seeking a better life in the United States. **Immigration reform** would be a major issue into the twenty-first century.

Clinton faced dissent in the mid-1990s with a conservative resurgence. A movement of young conservatives elected to Congress in 1994 promised a **Contract with America**, a conservative platform promising a return to lower taxes and traditional values. Clinton also came under fire for personal scandals: allegations of corrupt real estate investments in the Whitewater scandal and inappropriate personal behavior in the White House. These scandals fueled social conservatives and Christian fundamentalists who favored a return to the conservative era of the 1980s.

Despite these controversies and political division, society became increasingly liberal:

▶ New technology like the **internet** facilitated national and global communication, media, and business.

▶ Minority groups like the LGBTQ community engaged in more advocacy.

▶ Environmental issues became more visible.

THE TWENTY-FIRST CENTURY

By the end of the twentieth century, the United States had proved itself as the dominant global economic, military, and political power. Due to its role in global conflict from the Spanish-American War onwards, the US had established military bases and a military presence worldwide: in Europe, Asia, the Pacific, and the Middle East.

The US also dominated global trade: American corporations established themselves globally, taking advantage of free trade to exploit cheap labor pools and less restrictive manufacturing environments (at the expense of American workers).

American culture remained widely popular as well. Since the early twentieth century, American pop culture—music, movies, television shows, and fashion—was enjoyed by millions of people around the world.

However, globalization also facilitated global conflict. While terrorism had been a feature of the twentieth century, the United States had been relatively untouched by large-scale terrorist attacks. That changed on **September 11, 2001**, when the terrorist group **al Qaeda** hijacked airplanes, attacking New York and Washington, DC, in the largest attack on US soil since the Japanese bombing of Pearl Harbor.

The 9/11 attacks triggered an aggressive military and foreign policy under the administration of **President George W. Bush**, who declared a War on Terror, an open-ended global conflict against terrorist organizations and their supporters.

Figure 1.28. Attacks of September 11, 2001

Following the attacks, the US struck suspected al Qaeda bases in Afghanistan, beginning the **Afghanistan War**, during which time the US occupied the country. Suspected terrorist fighters captured there and elsewhere during the War on Terror were held in a prison in **Guantanamo Bay**, Cuba, which was controversial because it did not initially offer any protections afforded to prisoners of war under the Geneva Conventions.

President Bush believed in the doctrine of **preemption**: if the US is aware of a threat, it should preemptively attack the source of that threat. Preemption would drive the invasion of Iraq in 2003, when the US attacked the country, believing that it held **weapons of mass destruction** that could threaten the safety of the United States. This assumption was later revealed to be false. Still, the United States launched the **Iraq War**, deposing Saddam Hussein and supporting a series of governments until it withdrew its troops in 2011, leaving the country in a state of chaos.

At home, Congress passed the **USA Patriot Act** to respond to fears of more terrorist attacks on US soil. This legislation gave the federal government unprecedented—and, some argued, unconstitutional—powers of surveillance over the American public.

Tax cuts and heavy reliance on credit (especially in the housing market, which fueled the **Subprime Mortgage Crisis**) during the Bush administration helped push the country into the **Great Recession**.

Despite the tense climate, social liberalization continued in the US.

In 2008, the first African American president, **Barack Obama**, a Democrat, was elected. Under his presidency, the US emerged from the recession, ended its major combat operations in Iraq and Afghanistan, passed the Affordable Care Act, which reformed the healthcare system, and legalized same-sex marriage.

The Obama administration also oversaw the passage of consumer protection acts, increased support for students, and safety nets for homeowners. His administration was not without challenge, though. Over the course of his two terms, the Democratic party would go on to lose more than 1,000 seats to Republicans in state legislatures, Congress, and at the gubernatorial level.

PRACTICE QUESTIONS

28) **Which of the following BEST describes globalization?**

   A. cutting taxes to induce a "trickle down" of wealth to the middle class and the poor

   B. free trade among countries and easier international communication

   C. increased visibility and importance of environmental issues

   D. open-ended global conflict against terrorist organizations and their supporters

29) **How did Reagan's economic policies affect working class and poor Americans?**

   A. They had little effect on these classes because the United States has a free market economy.

   B. They increased taxes by eliminating the progressive income tax and cut social programs needed by many disadvantaged people.

   C. They benefitted the working and middle classes by cutting taxes and increasing investment opportunities.

   D. Despite Reagan's tax cuts, the government was able to fund all social programs, so lower income Americans who used them were unaffected by changes in revenue.

30) **How did the Bush doctrine of preemption affect US foreign policy in the early twenty-first century?**

    A.   The US believed that to contain terrorism, it had to occupy countries that might harbor terrorists.

    B.   Fearing that the entire Middle East would succumb to terrorists, the Bush administration established a presence in the centrally located country of Iraq to avoid a "domino effect" of regime collapse.

    C.   The Bush administration justified international intervention and foreign invasion without previous provocation to preempt possible terrorist attacks.

    D.   The US held prisoners captured during the War on Terror at Guantanamo Bay, where they were not given the protections and privileges entitled to prisoners of war under the Geneva Conventions.

Practice Questions Answer Key

1)   **B.** Powerful tribes controlled trade and territory; among these were the powerful Iroquois Confederacy.

2)   **B.** The Algonquin people were primarily located in what is today Quebec and southern Ontario, but the Algonquian language was spoken widely throughout North America among both settled and semi-settled non-Algonquin peoples.

3)   **B.** The Choctaw, Creek, Chickasaw, and others were Muskogean-speaking peoples; the Cherokee spoke an Iroquoian language. Both tribes were settled.

4)   **A.** The Great Plains tribes depended on buffalo, which were plentiful before European contact and settlement, for food; they also used buffalo parts for clothing and to make necessary items.

5)   **B.** The Ancestral Pueblo had settled in what is today the Four Corners region. The Navajo came to control land extending through present-day Arizona, New Mexico, and Utah.

6)   **A.** Spain established missions to spread Christianity, in addition to settling and exploiting the land; France worked to establish networks of trade and did not concentrate on religious conversion (although the Church was present and at work in its colonies). Both intermarried locally.

7)   **A.** The southern colonies featured a climate conducive to plantation agriculture. Crops like tobacco, cotton, and rice grew easily there, and led to demand for enslaved people.

8)   **C.** John Locke's *Second Treatise* was critical of absolute monarchy and became popular in the colonies.

9)   **B.** William Penn founded these colonies in the spirit of his tolerant Quaker faith.

10)   **C.** The Beaver Wars, the Chickasaw Wars, and later the French and Indian War (which was part of the Seven Years' War) are all examples of British-French conflict playing out in North America.

11)   **D.** Anger at being forced to provide shelter for British soldiers led

to protests; in 1770, British soldiers fired on protests against the Quartering Act in what came to be called the Boston Massacre.

12)   **B.** Shays' Rebellion, in which Daniel Shays led a rebellion of indebted farmers shortly after the end of the Revolution, showed the need for a stronger federal government to ensure national stability and was a major factor in planning the Constitutional Convention.

13)   **A.** Westward expansion accelerated after US independence. The Shawnee, Lenape, Miami, Kickapoo, and others organized to form the Northwest Confederacy.

14)   **C.** Universal manhood suffrage allowed all white males, whether or not they owned property, to vote; the "common man" had a voice in government, and Jackson enjoyed their support. Likewise, an influx of poor European immigrants changed the country's demographics, providing more workers for early industry, more settlers interested in populating the west, and a stronger voice in government against the wealthy.

15)   **B.** The Missouri Compromise allowed Missouri to join the union as a slave state but prohibited enslavement in any other new states north of the thirty-sixth parallel. By limiting the permissibility of enslaving people in new states, the Missouri Compromise showed how strongly the abolitionist movement affected politics.

16)   **D.** Legislation like the Missouri Compromise, the Compromise of 1850, and the Kansas-Nebraska Act represented ongoing efforts to bridge the gap between differences in views over slavery in determining the future of the country.

17)   **B.** The punitive Dawes Act forced assimilation by revoking federal recognition of tribes, taking lands allotted to tribes and dissolving reservations, and forcing children into assimilationist schools (thereby dividing families).

18)   **B.** Horizontal and vertical integration of industries allowed the same companies—and people—to control industries, or create monopolies. Those elites who monopolized specific markets organized trusts so that one group controlled entire sectors of the economy.

19)   **A.** Unions improved conditions for industrial workers; the Social Gospel imparted a sense of social responsibility that eventually manifested in laws and regulations protecting the rights and safety of workers, farmers, the poor, and others.

20)   **B.** US military successes showed European powers and other countries its strength as a military power.

21)   **A.** The sinking of the *Lusitania*, which resulted in numerous civilian deaths, was one factor causing the US to enter WWI.

22)   **A.** FDR focused on immediate economic stabilization upon taking office, then attacked poverty and unemployment on a sustainable basis.

23)   **B.** The Harlem Renaissance is one example of the emergence of African American culture in the public imagination; as US popular culture developed, African American contributions had a strong influence.

24)   **C.** Stalin's refusal to permit free elections or democracy in the countries of Eastern Europe was seen as a betrayal of the agreement reached by the Allies at Yalta, and a major reason for the collapse of the US-Soviet relationship.

25)   **A.** While the UN was modeled in part after the League of Nations, the Security Council was (and is) able to militarily intervene in cases of armed conflict that could pose a global threat, an ability the League of Nations did not have.

26)   **D.** Despite the end to legal segregation, discrimination was deeply entrenched, and laws still existed to prevent African Americans from voting. Civil rights activists worked to ensure the passage of the Voting Rights Act in 1965.

27)   **A.** LBJ believed in forming a Great Society and launched a War on Poverty, initiating federal government-sponsored social programs to support the disadvantaged; he also actively waged a war against the spread of communism in Southeast Asia, ultimately unsuccessfully.

28)   **B.** Globalization is the facilitation of global commerce and communication.

29)   **B.** Supply-side economics theorized that low taxes on the wealthy would encourage investment in the economy; as a result, wealth would "trickle down" to the middle and working classes and the poor. However, in practice, lower taxes meant less government revenue and many social programs that were needed by poor Americans were cut.

30)   **C.** Preemption was used to justify the 2003 invasion of Iraq, on the assumption that Iraq had weapons of mass destruction it intended to use or to provide for terrorist attacks against the United States.

Check Your Understanding Answer Key

Check Your Understanding #1

Great Plains peoples (e.g., **Sioux, Cheyenne, Apache, Comanche, Arapaho)**

Check Your Understanding #2

tobacco, rice, beaver pelts, fur

Check Your Understanding #3

Pontiac's Rebellion showed resistance to colonial incursions, accelerated European concerns that a stronger military presence was needed in the North American colonies, and resulted in an agreement not to settle land west of the Appalachians (Proclamation of 1763).

Check Your Understanding #4

1) admitted California as a free state; 2) allowed legality of slavery to be decided by popular sovereignty in Utah and New Mexico; 3) upheld the Fugitive Slave Act; 4) abolished the slave trade (but not slavery) in Washington, DC; 5) fixed the boundaries of Texas along its current lines

Check Your Understanding #5

heavy industry, petroleum/oil, westward expansion (railroads and steel)

Check Your Understanding #6

consumer credit, overspeculation on crops/land, weak banking protections

Check Your Understanding #7

economic weakness from the Great Depression, support for isolationism, the Neutrality Acts

Check Your Understanding #8

The initial goal of the Southern Christian Leadership Conference (SCLC) was desegregation.

Check Your Understanding #9

both unemployment and inflation are high at the same time

(Usually, when unemployment is low, inflation is high, and vice versa.)

2

World History

EARLY CIVILIZATIONS AND THE GREAT EMPIRES

PALEOLITHIC AND NEOLITHIC ERAS

The earliest humans were hunter-gatherers until the development of agriculture in about 11,000 BCE. They began migrating from Africa 60,000 – 70,000 years ago, gradually spreading out across the continents in several waves of migration throughout Europe and Asia and eventually into Australia, the Pacific Islands, and the Americas.

Human history begins with the **Paleolithic Era** followed by the **Neolithic period**.

Early **hominids** of the Paleolithic Era:

- *Australopithecus*

- *Homo habilis* (descended from *Australopithecus*)

- *Homo erectus* (descended from *Australopithecus*)

- *Homo neanderthalensis* (descended from *Australopithecus*)

Figure 2.1. Early Hominids

- *Homo sapiens sapiens* (descended from *Australopithecus*; the modern-day human)

All are now extinct, save for us, *Homo sapiens*.

DID YOU KNOW?

Evidence suggests that *Homo sapiens sapiens* and *Homo neanderthalensis* coexisted.

Table 2.1. The Paleolithic and Neolithic Eras

Paleolithic Era	Neolithic Era
▶ before agricultural development and settled communities ▶ the use of tools exhibited by hominids (up to and including our ancestors) ▶ rudimentary human technology based on stone; referred to as the **Old Stone Age**. ▶ took place before 11,000 BCE	▶ humans began settling communities, developing agricultural practices, and domesticating animals ▶ notable technological advancements (tools, weapons, and other metal objects) made by working with copper and tin; the start of the **Bronze Age** ▶ also referred to as the *New Stone Age* ▶ all species of humans extinct except *Homo sapiens sapiens* ▶ behavioral and technological changes, such as the invention of the wheel ▶ began approximately 11,000 – 10,500 BCE

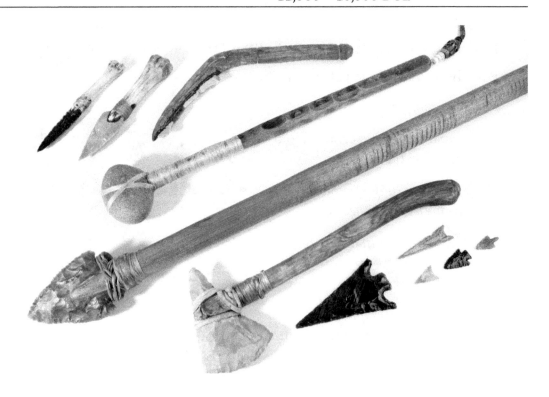

Figure 2.2. Early Tools

MIDDLE EAST AND EGYPT

Beginning in the Near East, settled societies organized into larger centralized communities. These were characterized by early social stratification and rule of law. The earliest known examples of these were in the **Fertile Crescent**, the area in North Africa and Southwest Asia stretching from Egypt through the Levant and into Mesopotamia.

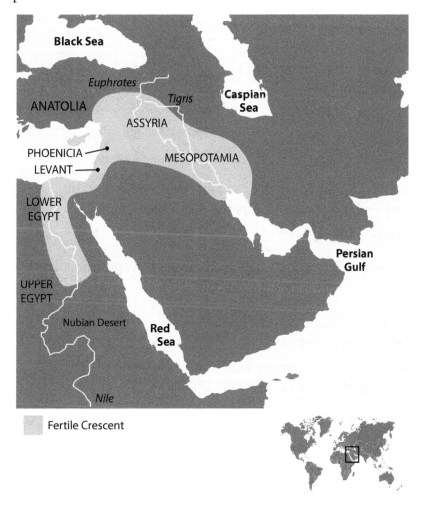

Figure 2.3. Fertile Crescent

Around 2500 BCE (or possibly earlier) the **Sumerians** emerged in the Near East (eventually expanding into parts of Mesopotamia). By developing irrigation and advanced agriculture, they were able to support settled areas that developed into city-states and eventually major cities like Uruk.

The Sumerians are known especially for the following:

▶   cuneiform: the earliest known example of writing to use characters to form words

▶ early education, literary, and artistic developments (the *Epic of Gilgamesh*, for example); made possible by the Sumerian's development of cuneiform

▶ architectural achievements (ziggurats, for example)

▶ the creation of city-states and advanced governance and administration; also facilitated by cuneiform as a written language

▶ the potter's wheel, early astronomy, mathematics, religious thought

Figure 2.4. Ziggurats

Eventually the Sumerians were overcome by Semitic-speaking, nomadic peoples in the Fertile Crescent: the result was the **Akkadian Empire**.

The Akkadian Empire:

▶ grew to encompass much of the Levant, Mesopotamia, and parts of Persia;

▶ includes the Semitic Akkadian language, which adopted cuneiform, as one of its major legacies.

Around the eighteenth century BCE, the Akkadians had given way to **Babylonia** in southern Mesopotamia and **Assyria** in the north. These two civilizations would develop roughly concurrently and remain at odds, with Babylonia eventually coming under Assyrian domination until the final defeat of Assyria by Babylonia in 612 BCE in the battle of Nineveh, the Assyrian capital.

Before its defeat, Assyria had developed as a powerful city-state in northern Mesopotamia. The Assyrians had based much of their culture on the Sumerian and Akkadian legacies, contributing unique sculpture and jewelry, establishing military dominance, and playing an important role in regional trade.

HELPFUL HINT

Settled communities needed the reliable sources of food and fresh water a temperate climate could provide. Surpluses of food enabled civilization and culture, not just survival.

At odds with Babylonia over the centuries, the Assyrian Empire had grown to encompass most of the Fertile Crescent. The Assyrian identity persists to this day among the (widely persecuted) Assyrian people in Iraq, Syria, Turkey, and Iran.

Around 1200 BCE, during a time of instability in Mesopotamia, the region became vulnerable to the **Hittites** from Anatolia.

The Hittites are especially known for the following:

▶ developing in the Bronze Age but flourishing in the **Iron Age**

▶ developing expertise in metallurgy to create strong weapons

▶ mastering horsemanship

▶ inventing chariots

▶ becoming a strong military power (due to their advancements in the Iron Age)

As a result, the Hittites became a threat to both the Assyrians and, later, the Egyptians (see below). Not only did these empires risk losing land, they also lost control of trade routes throughout the Fertile Crescent. Eventually, however, Assyria grew strong enough to overcome the Hittites.

Like Assyria, Babylonia inherited the Akkadian language and used the Sumerian language in religious settings; it also inherited other elements of Sumerian civilization and developed them further.

Major achievements in Babylonia included:

▶ the development of courts in the eighteenth century BCE by King Hammurabi

▶ the development of an early codified rule of law—**the Code of Hammurabi**—which meted out justice on an equal basis: "an eye for an eye, a tooth for a tooth"

▶ the continuation of settled urban development supported by organized agriculture, warfare, administration, and justice

▶ the creation of Babylon as a major ancient city

▶ the development of more advanced astronomy, medicine, mathematics, philosophy, and art (particularly in working with clay, building bricks, and bas relief)

▶ literature, including developing the Sumerian poetry that was the basis for the *Epic of Gilgamesh* into the extended work we know today

DID YOU KNOW?

According to the Smithsonian, more lines from the *Epic of Gilgamesh* have been discovered in stone fragments in Iraq as recently as 2011.

After the fall of Nineveh, Babylonia would control Mesopotamia until the fall of Babylon to the Persian Achaemenid Empire in Persia in 539 BCE (see below).

Meanwhile, development had been under way in the **Nile Valley** in ancient **Egypt**. Despite the surrounding Sahara Desert, the fertile land on the banks of the

Nile River lent itself to agriculture. The early Egyptians were able to develop settled communities thanks to agriculture and irrigation.

The ancient Egyptians:

▶ emerged as early as 5000 BCE

▶ are known for their pyramids, art, and pictorial writing (**hieroglyphs**)

▶ were united under one monarch, or **pharaoh**, dating to the First Dynasty, around 3000 BCE

Civilizations developed on the Upper and Lower Nile, unifying under the early dynasties, which established the Egyptian capital at **Memphis**.

By the Fourth Dynasty, Egypt's civilizational institutions, written language, art, and architecture were well developed. It was during this period that the famous **pyramids** were erected at Giza. These structures were actually burial tombs for the Pharaohs Khufu, Khafre, and Menkaure circa 2400 – 2500 BCE. In addition, the religious framework of ancient Egypt had become established, with a complex mythology of various gods.

CHECK YOUR UNDERSTANDING #1

What were the contributions of the early Middle Eastern civilizations? List several.

Following this period, around 2200 BCE, Egypt became increasingly unstable. Eventually fighters from the city of Thebes took over, establishing the Eleventh Dynasty. The subsequent Twelfth Dynasty took control of Nubia (now Sudan), an area rich in gold and other materials. Egypt grew in power and reached its apex during the Eighteenth Dynasty, between 1550 and 1290 BCE. Led by the powerful Pharaoh **Thutmose III**, Egypt expanded into the Levant.

Later, **King Akhenaten (Amenhotep IV)** abolished the Egyptian religion, establishing a cult of the sun—Aten—linked to himself. During this period Egypt saw a surge of iconoclastic art and sculpture. However, Akhenaten's successors, particularly Ramesses I and Ramesses II, founded the Nineteenth Dynasty and returned to traditional values.

Figure 2.5. Egyptian Hieroglyphs

Under **Ramesses II**, Egypt battled the aggressive Hittites in the Levant, reaching a stalemate. Egypt eventually fell into decline, losing control of the Levant and ultimately falling to Assyria.

ASIA

Meanwhile, early civilizations also developed farther east. The **Indus Valley Civilization** flourished in the Indian subcontinent and the Indus and Ganges river basins. The **Harappan** civilization was based in Punjab from around 3000 BCE.

The Harappan civilization is known for the following:

▶ creating the major cities of **Harappa** and **Mohenjo-daro**, which may be the earliest planned cities in the world and featured grid systems indicative of detailed urban planning

▶ trade links between the civilizations, as evidenced by Harappan objects found in Mesopotamia

Centuries later, concurrent with the Roman Empire, the **Gupta Empire** emerged in India. The Gupta Empire introduced the Golden Age of India, characterized by its strong economy due to active trade by sea with China, East Africa, and the Middle East.

▶ Traded goods included spices, ivory, silk, cotton, and iron, which was highly profitable as an export.

▶ The Guptas encouraged music, art, architecture, and Sanskrit literature and philosophy.

▶ The empire, practitioners of Hinduism, was tolerant of Buddhists and Jains.

Organized administration and rule of law made it possible for **Chandragupta II** to govern a large territory throughout the Subcontinent. However, by 550 CE, invasions from the north by the Huns and internal conflicts within the Subcontinent led to imperial decline.

DID YOU KNOW?

Chandragupta II was considered a benevolent ruler and earned admiration for providing free hospitals and rest houses.

In China, the **Shang Dynasty**, the first known dynasty, ruled the **Huang He** or **Yellow River** area around the second millennium BCE.

Achievements of the Shang Dynasty include:

▶ developing the earliest known Chinese writing, which helped unite Chinese-speaking people throughout the region

▶ the use of bronze technology, horses, wheeled technology, walled cities, and other advances beyond those of the Neolithic societies

Around 1056 BCE the Zhou Dynasty emerged. It succeeded the Shang and expanded Chinese civilization to the **Chiang Jiang (Yangtze River)** region.

The Zhou Dynasty is known for:

▶ developing a social and political infrastructure in China in which family aristocracies controlled the country, with the capital at Hao (near Xi'an)

▶ tracts of land throughout the country controlled by ancestral cults in a hierarchy similar to later European feudalism

▶ setting the foundation for hierarchical rule and social stratification

DID YOU KNOW?

Shared customs like the use of silkworms, jade, chopsticks, and the practice of Confucianism are also indications of early Chinese unity.

The unstable period toward the end of the Zhou Dynasty is known as the **Spring and Autumn Period**. During this time **Confucius** (c. 551 – 479 BCE) lived. His teachings would be the basis for Confucianism, the foundational Chinese philosophy emphasizing harmony and respect for hierarchy.

Figure 2.6. Confucius

DID YOU KNOW?

The concept of the **Mandate of Heaven**, in which the emperor had a divine mandate to rule, emerged from the understanding that land was divinely inherited.

Following the chaotic **Warring States Period** (c. 475 – 221 BCE) the short-lived but influential **Qin Dynasty** emerged, unifying disparate Chinese civilizations and regions under the first Emperor, **Qin Shi Huang** (also known as **Shihuangdi**).

The Qin dynasty (221 – 206 BCE) was characterized by:

▶   a centralized administration

▶   expanded infrastructure

▶   standardized weights and measures

▶   standardized writing

▶   standardized currency

▶   strict imperial control

The administrative bureaucracy established by the emperor was the foundation of Chinese administration until the twentieth century.

During the Qin Dynasty, China expanded as far south as Vietnam. In addition, Emperor Qin Shi Huang constructed the **Great Wall of China**. His tomb is guarded by the famous **terracotta figurines**.

Figure 2.7. Great Wall of China

Despite the short length of the Qin Dynasty, it had a lasting impact on Chinese organization. The **Han Dynasty** took over in 206 for the next 300 years (206 BCE – 220 CE), retaining Qin administrative organization and adding Confucian ideals of hierarchy and harmony.

The Han prized education in the Confucian tradition. The idea that educated men should control administrative government began to take root in China. Women were not included in politics or administration.

THE AMERICAS

Prehistoric peoples migrated to the Americas from Asia during the Paleolithic period, and evidence of their presence dates to 13,000 years ago. Remnants of the **Clovis** people from this time have been found in New Mexico; however, recent findings in Canada suggest that prehistoric peoples may have come to North America even earlier—about 13,300 years ago.

▶ Migration from Asia was gradual, probably occurring over hundreds or thousands of years.

▶ Early humans likely crossed by land from Siberia to Alaska, while some may even have had naval capabilities and arrived by boat.

▶ Gradually, humans spread throughout the hemisphere.

From around 1200 BCE, the **Olmec** civilization developed on the Mexican Gulf Coast. Its massive sculptures reflect complex religious and spiritual beliefs. Later civilizations in Mexico included the **Zapotecs**, **Mixtecs**, **Toltecs**, and **Mayas** in the Yucatán peninsula. Throughout Mesoamerica, civilizations had developed irrigation to expand and enrich agriculture, similar to developments in the Fertile Crescent.

Meanwhile, in South America, artistic evidence remains of the Chavin, Moche, and Nazca peoples, who preceded the later Inca civilization and Empire.

The art produced by the Chavin, Moche, and Nazca peoples each had distinct features:

▶ The **Chavin** style, which was complex, focused on animals and went on to influence Andean art.

▶ The **Moche** people left behind complicated ceramics that are comparable to Hellenic artifacts.

▶ Enormous sketches in the ground, known as the famous Nazca lines, are visible only from the air. How they were constructed by the **Nazca** peoples remains a mystery.

Figure 2.8. Nazca Lines

In North America, the remains of mounds in the Mississippi Valley region may be evidence of ancient spiritual structures. For more discussion of precolonial North American peoples, please see Chapter One, "United States History."

PERSIA AND GREECE

The Persian Emperor **Cyrus**, founder of the **Achaemenid Empire**, conquered the Babylonians in the sixth century BCE. His son **Darius** extended Persian rule from the Indus Valley to Egypt, and north to Anatolia by about 400 BCE, where the Persians encountered the ancient Greeks.

Known for its fundamental impact on Western civilization to this day, the neighboring Greek, or **Hellenic civilization**, included political, philosophical, and mathematical thought; art and architecture; and poetry and theater.

> **CHECK YOUR UNDERSTANDING #2**
>
> How is Greek philosophy and its focus on reason important in modern culture?

Greece was comprised of city states like Athens, the first known democracy, and the military state Sparta. Historically these city-states had been rivals; however, they temporarily united to come to the aid of Ionian Greeks in Anatolia under Persian rule and drive Persia from Greece.

In Anatolia, the Persian king Xerxes led two campaigns against Greek forces. The Greeks held the Persians at bay, and much of Greece became unified under Athens following the war. The Persians had been decisively defeated at the battles of **Marathon** (490 BCE) and Salamis (480 BCE) around 460 BCE. It was during this period, the **Golden Age** of Greek civilization, that much of the Hellenic art, architecture, and philosophy known today emerged.

Democracy in the Hellenic civilization was participatory rather than representative: instead of being elected, officials were chosen by groups. Of the many small political bodies, Athens was the strongest. Under the Athenian leaders Pericles and Ephialtes, Athens became a revolutionary democracy controlled by the poor and working classes.

> **DID YOU KNOW?**
>
> The word political comes from the Greek word **polis** meaning "city-state" or "community." The term democracy comes from the Greek word **demokratia**— "people power."

During the Golden Age and into the fourth century BCE, numerous achievements took place. Many of these would go on to influence western society:

▶ The **Parthenon** was built, as were other masterpieces of ancient Greek sculpture and architecture.

▶ **Socrates** began teaching philosophy, influencing later philosophers, like **Plato**, who founded the Academy where figures such as **Aristotle** emerged. This established the basis for modern western philosophical and political thought.

► Playwrights like Sophocles, Euripides, and Aeschylus emerged; their work influenced later western literature.

Figure 2.9. The Parthenon

Despite its status as a democracy, Athens was not fully democratic: women did not have a place in politics, and Athenians practiced slavery. Furthermore, those men eligible to participate in political life had to prove that both of their parents were Athenian (the criterion of double descent).

Toward the end of the fifth century BCE, Athens and Sparta were at odds once again during the **Peloponnesian War** (431 – 404 BCE), which involved most of the Hellenic world and ultimately crippled the Athenian democracy permanently.

Instability permitted the rise of the northern state of Macedon, and in the fourth century BCE, Philip II of Macedonia was able to take over most of Greece. His son **Alexander** (later known as Alexander the Great) would go on to conquer Persia, spreading Greek civilization throughout much of western and central Asia.

ROME

Meanwhile, in Italy, the ancient Romans had begun consolidating their power. The city of **Rome** was founded as early as the eighth century BCE and became strong thanks to its importance as a trade route for the Greeks and other Mediterranean peoples. Early Roman culture drew from the **Etruscans**, Indigenous inhabitants of the Italian peninsula, and the Greeks, from whom it borrowed elements of architecture, art, language, and even religion.

Originally a kingdom, Rome became a republic under Lucius Junius Brutus in 509 BCE. As a **republic**, Rome elected lawmakers (senators) to the **Senate**. Economically powerful Rome began conquering areas around the Mediterranean with its increasingly powerful military, expanding westward to North Africa in the **Punic Wars** (264 – 146 BCE) against its rival Carthage (in present-day Tunisia).

With the conquest of territory and expansion of trade came increased slavery and the displacement of Rome's working class (**Plebeians**). At the same time, the wealthy ruling class (**Patricians**) became more powerful and corrupt. Resulting protest movements led by the tribunes Gaius and Tiberius led to legislative reform and republican stabilization, strengthening the republic by the first century BCE.

The increasingly diversified republic, while militarily and economically strong, was still divided:

> **DID YOU KNOW?**
>
> The Romans developed highly advanced infrastructure, including aqueducts and roads. Some remain in use to this day!

- ▶ the wealthy ruling class (the **Optimates**, or "the best")

- ▶ the working, the poor, and the military (the **Populare**, "the people"), who favored more democratization

As the Senate weakened due to its own corruption, the First Triumvirate of the military leaders **Gaius Julius Caesar** and Gnaeus Pompeius Magnus (Pompey the Great), and the wealthy citizen Marcus Licinius Crassus consolidated their rule of the republic. Pompey and Crassus belonged to the Optimate class, while Julius Caesar, a popular military leader, was firmly of the Populare.

Caesar had proven himself in the widely chronicled conquest of Gaul (today, France), and was respected and beloved by the military for his personal devotion to his troops. Meanwhile, Crassus was the wealthiest man in Rome, controlling most of the political class. Despite his wealth and though he had played a role in the defeat of the widespread slave rebellion led by the gladiator **Spartacus**, Crassus was unpopular among the Populare and was not regarded as a military leader on the level of Caesar.

Pompey had led successful missions conquering territory for Rome in Syria and elsewhere in the Levant. He also took credit for defeating Spartacus, though he played less of a role than Crassus, which caused a rift between the two.

With resentment between Crassus and Pompey over credit for the defeat of Spartacus, Crassus's insecurity over his perception as a military leader, and Caesar's popularity among the Populare, the Triumvirate was short-lived. Crassus was killed fighting the Parthians in Turkey in 53 BCE, at which point Pompey and Caesar declared war upon each other. The two fought in Greece where Pompey was defeated, fled to Egypt, and assassinated.

Forcing the corrupt Senate to give him control, Caesar began to transition Rome from a republic (if, at that point, in name only) to what would become an empire. Caesar was assassinated by a group of senators led by Brutus and Cassius in 44 BCE. However, in that short time he had been able to consolidate and centralize imperial control.

His cousin, **Marcus Antonius (Mark Antony)**, his friend Marcus Aemilius Lepidus, and his nephew **Gaius Octavius Thurinus (Octavian)** defeated Brutus and Cassius two years later at the Battle of Philippi, forming the Second Triumvirate.

Lepidus was sent from Rome to Hispania (Spain) and Africa while Mark Antony and Octavian split control of Rome between east and west, respectively. However, the two went to war after Antony became involved with the Egyptian queen Cleopatra, upsetting the balance of power. Octavian defeated Antony and Cleopatra, taking control of Rome in 31 BCE. He took the name **Augustus Caesar** when the Senate gave him supreme power in 27 BCE, becoming the first Roman emperor and effectively starting the Roman Empire.

At this time, Rome reached the height of its power, and the Mediterranean region enjoyed a period of stability known as the **Pax Romana**. Rome controlled the entire Mediterranean region and lands stretching as far north as Germany and Britain, territory into the Balkans, far into the Middle East, Egypt, North Africa, and Iberia.

CHECK YOUR UNDERSTANDING #3

How did social divisions emerge in the republic of Rome and ultimately lead to the creation of the Roman Empire?

In this time of relative peace and prosperity, Latin literature flourished, as did art, architecture, philosophy, mathematics, science, and international trade throughout Rome and beyond into Asia and Africa.

A series of emperors would follow and Rome remained a major world power, but it would never again reach the height of prosperity and stability that it did under Augustus.

It was during the time of Augustus that a Jewish carpenter in Palestine, named Jesus, began teaching that he was the son of the Jewish God and that his death would provide salvation for all of humanity. Jesus was eventually crucified. Followers of **Jesus Christ**, called Christians, preached his teachings throughout Rome. Despite the persecution of Christians, the concept of forgiveness of sin became popular and **Christianity** would eventually become the official religion of Rome. Christianity's universal appeal and applicability to people of diverse backgrounds would allow it to spread quickly.

By 300 CE, Rome was in decline. Following a series of unstable administrations, **Diocletian** (284 – 305 CE) took over as emperor, effectively dividing the empire into two: the Western Roman Empire and the Eastern Roman Empire.

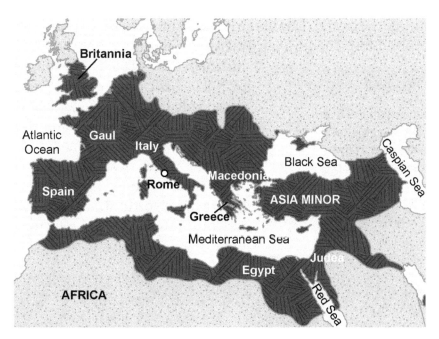

Figure 2.10. Pax Romana

Diocletian reestablished some stability and more effective administration, creating a loose power-sharing agreement throughout the empire. The Christian **Constantine** took over the eastern half of the empire, establishing a new capital at **Constantinople** and Christianity as an official religion. The ambitious Constantine reconquered the Western Roman Empire and reunited the empire in 324 CE. The capital remained at Constantinople, and the balance of power and stability shifted to the east.

This political shift enabled the western (later, Catholic) Church to gain power in Rome. One of Jesus Christ's followers, Peter, was considered to be the first **pope**, or leader of Christian ministry. He had been executed in Rome in 67 CE after a lifetime of spreading the religion. Since then, the city has been a base of Christianity and home to the **Vatican**, the seat of the Catholic Church. Over time, the Catholic Church would become one of the most powerful political entities in the world. Even today, following several schisms in Christianity, there are around one billion Catholics worldwide.

The western part of the Roman Empire gradually fell into disarray. A weakening Rome had created security agreements with different European clans like the **Anglo-Saxons**, the **Franks**, the **Visigoths**, the **Ostrogoths**, and the **Slavs**, among others, to protect its western and northern borders.

Eventually, these groups rebelled against the government and what was left of the Roman Empire in the west finally fell. In Western Europe, the last Roman emperor was killed in 476 CE, marking the end of the empire. The west dissolved into territories controlled by these and other tribes.

Meanwhile the eastern part of the Roman Empire, with its capital at Constantinople, evolved into the unified **Byzantine Empire**. The Byzantine Emperor **Justinian** (527 – 565 CE) re-conquered parts of North Africa, Egypt, and Greece, established rule of law, reinvigorated trade with China, and built the Hagia Sophia, the cathedral and center of orthodox Christianity. Ultimately, the Byzantines would control varying amounts of land in Anatolia, the Levant, and North Africa until the conquest of Constantinople by the Ottoman Turks in 1453.

DID YOU KNOW?

These clans and others from Central Asia were able to defeat the Romans in the north and settle in Europe, thanks to their equestrian skills, superior wheels, and iron technology.

Figure 2.11. Hagia Sophia

Justinian also continued the establishment of Christianity, rebuilding the Hagia Sophia and eliminating the last vestiges of the Greco-Roman religion and competing Christian sects. However, over time, differences in doctrine between the church in Rome and Christians in Constantinople would give way to a schism, creating the Roman Catholic Church and the Greek Orthodox Church.

During the early Middle Ages in Europe and the Byzantine Empire, the roots of another civilization were developing in the Arabian Peninsula. In the seventh century, the Prophet Muhammad began teaching **Islam**. Based on the teachings of Judaism and Christianity, Islam presented as the final version of these two religions, evolving its own set of laws and philosophical teachings. Like Christianity, it held universal appeal.

The process of converting to Islam and practicing the faith was (and is) considered easy. The religion transcends national and ethnic differences and offers the possibility of redemption, forgiveness of sins, and a pleasant afterlife. Furthermore, due to ideological similarities, Muslims were willing to accept Jews and Christians as **People of the Book** rather than forcing their conversion, enabling their later conquest of Southwest Asia and facilitating relationships in the region.

Leading a small group of followers out of the desert to conquer the Arabian cities of Mecca and Medina, where they would establish the beginnings of the **Caliphate**, Muhammad's followers would later come to control Southwest Asia and North Africa.

DID YOU KNOW?

The Caliphate is the political embodiment of the society envisioned in Islam.

PRACTICE QUESTIONS

1) **What is required for a settled community?**

    A. domesticated animals

    B. a source of fresh water

    C. technology

    D. weapons

2) **What is the earliest known form of writing to use characters to create words?**

    A. cuneiform, developed by the Egyptians

    B. cuneiform, developed by the Sumerians

    C. hieroglyphs, developed by the Egyptians

    D. hieroglyphs, developed by the Sumerians

3) **The Shang and Zhou Dynasties are particularly relevant in Chinese history for their contributions in**

    A. developing Chinese administration.

    B. centralizing Chinese imperial power as symbolized through the terracotta figurines in the imperial tombs.

    C. forming a Chinese identity through the development of written language, the emperor's Mandate of Heaven, and fostering Confucianism.

    D. ensuring China's safety by building the Great Wall of China.

4) **Which of the following did the Athenian concept of democracy embrace?**

A. participatory democracy, permitting the poor to dominate the process rather than the elites

B. an anonymous electoral process similar to that of the United States in which officials were elected

C. people of all backgrounds, so that all residents of Athens had a stake in the political process

D. an educated electorate in order to ensure the best possible decision-making

5) **How did Julius Caesar rise to and retain power?**

A. He invaded Rome with his armies from Gaul and used his military resources to control the empire.

B. He was elected president of the Senate by the people thanks to political support throughout the Republic.

C. He took control of the Senate and maintained control of Rome thanks to his charisma and widespread popularity among the people.

D. As part of the Triumvirate, he was guaranteed a leadership position and the support of Crassus and Pompey.

WORLD RELIGIONS

JUDAISM

Judaism was the first **monotheistic** religion. Its adherents believe in only *one* god , Yahweh. It is believed that God came to the Hebrew Abraham and that the Hebrews—the Jews—were to be God's *chosen people*, to serve as an example to the world.

Later, Moses would lead the Jews out of slavery in Egypt, and God gave him **Ten Commandments**, or laws, which would become the basis of Judeo-Christian and Islamic moral codes. Notably, these moral codes applied to all people, including slaves. In addition to confirming the singular nature of God, the Ten Commandments laid out social rules for an organized society under that one god: to refrain from theft and murder and to honor one's parents, among others.

Judaism's holy texts are the **Torah** and the **Talmud** (religious and civil law, respectively). There are different branches of Judaism with varying teachings, including Orthodox, Conservative, and Reform Judaism, among others.

CHRISTIANITY

In Roman Palestine, the Jewish carpenter Jesus taught that he was the son of the singular, Jewish God and gained many followers. According to Christian belief:

▶ Jesus was crucified and died so that all mankind may be forgiven for their sins.

- Jesus rose from the dead three days after his crucifixion (the **Resurrection**) and ascended to heaven

  ▷ Christians celebrate the Resurrection on Easter Sunday.

- Jesus was miraculously born from a virgin mother (the **Virgin Mary**)

- God is made up of the Father, the Son, and the Holy Spirit—the **Holy Trinity.**

The **Catholic Church** is led by the pope and descended from the early western Church that followed the Schism of 1054, when theological disagreement divided the Church into the western Catholic Church and **Eastern Orthodox** Christianity.

Later in Western Europe, the **Protestant Reformation** gave rise to other forms of Protestant, or non-Catholic, Christianity.

ISLAM

Islam is rooted in the Arabian Peninsula. Its faithful—Muslims—believe that the angel Gabriel spoke to the **Prophet Muhammad**, transmitting the literal word of **Allah** (God), which was later written down as the **Qur'an.**

Muhammad is considered by Muslims to be the final prophet of the god of the Jews and Christians, and Islam shares similar moral teachings. Islam recognizes leaders like Abraham, Moses, and Jesus, but unlike Christianity, views Jesus as a prophet, not as the son of God.

The Prophet Muhammad was a religious, military, and political leader. By conquering the Arabian Peninsula and eventually other parts of the Middle East, he protected the **People of the Book**—Jews and

> **CHECK YOUR UNDERSTANDING #4**
>
> Explain monotheism. What are the major monotheistic religions and who are their main figures?

Christians. After his death, discord among his followers resulted in the **Sunni-Shi'a Schism** over his succession and some teachings. To this day, deep divisions remain between many Sunnis and Shi'ites. Like Judaism, Islam also has a book of legal teachings called the Hadith.

HINDUISM

Major tenets of Hindu belief include:

- reincarnation, the belief that the universe and its beings undergo endless cycles of rebirth

- karma, the idea that people create their own destiny

The soul is reincarnated until it has resolved all karmas, at which point it attains moksha, or liberation from the cycle.

Hindus believe in multiple divine beings. Religion is based in the **Vedic scriptures**; other important texts include the Upanishads, the Mahabharata, and the Bhagavad Gita. Hinduism is the primary religion in India and is intertwined with the **caste system**, a hierarchical societal structure.

Buddhism

In Buddhism, the Prince **Siddhartha Gautama** is said to have sought **enlightenment** around the third century BCE, renouncing worldly goods and living as an ascetic in what is today northern India. Buddhism teaches that desire—the ego, or self—is the root of suffering, and that giving up or **transcending** material obsessions will lead to freedom, or nirvana—enlightenment. While Buddhism originated in India, it is practiced throughout Asia and the world.

The main Buddhist schools of theology include:

▶ Mahayana, prevalent in northern and eastern Asia (Korea, parts of China, Mongolia)

▶ Theravada, dominant in Southeast Asia and Indian Ocean regions

▶ Vajrayana, central to Tibetan Buddhism

Confucianism

Confucianism teaches obedience and adherence to tradition in order to maintain a harmonious society. Ideally, practicing integrity and respecting wisdom would ensure that authority would be used for beneficial purposes.

Confucius himself was a Chinese scholar in the sixth century BCE. His philosophy would go on to inform Chinese culture for centuries.

Feudalism through the Era of Expansion

The Middle Ages in Europe

The Byzantine Empire remained a strong civilization and a place of learning. Constantinople was a commercial center, strategically located at the Dardanelles, connecting Asian trade routes with Europe. Later, missionaries traveled north to Slav-controlled Russia, spreading Christianity and literacy.

The ninth-century missionaries Saints Cyril and Methodius are credited with developing what would become the **Cyrillic** alphabet used in many Slavic languages. In 988 CE, the Russian Grand Prince of Kiev, **Vladimir I**, converted to Christianity and ordered his subjects to do so as well. Russian Christianity was influenced by the Byzantine doctrine, what would become Greek Orthodox Christianity.

Despite the chaos in Western Europe, the Church in Rome remained strong and became a stabilizing influence. However, differences in doctrine between Rome and Constantinople became too wide to overcome.

Beginning in 1054, a series of **schisms** developed in the now-widespread Christian religion between the **Roman Catholic Church** and the **Greek Orthodox Church** over matters of doctrine:

▶ the role of the pope and papal authority

▶ the use of leavened versus unleavened bread in religious services

▶ other theological concepts

Eventually the two would become entirely separate churches.

In Europe, the early Middle Ages (or **Dark Ages**) from the fall of Rome to about the tenth century, were a chaotic, unstable, and unsafe time. The protection and stability that did exist were represented and maintained by the Catholic Church and the feudal system.

Society and economics were characterized by decentralized, local governance, or **feudalism**, a hierarchy where land and protection were offered in exchange for loyalty. Feudalism was the dominant social, economic, and political hierarchy of the European Middle Ages from the time of Charlemagne (discussed further below).

Economic and social organization consisted of:

▶ vassals, freemen who would pledge **fealty**, or pay homage to lords

▶ lords, landowners who would reward their vassals' loyalty with land, or **fiefs**

▶ manors, self-sustaining areas possessed by lords but worked by peasants

▶ serfs, peasants who were tied to the land and worked for the lord in exchange for protection

While not exactly enslaved, serfs were effectively controlled by the lord, though they were not required to fight. They were also usually granted some land for their own use.

Warriors who fought for lords were called **knights**. They were rewarded with land and could become minor lords in their own right. Lords

Figure 2.12. Depiction of a Medieval Knight

themselves could be vassals of other lords; that hierarchy extended upward to kings or the Catholic Church.

The Catholic Church itself was a major landowner and political power. In a Europe not yet dominated by sovereign states, the pope was not only a religious leader, but also a military and political one.

Small kingdoms and alliances extended throughout Europe, and stable trade was difficult to maintain. The **Celts** controlled Britain and Ireland until the invasion of the Saxons. Around 600 CE, the Saxons conquered Britain while the Celts were pushed to Ireland, Scotland, and Brittany in northwest France.

Though the Church was gaining power, it was insecure in Italy as the Germanic tribes vied for control in Germany and France. Monasteries in Ireland and England retained and protected classical documentation in the wake of the fall of Rome and insecurity in Italy. The Germanic tribes themselves were threatened by Asian invaders like the Huns. This caused further instability in central and eastern parts of Europe, where Slavs also fought for supremacy north of Byzantium.

One exception to the chaos was the Scandinavian **Viking** civilization. From the end of the eighth century until around 1100, the Vikings expanded their influence from Scandinavia.

Thanks to their extraordinary seafaring skills and technology, their influence ranged from the Baltic Sea to the east to the North Sea through the North Atlantic. The Vikings traded with the Byzantine Empire and European powers and were known to travel to—and sometimes raid—parts of Britain, Ireland, France, and Russia. The Icelandic Erik the Red established a settlement in Greenland, and his son **Leif Erikson** may have traveled as far as North America.

DID YOU KNOW?

Byzantine and Middle Eastern artifacts have been found among Viking excavations in Scandinavia.

In addition to military prowess and advanced shipbuilding technology, the Vikings had a complex religion with a pantheon of gods and well-developed mythology. They also developed a literary canon of sagas in Old Norse, the basis of some Scandinavian languages today. Viking achievements have been documented in literature from other European cultures like the Anglo-Saxons, as well as the Arab historian Ibn Fadlan.

Meanwhile, by the eighth century, the North African **Moors**, part of the expanding Islamic civilization, had penetrated Iberia and were a threat to Christian Europe. Charles Martel, leader of the Franks in what is today France, defeated the Moors at the **Battle of Tours (or Poitiers)** in 732 CE, effectively stopping any further Islamic incursion into Europe.

Martel, a Christian, had previously consolidated his control of France, leading the Franks in victory over the Bavarians, Frisians, and other tribes and supporting their conversion to Christianity. But instability followed Charles Martel's death. **Charlemagne**, the son of a court official, eventually took over the Merovingian kingdom following disputes over succession.

Charlemagne was able to maintain Frankish unity and consolidate his rule, extending Frankish control into Central Europe and defending the Papal States in central Italy. In what is considered the reemergence of centralized power in Europe, parts of Western and Central Europe were organized under Charlemagne, who was crowned emperor of the Roman Empire by Pope Leo III in 800 CE. While in retrospect this seems long after the end of Rome, at the time many Europeans still perceived themselves as somehow still part of a Roman Empire.

> **DID YOU KNOW?**
>
> Today, Charlemagne's rule is referred to as the Carolingian Empire.

Several notable achievements occurred under Charlemagne's rule:

- ▶ Charlemagne brought stability to Western and Central Europe during a period when two powerful, non-Christian, organized civilizations (the Vikings in the north and the Islamic powers in the south) threatened what was left of western Christendom.

- ▶ Charlemagne brought stability to Western and Central Europe at a time when insecurity was growing to the east with the decline of the Byzantines and the emergence of the Umayyad Caliphate based in Damascus.

- ▶ During Charlemagne's reign, the Roman Catholic Church was strengthened, enabling the reemergence of Roman and Christian scholarship that had been hidden in English and Irish monasteries.

- ▶ The feudal system became truly organized, resulting in increased stability in Western Europe.

The Catholic Church would dominate Europe from Ireland toward Eastern Europe, an area of locally controlled duchies, kingdoms, and alliances. In 962 CE, Otto I became emperor of the **Holy Roman Empire** in Central Europe, a confederation of small states which remained an important European power until its dissolution in 1806.

While the Holy Roman Empire remained intact, the Carolingian Empire did not. Spain and Portugal remained under Muslim control, and France dissolved into small fiefdoms and territories. Meanwhile, England and Scotland were controlled by Norsemen (Vikings), especially Danish settlers and various local Anglo-Saxon rulers, the remnants of the Germanic tribes that had come to rule Europe and led to the fall of Rome.

In 1066, **William the Conqueror** left Normandy in northwest France. The **Normans** established organization in England, including a more consolidated economy and kingdom supported by feudalism. They also consolidated Christianity as the local religion.

> **DID YOU KNOW?**
>
> There were limits on sovereign power. In 1215, long before the revolution, English barons forced King John to sign the **Magna Carta**, which protected their property and rights from the king and was the basis for today's parliamentary system in that country.

English possessions included parts of France, nominally a kingdom but consisting of smaller territories with some level of independence. Intermarriage and conquest resulted in English control of Anjou and Bordeaux in France; William had brought control of French Brittany with him when he arrived on the island of Britain. Conflict between Britain and France would continue for several centuries, while rulers in Scandinavia and Northwest Europe consolidated power.

THE ISLAMIC WORLD

Meanwhile, in the wake of the decline of the Byzantine Empire, **Arab-Islamic Empires**, characterized by brisk commerce, advancements in technology and learning, and urban development, arose in the Middle East.

Before the rise of Islam in the seventh century, the Arabian Peninsula was located at the intersection of the Byzantine Empire—a diverse collection of ethnicities ruled by Greek Orthodox Christians and the Sasanians (Persians), who practiced Zoroastrianism. Both of these empires sought to control trade with central and eastern Asia along the Silk Road. They also sought to establish trade ties with Christian Axum (Ethiopia).

In Arabia itself, Judaism, Christianity, and animist religions were practiced by the Arab majority. The Prophet Muhammad was born in Mecca around 570 CE. He began receiving messages from God (Allah), preaching them around 613 CE as the last affirmations of the monotheistic religions, and writing them as the Qur'an, the Islamic holy book. Driven from **Mecca** to Medina in 622 CE, Muhammad and his followers were able to recapture the city and other major Arabian towns by the time of his death, establishing Islam and Arab rule in the region.

After Muhammad's death in 632 CE, his followers were led by a Caliph, who was considered both a political and religious leader. The first Caliph was Abu Bakr who, along with his followers, went on to conquer land beyond Arabia north into the weakening Byzantine Empire. The well-organized Muslim Arabs, based in Arabia, led incursions into Syria, the Levant, and Mesopotamia, taking over these territories.

Thanks to military, bureaucratic, and organizational skills, as well as their ability to win over dissatisfied minorities, the Arabs eventually isolated the Byzantines to parts of Anatolia and Constantinople and crushed the Persian Sasanians.

Muhammad's cousin and son-in-law **Ali**, his wife, **Fatima** (Muhammad's eldest daughter), and their followers believed the leader of the Muslim Arabs should be a blood relative of Muhammad. Muhammad had no sons, so the logical choice was Ali. Meccan elites felt differently, and the popular Abu Bakr was chosen as the first caliph. The first four caliphs are known as the *Rashidun*, or "rightly guided ones":

> DID YOU KNOW?
>
> Ali's followers called themselves the Party of Ali or, in Arabic, the Shiat Ali, which is the origin of the word Shia or Shi'ite Muslims.

- ▶ Abu Bakr was succeeded by the second caliph, Umar.

- ▶ The third caliph, Uthman, took over when Umar died. Widely accused of corruption, Uthman was murdered in 656 CE.

- ▶ The Islamic leadership finally settled on Ali to take over as the fourth caliph.

Others in power felt differently. Muawiya, based in Damascus, led the opposition to Ali; this conflict is at the heart of the **Sunni-Shi'a Schism**.

Ali and Fatima established their base in Kufa, in Mesopotamia. Unable to come to an agreement over leadership, the Arabs became embroiled in the First Civil War (656 – 661 CE). The conflict ended when Ali was murdered in 661 CE. Unrest continued, and the bloody massacre of Ali's son Hussein and his family in Karbala (680 CE) triggered the Second Civil War (680 – 692 CE).

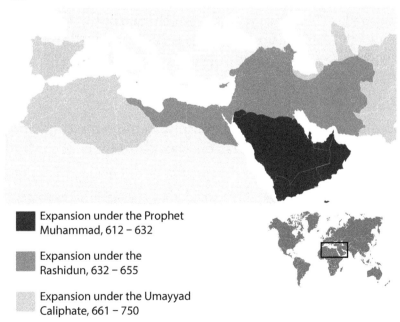

■ Expansion under the Prophet Muhammad, 612 – 632

■ Expansion under the Rashidun, 632 – 655

■ Expansion under the Umayyad Caliphate, 661 – 750

Figure 2.13. Islamic Expansion

The violence of these years cemented divisions in Islam, and **Shi'ite Islam** emerged in Mesopotamia. The Shi'ites believed that Ali was the rightful heir to Muhammad's early Islamic Empire, and maintained a focus on martyrdom, especially that of Ali and Hussein.

The followers of the Meccan elites became known as **Sunnis**, "orthodox" Muslims with a focus on community rather than genealogy. Over the centuries, other differences in theology and history would develop.

Muawiya is considered the first caliph of the **Umayyad Caliphate** (empire), named for the leading Meccan tribe that had supported Muhammad from the beginning. The Arabs already controlled Arabia; Spain (al-Andalus) was settled as early as 711 CE. By 750 CE, they would control parts of the following:

▶ Iberia

▶ North Africa

▶ Egypt

▶ the Levant

▶ Mesopotamia

▶ Persia

▶ Armenia

▶ Central Asia into Transoxiana (Uzbekistan)

▶ the Indus River Valley (areas of Pakistan)

Ongoing conflict among Arab elites resulted in the **Abbasid Caliphate** in 750 CE, based in Baghdad. The Umayyad were overthrown by the Arab-Muslim Abbasid family, which established a new capital in Baghdad. Caliph al-Mutasim professionalized the military. He created a group of professional soldiers called **mamluks**, who were freed slaves usually of Turkish origin. It was thought they would be more loyal with no family or national ties.

The mamluks helped the caliph consolidate imperial control and improve tax collection. Abbasid administration was also highly organized, allowing efficient taxation.

The administration and stability provided by the Caliphates fostered an Arabic literary culture. Stability permitted open trade routes, economic development, and cultural interaction throughout Asia, the Middle East, North Africa, and parts of Europe.

Furthermore, the Abbasid ruler al-Ma'mun fostered cultural and scientific study. This, combined with the universality of the Arabic language, lent itself to a number of cultural and scholastic contributions:

▶ Scientific and medical texts from varying civilizations—Greek, Persian, Indian—could be translated into Arabic and shared throughout the Islamic world.

▶ Arab thinkers studied Greek and Persian astronomy and engaged in further research.

▶ Arabs studied mathematics from around the world and developed algebra, which enabled engineering, technological, and architectural achievements.

▶ Islamic art, well known for its geometric designs, gained recognition during this time.

Around this time, the **Song Dynasty** (960 – 1276) controlled most of China. Under the Song, China experienced tremendous development and economic growth. The Song Dynasty is most notably characterized by the following:

▶ increased urbanization

▶ complex administrative rule, including the difficult competitive written examinations required to obtain prestigious bureaucratic positions in government

▶ the emergence of traditions now recognized as Chinese, such as the consumption of tea and rice and common Chinese architecture

▶ overland trade along the Silk Road with exports of silk, tea, ceramics, jade, and other goods

▶ sea trade with Korea, Japan, Southeast Asia, India, Arabia, and East Africa

CONFLICT AND CULTURAL EXCHANGE

Cultural exchange was not limited to interactions between Christian Europeans, Egyptians, and Levantine Muslims. Indeed, international commerce was vigorous along the **Silk Road**, trading routes which stretched from the Arab-controlled Eastern Mediterranean to Song Dynasty China, where science and learning also blossomed.

The Silk Road reflected the transnational nature of Central Asia:

▶ The nomadic culture of Central Asia lent itself to trade between the major civilizations of China, Persia, the Near East, and Europe.

▶ Buddhism and Islam spread into China.

▶ Chinese, Islamic, and European art, pottery, and goods were interchanged between the three civilizations, an example of early globalization.

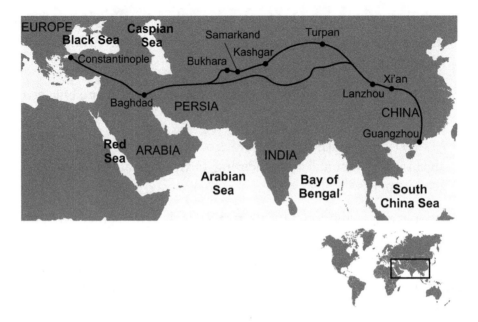

Figure 2.14. The Silk Road

The Islamic tradition of the **hajj**, or the pilgrimage to Mecca, also spurred cultural interaction. Islam had spread from Spain throughout North Africa, the Sahel, the Middle East, Persia, Central Asia, India, and China. Peoples from all these regions traveled and met in Arabia as part of their religious pilgrimage.

Islam also spread along trans-Saharan trade routes into West Africa and the Sahel. Brisk trade between the gold-rich **Kingdom of Ghana** and Muslim traders based in Morocco brought Islam to the region around the eleventh century. The Islamic **Mali Empire** (1235 – 1500), based farther south in **Timbuktu**, eventually extended beyond the original Ghanaian boundaries all the way to the West African coast and controlled the valuable gold and salt trades. It became a center of learning and commerce. At the empire's peak, the ruler **Mansa Musa** made a pilgrimage to Mecca in 1324. However, by 1500, the **Songhai Empire** had overcome Mali and eventually dominated the Niger River area.

> **CHECK YOUR UNDERSTANDING #5**
>
> How did the Silk Road and Islam both contribute to global cultural exchange?

Loss of Byzantine territory to the Islamic Empires meant loss of Christian lands in the Levant—including Jerusalem and Bethlehem—to Muslims. In 1095, the Byzantine emperor asked Pope Urban II for help defending Jerusalem and protecting Christians.

With a history of Muslim incursions into Spain and France, anti-Muslim sentiment was strong in Europe, and Christians there were easily inspired to fight them in the Levant (Holy Land). The pope offered lords and knights the chance to keep lands and bounty they won from conquered Muslims (and Jews) in this

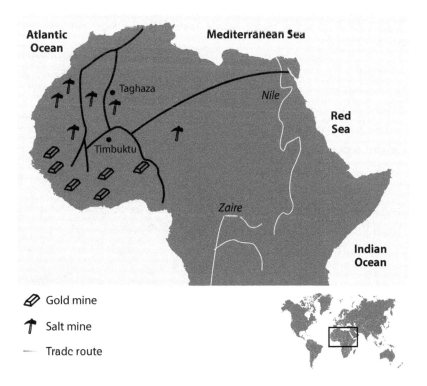

Figure 2.15. Trans-Saharan Trade Routes

crusade. He also offered Crusaders **indulgences**—forgiveness for sins committed in war and guarantees they would enter heaven.

Meanwhile, toward the end of the tenth century, the Abbasid Caliphate was in decline. The Shi'ite **Fatimids** took control of Syria and Egypt, addressing the Shi'ite claim to the Caliphate. Other groups took control of provinces in Mesopotamia, Arabia, and Central Asia.

In Spain, Abd al-Rahman III (891 – 961 CE) had defied the Abbasids and the Fatimids, taking over al-Andalus (Spain) himself and fostering a unique Hispano-Arabic culture where intellectual pursuits bloomed:

▶ Rahman was responsible for the Great Mosque of Cordoba.

▶ The Muslim philosopher Averroes developed his commentary on Aristotle.

▶ The Jewish philosopher Maimonides developed religious and philosophical thought.

Still, conflict persisted with the Carolingians and with smaller Christian kingdoms in northern Spain.

In Western Europe, instability had been ongoing as control over continental territories passed between England and France. France never regained the strength it had under Charlemagne. While the French monarchy existed, smaller states remained powerful, and power was decentralized. Despite internal divisions, organization in England accelerated upon William's 1066 conquest. The two civilizations were at odds.

Despite conflict in Europe, Christians found they had more in common with each other than with Muslims. European Christians united to follow the pope's call to arms to fight in the Middle East. The decline of the Abbasids had left the Levant vulnerable, and Christian Crusaders established settlements and small kingdoms in Syria and on the Eastern Mediterranean coast, conquering major cities.

Figure 2.16. Great Mosque of Cordoba

The Crusades continued over several centuries:

▶ By 1099, Jerusalem was captured by Christian Crusaders in the First Crusade as called for by Pope Urban II (see above).

▶ In 1171, the Kurdish military leader Salah al-Din (Saladin) abolished the Fatimid Caliphate. Following his death and a succession of rulers, elite slave troops took power.

▶ In 1187, Salah al-Din reconquered Jerusalem, driving European Christians out for good.

▶ The **Mamluks** (1250 – 1517) controlled Egypt and would later defeat the Mongols in 1260, protecting Egypt and North Africa from the Mongol invasions.

DID YOU KNOW?

The Egyptian rulers, the Mamluks, descended from Abbasid Caliph al-Mutasim's fighting force.

While the ongoing Crusades never resulted in permanent European control over the Holy Land, they did open up trade routes between Europe and the Middle East, stretching all the way along the Silk Road to China. This increasing interdependence led to the European Renaissance.

Ongoing interactions between Europeans and Muslims also had other societal effects as well:

- Europeans were exposed to improved education and goods, which they could now afford thanks to international trade.

- The **Bubonic (Black) Plague** spread to Europe as a result of global exchange, killing off a third of its population from 1347 – 1351, and having a worldwide impact, with empires falling in its wake.

Back in Europe, conflict reached its height throughout the thirteenth and fourteenth centuries, known as the **Hundred Years' War** (1337 – 1453):

- France was in political chaos during the mid-fourteenth century, decentralized and at times without a king.

- The region was suffering the effects of the Black Plague.

- France remained vulnerable to English attack and periodically found itself under English rule.

- After ongoing conflict, England lost its last territory, Bordeaux, France, in 1453 to the French King Charles VII.

> **DID YOU KNOW?**
>
> During the Hundred Years' War, Joan of Arc led the French in the 1429 Battle of Orléans, reinvigorating French resistance to English incursions.

In al-Andalus (Spain), despite some coexistence between Christians and Muslims under Muslim rule, raids and conflict were ongoing during the lengthy period of the **Reconquista**:

- From the zenith of Muslim rule under Abd al-Rahman, Christian raids continued, as did shifting alliances between the small kingdoms of Christian Spain and Portugal.

- By the second half of the thirteenth century, the only remaining Muslim power in Iberia was Grenada.

- By the fifteenth century, small Christian Spanish kingdoms were vying for dominance.

- The marriage of Ferdinand of Castilla and Isabella of Aragon in 1479 connected those two kingdoms, and the monarchs were able to complete the Reconquista by taking Grenada and uniting Spain.

- The period of the Reconquista ended in 1492 when Christian powers took Grenada.

Ferdinand and Isabella also launched the Inquisition, an extended persecution of Jews and Jewish converts to Christianity who continued to practice Judaism in secret. Jewish people were tortured, killed, and exiled; their belongings and property were confiscated. Muslims were also persecuted and forced to convert to Christianity or be exiled.

EMPIRES IN TRANSITION

Beyond Egypt and the Levant, the collapse of the Abbasid Caliphate led to instability and decentralization of power in Mesopotamia, Persia, and Central Asia:

▶ Smaller sultanates (territories ruled by regional leaders, or sultans) emerged, and production and economic development declined.

▶ Tang Dynasty China closed its borders, resulting in a decline in trade on the Silk Road.

▶ The nomadic **Seljuks**, Turks from Central Asia, nominally took over the region from Central Asia through parts of the Levant in the eleventh century, though they lacked effective administration or central authority.

▶ Political decentralization ultimately left the region vulnerable to the Mongol invasions of the twelfth and thirteenth centuries.

DID YOU KNOW?

During this period, Persian-influenced Sufi (mystical) Islam and poetry developed. Shi'ite theology and jurisprudence also developed as part of a strengthening independent Shi'ite identity.

Despite the lack of political cohesion, Islam remained a unifying force throughout the region, and political instability and decentralization paradoxically allowed local culture to develop, particularly Persian art and literature. Islam was also able to thrive during this period: local religious leaders (*ulama*) had taken up community leadership positions following the loss of any powerful central authority, and Islam became a guiding force in law, justice, and social organization throughout the region.

In the Near East, the **Mongol invasions** destroyed agriculture, city life and planning, economic patterns and trade routes, and social stability. After some time, new patterns of trade emerged, new cities rose to prominence, and stability allowed for prosperity, but the Mongol invasions dealt a blow to the concept that Islam was inherently favored by God.

Despite the rich history of transnational activity across Asia, the continent was vulnerable. Central Asia lacked one dominant culture or imperial power, and Southwest Asia was fragmented following the decline of the Abbasids. Combined with the disorganization of the Seljuks and the remnants of the Byzantines, these weaknesses allowed the Mongols to take over much of Eurasia.

Important facts about the **Mongol Empire** include:

▶ It was based in Central Asia.

▶ It was led by **Genghis Khan**.

▶ It expanded throughout Asia thanks to abilities in horsemanship and archery.

▶ It ultimately controlled Pannonia (Hungary) through the Middle East, Persia, Central Asia, Northern and Western China, and Southeast Asia.

The impact of the Mongol invasions was not limited to Eurasia. In China, the Mongols destroyed local infrastructure, including the foundation of Chinese society and administration—the civil service examinations.

In order to govern the vast territory effectively, the Mongols in China took a different approach. Genghis Khan's grandson Kublai Khan conquered China and founded the Mongol Yuan Dynasty in 1271.

> **CHECK YOUR UNDERSTANDING #6**
>
> What were the vulnerabilities on the continent of Asia that facilitated the Mongol invasions? How did these vulnerabilities come about?

The Yuan Dynasty:

▶ abolished the civil service examinations until 1315

▶ maintained most of the administrative policy of the preceding Song Dynasty

  ▷ the Six Ministries

  ▷ the Secretariat

  ▷ provincial administrative structure

▶ upended Chinese social hierarchy, placing Mongols at the top, followed by non-ethnic Han Chinese, and then Han Chinese

Mongol attempts at imperial expansion in China into Japan and Southeast Asia, coupled with threats from the Black Plague, financial problems, and flooding, led to the decline of the Yuan Dynasty and the rise of the native Chinese **Ming Dynasty** in 1368:

> **DID YOU KNOW?**
>
> Despite Mongol distrust of Confucianism and Confucian administrator-scholars, Kublai Khan educated his son in the Confucian tradition.

▶ Zhu Yuanzhang led the Chinese to victory and ruled as the first Ming emperor from Nanjing.

▶ The capital later moved to Beijing in 1421.

▶ Ming China controlled land throughout Asia, accepting tribute from rulers in Burma, Siam (Thailand), Annam (Vietnam), Mongolia, Korea, and Central Asia.

▶ The Ming reasserted Chinese control and continued traditional methods of administration; however the construction of the **Forbidden City**, the home of the emperor in Beijing, helped consolidate imperial rule.

▶ The Ming emphasized international trade: demand for ceramics in particular, in addition to silk and tea, was high abroad, and contact with seafaring traders like the Portuguese and Dutch in the sixteenth century was strong.

▶ The Ming also encouraged trade and exploration by sea; the Chinese explorer Zheng He traveled to India, Sri Lanka, and Asia.

Despite some decline in Mongol hegemony throughout Asia, the military leader **Timur (Tamerlane)** began conquering land in the area around 1364. By 1383, he occupied Moscow and turned toward Persia. Up to the turn of the century he would go on to conquer numerous areas:

▶ Persia

▶ Mesopotamia

▶ much of the Caucasus

▶ parts of India (Delhi)

His conquests continued into the early fifteenth century:

▶ Syria was taken.

▶ Anatolia was invaded.

▶ Tribute was exacted from Egypt.

DID YOU KNOW?

Tamerlane was a Mongol descendant from Transoxania, present-day Uzbekistan.

While rarely spending too much time in one place, Timur had contributed to the development of the capital of his empire, Samarkand, enriching Central Asia culturally. Timur died in 1405 on an expedition to China.

Mongol decline was not only isolated to China. In Russia, **Ivan the Great** brought Moscow from Mongol to Slavic Russian control:

▶ In the late fifteenth century, Ivan had consolidated Russian power over neighboring Slavic regions.

▶ Through both military force and diplomacy, Ivan achieved Moscow's independence in 1480, despite Muscovy's status as a vassal state.

▶ He set out to bring other neighboring Slavic and Baltic lands, including Poland-Lithuania, and later, parts of Ukraine, under Russian rule.

▶ Ivan achieved a centralized, consolidated Russia that was the foundation for an empire and a sovereign nation that sought diplomatic status with Europe.

Figure 2.17. The Forbidden City

A century later, **Ivan the Terrible** set out to expand Russia further, integrate it into Europe, and strengthen Russian Orthodox Christianity. Named the first **tsar**, or emperor, Ivan is known for:

▶ reforming government, strengthening centralization and administrative bureaucracy and disempowering the nobility

▶ leading the affirmation of orthodox Christianity, calling councils to organize the church and canonize Russian saints

▶ reorganizing the military, including promoting officials based on merit rather than status

▶ expanding and improving foreign policy and relations

▶ developing Russian culture and religion

However, overextension of resources and his oppressive entourage, the *oprichnina*, depopulated the state and gave him the reputation as a despotic ruler. Despite this, Ivan's reforms strengthened the apparatus of the Russian state.

Farther south in Central Asia, one of Timur's descendants, Babur, laid claim to Timur's dominions. Despite his Mongol roots, Babur identified as Turkic due to his tribal origins and enjoyed support from the powerful Ottoman Empire in Turkey (see below). He founded the **Mughal Empire** of India:

Figure 2.18. The Taj Mahal

▶ In 1525, Babur set out for India.

▶ By 1529, Babur had secured land from Kandahar in the west to Bengal in the east.

▶ Babur's grandson, Akbar, consolidated the empire, which at the time consisted of small kingdoms.

▶ The Mughals would rule India until the eighteenth century and nominally control parts of the country until British takeover in the nineteenth century.

During Mughal rule in India, the Ming Dynasty fell in China in 1644 to a peasant revolt and the Qing took over:

▶ The **Manchu**, a non-Han group from the north, took the opportunity to seize Beijing and take the country.

▶ Despite their status as non-Han Chinese, the Manchu were accepted, thus beginning the **Qing Dynasty**.

▶ The first Qing emperor, the Kangxi Emperor, promoted the arts and education.

▶ Under the reign of the Qianlong Emperor (1736 – 1796), China grew to its largest size, including Tibet, Mongolia, Xinjiang, and parts of Russia.

▶ Like the Kangxi Emperor, the Qianlong Emperor was a patron of the arts.

▶ China became the dominant power in East Asia and a successful multi-ethnic state.

▶ The Qing would be the last of China's imperial rulers after losing power in 1911.

Meanwhile, in Persia, the **Safavids** emerged in 1501 in the wake of the Timurid Empire:

▶ This dynasty would rule from Azerbaijan in the west through to modern-day Pakistan and Afghanistan.

▶ A major rival of the Ottoman Empire, the Safavids were a stabilizing force in Asia.

▶ Following Sufism, the Safavids supported art, literature, architecture, and other learning.

▶ Their organized administration brought order and stability to Persia throughout their rule, which lasted until 1736, when the **Qajar Dynasty** took over.

Despite the instability inland, Indian Ocean trade routes had continued to function since at least the seventh century.

These oceanic routes connected the following areas:

▶ the Horn of Africa

▶ the East African Coast

▶ the Arabian Peninsula

▶ Southern Persia

▶ India

▶ Southeast Asia

▶ China

The ocean acted as a unifying force throughout the region, and the **monsoon winds** permitted Arab, Persian, Indian, and Chinese merchants to travel to East Africa in search of goods such as ivory and gold—and people to enslave.

Despite the civilizational achievements of the Islamic Empires, Tang, and later Ming Dynasty China, and the Central Asian and Indian Empires that would emerge from the Mongols, the **East African slave trade** endured until the nineteenth century:

▶ Arabs, Asians, and other Africans kidnapped African people and enslaved them throughout the Arab world and South Asia.

▶ Europeans would later take part in the trade as well, forcing Africans into slavery in colonies throughout South and Southeast Asia, and on plantations in Indian Ocean islands like Madagascar.

▶ The major East African port was Zanzibar, from which gold, coconut oil, ivory, and other African exports—including enslaved people—traveled to Asia and the Middle East.

▶ Enslaved persons from Sub-Saharan Africa were also forced north overland to markets in Cairo, where they were sold and dispersed throughout the Arab-Islamic, Fatimid, and Ottoman Empires.

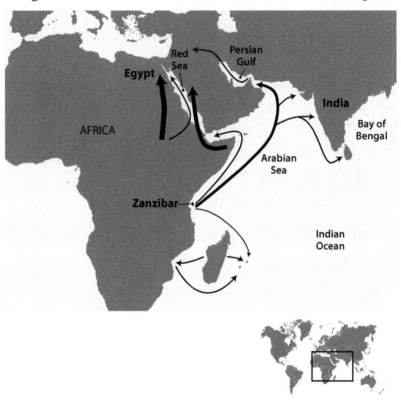

Figure 2.19. Indian Ocean Slave Trade

Islam also spread throughout the African coast and inland. Given the cosmopolitan nature of the coastline, the **Swahili** language adopted aspects of Arabic and other Asian languages.

Farther north, the Ottoman Turks represented a threat to Central Europe:

▶ After controlling most of Anatolia from the late thirteenth century, the Ottomans spread west into the Balkans.

▶ They consolidated their rule in 1389 at the Battle of Kosovo.

▶ In 1453 they captured Istanbul, from which the Ottoman Empire would come to rule much of the Mediterranean world.

▶ Under the leadership of **Mehmed the Conqueror** and his successors in the fifteenth century, the Ottomans conquered Pannonia (Hungary), North Africa, the Caucasus, the Levant and Mesopotamian regions, western Arabia, and Egypt.

▶ Under **Suleiman the Magnificent** (1520 – 1566), the **Ottoman Empire** consolidated control over the Balkans, the Middle East, and North Africa and would hold that land until the nineteenth century.

The capture of Istanbul (Constantinople) represented the true end of the Byzantine Empire. The remaining Christian Byzantines—mainly isolated to coastal Anatolia, Constantinople, and parts of Greece—fled to Italy, bringing Greek, Middle Eastern, and Asian learning with them and enriching the emerging European Renaissance.

THE EUROPEAN RENAISSANCE

The **Renaissance**, or *rebirth*, included the revival of ancient Greek and Roman learning, art, and architecture. However, the roots of the Renaissance stretched further back to earlier interactions between Christendom, the Islamic World, and even China, during the Crusades and through Silk Road trade.

Key characteristics of the Renaissance included:

▶ inspiring new learning and prosperity in Europe

▶ enabling exploration, colonization, profit, and imperialism

▶ scientific and religious questioning

▶ rebellion against the Catholic Church and, later, monarchical governments

Russia would not experience these cultural changes until the eighteenth century, when **Peter the Great** and **Catherine the Great** copied modern European culture, modernized the military, and updated technology, including building the new capital city of St. Petersburg, a cultural center.

Reinvigoration of classical knowledge was triggered in part by Byzantine refugees from the Ottoman conquest of Constantinople, including scholars who brought Greek and Roman texts to Italy and Western Europe.

The fall of Constantinople precipitated the development of **humanism** in Europe:

▶ Humanism is a mode of thought emphasizing human nature, creativity, and an overarching concept of truth in all philosophical systems (the concept of **syncretism**).

▶ Emerging in Italy, the seat of the Catholic Church, humanism was supported by some popes, including Leo X.

▶ In the long term, humanism represented a threat to religious— especially Catholic—orthodoxy, since it allowed religious teaching to be questioned.

▶ Figures associated with humanism included Dante, Petrarch, and Erasmus.

▶ Humanism is at the root of the Reformation of the sixteenth century.

Art, considered not just a form of expression but also a science in itself, flourished in fifteenth century Italy, particularly in Florence. Major figures explored design and perspective, innovation in architecture, and anatomy in sculpture:

▶ Leonardo da Vinci (known for scientific pursuits in addition to artistic achievement)

▶ Bramante

▶ Michelangelo

▶ Rafael

▶ Donatello

While artists worked throughout Italy and found patrons in the Vatican, among other places, the Florentine **Medici family** supported Renaissance art in that city by funding extensive civic projects, construction, décor, and public sculpture throughout Florence.

Figure 2.20. Michelangelo's *The Creation of Adam*

Meanwhile, scholars like Galileo, Isaac Newton, and Copernicus made discoveries in what became known as the **Scientific Revolution**:

▶ The Scientific Revolution was rooted in the scientific knowledge of the Islamic Empires, which had been imported through economic and social contact initiated centuries prior during the Crusades.

▶ Scientific study and discovery threatened the power of the Church, whose theological teachings were often at odds with scientific findings and logical reasoning.

Also in the mid-fifteenth century, in Northern Europe, Johann Gutenberg invented the **printing press**. With the advent of printing, texts could be more widely and rapidly distributed, and people had more access to information beyond what their leaders told them.

Figure 2.21. Gutenberg Bible

Combined with humanism and an increased emphasis on secular thought, the power of the Church and of monarchs who ruled by divine right was under threat. Here lay the roots of the **Enlightenment**, the basis for reinvigorated European culture and political thought that would drive its development for the next several centuries—and inspire revolution.

Transnational cultural exchange had also resulted in the transmission of technology to Europe:

DID YOU KNOW?

The Bible was the first book to be published using the printing press.

▶ During the sixteenth century, European seafaring knowledge, navigation, and technology benefitted from Islamic and Asian expertise.

▶ With this advanced technology, European explorers and traders could now venture beyond the Mediterranean.

▶ Portuguese and Dutch sailors eventually reached India and China, where they established ties with the Ming Dynasty.

CHECK YOUR UNDERSTANDING #7

The Scientific Revolution changed European thinking. What was the impact of using reason and scientific methodology rather than religion to understand the world?

▶ Advances in technology also allowed for trade that was no longer dependent on the Silk Road.

▶ Improved technology empowered Europeans to explore overseas, eventually landing in the Western Hemisphere, unknown to the peoples of Eurasia and Africa until this time.

MESOAMERICAN AND ANDEAN CIVILIZATIONS

In the Americas, the **Maya**, who preceded the Aztecs in Mesoamerica, came to dominate the Yucatan peninsula around 300 CE:

▶ The Maya developed a complex spiritual belief system accompanied by relief art and built pyramidal temples that still stand today.

▶ The Maya developed a detailed calendar and a written language using pictographs similar to Egyptian hieroglyphs.

▶ Astronomy and mathematics were studied by the Maya.

▶ Maya political administration was organized under monarchical city-states from around 300 until around 900, when the civilization began to decline.

▶ There is evidence of interaction throughout Mayan history with the Mesoamerican city-state of **Teotihuacan**, a major city likely comprised of various Mesoamerican peoples such as Toltecs, Mixtecs, Zapotecs, some Mayans, and other peoples.

By around 1400, two major empires dominated Central and South America: the Incas and the Aztecs. These two empires would be the last Indigenous civilizations to dominate the Americas before European colonization of the Western Hemisphere.

As smaller Mesoamerican civilizations had weakened and collapsed, the **Aztecs** had come to dominate Mexico and much of Mesoamerica, throughout which the same calendar was used. Characteristics of the Aztec civilization include the following:

▶ a military power and militaristic culture that allowed the Aztecs to dominate the region

▶ a dominance in regional trade in precious objects like quetzal bird feathers

▶ a main city, **Tenochtitlan**, founded in 1325 that served as a major world city home to several million people at its height

▸ a society divided on a class basis:

  ▹ slaves

  ▹ indentured servants

  ▹ serfs

  ▹ an independent priestly class

  ▹ military and ruling classes

Figure 2.22. Quetzalcoatl

▸ upward mobility for classes, especially those who had proven themselves in battle

▸ sharing many beliefs with the Mayans

▸ worship of the god **Quetzalcoatl**, a feathered snake, central to its religion

Meanwhile, in the Andes, the **Incas** had emerged. This Indigenous civilization is especially known for the following:

▸ The Inca civilization was based in **Cuzco**.

▸ Around 1300, the Incas had consolidated their power and strengthened in the area, likely due to a surplus of their staple crop maize.

▸ They were able to conquer local lords and, later, peoples farther south.

▸ Domesticated llamas and alpacas, which allowed the military to transport supplies through the mountains, contributed to their dominance.

▸ In addition to the citadel of **Machu Picchu**, Inca engineers built imperial infrastructure, including roads throughout the Andes.

▸ The Incas developed mountain agriculture; they were able to grow crops at high altitudes and maintain way stations on the highways stocked with supplies.

▸ To subdue local peoples, they moved conquered groups elsewhere in the empire and repopulated conquered areas with Incas.

DID YOU KNOW?

The Incas used a system called *quipus*, knotted cords, to keep track of inventories and other data, such as population.

Figure 2.23. Machu Picchu

COLONIZATION OF THE WESTERN HEMISPHERE

Interest in exploration grew in Europe during the Renaissance period. Numerous factors would eventually lead to the discovery of the Western Hemisphere:

▶ Technological advancements made complex navigation and long-term sea voyages possible.

▶ Economic growth resulting from international trade drove interest in market expansion.

▶ Global interdependence was boosted by Spain when King Ferdinand and Queen Isabella sponsored **Christopher Columbus's** exploratory voyage in 1492 to find a sea route to Asia, in order to speed up commercial trade there.

▶ Christopher Columbus would instead stumble upon the Western Hemisphere, which was unknown to Europeans, Asians, and Africans to this point.

▶ Columbus landed in the Caribbean. He and later explorers would claim the Caribbean islands, Central, and South America for Spain and Portugal; however, those areas were already populated by the major American civilizations (discussed above).

Spanish colonization would eventually lead to the fall of the Aztec Empire:

▶ The Aztec ruler **Montezuma II** led the Aztecs during their first encounter with Spain.

▶ Explorer **Hernan Cortés** met with Montezuma II in Tenochtitlan after invading other areas of Mexico in 1519.

▶ Due to Spanish superiority in military technology, Montezuma attempted to compromise with Cortés.

▶ Cortés was in no position to compromise with the Aztecs: he was seeking wealth and prestige in Mexico and disobeyed Spanish colonial authorities by unlawfully leaving the Spanish stronghold of Cuba.

▶ A few days later Cortés arrested Montezuma and took over the city.

▶ Spain was especially interested in controlling Mexican and Mesoamerican gold and subduing the Aztec religion, which included ceremonies with human blood and human sacrifice.

▶ Spain then began the process of colonizing Mexico and Central America, and the Aztec Empire collapsed.

Though the Inca Empire remained nominally intact for several years after the Spanish gained access to South America, a number of factors would eventually lead to the empire's decline:

▶ The Spanish accessed the continent in the early sixteenth century and were interested in economic exploitation and spreading Christianity, as was the case in Mexico and Central America.

▶ In 1533, the Spanish conquistador **Francisco Pizarro** defeated the Inca king **Atahualpa** and installed a puppet ruler; this marked the decline of the Inca Empire.

▶ The Spanish desecrated important religious artifacts—such as mummies essential for ancestor worship—installed Christianity, and took economic and political control of the region.

Spreading Christianity was one important reason for European expansion. By taking over the silver- and gold-rich Mesoamerican and Andean territories, as well as the Caribbean islands—where sugar became an important cash crop—Spain also contributed to the development of new economic practices that would eventually lead to the rise of a new era in slavery:

▶ **Mercantilism** was introduced, whereby the colonizing, or "mother country," took raw materials from the territories they controlled for the colonizers' own benefit.

- ▶ Governments amassed wealth through protectionism and increasing exports at the expense of other rising colonial powers, which eventually involved developing goods and then selling them back to those colonized lands at an inflated price.

- ▶ The **encomienda** system developed, granting European landowners the "right" to hold lands in the Americas and demand labor and tribute from the local inhabitants. Local civilizations and resources were exploited and destroyed.

- ▶ The **Columbian Exchange** began, which enabled mercantilism to flourish.

- ▶ Conflict and illness brought by the Europeans—especially **smallpox**—decimated the Native Americans; Europeans were left without labor to mine the silver and gold or to work the land.

- ▶ **African slavery** was the Europeans' solution to fill the need for labor.

CHECK YOUR UNDERSTANDING #8

What was destructive about the encomienda system?

Slavery was an ancient institution in many societies worldwide; however, with the Columbian Exchange slavery came to be practiced on a mass scale the likes of which the world had never seen.

Throughout Africa and especially on the West African coast, Europeans traded for slaves with some African kingdoms and also raided the land, kidnapping people. European enslavers took captured Africans in horrific conditions to the Americas; those who survived were enslaved and forced to work in mining or agriculture for the benefit of expanding European imperial powers.

The Columbian Exchange described the **triangular trade** across the Atlantic: European slavers took kidnapped African people from Africa to the Americas, sold them at auction and exchanged them for sugar and raw materials; these materials were traded in Europe for consumer goods, which were then exchanged in Africa for slaves, and so on.

DID YOU KNOW?

The historian Alfred Crosby published *The Columbian Exchange* in the 1970s, coining the term used today to describe the tremendous interchange of people, plants, animals—and diseases—that took place between the hemispheres.

Enslaved Africans suffered greatly and were forced to endure ocean voyages crammed on unsafe, unhygienic ships—sometimes among the dead bodies of other kidnapped people—only to arrive in the Americas to a life of slavery in mines or on plantations.

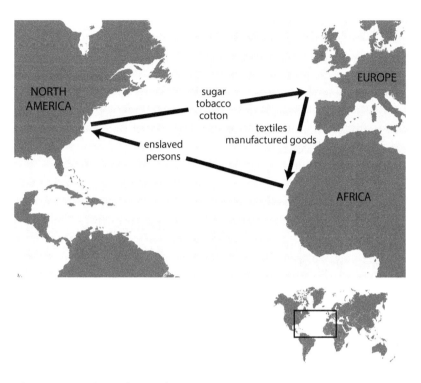

Figure 2.24. Triangular Trade

Throughout this period, Africans did resist both on ships and later, in the Americas:

▶ **Maroon communities** of escaped slaves formed throughout the Western Hemisphere.

▶ The **Underground Railroad** in the nineteenth-century United States helped enslaved persons escape the South.

▶ **Toussaint L'Ouverture** led a successful slave rebellion in Haiti, winning independence from the French for that country in 1791.

Despite this resistance, the slave trade continued for centuries. The colonies and later independent countries of the Western Hemisphere continued to practice slavery until the nineteenth century. Oppressive legal and social restrictions based on race continue to affect the descendants of enslaved African people to this day.

During the eighteenth century, Spain and Portugal were preeminent powers in global trade thanks to colonization and **imperialism**, the possession and exploitation of land overseas. However, Great Britain became an important presence on the seas. It would later dominate the oceans throughout the nineteenth century.

Though Britain would lose its territories in North America after the American Revolution, it maintained control of the resource-rich West Indies and went on to dominate strategic areas:

▶ South Africa

▶ New South Wales in Australia

▶ Mauritius in the Indian Ocean

▶ Madras and Bengal in the Indian Subcontinent

Britain would further expand its empire in the nineteenth century. Likewise, France gained territory in North America and the West Indies. Despite losses to Britain in the eighteenth century, that country would also expand its own global empire in the nineteenth century.

PRACTICE QUESTIONS

6) **Which of the following explains why the Eastern Roman Empire remained stable and transitioned to the Byzantine Empire while Rome in Western Europe collapsed?**

   A. Feudalism contributed to instability in Western Europe, so that part of the continent disintegrated into a series of small states.

   B. The schism between the Catholic and Greek Orthodox Churches tore the empire apart.

   C. Muslims entered Constantinople and took it from Christian Roman control.

   D. Imprudent alliances in the West led to Roman collapse, while strong leadership and centralization in the East developed a new empire.

7) **Following the death of Muhammad, Muslim leadership became so divided that the religious movement eventually split into Sunnis and Shi'ites. This was due to**

   A. disagreement over secession to his place as leader.

   B. disagreement about the importance of conquest.

   C. disagreement over the theological nature of Islam.

   D. disagreement over whether to accept Christians and Jews as *People of the Book*.

8) **Which of the following best explains the Atlantic Triangular Trade?**

   A. American raw materials were transported to Africa, where they were exchanged for enslaved persons; enslaved persons were taken to the Americas, where they turned raw materials to consumer goods for sale in Europe.

   B. European consumer goods were sold in the Americas at a profit; these goods were also sold in Africa in exchange for raw materials and for enslaved persons, who were taken to the Americas.

   C. European raw materials were sent to the Americas to be transformed into consumer goods by people who had been kidnapped from Africa and enslaved. These consumer goods were then traded in Africa for more slaves.

D.   Enslaved African people were traded in the Americas for raw materials; raw materials harvested by slaves went to Europe where they were utilized and turned to consumer goods; European consumer goods were exchanged in Africa for enslaved people.

9)   **Despite the violence of the Crusades, they were also beneficial for Europe in that they**

A.   resulted in substantial, long-term land gains for European leaders in the Middle East.

B.   introduced European powers to the concept of nation-states, the dominant form of political organization in the Middle East.

C.   exposed Europe to Islamic and Asian science, technology, and medicine.

D.   enhanced tolerance of Islam throughout Europe.

10)   **Which of the following was a result of the rise of the Ottoman Turks?**

A.   Christians left Constantinople for Western Europe, bringing classical learning with them.

B.   European powers were driven to colonize the Americas, fleeing Ottoman approach.

C.   Islam became the dominant religion in Europe, threatening the power of the Catholic Church.

D.   The Vikings ventured deeper into Europe.

ARMED CONFLICTS

REFORMATION AND NEW EUROPE

While Spain and Portugal consolidated their hold over territories in the Americas, conflict ensued in Europe. With the cultural changes of the Renaissance, the power of the Catholic Church was threatened. New scientific discoveries and secular Renaissance thought were at odds with many teachings of the Church, eventually leading to the **Reformation**, or movement for reform of the Church:

▶   In 1517, the Catholic monk **Martin Luther** wrote a letter of protest to the pope known as the **Ninety-Five Theses**, which outlined ways he believed the Church should reform.

▶   Luther's ideas gained support, especially among rulers who wanted more power from the Church, triggering the Reformation.

DID YOU KNOW?

Martin Luther translated the New Testament into German. Previously the Bible was in Latin, and priests were usually the only ones able to read it.

▶ These ideas led to offshoots of new versions of Christianity in Western Europe, separate from the Orthodox Churches in Russia and Greece.

▶ Protestant thinkers like Luther and **John Calvin** addressed particular grievances, condemning the **infallibility** of the pope (its teaching that the pope was without fault) and the selling of indulgences (guarantees of entry into heaven).

▶ The English **King Henry VIII** developed the Protestant **Church of England,** further consolidating his own power, famously allowing divorce, and marrying several times himself.

▶ The reign of Henry VIII, of the **House of Tudor**, initiated a chain of events leading to the consolidation of Protestantism in England, and eventually civil war and the empowerment of Parliament.

In Britain, religious and ethnic diversity between Protestant England and Scotland, and Catholic Ireland, made the kingdom unstable:

▶ The Catholic **Mary Queen of Scots**, who was the daughter of the Scottish King James V and half French, had been betrothed to Henry VIII's son, Edward; however her guardians canceled the arrangement, causing conflict with England.

▶ Mary Queen of Scots temporarily married Francis of France, uniting Scotland with that Catholic country, but he quickly died from illness.

▶ Mary then married her Protestant cousin the Earl of Darnley, with whom she had a son, **James**.

▶ Darnley forced Mary to abdicate the Scottish throne in 1567 and she fled to England, seeking safety with her Protestant cousin **Elizabeth I**, daughter of Henry VIII and queen of England.

▶ Mary's son, still a baby, became **King James VI** of Scotland.

▶ The Tudor Queen Elizabeth imprisoned the Catholic Mary in England as she—and her son—represented a threat to her power.

▶ Not only was James's male sex a liability for Elizabeth's inheritance to the throne, but their religious identities as Catholics threatened Elizabeth's hold over the Catholics of England and Scotland, as well as her tenuous grip on Catholic Ireland.

▶ In 1587, Elizabeth had Mary executed following revelations of a Catholic plot to overthrow Elizabeth.

▶ Despite Mary's execution, James succeeded Elizabeth upon her death in 1603. As **King James I** of England and Ireland, he would usher in the **House of Stuart**.

James I attempted to balance the diverse ethnic and religious groups in England, Scotland, and Ireland, including the Catholic majority in Ireland and the Calvinist Scots, who disagreed on many points with the more liberal Church of England (Anglicans). Despite his efforts at maintaining a delicate political balance, instability grew. In fact, though James's roots were in Catholicism (with his mother having been the Catholic Mary), oppression of Catholics continued. Furthermore, James' daughter married into the Bohemian royal family, forcing English involvement in the Thirty Years' War as that family lost power to Catholics in Central Europe—foreign involvement James was loath to initiate.

> **DID YOU KNOW?**
>
> The Gunpowder Plot to blow up the House of Lords and execute King James in the process was planned by Catholic fighters for November 5, 1605. This plot was conceived by a group including the famous Guy Fawkes, who represents rebellion to this day.

James's son **Charles I** continued the anti-Catholic conflict in 1625 upon his succession to the throne; however, upon his withdrawal in 1630, conservative Protestants in England and Scotland (**Puritans**) began to suspect a royal movement to weaken Protestantism and even restore Catholicism in the kingdom. Many began moving to North America as a result.

Conflict between Protestants and Catholics was fierce on the Continent as well:

- The **Thirty Years' War** (1618 – 1648) began in Central Europe between Protestant nobles in the Holy Roman Empire who disagreed with the strict Catholic Ferdinand II, King of Bohemia and eventually Archduke of Austria and King of Hungary (what was not under Ottoman domination).

  - Elected Holy Roman emperor in 1619, Ferdinand II was a leader of the **Counter-Reformation**, attempts at reinforcing Catholic dominance throughout Europe during and after the Reformation in the wake of the Renaissance and related social change.

  - Ferdinand was closely allied with the Catholic **Habsburg** Dynasty, which ruled Austria and Spain.

- Interference in 1625 by Protestant Denmark and Sweden in Poland and Germany stirred further anti-Catholic discontent among local nobles in Germany, who yearned for independence from the imperial Holy Roman Empire.

  - Despite Danish, Dutch, Swedish, and British support, the imperial military leader Albrecht von Wallenstein took control of most Protestant German states and Denmark.

- ▷ Ferdinand II issued the **Edict of Restitution**, restoring rebellious Protestant German territory to imperial, Catholic control.

- ▷ The defeat of Denmark in 1629 marked the defeat of Denmark as an important European power at that point in history.

▶ Protestant Sweden engaged in further conflict with Catholic Poland.

- ▷ Polish political ambition drove it to take advantage of instability throughout the region, venturing east into Russia until the 1634 Peace of Polyanov.

- ▷ After the Peace of Polyanov, Poland battled Sweden for control over Baltic territory.

▶ Sweden quickly reemerged in 1630 to reignite the Protestant cause.

- ▷ Allied with the Netherlands, Sweden reestablished a Protestant revival throughout Germany, driving imperial forces south.

- ▷ Ferdinand sought aid from the Catholic Spanish Hapsburgs and the Papacy.

- ▷ Sweden was defeated at Nordlingen in 1634, and Catholicism was reestablished in the south.

▶ Despite France's status as a Catholic country, it came into conflict with its neighbors—Hapsburg-ruled Spain and Austria.

- ▷ Spain's victory in Central Europe in 1634 cemented its power in the region.

- ▷ Hapsburg dominance to France's south and east represented a threat to that country, which was now surrounded by a strong military power.

- ▷ Despite their religious commonalities, France declared war on Spain in 1635 and, shortly after, the country also declared war on the Hapsburg-supported Holy Roman Empire.

- ▷ This political tactic represented a break from the prioritization of religious alliances and a movement toward emphasis on state sovereignty.

▶ The tangled alliances between European powers also resulted in war between Sweden and Austria, with the small states of the weakening Holy Roman Empire caught in the middle.

- ▷ The war had been centered on alliances and concerns about the nature of Christianity within different European countries.

- ▷ Upon signing the 1648 **Treaty of Westphalia**, the European powers agreed to recognize **state sovereignty** and practice **noninterference** in each other's matters—at the expense of family and religious allegiance.

- ▷ The year 1648 marked a transition into modern international relations, when politics and religion would no longer be inexorably intertwined.

The end of the Thirty Years' War represented the end of the domination of the Catholic Church over Europe and the concept of religious regional dominance, rather than ethnic state divisions. Over the next several centuries, the Church—and religious empires like the Ottomans—would eventually lose control over ethnic groups and their lands, later giving way to smaller **nation-states**.

As state sovereignty became entrenched in European notions of politics, so too did conflict between the states, which would eventually reflect the Continent's overseas competition:

- ▶ Upon the death of the Hapsburg Holy Roman Emperor Charles VI in 1740, the **War of the Austrian Succession** began, which was a series of Continental wars over who would take over control of the Hapsburg territories; these conflicts would lead to the Seven Years' War.

  - ▷ Though there was dispute over whether a woman—Charles's daughter **Maria Theresa**—could inherit the Austrian throne, it is more likely that **Frederick II** (or **Frederick the Great**) of Prussia took advantage of the instability following Charles's death in 1740 to capture the resource-rich province of Silesia from Hapsburg Austria.

  - ▷ Prussia allied with France, Bavaria, and Spain.

  - ▷ Maria Theresa sought help from Britain, which would be threatened by French dominance of Europe.

  - ▷ Britain and Spain had been in conflict over territory beyond Europe for decades: Britain and France were rivals on the North American continent, in Asia, and in the West Indies.

  - ▷ Forced to the negotiating table by dwindling finances, the European powers signed the Treaty of Aix-la-Chappelle in 1748, which granted Maria Theresa most Austrian possessions and gave Silesia to Prussia.

However, it was clear that Austria intended to regain Silesia. In an effort to protect its allies in Hanover during Continental instability, Britain formed a pragmatic alliance with Prussia, despite its traditional friendship with Austria. As a result, Austria allied with its former enemy France, in a development known as the *Diplomatic Revolution.*

In 1756, Austria was set to attack Prussia, but Frederick the Great attacked first, launching the Seven Years' War:

▶ In Europe, this war further cemented concepts of state sovereignty and delineated rivalries between European powers engaged in colonial adventure and overseas imperialism—especially Britain and France.

▶ It would kick-start British dominance in Asia and lead to Britain's loss of its North American colonies, nearly bankrupting the Crown (as discussed below).

Frederick the Great invaded Silesia and then Bohemia in 1787; however he was repelled by Austria.

Meanwhile, as the English led a Hanoverian army against the French in the west, they too were defeated and the French marched on Prussia:

▶ Sweden attacked from the north; Russia attacked from the east.

▶ Frederick called on Britain for more support.

▶ William Pitt the Elder, the British political leader (essentially prime minister) authorized enormous financial contributions to Prussia.

▶ William Pitt the Elder also began focusing the war overseas against France on imperial possessions in the Western Hemisphere and Asia.

Fortunately for the Anglo-Prussian alliance in Europe, changes in Russian leadership led to Catherine the Great's takeover. Catherine ended hostilities with Prussia and focused on development in Russia instead. This time of change in Europe would affect Asia:

▶ European concepts of social and political organization became constructed around national sovereignty and nation-states.

▶ European economies had become dependent upon colonies and were starting to industrialize, enriching Europe at the expense of its imperial possessions in the Americas, in Africa, and increasingly in Asia.

▶ Industrialization and political organization allowed for improved militaries, which put Asian governments at a disadvantage.

▶ The major Asian powers—Mughal India, Qing China, the Ottoman Empire, and Safavid (and later, Qajar) in Persia—would eventually succumb to European influence or come under direct European control.

While hostilities died down in Europe, the conflict overseas set the stage for the creation of an empire (see below).

THE AGE OF REVOLUTIONS

Monarchies in Europe had been weakened by the conflicts between Catholicism and Protestant faiths. Despite European presence and increasing power overseas, as well as its dominance in the Americas, instability on the continent and in the British Isles made the old order vulnerable.

In England, Puritans and Separatists—strict, conservative Protestants—were suspicious of King Charles I, believing he was weakening Protestantism and even possibly supporting Catholic plots. At the same time, more moderate Protestant leaders, including the weak Parliament and aristocratic class, were upset by Charles' dictatorial reign.

A combination of Enlightenment ideals and political instability would trigger revolution against **absolute monarchy** and mark the early days of the **Age of Revolutions**. Revolutionary actors drew on the philosophies of Enlightenment thinkers:

▶ John Locke

▶ Jean-Jacques Rousseau

▶ Montesquieu

▶ Voltaire

Core beliefs of Enlightenment thinkers:

▶ **republicanism** and democracy

▶ the **social contract** between the people and government

▶ the **separation of powers**

▶ the natural **rights of man**

In 1642, the **English Civil War** broke out between the **Royalists**, who supported the monarchy, and the **Parliamentarians**, who wanted a republic:

▶ Charles I was despotic and sidelined Parliament, causing political and military unrest.

▶ Conflict between England and Scotland in the late 1630s and an Irish uprising in 1641 weakened Charles further.

▶ Disgruntled English aristocracy, who felt that Charles had become a tyrannical ruler, withdrew support and began consolidating their own power.

▶ The Royalists succumbed to the Parliamentarians; Charles was executed in 1649.

Meanwhile, England had lost control over Ireland, and the Parliamentarian military leader Oliver Cromwell was sent to reestablish control over the island:

▶ Charles II, son of Charles I, had established control as King of Scotland.

▶ Cromwell defeated him, and England took back control of Scotland in 1651.

▶ By 1653, England once again controlled Britain and Ireland; Cromwell was installed as Lord Protector.

Following Cromwell's death, Charles II restored the Stuart monarchy; however, stability was short lived once his Catholic brother James II succeeded him in 1685.

By 1688, English Protestants asked the Dutch William of Orange, husband of James II's daughter Mary, to help restore Protestantism in Britain:

▶ William and Mary defeated James and consolidated Protestant control over England, Scotland, and Ireland under a Protestant constitutional monarchy in the **Glorious Revolution**.

▶ The 1689 English Bill of Rights established constitutional monarchy, in the spirit of the Magna Carta.

DID YOU KNOW?

Louis XIV built the palace of Versailles, to centralize the monarchy—and also to contain and monitor the nobility.

The **American Revolution**, also heavily influenced by Locke, broke out a century later.

The French Revolution was the precursor to the end of the feudal order in most of Europe. **King Louis XIV**, the *Sun King* (1643 – 1715), had consolidated the monarchy in France, taking true political and military power from the nobility. Meanwhile, French Enlightenment thinkers like Jean-Jacques Rousseau, Montesquieu, and Voltaire criticized absolute monarchy and the repression of freedom of speech and thought. In 1789, the French Revolution broke out.

Numerous factors were in play in the lead-up to the French Revolution:

▶ The power of the Catholic Church had weakened.

▶ The Scientific Revolution and the Enlightenment had fostered social and intellectual change.

▶ Colonialism and mercantilism were fueling the growth of an early middle class: people who were not traditionally nobility or landowners under the feudal system were becoming wealthier and more powerful thanks to early capitalism.

▶ This new middle class, the **bourgeoisie**, earned their wealth in business and chafed under the rule of the nobility, who had generally inherited land and wealth.

▶ France had entrenched nobilities and one of the most centralized monarchies in Europe.

▶ With a growing bourgeoisie and peasant class paying increasingly higher taxes to the nobility, resentment was brewing.

▶ The problem was most acute in France since it had the largest population in Europe at the time.

▶ Louis XIV had strengthened the monarchy by weakening the nobility's control over their land and centralizing power under the king.

▶ Louis XIV's successors failed to govern effectively or win the loyalty of the people, causing wide resentment of both the nobility and the monarch.

DID YOU KNOW?

A Tale of Two Cities, by Charles Dickens, features a fictional account of the storming of the Bastille. Contrary to popular belief, Victor Hugo's *Les Misérables* takes place several decades after the French Revolution.

▶ The bourgeoisie resented their lack of standing in government and society.

▶ Advances in medicine had permitted unprecedented population growth, further empowering the peasantry and bourgeoisie.

Having supported the American Revolution, the French government was struggling financially. In desperation, the controller-general of finances suggested reforms that would tax the nobility. An unwilling council of nobles instead called for the **Estates-General** to be convened in 1787; this toothless body had not come together since 1614.

The Estates-General was a weak representative assembly that reflected French society:

▶ the clergy

▶ the nobility

▶ the **Third Estate**: the middle class and the poor peasants, or *commoners*

DID YOU KNOW?

The burden of taxation traditionally fell on the Third Estate. In fact, peasants had to **tithe**, paying ten percent of their earnings to the nobles.

After a poor harvest in 1788, unrest spread throughout the country:

▶ King Louis XVI permitted elections to the Estates-General and some free speech; resentment against the elites gained momentum.

▶ Disagreement between the nobility and the elite clergy, on the one hand, and the Third Estate and lower-level parish priests, on the other, erupted once the Estates-General convened at Versailles in 1789.

▶ The two sides came to terms and formed the National Constituent Assembly.

▶ The king and nobility were suspicious of the other side and Louis XVI planned to dissolve it.

At the same time, panic over dwindling food supplies and suspicion over a conspiracy against the Third Estate triggered the **Great Fear** among the peasants in July 1789:

▶ Suspicion turned to action when the king sent troops to Paris.

▶ On July 14 the people stormed the **Bastille** prison in an event symbolic of the overthrow of tyranny and still celebrated in France.

▶ Peasantry revolt in the countryside resulted in the National Constituent Assembly's official abolishment of the feudal system and tithing.

▶ The Assembly issued the **Declaration of the Rights of Man and the Citizen**, the precursor to the French constitution assuring liberty and equality, in the model of Enlightenment thought.

Louis XVI refused to accept these developments; as a result, the people marched on Versailles and brought the royals back to Paris, effectively putting the Assembly in charge.

Members of the **Jacobins**, revolutionary political clubs, became members of the Assembly. The more extreme of these political figures would play key roles in the immediate future of the country.

The Assembly continued reforms:

▶ Lands of the Catholic Church were nationalized to pay off debt, disempowering the Church.

▶ The administration of the *ancien régime* (the old government) was reorganized and allowed the election of judges.

▶ When Louis XVI attempted to escape France, he was detained.

The French Revolution inspired revolutionary movements throughout Europe and beyond; indeed, the revolutionary principle of self-determination drove revolutionary France to support its ideals abroad:

▶ The country declared war on Austria in 1792.

▶ Following severe defeats by joint Austrian-Prussian forces, the people became suspicious of the unpopular queen **Marie Antoinette**.

> ▷ Marie Antoinette was originally from Austria and had encouraged an invasion, hoping to suppress the revolution.

- ► The people imprisoned the royal family.

- ► The Jacobins abolished the monarchy, establishing the republic later that year.

War in Europe dragged on into 1793, with considerable French losses against an alliance between Austria, Prussia, and Great Britain.

Within France, the Jacobins—essentially, the government of the Republic—were breaking into two main factions:

- ► Girondins

  - ▷ moderate

  - ▷ favored concentrating power in the hands of the bourgeoisie

- ► Montagnards

  - ▷ more extreme

  - ▷ led by Robespierre

  - ▷ favored radical social policy that empowered the poor

> **DID YOU KNOW?**
>
> An important tenet of the revolutionary ethos in France was the concept of self-determination, or the right of a people to rule themselves, which threatened rulers fearing revolution in their own countries.

Fearful of counterrevolutionaries in France and instability abroad, the republican government created the Committee of Public Safety in 1793:

- ► Robespierre led the Committee.

- ► The **Reign of Terror** began in France:

  - ▷ Thousands of people were executed by **guillotine**, including Louis XVI and Marie Antoinette.

  - ▷ Robespierre himself was executed a year later.

Ongoing war in Europe and tensions in France between republicans and royalists continued to weaken the revolution, but France had military successes in Europe:

- ► France had continued its effort to spread the revolution throughout the continent.

- ► These efforts were led by **Napoleon Bonaparte**, who even occupied Egypt in an attempt to threaten British power abroad.

- ► In 1799, Napoleon took power in France: the revolution was over.

In 1804 **Napoleon Bonaparte** emerged as emperor of France and proceeded to conquer much of Europe throughout the **Napoleonic Wars**, changing the face of the continent:

- ► French occupation of Spain weakened that country enough that revolutionary movements in its colonies strengthened; eventually Latin American colonies, inspired by the Enlightenment and revolution in Europe, won their freedom.

- ► Napoleon's movement eastward triggered the collapse of the Holy Roman Empire.

  - ▷ The powerful state of **Prussia** emerged in its wake, and a strong sense of militarism and Germanic nationalism took root in the face of opposition to seemingly unstoppable France.

  - ▷ Prussia would later go on to unify the small kingdoms of Central Europe that had made up the Holy Roman Empire, forming Germany, as discussed below.

Napoleon was finally defeated in Russia in 1812 and was forced by the European powers to abdicate in 1813. He escaped from prison on the Mediterranean island of Elba and raised an army again, overthrowing the restored monarch of Louis XVIII. Defeated at Waterloo by the British, he was once again exiled, this time to St. Helena in the southern Atlantic Ocean.

By 1815, other European powers had managed to halt his expansion:

- ► At the **Congress of Vienna** in 1815, a **balance of power** on the continent was agreed upon by European powers that included:

  - ▷ unified Prussia

  - ▷ the Austro-Hungarian Empire

  - ▷ Russia

  - ▷ Britain

DID YOU KNOW?

The Congress of Vienna was the first real international peace conference and set the precedent for European political organization, despite Napoleon's brief reemergence.

In the early part of the nineteenth century, Latin American countries joined Haiti and the United States in revolution against colonial European powers. These movements were inspired by the American and French Revolutions.

Independence movements were led or influenced by **Simón Bolivar** in:

- ► Venezuela

- ► Colombia (including present-day Panama)

CHECK YOUR UNDERSTANDING #9

How did the emergence of a new middle class—the bourgeoisie—set the stage for revolution in Europe and beyond?

- Ecuador

- Peru

- Bolivia

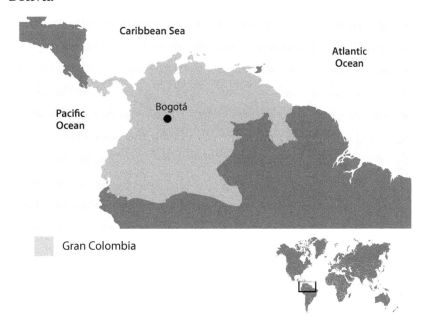

Figure 2.25. Gran Colombia

EUROPEAN DIVISION

The nineteenth century was a period of change and conflict, and the roots of the major twentieth-century conflicts—world war and decolonization—are found in it:

- Nationalism and the nation-state would begin to emerge, becoming a part of modern European social and political norms.

- Economic theories based in the Industrial Revolution like **socialism** and eventually **communism** gained traction.

- **Urbanization** and industry led to stark class divisions (which also helped fuel interest in socialism and communism).

Following the Napoleonic Wars, Prussia had come to dominate the German-speaking states that once comprised the Holy Roman Empire. Prussia, a distinct kingdom within the Holy Roman Empire since the thirteenth century, had become a powerful Central European state by the eighteenth century:

- Prussia became the main rival of Austria for influence in the Germanic lands of Central Europe.

- By the nineteenth century and due in part to emphasis on military prowess, Prussia became an important military power—and a key ally in the efforts against Napoleon.

- Prussia had a particular rivalry with France after losing several key territories during the Napoleonic Wars.

- In 1870, the militarily powerful kingdom went to war against France in the **Franco-Prussian War**.

  ▷ Prussia took control of Alsace-Lorraine, mineral rich and essential for industrial development.

Prussian power would continue to grow in the wake of the Franco-Prussian War:

- **Nationalism** and the **nation-state**—the idea that individuals with shared experience (including ethnicity, language, religion, and cultural practices) should be unified under one government—fueled Prussian power.

- In 1871, the **German Empire** became a united state.

- **Otto von Bismarck** unified those linguistically and culturally German states of Central Europe:

  ▷ Economic cooperation was encouraged.

  ▷ Army reforms were instituted.

  ▷ An image of Prussia as a defender of German culture and nationhood was created.

Nationalism also led to **Italian Unification**:

- Italy, a region of small independent states, was occupied by France and then Austria toward the end of the eighteenth century.

- After being invaded and occupied by Napoleon, the Italian peninsula was divided into three regions.

- Napoleonic concepts of nationalism, freedom, equality, and justice under the law spread throughout the peninsula; what was left of feudalism faded.

Despite re-fragmentation throughout the nineteenth century following the fall of Napoleon, a secret movement for reorganization—the **Risorgimento**—began working toward Italian unification:

- Following the 1859 Franco-Austrian War, Austria's loss of territorial control in northern Italy allowed Italian states to unite via elections.

- Giuseppe Garibaldi led the Northern Italian overthrow of Southern Italian monarchies, uniting the Peninsula with the exception of Rome and Venice.

- The Kingdom of Italy was declared in 1861, under Victor Emmanuel II.

▶ An Italian alliance with Prussia during the **Austro-Prussian War** in 1866 (in which Austria lost even more territory) allowed Italy to take control of Venice.

▶ The Kingdom of Italy entered Rome and incorporated that city and the Papal States during the Franco-Prussian War.

CONFLICT IN THE BALKANS

Farther east, as European kingdoms and empires consolidated their power, the Ottoman Empire was in decline:

▶ The Ottoman Empire had long been a major force in Europe and controlled the bulk of the Balkans.

▶ The empire had lost land in Europe to the Austrians and in Africa to British and French imperialists.

▶ In the Balkans, rebellion among small nations supported by European puppet masters would put an end to Ottoman power in Europe for good.

Despite previous conflict between some of these powers, deeper rivalries throughout the continent inspired Russia, Germany, and Austria-Hungary to form the **Three Emperors' League** in 1873:

▶ If one country went to war, the others would remain neutral, and the powers would consult each other on matters of war.

▶ The **First Balkan Crisis** in 1874 put an end to this alliance:

  ▷ Bosnia Herzegovina rebelled against Ottoman rule.

  ▷ Christian peasants in Herzegovina were unwilling to submit to Muslim landlords.

  ▷ Regional Christians and Bosnian Muslims were no longer willing to submit to rule by the ethnically different Turks, thus beginning the First Balkan Crisis.

Two years later, the Ottoman autonomous principality of Serbia, joined by Montenegro, rebelled in support of Bosnia:

▶ Serbian rebellion attracted Russian attention after Serbia came under Russian influence due to Pan-Slavism.

  ▷ **Pan-Slavism** is the concept that Slavic ethnic groups throughout Eastern and Southeastern Europe should embrace their Slavic heritage and turn toward Russia for support.

- When the Ottoman **Sultan Hamid II** refused to institute reforms to protect Balkan Christians, Russia declared war.

- The **Russo-Turkish War** ended in 1878 with the **Treaty of San Stefano**, which favored Russian territorial gains.

- Austro-Hungarian and British objections to the treaty, which threatened their influence in the region, led to the **1878 Congress of Berlin**, hosted by Otto von Bismarck.

- Unfortunately for Russia, which was the militarily and financially weaker power, Britain and Austria-Hungary changed the outcome of the war with the **Treaty of Berlin**, which replaced the Treaty of San Stefano.

  ▷   While the independence of Serbia and Montenegro was decided, Russia lost influence in Bulgaria as well as territorial gains in Asia. These insults would not be forgotten.

Given developments in the Balkans, Germany and Austria-Hungary secretly formed the Dual Alliance to respond to fears of Pan-Slavism. In 1882, Italy asked these countries for assistance against France, which had upset Italian imperial ambition in North Africa; the **Triple Alliance**, a secret political and military alliance was formed.

Stability in the Balkans and among the great powers was further threatened by the 1885 **Second Balkan Crisis**:

- Bulgaria declared unification and independence, violating the Treaty of Berlin and Russian interests.

- Serbia went to war against Bulgaria, requiring Austro-Hungarian support.

Eventually, tension between Russia and Austria-Hungary—which was supported by Germany—led to the breakdown of Russian relationships with those countries. Russian relations improved with Great Britain and France.

CHECK YOUR UNDERSTANDING #10

List some important European alliances in the nineteenth century.

In 1894, Russia and France became allies. Great Britain would join this alliance in the 1907 **Triple Entente**, setting the stage for the system of alliances at the heart of the First World War.

Continued European involvement in the Balkans accelerated the ongoing loss of Ottoman influence there due to phenomena like nationalism, ethnocentrism (Pan-Slavism), military and political power, and religious influence. The small Balkan nations were empowered to continue rebellion against Ottoman rule, and European powers proceeded into the area:

▶ In 1908, Austria-Hungary annexed Bosnia-Herzegovina, disregarding Russian objections.

▶ Russia helped form the **Balkan League**, comprised of Serbia, Montenegro, Greece, and Bulgaria, which went to war with the Ottomans in the 1912 **First Balkan War**.

▶ The Ottomans were defeated and lost nearly all their European possessions.

The following year, disagreement over the division of land led to the **Second Balkan War**:

▶ The Second Balkan War was between Bulgaria and a Serbian-Greek alliance.

▷ Serbia wanted to keep Albanian territory, which Austria-Hungary insisted remain independent.

▷ Bulgaria wanted control over more land in Macedonia (which had come mainly under Greek and Serbian rule).

▶ This instability would eventually lead to the First World War.

IMPERIALISM

Colonialism and imperialism contributed to ongoing tensions between nation-states on the continent of Europe:

Table 2.2. Causes of Colonialism and Imperialism over the Centuries

Century	Colonialism	Imperialism
Fifteenth century	• mercantilism	
Sixteenth century	• conquest • Christian conversion	
Seventeenth century		• capitalism
Eighteenth century		• European competition
Nineteenth century		• conceptions of racial superiority

Britain and France, historic rivals on the European continent, were also at odds colonizing North America and in overseas trade, and helped fuel the **Seven Years' War** (1756 – 1763):

▶ Britain and France fought in Europe and overseas colonies and interests in North America and Asia.

DID YOU KNOW?

The Seven Years' War is considered by many historians to be the first truly global conflict.

- ▶ Alliances:
  - ▷ Britain, Prussia, and Hanover
  - ▷ France, Austria, Sweden, Russia
- ▶ The war's extension into the imperial realm made it a global conflict.

In North America, Britain and France had explored the region and controlled tremendous amounts of territory in what later would become Canada and the United States.

Table 2.3. British and French Control in North America

	Territory	Major Ports	Major Exports
Britain	• Thirteen Colonies (Atlantic coast)	• New York • Philadelphia • Boston	• tobacco • rice • vegetables • various crops
France	• Quebec • Northeastern territories • territory in the Midwest that included interior trade routes through much of **the Great Lakes** region	• Major Ports: • Montreal • Quebec City • St. Lawrence River (leading to Atlantic Ocean) • Detroit River (leading to the St. Lawrence River) • Mississippi River • Port of New Orleans (leading to the Gulf of Mexico)	• beaver pelts (valuable in Europe for their water-repellant properties) • timber • various natural resources

The **French and Indian War**, as the Seven Years' War is called in North America, resulted in net gains for Britain:

- ▶ France formed an important alliance with the powerful Algonquin in the Northeast.
- ▶ Britain was allied with the Iroquois.
- ▶ Strong military leaders like **George Washington** helped Britain take control of French Canada.

The conflict in Europe, however, would put a strain on Britain:

- ▶ Financially exhausted from the costly conflict in Europe, Britain ceded control of the Northwest Territories (Michigan, Ohio, Indiana) to various tribes in the **Treaty of Paris in 1763** (agreements later not honored by the United States).

▶ The financial and military strain suffered by Britain in the Seven Years' War made it particularly vulnerable to later rebellion in the Colonies, helping the Americans win the Revolutionary War there.

According to Pitt the Elder's plan, Britain went to war with France in Asia as well:

▶ The decline of the **Mughal Empire** in India and the rising power of colonial companies specializing in exporting valuable resources like spices and tea, led to the formation of smaller Indian kingdoms that formed alliances with those increasingly influential corporations.

▶ By the mid-eighteenth century, violence broke out between the British East India Company and the French East India Company and their allies among the small Indian states in a series of wars known as the **Carnatic Wars** (1746 – 1763).

▶ With the end of the Seven Years' War, the Treaty of Paris established British dominance in the Subcontinent.

  ▷ France was allowed some trading posts in the region but was forced to recognize British power there.

  ▷ By 1803, British interests effectively took control of the Subcontinent and the Mughals were pushed to the north.

> **DID YOU KNOW?**
>
> The Netherlands was already coming to dominate Indonesia (at the time, the Dutch East Indies) thanks to similar actions by the Dutch East India Company.

Despite losing the Thirteen Colonies, at the dawn of the nineteenth century Britain retained control of Canada, rich in natural resources like beaver pelts and timber. In addition, it controlled the resource-rich and strategically important Indian Subcontinent. Britain would become the strongest naval power in the world and continue to expand its empire, especially in the search for new markets for its manufactured goods to support its industrial economy.

During the reign of **Queen Victoria** (1837 – 1901), the British Empire would expand to lengths not seen up to this time:

▶ In 1788, Britain had begun sending convicts to the penal colony of Australia.

  ▷ Gold was discovered there in 1851, and British subjects began to voluntarily settle Australia and the Pacific.

- ▶ In 1857, the **Indian Mutiny** against private British troops controlled by the East India Company caused the British government to intervene and send in military.

  ▷ Victoria would eventually take the title of **Empress of India**, cementing the imperial nature of government and the Raj (imperial administration).

- ▶ In 1877, the British annexed South Africa.

  ▷ Following the Boer Wars, Britain would retain control of diamond- and gold-rich South Africa (see below).

- ▶ Victoria chartered the imperialist **Cecil Rhodes** and his company, the British South Africa Company (BSAC) to explore north from South Africa to mine the land.

  ▷ This charter was ordered despite numerous factors:

    ▷ conflicting European claims to the land

    ▷ claims by the Afrikaaners, (see below)

    ▷ the residence of the Matabele, who had lived there for centuries

- ▶ Rhodes and the BSAC forcefully took over and brought the following territories under English rule using treaties, diplomacy, and violence:

  ▷ Northern Rhodesia (Zambia)

  ▷ Rhodesia (Zimbabwe)

  ▷ Nyasaland (Malawi)

  ▷ Bechuanaland (Botswana)

In East Africa, the British explorer **David Livingstone** had been working in Kenya; the government had influence over the Sultan of Zanzibar. However, secret German agreements with coastal leaders and the establishment of the German colony of Tanganyika forced the British into more activity in the region. In an agreement with the Germans, the British took control over what would become Kenya and Uganda, while Germany maintained Tanganyika. Borders were drawn without regard for the Kikuyu, Masai, Luo, and other tribes living in the area.

The racist concept of the **white man's burden** drove imperialism. White Europeans were "obligated" to bring what they considered their superior culture to other civilizations around the globe. This idea was popular in Britain and elsewhere in Europe.

Despite its small size, Belgium controlled the Congo, along with its vast resources in Central Africa. Coming into conflict with Rhodes at its southern edges, the Belgian Congo, which reached its heights under **King Leopold II**, was rich in rubber, timber, minerals, and diamonds. Furthermore, this territory was strategically important: controlling the Congo meant controlling the Congo River basin, allowing for the extraction of materials from the interior to the Atlantic Coast.

CHECK YOUR UNDERSTANDING #11

List some of the European powers' justifications for imperialism.

To gain access to closed Chinese markets, Britain forced China to buy Indian opium:

▶ The Opium Wars ended with the **Treaty of Nanking (1842)**, signed between the British and the increasingly impotent Qing government.

▶ As a result, China lost great power to Britain and other European countries, which gained:

▷ **spheres of influence** (areas of China they effectively controlled)

▷ **extraterritoriality** (privileges in which their citizens were not subject to Chinese law)

Even though nominally Chinese leadership still governed, discontent with the Qing Dynasty was growing as Chinese people perceived that their country was coming under control of European imperialists:

▶ The combination of economic hardship and huge casualties in the Opium Wars and in the **Sino-Japanese War of 1896** (see below) led to a violent uprising.

▷ In 1900, the **Boxer Rebellion**, an uprising led by a Chinese society against the emperor, was only put down with Western (including American) help.

▷ The Qing were humiliated further by being forced to pay the West enormous reparations for their assistance.

DID YOU KNOW?

The Boxers were so called because of their belief that physical exercises, like shadow boxing, would make them impervious to bullets. This rebellion was led by a secret society called the Yihequan, or The Society of Righteous and Harmonious Fists.

▷ Living conditions for Chinese people continued to deteriorate.

The European powers were immersed in what became known as the *Scramble for Africa*. The industrial economies of Europe would profit from the natural resources abundant on that continent, and the white man's burden continued to fuel colonization.

At the **1884 Berlin Conference**, control over Africa was divided among European powers. (Africans were not consulted in this process.)

The **Boer War** (1899–1902) between Afrikaaners of Dutch origin and the English, resulted in Britain officially gaining control of South Africa. Whites would rule the country until the end of **Apartheid** in the early 1990s.

France would eventually control the following:

▶   West Africa

▶   North Africa

▷   Algeria

▷   Mali

▷   Niger

▷   Chad

▷   Cameroon

▷   present-day Republic of the Congo (not to be confused with Belgian Congo, now the Democratic Republic of the Congo)

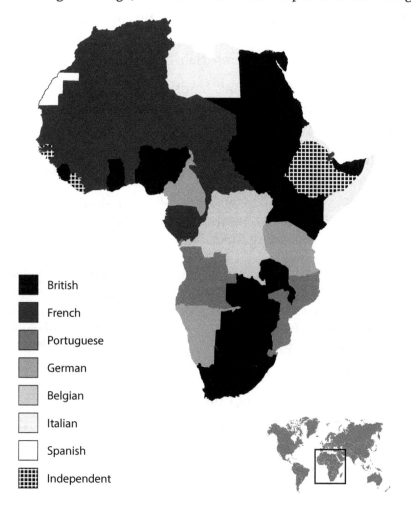

British

French

Portuguese

German

Belgian

Italian

Spanish

Independent

Figure 2.26. Imperial Africa

However, not all non-European countries fell to European imperialism:

▶ Emperor Meiji promoted the modernization of technology, especially the military, during the **Meiji Restoration** in Japan in 1868.

▶ Japan proved itself a world power when it defeated Russia in the **Russo-Japanese War** in 1905.

▶ Japan would go on to play a central role in twentieth century conflict.

INDUSTRIAL REVOLUTION

Throughout this entire period, raw goods from the Americas fueled European economic growth and development, leading to the **Industrial Revolution** in the nineteenth century:

▶ This economic revolution began with textile production in Britain, fueled by cotton from its overseas territories in North America, and later India and Egypt.

▶ The first factories were in Manchester, where **urbanization** began as poor people from rural areas flocked to cities in search of higher-paying unskilled jobs in factories.

▶ Early industrial technology sped up the harvesting and transport of crops and their conversion to textiles.

This accelerated manufacturing was based on **capitalism**, the **laissez-faire** (or **free market**) theory developed by Adam Smith, who believed that an *invisible hand* should guide the marketplace: government should stay out of the economy regardless of abuses since the economy would eventually automatically correct for inequalities, price problems, and any other problematic issues.

Advances in technology also helped accelerate manufacturing:

▶ The spinning jenny and flying shuttle exponentially increased the amount of cotton that workers could process into yarn and thread.

▶ The steam engine efficiently powered mills and ironworks; factories no longer had to be built near running water to access power.

Figure 2.27. Spinning Jenny

▶ Improvement in iron technology allowed for stronger machinery; it would also support the **Second Industrial Revolution** in the late nineteenth and early twentieth centuries, which was based on heavy industry, railroads, and weapons.

To access the raw materials needed to produce manufactured goods, Britain and other industrializing countries in Western Europe needed resources—hence the drive for imperialism as discussed above:

- Cotton was harvested in India and Egypt for textile mills.

- Minerals mined in South Africa and the Congo were used to support metallurgy.

Industrialization and urbanization led to the development of early middle classes in Europe and North America, resulting in increased imports of luxury goods like tea, spices, silk, precious metals, and other items from Asia to meet consumer demand.

Colonial powers also gained by selling manufactured goods back to the colonies from which they had harvested raw materials in the first place, for considerable profit.

Largely unbridled capitalism had led to the conditions of the early Industrial Revolution; workers suffered from abusive treatment, overly long hours, low wages (or none at all), and unsafe conditions, including pollution. The German philosophers Karl Marx and Friedrich Engels, horrified by conditions suffered by industrial workers, developed **socialism**:

- Socialism is the philosophy that workers, or the **proletariat**, should own the means of production and reap the profits.

- The **bourgeoisie**, who had no interest in the rights of the workers at the expense of profit and who did not experience the same conditions, should not own the means of production nor claim its profits.

- Marx wrote *Das Kapital*:

  ▷ He offered arguments for the abolition of the class system, wages, and private property.

  ▷ He favored collective ownership of both the means of production and products, with equal distribution of income to satisfy the needs of all.

- Later, Marx and Engels wrote the *Communist Manifesto*:

  ▷ The *Communist Manifesto* outlined their ideas and called for revolution.

  ▷ It inspired the formation of socialist groups worldwide.

A different version of socialism would later help Russia become a major world power. The Russian intellectuals **Vladimir Lenin** and **Leon Trotsky** would take Marx and Engels' theories further, developing Marxism-Leninism:

▶ They embraced socialist ideals and believed in revolution.

▶ They felt that communism could not be maintained under a democratic governing structure.

> **DID YOU KNOW?**
>
> The Communist Manifesto contained the famous words, "Workers of the world, unite!"

▶ Lenin supported dictatorship, more precisely the **dictatorship of the proletariat**, paving the way for the political and economic organization of the Soviet Union.

PRACTICE QUESTIONS

11) **What did the Treaty of Westphalia do?**

   A. laid out the final borders of Europe, setting the stage for modern foreign policy

   B. established the notion of state sovereignty, in which states recognized each other as independent and agreed not to interfere in each other's affairs

   C. gave the Catholic Church more power in the affairs of Catholic-majority countries

   D. established the notion of the nation-state, in which culturally and ethnically similar groups would control their own territory as sovereign countries

12) **What was an important factor that led to the French Revolution?**

   A. the corruption of Louis XIV

   B. the strong organization of the Estates-Genera

   C. support from the United States of America

   D. the anti-monarchical philosophies of Enlightenment thinkers like Rousseau and Voltaire

13) **How did Pan-Slavism affect the crises in the Balkans?**

   A. Pan-Slavism led Russia to directly intervene militarily throughout the nineteenth century in the Balkans, leading to violent conflict.

   B. Pan-Slavism generally ensured Russian support for Slavic ethnic groups in the Balkans, which contributed to ongoing tensions there already fueled by competing European and Ottoman interests and diverse nationalities.

   C. Russian interests in Slavic groups in the Balkans strengthened its alliance with Turkey.

   D. Pan-Slavism did not have a major effect on the Balkans, as the major Slavic cultures are located farther north in Europe.

14) **Which of the following is NOT a way that the white man's burden influenced imperialism?**

A. It inspired Europeans to settle overseas in order to improve what they believed to be "backward" places.

B. Europeans believed imperialism was in the best interest of Indigenous peoples, who would benefit from adopting European languages and cultural practices.

C. Europeans believed it burdensome to be forced to tutor non-Europeans in their languages and customs.

D. Many Europeans supported the construction of schools for colonial subjects and even the development of scholarships for them to study in Europe.

15) **Which of the following did Marx and Engels believe?**

A. The proletariat must control the means of production to ensure a wageless, classless society to equitably meet the needs of all.

B. The workers would control the means of production in the dictatorship of the proletariat.

C. An organized revolution directed by a small group of leaders was necessary to bring about social change and a socialist society.

D. The bourgeoisie would willingly give up control of the means of production to the proletariat.

GLOBAL CONFLICTS

PRE-REVOLUTIONARY RUSSIA

Russia had gone to war with Japan in 1904 to secure access to the Pacific as well as its interests in Asia. **Tsar Nicholas II**, unpopular at home, also believed that a victory would improve his security as a ruler. Japan, concerned about losing influence in Korea and seeking influence in China, attacked Russia; the **Russo-Japanese War** quickly ended in 1905 due to superior Japanese military technology, including naval technology, training, and leadership.

Russia's loss to Japan in the 1905 Russo-Japanese War was just another example of its difference from other European powers:

▶ While technically a European country, Russia had been slow to industrialize, due in part to its size and terrain.

▶ A largely agrarian country at the turn of the century, **serfdom**, the practice of "tying" peasants to the land and the last vestiges of feudalism, had only been abolished in 1861.

▶ Most Russians were still poor, rural farmers, and industrialization brought wretched conditions to workers in the cities.

▶ Russia also continued to have an absolute monarchy, unlike many European powers whose governments had shifted during the Age of Revolution.

Numerous factors caused Tsar Nicholas to face dissent at home:

▶ the humiliating defeat by the Japanese

▶ discontent fueled by longer-term economic hardship in the face of a strengthening European industrial economy

▶ limited freedoms in comparison to those enjoyed elsewhere in Europe

As a result, unlawful trade unions appeared, workers began striking, and peasants rose up in protest of oppressive taxation.

Figure 2.28. Bloody Sunday

Still, many Russians blamed the Tsar's advisors and minor officials for conditions, believing that the Tsar himself would act to improve conditions for Russians. These ideas were shattered in 1905 when a peaceful protest of working conditions in St. Petersburg ended in a bloody massacre of civilians by the Tsar's troops. **Bloody Sunday**, as the event came to be called, resulted in the **Revolution of 1905**, during which the Tsar temporarily lost control of Russia and was discredited.

Following the Revolution of 1905, the Tsar made some reforms in Russia, including the establishment of a **Duma**, or Parliament. However, economic hardship and social discontent continued in the country.

While not directly involved with the failed Revolution of 1905, the Marxist Social Democrats—made up of the **Bolsheviks**, led by **Lenin**, and the **Mensheviks**—would gain power. They would eventually take over the country in 1917.

WORLD WAR I

Instability in the Balkans and increasing tensions in Europe culminated with the assassination of the Austro-Hungarian Archduke **Franz Ferdinand** by the Serbian nationalist **Gavrilo Princip** in Sarajevo on June 28, 1914.

In protest of continuing Austro-Hungarian control over Serbia, Princip's action kicked off the **system of alliances** that had been in place among European powers:

▶ Austria-Hungary declared war on Serbia; Russia came to Serbia's aid.

▶ As part of the Triple Alliance and an ally of Austria-Hungary, Germany declared war on Russia.

▶ Russia's ally France prepared for war.

▶ As Germany traversed Belgium to invade France, Belgium pleaded for aid from other European countries, which led Britain to declare war on Germany.

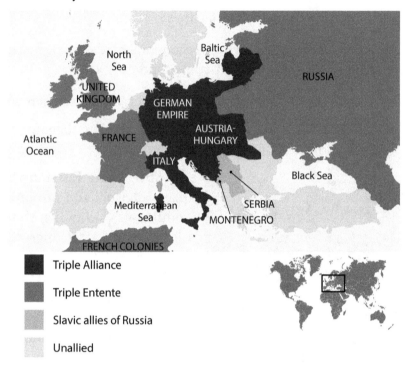

Figure 2.29. WWI Alliances

Germany had been emphasizing military growth since the consolidation and militarization of the empire under Bismarck in the mid-nineteenth century. Germany was a militarized state and an important European power in its own right, and the country was now under **Kaiser Wilhelm II**:

▶ Wilhelm took over the German Empire in 1888.

▶ He was the grandson of Frederick II (on his father's side) and Queen Victoria.

▶ He focused on improving naval power and expanding German territory overseas (including the potential capture of overseas British and French colonies).

Despite Wilhelm's connections to Britain, Germany's threat to British overseas power brought the war beyond Europe to Africa and Asia:

▶ In Togo, Britain and France took over an important German communications point.

▸ In China, Japan allied with Britain and France and took control of the German settlement of Tsingtao and German colonies in the Pacific Islands.

▸ Britain's imperial power allowed it to call on troops from all over the globe—Indians, Canadians, Australians, South Africans, and New Zealanders all fought in Europe.

▸ France also imported colonial fighters from North Africa.

Table 2.4. Important Military Campaigns of WWI

Battle	Year	Description	Impact
Battle of the Marne	1914	• German, French, and British forces defended France.	• trench warfare that would continue for years, marking the Western Front
Gallipoli	1915	• Australian and New Zealander troops fought the Ottoman Empire, allies of Germany, near Istanbul.	• heavy casualties sustained by the British Commonwealth • The reputation of the Allies' military force was weakened.
Battle of Verdun	1916	• the longest battle of the war	• The Germans failed to defeat the French army.
Battle of Jutland	1916	• The British navy pushed back the German navy. • heavy losses suffered by the British	• Britain was able to ensure that German naval power was diminished for the rest of the war.
Battle of the Somme	1916 (July 1)	• part of an allied effort to repel Germany using artillery to end the stalemate on the Western Front	• After four months, the Front moved only five miles.

Finally, in 1917, the United States learned of the **Zimmerman Telegram**, in which Germany secretly proposed an alliance with Mexico to attack the US. This finally spurred US intervention in the war. Despite Russian withdrawal after the Bolshevik Revolution in October 1917, Germany was forced to surrender in the face of invasion by the US-supported allies.

According to the **Schlieffen Plan**, Germany had planned to fight a war on two fronts against both Russia and France; however, Russia's unexpectedly rapid mobilization stretched the German army too thin on the Eastern Front, while it became bogged down in **trench warfare** on the Western Front against the British, French, and later the Americans.

DID YOU KNOW?

In 1915, a German submarine (U-boat) sank the *Lusitania*, a passenger ship in the Atlantic, killing many American civilians. This event strained relations with a neutral US, which would enter the war in 1917.

Germany lost the war and was punished with the harsh **Treaty of Versailles,** which held it accountable for the entirety of the war:

▶ The Treaty brought economic hardship on the country by forcing it to pay **reparations**.

▶ Wilhelm was forced to abdicate and never again regained power in Germany.

▶ The Treaty resulted in German military failure and consequent economic collapse. These, combined with later worldwide economic depression, set the stage for the rise of fascism and Adolf Hitler.

▶ The Treaty created the **League of Nations**, an international organization designed to prevent future outbreaks of international war. It was largely toothless, especially because the powerful United States did not join.

Change in the Middle East

The end of WWI also marked the end of the Ottoman Empire. A number of factors led to the empire's eventual dissolution:

▶ An ally of Germany, the Ottoman Empire had been defeated in the war.

▶ Tremendous losses led to the collapse of many Ottoman institutions.

▶ Poor organization and refugee movements led to starvation and chaos throughout the region.

▶ In 1908, the Young Turks, a military government, effectively took over the empire in an effort to modernize it.

▷ They were especially concerned with nationalism and promoting *Turkishness*, a focus on Turkish ethnicity and culture, throughout the diverse empire.

▶ The Ottomans had already lost their North African provinces to France in the mid-nineteenth century.

▶ From the end of the nineteenth century, the British had been increasing their influence throughout Ottoman territory in Egypt and the Persian Gulf, seeking control over the Suez Canal and petroleum resources in the Gulf.

▶ In 1916, France and Britain concluded the **Sykes-Picot Agreement**, which secretly planned for the Middle East following the defeat of the Ottoman Empire.

▷ The Agreement divided up the region now considered the Middle East into spheres of influence to be controlled by each power; Palestine would be governed internationally.

▶ In 1917, the secret **Balfour Declaration** promised the Jews an independent state in Palestine, but Western powers did not honor this agreement; in fact it conflicted directly with the Sykes-Picot Agreement. The state of Israel was not established until 1948.

▶ The Ottoman Empire was officially dissolved in 1923.

At the end of the war the area was indeed divided into **mandates**, areas nominally independent but effectively controlled by Britain and France. The borders drawn are essentially those national borders that divide the Middle East today.

After the First World War, the nationalist **Mustafa Ataturk**, one of the Young Turks who pushed a secular, nationalist agenda, kept European powers out of Anatolia and abolished the Caliphate in 1924, establishing modern Turkey.

After the dissolution of the Ottoman Empire, the future of the Middle East was uncertain.

> **DID YOU KNOW?**
>
> In 1915, the Ottoman Empire launched a genocide against the Christian Armenian people, part of a campaign to control ethnic groups it believed threatened the Turkish nature of the empire. An estimated 1.5 million Armenians were removed from their homes and killed. The Turkish government still denies the Armenian Genocide.

Table 2.5. The Middle East During and After the Ottoman Empire

During the Ottoman Empire	After the Ottoman Empire
• Ottoman caliphate represented the symbolic center of Islam • Ottoman caliphate controlled the holy cities of Mecca and Medina • unifying religious leadership (caliph was entrusted with the leadership of those two holy cities)	• broken up into European-controlled protectorates • Turkey—nationalist, secular, and independent—turned toward Europe • unraveling of the social and political fabric of the region • no longer a caliph/unifying religious leader • refugees and migrants suddenly restricted by international borders from their places of origin • people needed—and lacked—identification papers • ethnic and religious groups divided by what would become the borders of the modern Middle East

France and Britain backed different political factions in their mandates:

▶ Nominally autonomous Egypt and its ruler, King Fuad, were close allies of the British, having essentially been under their control.

▶ Husayn ibn Ali (King Hussein), the sharif (ruler) of Mecca, claimed the title of caliph, but was driven out and made king of Jordan by the British. (His family controls the monarchy to this day.)

▶ The rest of the Arabian Peninsula, where oil had not yet been discovered, was taken by the Saudis, a tribe from the desert which followed an extreme form of Islam, the **Wahhabi Movement**.

  ▷ King Saud would eventually conquer Mecca and Medina but never take the title of Caliph.

The roots of two competing ideologies, Pan-Arabism and Islamism, developed in this context.

▶ **Pan-Arabism** became an international movement espousing Arab unity in response to European and US influence and presence later in the twentieth century.

  ▷ Arabs and Arabic speakers should be aligned regardless of international borders.

▶ **Islamism** began as a social and political movement.

  ▷ The Muslim Brotherhood was established in Egypt in the 1920s, filling social roles that the state had abandoned or could not fill.

  ▷ Eventually taking a political role, the Muslim Brotherhood's model later inspired groups like Hamas and Hezbollah.

RUSSIAN REVOLUTION

During WWI, a combination of failures at home and on the front only added to widespread dissatisfaction with the rule of the tsar:

▶ Russia was suffering from widespread food shortages and economic crisis.

▶ Morale was low due to conscription.

▶ The military suffered losses and defeats under the command of Nicholas II.

An enormous strike in Petrograd in January 1917 commemorating Bloody Sunday ended in revolt.

▶ Soldiers refused to fire on protesters.

- ▶ The people formed the elected Petrograd Soviet (Petrograd Council) in the **February Revolution**.

- ▶ The Tsar was forced to abdicate.

- ▶ The revolutionary movement resulted in the fall of his family, the Romanovs.

A weak provisional government was formed until elections could be held.

- ▶ It was widely regarded as working in the interests of the elite, making unpopular decisions like continuing to engage in WWI and putting off land reform.

- ▶ The Provisional Government was ineffective in solving economic problems.

Meanwhile, other Soviets (councils) formed beyond Petrograd. The elected Soviets seemed to better represent the interests of the workers and peasants who suffered the most, and so they became more powerful. At the same time, the Soviets appealed to discontented soldiers fighting in the unpopular war.

Unlike the Mensheviks, the Bolsheviks, led by Lenin, believed that revolution must be planned and instigated at the right moment—not a phenomenon meant to occur naturally. Consequently, they were not involved in the February Revolution.

Ideologies of Lenin and the Bolsheviks:

- ▶ Lenin believed that revolution must be planned, and that the proletariat needed direction in beginning and pursuing a revolution.

- ▶ Later in 1917, the Bolsheviks had become a stronger force, and Lenin believed that the time was right to trigger revolution in Russia.

Lenin and the Bolsheviks proposed a number of changes:

- ▶ power would be concentrated in the Soviets, not in the Duma

- ▶ Russia would make peace and withdraw from European hostilities

- ▶ land would be redistributed among the peasants

- ▶ economic crises in the cities would be solved

Lenin's plan was to take control of the Petrograd Soviet, of which Leon Trotsky had become chairman.

In the **October Revolution** Lenin, Trotsky, and the Bolsheviks took control of Russia, defeating the Provisional Government in a coup.

In 1918, despite withdrawal from WWI, the **Russian Civil War** was underway:

- ▶ The White Armies, former supporters of the Tsar, were in conflict with the Bolshevik Red Army.

- ▶ During the war, the communists consolidated their power by nationalizing industry, developing and distributing propaganda portraying themselves as the defenders of Russia against imperialism, and forcefully eliminating dissent.

- ▶ For many, it was more appealing to fight for a new Russia with hope for an improved standard of living than to return to the old times under the Tsar.

- ▶ Many Russians feared the specter of imperialism or interference by foreign powers.

- ▶ By 1921, the Bolsheviks were victorious and formed the **Soviet Union** or **Union of Soviet Socialist Republics (USSR)**.

Following Lenin's death in 1924, Trotsky and the Secretary of the Communist Party, **Josef Stalin**, struggled for power. Stalin ultimately outmaneuvered Trotsky, who was exiled and assassinated.

Under Stalin's totalitarian dictatorship, the USSR became socially and politically repressive:

- ▶ The Communist Party and the military underwent **purges** where any persons who were a potential threat to Stalin's power were imprisoned or executed.

- ▶ Stalin's paranoia and oppression extended to the general population.

  - ▷ Russians suffered under the Great Terror throughout the 1920s.

  - ▷ Any hint of dissent was to be reported to the secret police—the NKVD—and usually resulted in imprisonment for life.

- ▶ Stalin enforced **Russification** policies, persecuting ethnic groups.

  - ▷ People throughout the USSR were forced to speak Russian and limit or hide their own cultural practices.

  - ▷ Religious practices were restricted or forbidden.

- ▶ In 1931, Stalin enforced the **collectivization** of land and agriculture in an attempt to consolidate control over the countryside and improve food security.

  - ▷ He had the *kulaks*, or landowning peasants, sent to the *gulags*, enabling the government to confiscate their land.

  - ▷ By 1939, most farming and land was controlled by the government, and most peasants lived on collective land.

▷ Collectivizing the farms enabled Stalin to encourage more peasants to leave the country and become industrial workers, produce agricultural surpluses to sell overseas, and eliminate the *kulaks*.

▶ Systemic disorganization in the 1920s and early 1930s resulted in famine and food shortages.

As part of modernizing Russia, Stalin focused on accelerating industrial development:

▶ He targeted heavy industry with **Five Year Plans**.

▷ Production in industrial materials and staples like electricity, petroleum, coal, and iron increased.

▷ Construction of major infrastructure throughout the country took place from 1929 – 1938.

▶ These developments provided opportunities for women, but conditions for the workers were dismal.

▶ The USSR quickly became an industrial power, but at the expense of millions of Russians, Ukrainians, and other groups who lost their lives in purges, forced labor camps, and famine.

> **DID YOU KNOW?**
>
> In the 1920s, around twenty million Russians were sent to the gulags, or prison labor camps, usually in Siberia, thousands of miles from their homes. Millions died.

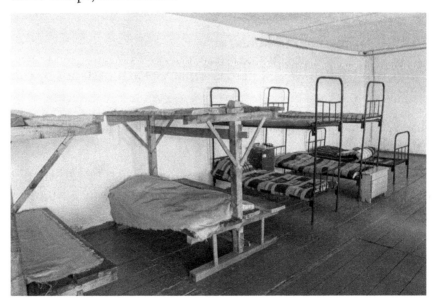

Figure 2.30. Gulag

CHANGE IN EAST ASIA

Japan had undergone rapid modernization after being closed off from 1600 until the mid-nineteenth century under the Tokugawa Shogunate.

Following its victory in the Russo-Japanese War, Japan:

- had become more visible internationally in the early part of the twentieth century

- was now recognized as a military power for defeating Russia

- joined a world focused on industry and imperialism

Japan, having already embraced industrialization and modern militarization, turned toward imperialism throughout Asia:

- From 1894 – 1895, Japan fought the **First Sino-Japanese War** with Qing Dynasty China.

- The First Sino-Japanese War revealed Chinese military and organizational limitations and showed Japanese military superiority.

- The 1895 Treaty of Shimonoseki ended the First Sino-Japanese War.

  ▷   It established trading rights for Japan on Chinese territory.

  ▷   Japan gained influence over China's vassal Korea.

  ▷   Japan gained control of Taiwan.

The later **Russo-Japanese War** (1904 – 1905) confirmed Japan's status in the eyes of European empires as a world power. It also solidified Japanese influence in Korea and Manchuria.

- In 1910, Japan annexed Korea.

- After WWI, Japan was granted Germany's Pacific islands by the League of Nations.

- In 1931, Japan invaded Manchuria, creating the puppet state *Manchukuo*.

Following WWI, and despite having provided assistance to the French and British in Asia, Japan began its own imperialist adventure in East and Southeast Asia. Japan intended:

- to gain power

- to access raw materials

- to limit and expel European rule in what Japan considered its sphere of influence

While Japan was building its global reputation, military, and economic strength in Asia, China was undergoing political change.

The Xinhai Revolution broke out in 1911. Led by **Sun Yat-sen**, the revolutionaries had the support of disaffected Chinese people as well as the financial support of millions of Chinese living abroad.

- The Qing was overthrown.
- Dynastic Chinese rule ended.
- The short-lived **Republic of China** was established.

DID YOU KNOW?

China felt betrayed by European powers, which had awarded German possessions in China to Japan in the Treaty of Versailles. China refused to sign the treaty, and communism became popular among some Chinese leaders.

The Republic of China was recognized by major international powers. But the power vacuum left by the end of imperial China allowed for the rise of warlords throughout the enormous country. Republican government was unable to establish total control. Two major parties would emerge: the **Kuomintang (KMT)** and the **Chinese Communist Party (CCP)**.

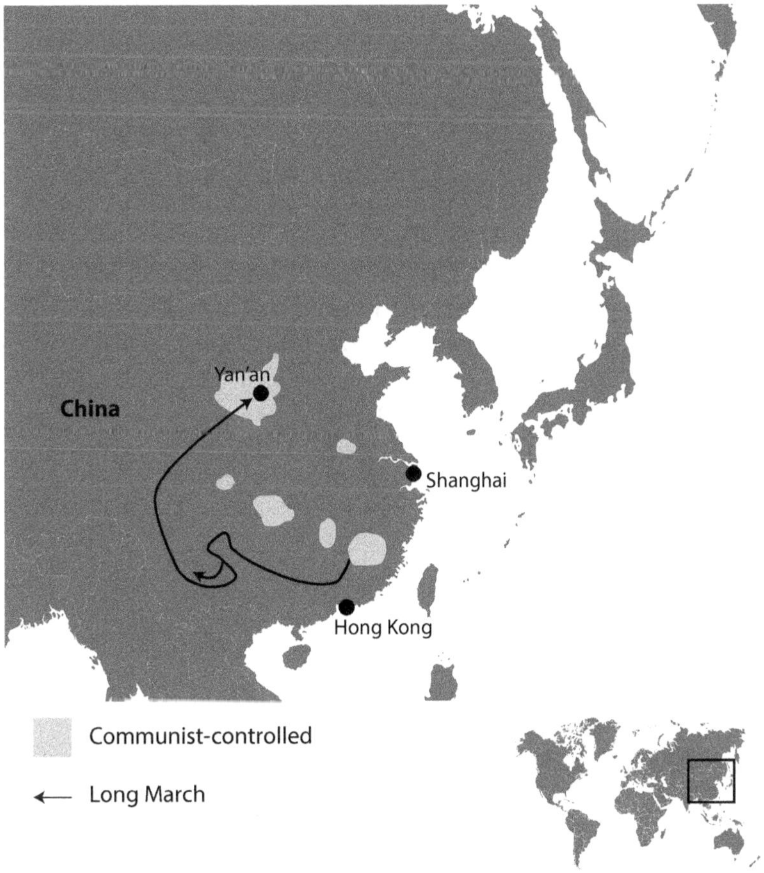

Figure 2.31. The Long March

Kuomintang (KMT)	Chinese Communist Party (CCP)
• Nationalist Party of the revolutionary government • worked to consolidate government power • KMT leader Chiang Kai-shek (Jiang Jieshi) took back control of much of China from the warlords after Sun Yat-sen's death in 1925. • temporarily worked with the CCP to bring Chinese territory back under the control of the Republic • Chiang turned against the CCP in 1927, driving it south.	• emerged after country felt betrayed by European powers • focused its organizing activities in the countryside on the peasants, becoming powerful in southern China • KMT attacks on the CCP in the south in 1934 forced the CCP to retreat on the **Long March** north. • **Mao Zedong** emerged as the leader of the movement.

Table 2.6. The KMT and CCP

WORLD WAR II

While China was in the midst of political change, Germany was suffering under the provisions of the Treaty of Versailles. In 1919, a democratic government was established at Weimar—the **Weimar Republic**.

Germany was in chaos. The Kaiser had fled, the country was torn apart by the war, and the new government could not bring stability.

▶ Germany was blamed for WWI and owed huge **reparations** according to the treaty to pay for the cost of the war, setting off **hyperinflation** and impoverishing the country and its people.

▶ The rise of communists and a workers' party that came to be known as the National Socialist Party, or **Nazi Party**, led to further political instability.

▶ Following the crash of the stock market in 1929, German unemployment reached six million; furthermore, the United States had called in its foreign loans.

▶ Unemployed workers began supporting communism.

▶ The Nazis, led by **Adolf Hitler**, gained support from business interests, which feared communist power in government, leading the Nazis to become an important force in the Weimar Republic at the beginning of the 1930s.

Hitler maneuvered into the role of chancellor by 1933:

▶ His charisma and popular platform—to cancel the Treaty of Versailles —allowed him to rise.

▶ The Nazi Party enjoyed the support of the wealthy and big business, which feared communism (especially with the development of Soviet Russia).

▶ Nazi ideals appealed strongly to both industry and the workers in the face of global economic depression.

▶ The Nazi Minister of Propaganda Joseph Goebbels executed an effective propaganda campaign, and would do so throughout Hitler's rule, known as the Third Reich.

In 1934, Hitler became the *Führer*, or leader, of Germany. A series of chaotic events followed:

▶ a fire in the Reichstag (German Parliament), which allowed Hitler to arrest communist leaders

▶ the rise of the Gestapo, or secret police (which violently enforced Nazi rule among the people)

▶ the banning of political parties and trade unions.

As a result of these events, Hitler and the Nazis consolidated total control. They also set into motion their agenda of racism and genocide against "non-Aryan" (non-Germanic) or "racially impure" people.

Jewish people were particularly targeted. Germany had a considerable Jewish population as did the other Central and Eastern European countries that Germany would come to control. Throughout the 1930s, the Nazis passed a series of laws limiting Jewish rights, including:

▶ jobs that Jewish people could hold

▶ rights to citizenship

▶ places they could go

▶ public facilities they could use

▶ whom they could marry

▶ the names they could have

DID YOU KNOW?

Kristallnacht, an organized series of attacks on Jewish businesses, homes, and places of worship, took place in 1938. It is so called because the windows of these places were smashed.

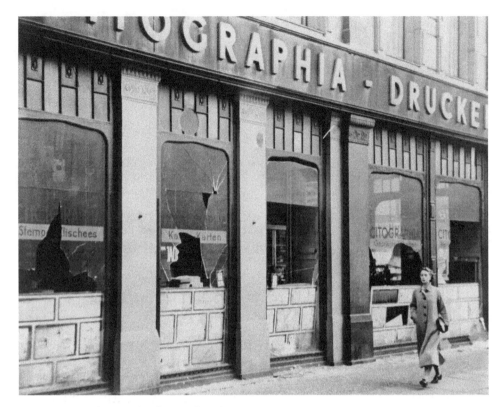

Figure 2.32. Aftermath of Kristallnacht

Jewish people would endure continued repression and horrific events in the years to follow:

▶ In 1939, Jews were forced from their homes into **ghettos**, isolated and overcrowded urban neighborhoods.

▶ In 1941, they were forced to wear yellow stars identifying them as Jewish.

▶ Millions of Jewish people were sent to **concentration camps**.

▶ The Nazis decided on the Final Solution to the "Jewish Question": to murder Jewish people by systematically gassing them at death camps.

▶ At least six million European Jews were murdered by the Nazis in the **Holocaust**.

Roma, Slavic people, homosexuals, disabled people, people of color, prisoners of war, communists, and others not considered "Aryan" were also forced into slave labor in concentration camps and murdered there. Later, this concept of torturing and killing people based on their ethnicity in order to exterminate them would become defined as genocide.

Hitler was a **fascist**: he believed in a mostly free market accompanied by a dictatorial government with a strong military.

He sought to restore Germany's power and expand its reach by annexing Austria (the *Anschluss*, or *union*) and the Sudetenland, German-majority areas in part of what is today the Czech Republic.

DID YOU KNOW?

Given the threat posed by the new Soviet Union, Britain and France believed at the time that a stronger Germany would be in their interests.

With the collapse of the Weimar Republic and the League of Nations at its weakest state, France and Britain granted the Sudetenland to Hitler in 1938 in a policy called **appeasement** in an effort to maintain stability in Europe and avoid another war. Appeasement failed when Hitler invaded the rest of Czechoslovakia and formed an alliance with Italy the next year.

In 1939 the Soviet Union made a pact with Germany: Germany would not invade the USSR, and the two countries would divide Poland. Germany then invaded Poland. Its 1939 invasion is commonly considered the beginning of the **Second World War**.

War exploded in Europe in 1939 as Hitler gained control of more land than any European power since Napoleon:

DID YOU KNOW?

Some historians consider the Japanese invasion of Manchuria in 1931 to be the beginning of WWII.

▶ In 1940, Germany took Paris.

▶ The Battle of Britain began in July 1940.

▷ Germany suffered its first defeat and was unable to take Britain.

▶ Despite staying out of combat, in 1941 the United States enforced the **Lend-Lease Act** which provided support and military aid to Britain.

▶ The two also released the Atlantic Charter in 1941, which outlined common goals.

When Japan joined the **Axis** powers of Germany and Italy, the **Second Sino-Japanese War of 1937** would also be subsumed under the Second World War, ending in 1945. The **Chinese Civil War** between communists led by Mao Zedong and nationalists led by Chiang Kai-shek was interrupted by the Second Sino-Japanese War, when Japan tried to extend its imperial reach deeper into China, resulting in atrocities like the Rape of Nanking (1937 – 1938).

DID YOU KNOW?

The **Atlantic Charter** described values shared by the US and Britain, including restoring self-governance in occupied Europe and liberalizing international trade.

At this time, Chiang was forced to form an alliance with Mao and the two forces worked together against Japan. By the end of the war, the CCP was stronger than ever, with widespread support from many sectors of Chinese society, while the KMT was demoralized and had little popular support.

In December of 1941, Japan, now part of the **Axis powers** along with Germany and Italy, attacked the United States at Pearl Harbor. Consequently, the US joined the war in Europe and in the Pacific, deploying thousands of troops in both theaters.

Meanwhile, in Asia, Japan continued its imperialist policies. In the early 1940s, it took advantage of chaos in Europe and the weakened European colonial powers to invade and occupy French Indochina, Indonesia, and Burma; it also occupied the Philippines.

Controlling these strategic areas meant the Axis was a direct threat to British India, Australia, and the eastern Soviet Union, not to mention European imperial and economic interests.

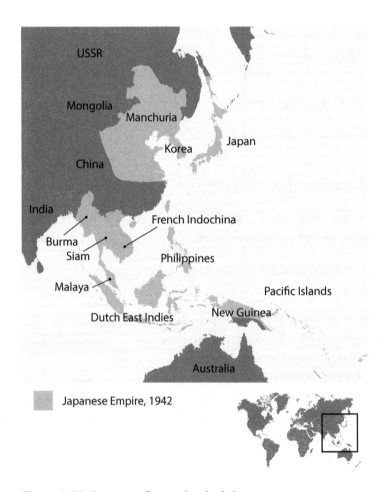

Figure 2.33. Japanese Expansion in Asia

Table 2.7. Major Military Events of WWII

Event	Year	Impact
German invasion of the Soviet Union	1941	Hitler broke his promise to the USSR by invading it, spurring the USSR's alliance with Britain and the US.
Battle of Stalingrad	1942	The USSR defeated Germany, a turning point in the war during which the Nazis were forced to turn from the Eastern Front.
Tehran Conference	1943	• Churchill, Roosevelt, and Stalin met in Tehran to discuss the invasion of Italy. • The Allies took Rome later that year.
D-Day	1944	The Allies invaded France, liberating Paris in August.
Battle of the Bulge	1944 – 1945	• a costly battle that lasted from December 1944 to January 1945 • thousands of US casualties • Hitler's forces were pushed back.
USSR invasion of Berlin; US crosses the Rhine	spring 1945	• Hitler committed suicide. • The Allies accepted German surrender.
Battles of Saipan and Iwo Jima	1944 and 1945, respectively	strategic battles to secure landing strips for American bombers
Battle of Leyte	1944	• The US destroyed most of the Japanese Navy. • Despite casualties of up to 400,000, Japan continued to fight the US for territory in the Philippines.
Battle of Okinawa	1945	• The US planned to use Okinawa as a staging point for an invasion of Japan in order to force Japanese surrender, which would have likely resulted in hundreds of thousands of American troop casualties. • This battle would sway **President Truman** (who succeeded Roosevelt) to drop the atomic bombs to force the Japanese to surrender.
Hiroshima and Nagasaki bombings	1945	The US dropped the atomic bomb on these Japanese cities, causing tremendous civilian casualties, forcing the emperor to surrender, and concluding WWII.

That year in China, the Chinese Civil War recommenced:

▶ By 1949 the communists had emerged victorious.

▶ The KMT withdrew to Taiwan.

▶ Mao and the CCP took over China, which became a communist country.

WWII and the period immediately preceding it saw horrific violations of human rights in Europe and Asia, including the atrocities committed during the Japanese invasions of China, Korea, and Southeast Asia, and the European Holocaust of Jews and other groups like Roma and homosexuals.

The war finally ended with the US atomic bombings of Hiroshima and Nagasaki in 1945, ending years of firebombing civilians in Germany and Japan; devastating ground and naval warfare throughout Europe, Asia, the South Pacific, and Africa; and the deaths of millions of soldiers and civilians all around the world.

The extreme horrors of WWII helped develop the concept of **genocide**—the effort to extinguish an entire group of people because of their ethnicity—and the idea of **human rights**.

The **United Nations** was formed, based on the League of Nations, as a body to champion human rights and uphold international security. Its **Security Council** is made up of permanent member states which can intervene militarily in the interests of international stability.

Allied forces took the lead in rebuilding efforts: the US occupied areas in East Asia and Germany, while the Soviet Union remained in Eastern Europe. The Allies had planned to rebuild Europe according to the Marshall Plan. However, Stalin broke his promise made at the 1945 **Yalta Conference** to allow Eastern European countries to hold free elections. Instead, the USSR occupied these countries and they came under communist control. The **Cold War** had begun.

THE COLD WAR

In February 1945, Stalin, Churchill, and Roosevelt came to numerous agreements at the Yalta Conference:

▶ the division of Germany

▶ the free nature of government in Poland

▶ free elections in Eastern Europe

However, at the Potsdam Conference in July 1945, things had changed:

▶ Harry Truman had replaced Franklin D. Roosevelt, who had died in office.

▶ Clement Atlee had replaced Winston Churchill.

▸ Stalin felt betrayed by the US use of the atomic bomb.

▸ The US and the British felt that Stalin had violated the agreement at Yalta regarding democracy in Eastern Europe.

Stalin ensured that communists came to power in Eastern Europe, setting up satellite states at the Soviet perimeter in violation of the Yalta agreement. The Soviet rationale was to establish a buffer zone following its extraordinarily heavy casualties in WWII—around twenty million. With Stalin's betrayal of the Allies' agreement, in the words of the British Prime Minister Winston Churchill, an **iron curtain** had come down across Europe, dividing east from west.

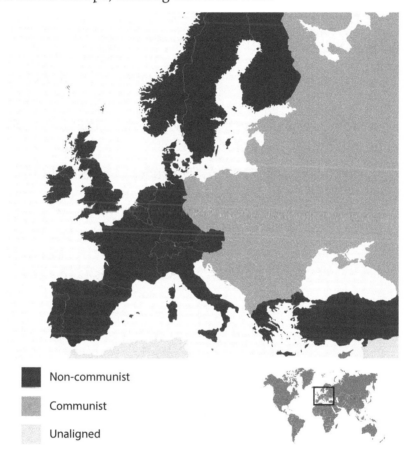

■ Non-communist

■ Communist

▫ Unaligned

Figure 2.34. Cold War Europe

As a consequence, western states and the Soviet Union created organizations and policies to support their interests:

▸ Western states formed **NATO**, the North Atlantic Treaty Organization.

▹ It served as an agreement wherein an attack on one was an attack on all.

▹ It provided for **collective security** in the face of the Soviet expansionist threat.

▶ The United States adopted a policy of **containment**, the idea that communism should be *contained*, as part of the **Truman Doctrine** of foreign policy.

▶ The United States also sponsored the **Marshall Plan**, which provided aid to European countries in an effort to restart the European economy and rebuild the continent. Stalin did not permit Soviet-controlled countries to take Marshall aid.

▶ In response, the Soviet Union created the **Warsaw Pact**, a similar organization consisting of Eastern European communist countries.

Nuclear weapons, especially the development of the extremely powerful hydrogen bomb, raised the stakes of the conflict.

Germany itself had been divided into four zones, controlled by Britain, France, the US, and the USSR. Berlin had been divided the same way. Once Britain, France, and the US united their zones into West Germany in 1948 and introduced a new currency, the USSR cut off West Berlin in the **Berlin Blockade**. Viewing this as an aggressive attempt to capture the entire city, western powers provided supplies to West Berlin by air in the **Berlin Airlift** for nearly a year.

CHECK YOUR UNDERSTANDING #12

How did the Cold War erupt between the Allies and the Soviet Union?

Berlin continued to be a problem for the USSR:

▶ Until 1961, refugees from the Eastern Bloc came to West Berlin, seeking better living conditions in the West.

▶ West Berlin was a center for Western espionage.

▶ In 1961, the USSR, now led by **Nikita Khrushchev**, closed the border and constructed the **Berlin Wall**.

Following the Second World War, Korea had also been divided:

▶ In the northern part of the country, the communist **Kim il Sung** controlled territory.

▶ South of the thirty-eighth parallel, the non-communist Syngman Rhee controlled the rest of the country.

▶ In 1950, Kim il Sung invaded the south with Russian and Chinese support, intending to create a communist Korea.

According to the Truman Doctrine, communism needed to be contained. Furthermore, according to **domino theory**, if one country became communist, then more would, too, like a row of dominoes falling. Therefore, the United States, by way of the United Nations, became involved in the **Korean War** (1950 – 1953):

▶ UN troops dominated and led by the US came to the aid of the nearly defeated South Koreans, pushing back Kim il Sung's troops.

▶ China supported Kim il Sung, and war on the peninsula continued until 1953.

▶ In 1953, US President Eisenhower threatened to use the nuclear bomb, ending the war in a stalemate.

In 1959, the revolutionary **Fidel Castro** took over in Cuba. Allied with the Soviet Union, he allowed missile bases to be constructed in Cuba, which threatened the United States. During the **Cuban Missile Crisis** in 1962, the world came closer than ever to nuclear war when the USSR sent missiles to Cuba:

Figure 2.35. Fidel Castro

▶ Cuba-bound Soviet ships faced an American blockade and tension grew as the US considered invading Cuba.

▶ President Kennedy and Premier Khrushchev were able to come to an agreement: the USSR promised to dismantle its Cuban bases as long as the US ended the blockade and secretly dismantled its own missile bases in Turkey.

▶ Nuclear war was averted.

Despite this success, the United States engaged in a lengthy violent conflict in Southeast Asia. Supporting anti-communist fighters in Vietnam in keeping with containment and Domino Theory, the United States pursued the **Vietnam War** for almost a decade:

▶ The **Gulf of Tonkin Resolution** authorized the US president to manage the ongoing conflict without consulting Congress.

▷ For a period of years, troops continued to be deployed to the region, fueling the conflict.

▶ The US became involved in the war after coming to the aid of Vietnam's old colonial master, France.

▶ Ho Chi Minh, the revolutionary Vietnamese leader, led North Vietnamese forces, including the guerrilla fighters called **Viet Cong**, in a war for independence throughout the 1960s.

▷ Despite being outnumbered, Viet Cong familiarity with the difficult terrain, support from Russia and China, and determination eventually resulted in their victory.

DID YOU KNOW?

Ho Chi Minh had actually originally approached the Americans for assistance in asserting Vietnamese independence.

▶ Bloody guerrilla warfare demoralized the American military; the 1968 **Tet Offensive** was a turning point.

▷ Despite enormous losses, the North Vietnamese won a strategic victory in this coordinated, surprise offensive.

▶ Extreme objection to the war within the United States, high casualties, and demoralization eventually resulted in US withdrawal in 1973.

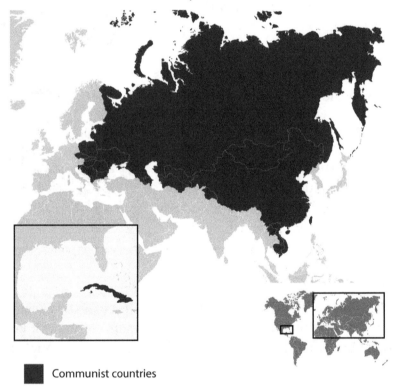

■ Communist countries

Figure 2.36. The Communist World

Toward the end of the 1960s and into the 1970s, the Cold War reached a period of **détente**, or a warming of relations:

- The US and USSR signed the **Nuclear Non-Proliferation Treaty**, in which they and other nuclear power signatories agreed not to further spread nuclear weapons technology.

- Later, the USSR and the US signed the **SALT I Treaty** (Strategic Arms Limitation Treaty), limiting strategic weaponry.

- Some cultural exchanges and partnerships in outer space also took place.

At the same time, the United States began making diplomatic overtures toward communist China. This was, however, part of a different Cold War strategy:

- Despite its status as a communist country, China and the USSR had difficult relations due to their differing views on the nature of communism.

  ▷ While Khrushchev took a more moderate approach to world communism, Mao believed in more aggressive policies.

- Following the **Sino-Soviet Split** of the 1960s, China had lost much Soviet support for its modernization programs, and despite advances in agriculture and some industrialization, Mao's programs like the **Great Leap Forward** had taken a toll on the people.

- In 1972, President Nixon visited China, establishing relations between the communist government and the United States.

  ▷ Communist China was permitted to join the UN. (Previously, China had been represented by the KMT, which was isolated to Taiwan.)

The climate would change again, however, in the 1970s and 1980s:

- The US and USSR found themselves on opposite sides in proxy wars throughout the world (see below).

- The **arms race** was underway.

  ▷ **President Ronald Reagan** pursued a militaristic policy, prioritizing weapons development with the goal of outspending the USSR on weapons technology.

DID YOU KNOW?

Perhaps the most famous proposal in weapons technology during this time was the Strategic Defense Initiative. Popularly known as Star Wars, this outer space-based system would have intercepted Soviet intercontinental ballistic missiles.

DECOLONIZATION

Meanwhile, the former colonies of the fallen European colonial powers had won or were in the process of gaining their independence. One role of the United Nations was to help manage the **decolonization** process.

▶ In 1949, **Mohandas Gandhi** led a peaceful independence movement in India against the British, winning Indian independence.

▶ His assassination by Hindu radicals led to conflict between Hindus and Muslims in the Subcontinent, resulting in **Partition**, the bloody division of India.

  ▷ Hindus fled into what is today India.

  ▷ Muslims fled to East Pakistan (now Bangladesh) and West Pakistan.

  ▷ Instability is ongoing on the Subcontinent.

Bloody conflict resulted in many African countries gaining independence in the 1950s, 1960s, and 1970s:

▶ the Algerian War against France (1954 – 1962)

▶ the Mau Mau Rebellion against the British in Kenya in the 1950s

▶ violent movements against Belgium in the Congo

Likewise, strong leadership by African nationalist leaders and thinkers like Jomo Kenyatta, Julius Nyerere, and Kwame Nkrumah contributed to this independence.

The apartheid regime in South Africa, where segregation between races was legal and people of color lived in oppressive conditions, was not lifted until the 1990s; **Nelson Mandela** led the country in a peaceful transition process.

In the Middle East, following the fall of the Ottoman Empire after WWI, European powers had taken over much of the area:

▶ These **protectorates** became independent states with arbitrary borders drawn and rulers installed by the Europeans.

▶ The creation of the state of Israel was especially contentious.

  ▷ In the 1917 **Balfour Declaration**, the British had promised the Zionist movement of European Jews that they would be given a homeland in the British-controlled protectorate of Palestine.

  ▷ The US meanwhile assured the Arabs in 1945 that a Jewish state would not be founded there.

▶ Israel emerged from diplomatic confusion, chaos, and tragedy after the murder of millions of Jews in Europe, and violence on the ground in Palestine carried out by both Jews and Arabs.

▶ This legacy of conflict lasts to this day in the Middle East.

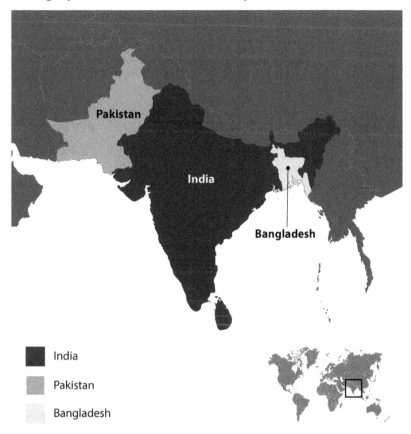

Figure 2.37. Partition

While the Middle East had been divided into protectorates or into nominally independent states like Egypt that were still under strong European influence, these areas had become independent after the Second World War.

Liberal activists against monarchical and dictatorial regimes and popular movements like Pan-Arabism and Islamism put pressure on Middle Eastern monarchies. Countries created by artificial borders based on the Sykes-Picot Agreement and comprised of divided and diverse ethnic and religious groups were already vulnerable to political instability; with added unrest, Middle Eastern governments fell. Furthermore, the Middle East became a Cold War battleground, with regimes courting the support of the Cold War powers:

▶ In Egypt, Gamal Abdul Nasser led the Pan-Arabist movement in the region, which included creating an Arab alliance against Israel.

- ▶ In 1967, Arab allies launched a war against Israel.

  - ▷ They were badly beaten in the **Six Day War**, an embarrassing defeat for the Arab states and one from which Nasser never truly recovered.

  - ▷ Israel took control of the Sinai Peninsula, the Golan Heights, and the West Bank of the Jordan River.

- ▶ During the 1973 **Yom Kippur War**, the US supported Israel while the USSR supported Syria and Egypt.

  - ▷ Syria and Egypt had launched a surprise attack on Israel on the holiest day of the Jewish year in an attempt to gain back territory lost years prior.

  - ▷ Israel was able to maintain its defenses.

- ▶ In 1978, the American president Jimmy Carter was able to broker a peace agreement between the Egyptian leader Anwar Sadat and the Israeli leader Menachem Begin known as the **Camp David Accords**.

  - ▷ Other Arab countries, aside from Jordan, did not make peace with Israel.

  - ▷ By the 1970s, Pan-Arabism was no longer the popular, unifying movement it had once been.

The **Non-Aligned Movement** arose in response to the Cold War. Instead of the bipolar world of the Cold War, the Non-Aligned Movement sought an alternative: the **Third World**.

DID YOU KNOW?

The bipolar world of the Cold War describes one as democratic, led by the US, and the other communist, led by the USSR.

- ▶ Non-Aligned, or Third World countries, wanted to avoid succumbing to the influence of either of the superpowers.

- ▶ Many found a forum in the United Nations in which to strengthen their international profiles.

Throughout the Cold War, proxy wars between the US and the USSR were fought around the world:

- ▶ In the 1980s, the US began supporting the anti-communist Contras in Nicaragua, who were fighting the communist Sandinista government.

▶ In 1979, the USSR invaded Afghanistan, an event which would contribute to the Soviet collapse.

   ▷ In response, the US began supporting anti-Soviet *mujahideen* forces, some of whose patrons would later attack the US as part of international terrorist groups.

▶ the Angolan Civil War

▶ the Mozambican Civil War

In the Horn of Africa, Somalia was formed when the Italian-administered UN trust territory of Somalia united with the British protectorate of Somaliland in 1960:

▶ Initially supported by the USSR for its socialist leanings, Somalia and its leader, Mohamed Siad Barre, initiated a war against Ethiopia in 1977.

CHECK YOUR UNDERSTANDING #13

What is a proxy war? Why were proxy wars important in the context of the Cold War?

▶ The USSR supported Ethiopia.

▶ The United States supported Somalia.

While never officially colonized, Iran had been under the oppressive regime of the western-supported **Shah Reza Pahlavi** for decades:

▶ During its imperial era, Britain began exploring petroleum interests in what was then Persia; Western oil companies had remained powerful in that country.

▶ The Pahlavi Dynasty took over Persia in 1920 from the Qajars, who had ruled since 1785, and who themselves had been important in administration under the Safavids since the sixteenth century.

▶ By the 1970s, the Shah's corrupt, oppressive regime was extremely unpopular in Iran, but it was propped up by the West.

▶ Several underground movements worked against the Shah, including communists and Islamic revolutionaries inspired by the Islamism of the early twentieth century.

▶ In the 1979 **Iranian Revolution**, these forces overthrew the Shah; shortly afterward, Islamist revolutionaries took over the country.

   ▷ The new theocracy was led by a group of clerics led by the Supreme Leader **Ayatollah Khomeini**.

▷ The Ayatollah instituted political and social reforms, including stricter interpretations of Islamic laws and traditions and enforcing those throughout the country as national and local law.

▷ Later that year, radical students who supported the revolution stormed the US Embassy and held a number of staff hostage for over a year. Known as the **Iran Hostage Crisis**, it would humiliate the United States.

Following the Iranian Revolution, the Iraqi leader **Saddam Hussein**, an ally of the United States, declared war against Iran:

DID YOU KNOW?

The revolutionary Iranian government would go on to support Shi'a militants (the Hezbollah, or the Party of God) in the Lebanese Civil War throughout the 1980s; this group is also inspired by Islamism.

▶ While governed by Sunnis, Iraq was actually a Shi'ite-majority country.

▶ Saddam feared Iran would trigger a similar revolution there.

▶ Iraq also sought control over the strategic Shatt al-Arab waterway and some oil-rich territories inland.

▶ The war raged from 1980 – 1990.

PRACTICE QUESTIONS

16) **Which of the following was a weakness of the Schlieffen Plan?**

    A.   It overstretched the German army.

    B.   It failed to anticipate a stronger resistance in France.

    C.   It underestimated Russia's ability to mobilize its troops.

    D.   all of the above

17) **According to the Sykes-Picot Agreement,**

    A.   Israel would become an independent state.

    B.   Husayn ibn Ali would become Caliph.

    C.   Ataturk would lead an independent Turkey.

    D.   Palestine would be under international supervision.

18) **Which of the following led to the rise of the Nazis in early 1930s Germany?**

    A.   the impact of reparations and the support of German industrialists

    B.   the impact of the Great Depression and the support of the workers

    C.   support from the international communist movement and the impact of reparations on the German economy

    D.   support from German industrialists and strong backing from other political factions in the Reichstag

19) Which of the following describes the roots of the Cold War?

   A. Stalin's unwillingness to cede control of East Berlin to the allies following the fall of the Nazis

   B. the erection of the Berlin Wall

   C. Stalin's failure to honor the Yalta agreement, installing communist regimes in Eastern Europe

   D. the Cuban Missile Crisis

20) Which of the following precipitated the end of the Cold War?

   A. the Iran Hostage Crisis

   B. the Soviet War in Afghanistan

   C. the Iran-Iraq War

   D. the Yom Kippur War

POST–COLD WAR WORLD

In 1991, the Soviet Union fell when Soviet Premier **Mikhail Gorbachev**, who had implemented reforms like **glasnost** and **perestroika** (or *openness* and *transparency*), was nearly overthrown in a coup. A movement led by **Boris Yeltsin**, who had been elected president of Russia, stopped the coup. The USSR was dissolved later that year and Yeltsin became president of the Russian Federation. The war in Afghanistan and military overspending in an effort to keep up with American military spending had weakened the USSR to the point of collapse, and the Cold War ended.

Figure 2.38. Gorbachev and Reagan

COLD WAR CONSEQUENCES

In 1990, Saddam Hussein, the leader of Iraq, invaded Kuwait and took over its oil reserves and production facilities. In response, the United States and other countries went to war—with a UN mandate—to expel Iraq from Kuwait and to defend Saudi Arabia in order to regain control of the world's petroleum reserves in the **Gulf War**. This event cemented the US status as the sole world superpower; the global balance of power had changed.

Despite stability throughout most of Europe, the changes following the fall of the Iron Curtain led to instability in the Balkans:

▶   In 1992, Bosnia declared its independence from the collapsing state of Yugoslavia, following Croatia and Slovenia.

▶   Violence broke out in Bosnia between Bosnian Serbs on one side, and Bosnian Muslims (Bosniaks) and Croatians on the other.

▶   The **Bosnian War** raged from 1992 to 1995, resulting in the deaths of thousands of civilians and another European genocide—this time, of Bosnian Muslims.

Also following the Cold War, proxy wars throughout the world and instability in former colonies continued. In 1994, conflict in Central Africa resulted in the **Rwandan Genocide**. Hutus massacred Tutsis. Violence continued on both sides.

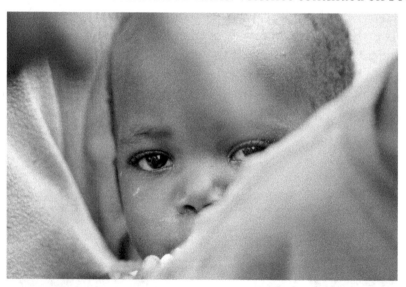

Figure 2.39. Rwandan Genocide

In Zaire, the country descended into instability following the fall of Mobutu Sese Seko, the US-supported dictator, in 1997. Renamed the **Democratic Republic of the Congo**, parts of this country and others in Central Africa would remain wracked by poverty and torn by violence for decades.

In the 1980s, drought in the **Horn of Africa** led to widespread famine. Humanitarian affairs and issues came into the eye of the general public, especially wealthier countries, who became more concerned about providing foreign aid to the suffering.

▶   The Somali leader Mohamed Siad Barre was overthrown in 1991.

- ▶ Somalia was broken up under the control of various warlords and clans.

- ▶ The people suffered from starvation with the breakdown of social order.

The United States intervened as part of a UN peacekeeping mission in an attempt to provide humanitarian aid. Strong military resistance from the warlord Muhammad Aideed impacted US public opinion, and the effort failed.

- ▶ There is no central government in Somalia, and much of the country is still dependent on aid.

- ▶ Some autonomous areas function independently.

COOPERATION AND CONFLICT

Following the end of the Cold War and post-decolonization, the balance of economic and political power began to change:

- ▶ The **G-20**, the world's twenty most important economic and political powers, includes many former colonies and non-European countries.

- ▶ The **BRICS**—Brazil, Russia, India, China, and South Africa—are recognized as world economic and political leaders.

  - ▷ With the exception of Russia, all of these countries were only recently classified as developing countries.

  - ▷ While still wrestling with considerable social, economic, and political challenges, the BRICS are world powers in their own right as independent nations—unthinkable developments a century ago.

Steps toward European unification had begun as early as the 1950s:

The **European Union**, as it is known today, was formed after the Maastricht Treaty was signed in 1992. As the former Soviet satellite states moved from communism to more democratic societies and capitalistic economies, more countries partnered with the EU and eventually joined it.

- ▶ As of 2015, twenty-seven countries are members, with more on the path to membership.

- ▶ European Union countries remain independent but cooperate in international affairs, justice, security and foreign policy, environmental matters, and economic policy.

- ▶ Many EU member states share a common currency, the **euro**.

- ▶ According to the Schengen Agreement, some EU countries have open borders.

Figure 2.40. European Union Headquarters

Continental integration exists beyond Europe:

▶   In Africa, the **African Union**, originally the Organization of African Unity, has become a stronger political force in its own right.

    ▷   It organizes peacekeeping missions throughout the continent.

    ▷   Similar to the EU, the AU is a forum for African countries to organize and align political, military, economic, and other policies.

Figure 2.41. African Union Headquarters

In this era of **globalization**, international markets became increasingly open through free-trade agreements. Technological advances such as improvements in transportation infrastructure and the **internet** made international communication faster, easier, and less expensive.

Table 2.8. Free Trade Agreements

Agreement	Description
NAFTA	the North American Free Trade Agreement
Mercosur	the South American free-trade zone
Trans-Pacific Partnership	a proposed free-trade zone between nine countries on the Pacific Ocean
World Trade Organization	international trade oversight

However, more open borders, reliable international transportation, and faster, easier worldwide communication brought risks, too.

In the early twenty-first century, the United States was attacked by terrorists on **September 11, 2001**, resulting in thousands of civilian casualties. Consequently, the US launched a major land war in Afghanistan and another later in Iraq.

Following the attacks on 9/11, the US attacked Afghanistan as part of the **War on Terror**. Afghanistan's radical Islamist Taliban government was providing shelter to the group that took responsibility for the attacks, al Qaeda. Led by **Osama bin Laden**, al Qaeda was inspired by Islamism and the radical Wahhabism of the remote Arabian desert followed by the Saudis.

> **DID YOU KNOW?**
>
> While benefits of international trade include lower prices and more consumer choice, unemployment often rises in more developed countries while labor and environmental violations are more likely in developing countries.

- Bin Laden had fought the Soviets with the US-supported Afghan *mujahideen* during the 1980s.

- Bin Laden and his followers were angered by US presence in Saudi Arabia throughout the 1990s and its support of Israel.

- Osama bin Laden was killed by the United States in 2011.

- Afghan security was turned over from the US to the US-backed government in 2014.

The US began withdrawing troops from Afghanistan in 2020, continuing into 2021. During the withdrawal, the Taliban had a resurgence and officially took control of the country in August 2021.

The Iraq War began in 2003. The US invaded Iraq, arguing that it supported international terrorism, and under faulty premises:

▶ that Saddam Hussein's regime was involved with al Qaeda

▶ that Iraq possessed weapons of mass destruction that it intended to use

Iraq descended into chaos, with thousands of civilian and military casualties, Iraqi and American alike. While Iraq technically and legally remains intact under a US-supported government, the ethnically and religiously diverse country is de facto divided as a result of the disintegration of central power.

Elsewhere in the Middle East, reform movements began via the 2011 **Arab Spring** in Tunisia, Egypt, Bahrain, and Syria:

HELPFUL HINT

One consequence of the Syrian Civil War has been enormous movements of refugees into other Middle Eastern countries and Europe.

▶ Some dictatorial regimes have been replaced with democratic governments; other countries still enjoy limited freedoms or even civil unrest.

▶ In Syria, unrest erupted into civil war between Bashar al Assad, who inherited leadership from his father, and opposition fighters.

Figure 2.42. Arab Spring

Today, a new group known as the Islamic State of Iraq and al Sham (**ISIS**), referring to Iraq and Syria (or Islamic State of Iraq and the Levant—ISIL), has filled the vacuum in parts of northern and western Iraq and eastern Syria: it has established a de facto state in Iraq and Syria with extremist Islamist policies and presents a global terror threat.

Uprisings in Israeli-occupied West Bank and Gaza have continued sporadically:

▶ Israel passed control of Gaza to the Palestinian Authority in 2005.

  ▷ Following political divisions within Palestinian factions, Gaza is controlled by Hamas while the Palestinian Authority represents Palestinian interests abroad and in the West Bank.

▶ In 1999, US President Clinton attempted to broker a final peace deal between the Israelis and Palestinians, delineating borders as part of a two-state solution.

  ▷ These efforts failed and conflict continues.

PRACTICE QUESTIONS

21) **Though the US emerged as the sole superpower immediately after the fall of the Soviet Union, which phenomenon in the twenty-first century has characterized global governance so far?**

   A. international terrorism

   B. international economic and political organizations

   C. international conflict

   D. the European Union

22) **What was one reason for the Bosnian War?**

   A. attacks by Bosnian Islamic extremists

   B. the dissolution of Yugoslavia

   C. the separation of Yugoslavia from the USSR

   D. attacks by Middle Eastern Islamic extremists

23) **What is one major role that the African Union plays?**

   A. The AU is a free trade area.

   B. The AU manages a single currency.

   C. The AU manages several peacekeeping forces.

   D. The AU represents individual African countries in international diplomacy.

24) **Which of the following is NOT a reason that the Soviet Union collapsed?**

   A. glasnost

   B. perestroika

   C. the war in Afghanistan

   D. the rise of the Taliban

25) **Why did Osama bin Laden sponsor attacks against the United States?**

   A.   He opposed US military presence in Saudi Arabia.

   B.   He wanted to fight the United States in a proxy war on behalf of Russia.

   C.   He wanted to build an empire from Afghanistan overseas.

   D.   He wanted oil resources in the Middle East that the United States controlled.

PRACTICE QUESTIONS ANSWER KEY

1) **B.** Fresh water permits a reliable food source, which allows for settlement; people need not travel in search of food.

2) **B.** The Sumerians developed cuneiform.

3) **C.** Written Chinese developed under the Shang Dynasty, and the Mandate of Heaven emerged under the Zhou Dynasty; furthermore, traditions like the use of chopsticks also came about during these periods.

4) **A.** The Athenian notion of *demokratia*, or people power, was participatory rather than representative.

5) **C.** The Senate's corruption and weakness, and Caesar's popularity with the plebeians, support of the military, and strong leadership, enabled him to take and retain control.

6) **D.** Security alliances with Germanic and Gothic tribes left Western Rome vulnerable to their attack; meanwhile in the east, centralized power in Constantinople and strong leadership, particularly under Justinian, led to the rise of the powerful Byzantine Empire.

7) **A.** The Meccan elites believed that they should take over leadership of Islam and continue the movement beyond the Arabian Peninsula; however Ali and Fatima, Muhammad's cousin and daughter, believed Ali was Muhammad's rightful successor as his closest living male relative.

8) **D.** American raw materials (like sugar and tobacco) were used in Europe and also turned into consumer goods there. European goods (as well as gold extracted from the Americas) were exchanged in Africa for enslaved persons, who were forced to harvest the raw materials in the Americas.

9) **C.** Europeans who traveled to the Levant to fight returned home with beneficial knowledge and technology.

10) **A.** Byzantine Christians left Constantinople with the rise of the Ottomans. They traveled to Western Europe, bringing classical learning with them.

11) **B.** The Treaty of Westphalia was based on state sovereignty and non-interference, the core principles of modern international relations.

12) **D.** Enlightenment thinking fueled the Age of Revolutions, and revolutionary French thinkers and writers like Rousseau, Voltaire, and others influenced revolutionary French leaders.

13) **B.** Russian support for Slavic ethnic groups in the Balkans—especially Serbia—helped fuel nineteenth century tensions in the region (and continued to do so throughout the twentieth century).

14) **C.** The idea of the white man's burden was not meant to suggest a literal burden; it was a paternalistic concept of responsibility used to justify imperial dominance.

15) **A.** Marx and Engels believed in abolishing wages and the class structure in exchange for a socialist society where the means of production were commonly held and in which income was equally distributed.

16) **D.** All of the answer choices are true.

17) **D.** Sykes-Picot put Palestine under the supervision of various international powers.

18) **A.** The Nazis planned to cease paying reparations, so their nationalist approach appealed to many Germans suffering from the hyperinflation that reparations had triggered. Furthermore, the Nazis had the support of German industrialists, who feared the rise of communism among the working classes.

19) **C.** The Cold War was rooted in Stalin's creation of communist satellite states in Eastern and Central Europe.

20) **B.** The Soviet invasion of Afghanistan and the subsequent ten-year war sapped Soviet financial and military resources—and morale. This draining war, plus the high price of the arms race with the United States, contributed significantly to the fall of the Soviet Union.

21) **B.** While the United States remains a leading world power, the emergence of international organizations like the BRICS, the EU, the G-20, and the AU has empowered other countries; furthermore, international trade agreements are helping mold the international balance of power.

22) **B.** One reason for the Bosnian War was the Yugoslav government's attempt to force the country to stay together; following the end of the Cold War and the collapse of communism, the formerly communist Yugoslavia had started to break up.

23) **C.** The AU organizes and manages peacekeeping forces in Africa; it also cooperates with the United Nations in peacekeeping.

24) **D.** The Taliban did not emerge in Afghanistan until well after Soviet withdrawal from the country.

25) **A.** Bin Laden was against the presence of the United States in Saudi Arabia, especially because that country is home to Mecca and Medina. He also wanted to expand his extremist ideology and opposed US support of Israel.

CHECK YOUR UNDERSTANDING ANSWER KEY

Check Your Understanding #1

social stratification, city-states, administration, irrigation, writing (cuneiform, hieroglyphs), literature (the *Epic of Gilgamesh*), codified rule of law (the Code of Hammurabi), art and architecture (ziggurats, pyramids), the potter's wheel, early astronomy, mathematics, religious thought, metallurgy (weaponry), horsemanship, chariots

Check Your Understanding #2

Greek ideas like reason and democracy informed modern Western thought and governance (rule of law, not rule of man). European literature was inspired by Greek plays and mythology.

Check Your Understanding #3

The republic was divided between the Optimates and the Populare. In addition, the Senate was extremely corrupt. Supported by the Populare, Julius Caesar forced the corrupt Senate to give him control, beginning the transition to an empire.

Check Your Understanding #4

Monotheism is the belief in one god. Major monotheistic religions include Judaism (Yahweh), Christianity (Jesus Christ), and Islam (Prophet Muhammad).

Check Your Understanding #5

The Silk Road spread art, pottery, and goods around Europe and Asia. It also helped Islam and Buddhism spread into China. The Islamic tradition of the hajj spurred cultural interaction as Muslims from around the world came together in Mecca. Islam spread along trans-Saharan trade routes in West Africa, spreading language, literature, goods, and art.

Check Your Understanding #6

There was no real dominant power in Asia. Central Asia lacked one dominant culture. The Abbasids, Seljuks, and Byzantines were in decline, making the Middle East vulnerable.

Check Your Understanding #7

Scientific study and discovery threatened the power of the Catholic Church and monarchs who ruled by divine right.

Check Your Understanding #8

The encomienda system allowed the exploitation and destruction of Indigenous American people and societies.

Check Your Understanding #9

The bourgeoisie earned their wealth but paid taxes and did not have government representation. Resentment grew against the nobility, who inherited wealth and power, driving revolutions.

Check Your Understanding #10

Russia, Germany, and Austria-Hungary (the Three Emperors' League); Germany and Austria-Hungary (the Dual Alliance); Germany, Austria-Hungary, and Italy (the Triple Alliance); Russia, France, Great Britain (the Triple Entente)

Check Your Understanding #11

spreading Christianity, natural resources (gold, opium, tea, beaver pelts, timber, rubber, diamonds); controlling strategic areas, white man's burden

Check Your Understanding #12

Stalin failed to allow Eastern European countries to hold free elections; USSR required a buffer zone in Eastern Europe after WWII; US use of nuclear weapons threatened USSR.

Check Your Understanding #13

In a proxy war, opposing countries fight each other indirectly by supporting sides in a third-party conflict. The US and USSR were never in direct combat during the Cold War, but they fought many proxy wars worldwide.

3

Principles of American Democracy (Civics)

POLITICAL THEORY

Political theory is the study of the principles and ideas used to describe, explain, and analyze political events and institutions. At its core, political theory explores the purpose of government.

There are two basic reasons for government:

▶ to provide law and order

▶ to protect people from conflicts

The first arises out of the second: to prevent and settle disputes between individuals, concrete rules of governance must be established. These goals are complicated, however, and lead to more questions that political theorists have grappled with throughout history:

▶ What kind of conflicts?

▶ How should conflict be prevented or managed?

▶ Who creates and enforces the rules that manage it?

▶ How far does that authority extend?

▶ To what extent should government intercede?

▶ What is the relationship between the government and the people?

FUNDAMENTAL CONCEPTS IN POLITICAL THEORY

Regardless of how they respond to these questions, all formal governments require recognition of their authority in order to exist. This recognition must come from both internal and external forces.

Table 3.1. External Recognition of Governmental Authority

Description	Example
External recognition comes in the form of sovereignty—the right of a group to be free of outside interference. • A group is sovereign when others outside of it recognize and respect that group's right to govern its own affairs and manage its own conflicts. • Sovereignty can exist at different levels and to different degrees.	• The US has complete national sovereignty because other nations recognize the US government's right to rule its own people and manage its own affairs. • Any attempt by another country to impose rules or regulate internal conflict would be viewed as a violation. • Many wars have begun based on conflicts over sovereignty.

The sovereignty of groups—and more specifically of states—is an ongoing question within the United States.

Table 3.2. Internal Recognition of Governmental Authority

Description	Examples

• Internal recognition is called legitimacy—the extent to which the people accept their government's authority.
 	
 • If the people within the group do not believe in the government's right to power, it cannot function.
 	
 • Legitimacy can be derived from:
   • God (in a theocracy)
   • military might (in a dictatorship)
   • the people (in a democracy or a republic)
	1. During the Age of Reason, rationality undermined popular belief in divine right (the idea that the king was chosen by God).
	   • This destroyed the legitimacy of the French monarchy.
	   • It allowed for the unrest brewing in France to erupt into the French Revolution.
	 2. The Confederate states in the US South broke away from the Union at the outbreak of the Civil War.
	   • They believed the federal government no longer represented their issues and was therefore an illegitimate government.

DID YOU KNOW?

Organizations like the National Rifle Association have limited sovereignty. They are subject to state and federal laws and oversight. They may make some rules regarding their internal organization and affairs, but that level of sovereignty exists only to the extent that those rules do not interfere with those of the larger society.

Without legitimacy, a government cannot continue. A loss of legitimacy is at the center of every failed government and state.

PRACTICE QUESTIONS

1) Which of the following is NOT an example of the US protecting Its national sovereignty?

    A.   declaration of war after the bombing of Pearl Harbor

    B.   signing of the Treaty of Paris at the end of the Revolutionary War

    C.   President Eisenhower sending troops to Little Rock, Arkansas, to integrate the schools

    D.   patrolling of the US-Mexico border

2) Which of the following is an example of a legitimate government?

    A.   the German Federal Republic in the 1990s

    B.   the Dole government in Hawaii in the 1890s

    C.   Mexican rule of Texas in the 1830s

    D.   the rule of Maximilian I in Mexico in the 1860s

MAJOR POLITICAL THEORISTS

Our understanding of government today is based upon the ideas of key political theorists. Each questioned the purpose of government and came to different conclusions. While there are many significant theorists, the most important to note follow.

Niccolò Machiavelli (1469 – 1527) believed that legitimacy is derived from power. According to Machiavelli:

▶ maintenance of power is the most important priority for any leader

▶ public morality and private or personal morality are two very different ideas

▶ a good ruler understands that sometimes immoral acts must be done to ensure the public good

Machiavelli is best known for his work *The Prince.*

▶ a book of political advice for a new prince seeking power

▶ discusses how government's purpose should be fulfilled

▶ guided politics throughout the Western world until the twentieth century

DID YOU KNOW?

Some later readers have argued that *The Prince* was written as a satire, or at least with exaggerated ruthlessness.

John Locke (1632 – 1704) argued that, by nature, all men (women were not widely considered until later in history) are free and equal and endowed with certain natural rights: life, liberty, and property—the **social contract**. Locke is considered:

▶ one of the most influential Enlightenment thinkers

▶ a major influence on central figures of the American and French Revolutions

▶ responsible for several of the foundational ideas of the American government

Figure 3.1. John Locke

Locke challenged the traditional view that men were bound by God to obey the monarchy. He argued instead that government was a natural outgrowth of the desire of individuals to protect their natural rights.

Because of this desire, men turn over certain individual sovereignty to a neutral party (a government), which holds the responsibility to maximize the individual enjoyment of rights as well as the public good. As a result, a government's legitimacy derives from the consent of the people.

This also means that when a government is no longer fulfilling its purpose and loses the people's consent, revolution is an appropriate and justified response.

Baron de Montesquieu (1689 – 1755) was a strong proponent of republican government, despite being a member of the French upper class. He advocated for **divided government: the separation of powers.**

DID YOU KNOW?

John Locke was not the first to consider the idea of the **social contract**, but his conception of it strongly impacted later thinkers and is fundamental to the modern republic.

HELPFUL HINT

A government's authority comes from the consent of the people it governs. Originally conceived by Thomas Hobbes, John Locke's version of this idea most influenced the founders.

Montesquieu argued that the most effective governments divided power among three different bodies or branches. He believed that powers should be equal but differ in nature, saying, "When the [law making] and [law enforcing] powers are in the same person, there can be no liberty."

Montesquieu's philosophy was in line with other Enlightenment thinkers. He focused on the importance of balance of power in the success of a republic.

Figure 3.2. Montesquieu

Montesquieu is best known for his philosophical contributions to the political structure of the United States. Separation of powers, using a three-branch structure, is the central organizing principle of the American government.

Like John Locke, **Jean-Jacques Rousseau** (1712 – 1778) believed that government was a natural extension of the desire of individuals to protect and best enjoy their natural rights. Rousseau believed that a general will exists, and that this general will should be the basis of all laws.

He extended the idea of the social contract in his writing entitled *The Social Contract* and argued for government built on the rule of law, the idea that laws would apply to and benefit all equally.

Rousseau believed that allowing laws (rather than an individual or group of individuals) to govern society, make decisions, and settle disputes, could prevent the inequities and subsequent revolution Locke feared.

Alexis de Tocqueville (1805 – 1859), an avid proponent of liberty and democracy, is best known for his 1835 work *Democracy in America,* which:

> HELPFUL HINT
>
> Rule of law was another Enlightenment idea that became a central tenet of the new United States government.

- ▶ details his travels throughout the United States

- ▶ chronicles his political analysis of what he saw

- ▶ celebrated the democratic underpinnings he saw in America—the emphasis on hard work and merit—and saw it as unique from the European experience

His views on equality were more complicated. He believed:

- ▶ inequality drove economic growth

- ▶ "radical equality" led to mediocrity

His writings are often referenced as an accurate and detailed analysis of the early stages of American democracy.

PRACTICE QUESTIONS

3) **Which political theorist argued for the separation of powers?**

   A. Jean-Jacques Rousseau

   B. Baron de Montesquieu

   C. John Locke

   D. Alexis de Tocqueville

4) **The Declaration of Independence was most greatly influenced by which political theorist?**

   A. John Locke

   B. Jean-Jacques Rousseau

   C. Niccolò Machiavelli

   D. Alexis de Tocqueville

5) **Which best describes social contract theory?**

   A. Government is a necessary evil to provide order for the people.

   B. Government is an agreement between a ruler and his or her subjects.

   C. Government exists as a promise to the people.

   D. Government exists at the will of the people.

6) **Which of the following is NOT true or consistent with Machiavelli's argument in *The Prince*?**

   A. For a ruler to maintain power, the ends always justify the means.

   B. Divine right is essential for a monarch to maintain legitimacy.

   C. *The Prince* provides a blueprint for gaining and keeping power.

   D. Rulers should not be judged by moral standards.

Political Orientations

In modern government, political ideology can be sorted into two main categories: liberal and conservative.

What these terms mean vary slightly from state to state; however, **liberals** generally have a more expansive view of government, whereas **conservatives** have a more restrictive view. In the United States, the ideological views of each are as follows.

Table 3.3. Liberal and Conservative Ideologies

Liberals	Conservatives
• also known as the Left	• also known as the Right
• believe in the power and responsibility of government to effect positive change	• believe in the individual's (and private sector's) power and responsibility to effect positive change
• see the government as essentially effective and view it as a protector of and provider for its citizens	• see the government as essentially ineffective at solving society's problems
• generally support a government that actively regulates the economy and implements extensive social programs	• believe the government's reach should be limited
• believe the government should not curtail the rights of its citizens	• believe that the government should only interfere to the extent that it makes it easier for the individual or private entity to better operate
• support the existence of implied rights, like the right to privacy	• support free-market solutions to economic problems and a decrease in the regulation of business
• believe the government should intervene to control economic factors that impede equality	• generally oppose government-run social programs

Table 3.4. Examples of Differing Views Between Liberals and Conservatives

Policy	Liberal Viewpoint	Conservative Viewpoint
National Health Care	• advocate for a national health care system	• believe a national health care system would lead to a decrease in the quality of care
Military	• support decreased military spending • support a decrease in committing troops abroad • often make exceptions for humanitarian or human rights purposes	• advocate increased military spending • believe military power is necessary to maintain national sovereignty • tend to be quicker to commit troops abroad

While the liberal-conservative dichotomy generally covers opposing political ideologies in American politics, it is simplistic. Many American politicians are **moderates** and fall in between these two camps:

▶ Moderates hold some views from each side of the spectrum.

▷ For example, a moderate might support increased military spending but also support some social programs.

There are also more extreme ideologies on each side of the spectrum.

On the far left, **socialists** advocate for a complete overhaul of the American economic and political system. Socialists:

▶ believe that the free market creates inequality, and that the market should be closely controlled by government to eliminate that inequality

▶ advocate far-reaching government-run programs from health care to schools to utilities

On the far right, **libertarians** support an extremely limited government, economically and socially. Libertarians:

▶ do not support government programs of any kind

▶ believe a completely unfettered market is most efficient and effective

▶ believe the government should not intervene to curtail or protect individual rights

▶ believe an ideal government would maintain only the most basic functions in order to ensure the functioning of the nation

PRACTICE QUESTIONS

7) Which of the following would most likely be supported by liberals?
   A. an open trade agreement with China
   B. funding a new stealth bomber
   C. a law restricting the use of national forests
   D. vouchers for students to attend private schools

8) Which of the following would a libertarian vote for, but not a liberal?
   A. regulation of business
   B. abortion rights
   C. criminal rights
   D. lower taxes

CONSTITUTIONAL UNDERPINNINGS OF THE US GOVERNMENT

Any study of the United States government must begin with its founding document: the Constitution.

Figure 3.3. The US Constitution

The **US Constitution** was written as both an expression of ideals and a practical framework for the functioning of the country. Designed to be a "living document," the Constitution and how it is interpreted has changed in the almost 230 years since it was written.

The core principles of the Constitution have not changed; they continue to serve as the foundation and guiding light of American government and politics.

While it is tempting to view the Constitution as a timeless document, it is important to understand that it was actually very much a product of the time in which it was written:

▶   The ideals that inform it grew directly out of the Enlightenment.

▶   The governing structure it created was in direct response to both colonial discontent under Britain and problems faced by the new republic.

In order to understand the government that emerged, it is necessary to understand this context.

HISTORICAL CONTEXT OF THE CONSTITUTION

While influenced by philosophy, the Constitution is actually a very practical document. It lays out the overarching structure of the government without excessive detail, explanation, or justification. However, each decision made about the structure of the government was an attempt to either prevent the re-emergence of tyranny or fix the mistakes of the first failed government.

In 1781, when it was all but assured that the colonies would win the Revolution, the Second Continental Congress convened.

The goal of the Second Continental Congress was to organize a government for the emerging nation.

▶   The colonies had broken away from Britain, in short, because of what they viewed as the oppressive rule of an over-bearing central government.

▶   As a result, the first government they created, whose framework was called the Articles of Confederation, was intentionally weak.

The **Articles of Confederation** were called a "firm league of friendship."

▶   They were designed to create a loose confederation between the colonies (now states) while allowing them to retain much of their individual sovereignty.

▶   They established a political system which consisted of a **unicameral legislature** (only one house) with extremely limited authority: the Congress of the Confederation.

The Congress of the Confederation:

▶   did not have the power to levy taxes or raise an army

▶   any laws had to be passed by a two-thirds vote

▶   any changes to the Articles had to be passed unanimously—essentially an impossible feat

▶   intentionally and clearly subordinate to the states

▶   representatives selected and paid by state legislatures

It quickly became clear that this government was too weak to be effective, and by 1787, the new government of the United States, only six years old, was already in crisis:

▶   Without the power to levy taxes, the federal government had no way to alleviate its debt burden from the war.

▶   Without an organizing authority, states began issuing their own currencies and crafting their own competing trade agreements with foreign nations.

▷   Trade was halted; inflation went through the roof.

▶ Without a national judicial system, there was no mechanism to solve the inevitable economic disputes.

Discontent was particularly strong among farmers, who were losing their property at devastating rates. Their unhappiness exploded into violence in 1786 when Daniel Shays led a rebellion against Massachusetts tax collectors and banks.

CHECK YOUR UNDERSTANDING #2

What were the three major problems with the Articles of Confederation?

Unable to raise an army, the Congress of the Confederation was powerless to intervene. The rebellion was finally suppressed when citizens of Boston contributed funds to raise a state militia. **Shays' Rebellion** made it clear that the new government was unable to maintain order.

PRACTICE QUESTIONS

9) **Why did the framers of the Articles of Confederation create a decentralized political system?**

   A. to cancel the debts the states owed from the Revolution

   B. to ensure that abuses of power like those that existed under British rule did not exist

   C. to delay the question of slavery

   D. to promote national sovereignty

10) **Which of the following ideas most influenced the framers of the Articles of Confederation?**

   A. In order to have the consent of the people, all people must be allowed to vote.

   B. Three separate and balanced branches of government are essential for the protection of liberty.

   C. The central government's primary authority should be in monitoring trade.

   D. A strong central government threatens the liberty of the people.

11) **Shays' Rebellion was considered a crisis of government because**

   A. people were previously unaware of the amount of debt that remained from the Revolution.

   B. it illustrated the national government's inability to maintain order.

   C. it allowed foreign intervention in American affairs.

   D. civil liberties were once again threatened as they had been under British rule.

12) **Which of the following groups had the most to gain from a revision of the Articles of Confederation?**

    A.   small farmers

    B.   members of state legislatures

    C.   women

    D.   merchants

ENLIGHTENMENT IDEAS

The founders of the United States were all very learned men who were educated in the philosophy of the Enlightenment. Several key elements of this philosophy are reflected in the Constitution.

Rule of Law: The very desire for a written constitution—a law above all others—reflected Enlightenment thinking, as it ensures a rule of law, rather than a rule of man. In a nation ruled by man, governance is at the whim of an individual or small group of individuals. Decisions are arbitrary based on the interests and needs of those in authority. In a nation ruled by law, governance is based on a body of written, or otherwise codified, law (such as the Constitution). No individual can make a governing decision in conflict with those laws.

Reason: The Constitution is a document based on reason and is therefore relatively simple and straightforward. It lays out the structure of government without detailing every single function of that government. Rather than simply empowering authority, the Constitution aims to limit government while still allowing it to fulfill its function. It also insists that governing decisions are made outside the scope of religion by actively separating the two.

Social Contract: The document begins "We the People..." because the founders believed that government was a social contract, legitimized only by the consent of the people. This is also known as **popular sovereignty**. The Constitution protects individual liberty, life, and property, the fundamental natural laws laid out by John Locke.

Social Progress: Enlightenment thinkers believed strongly that social progress was possible. As a result, the writers of the Constitution built in a means for amending the Constitution, allowing it to progress with the nation it governed.

PRACTICE QUESTIONS

13) **Which of the following aspects of the Constitution reflects the social contract philosophy?**

    A.   the presidential cabinet

    B.   checks and balances

    C.   judicial review

    D.   direct election of representatives

14) **Which of the following best demonstrates the rule of law?**

    A.   The president and members of Congress can be charged with crimes.

    B.   A government passes a law raising taxes, but later it does not require the wealthy to pay.

    C.   Congress passes a law declaring the Constitution null and void.

    D.   A king sentences his rival to death.

THE CONSTITUTION

A convention of the states was called to address problems in the young United States. At the **Constitutional Convention** in 1787, a decision was made to completely throw out the old Articles and write a new governing document from scratch. There were five main goals for the new Constitution:

▶ the protection of property

▶ granting increased, but limited power to the federal government

▶ the protection of and limitations on majority rule

▶ the protection of individual rights

▶ the creation of a flexible framework for government

Each of these reflect the desire to balance authority and liberty. It is this balance that is at the core of the framework of the American government.

STRUCTURE OF THE FEDERAL GOVERNMENT

The crises of the 1780s made it clear that a stronger central government was needed. However, the states did not want a central government that was so strong that it would oppress the states or the people. The solution? Increase the power of the government but prevent the concentration of power by dividing it.

The federal government was reorganized under the Constitution, shifting from a one-body political system to a three-branch system as conceived by Montesquieu:

▶ bicameral (two-house) legislature

▶ a legitimate executive branch

▶ a judicial branch

Following Montesquieu's model of **separation of powers**, the now-increased powers of the federal government were divided between these branches. In addition, each branch was given powers that would limit the power of the other branches in a system called **checks and balances**.

Table 3.5. The Separation of Powers and Checks and Balances

Function of Branch	Description of Checks and Balances
Executive Branch	
• has the power to appoint justices to the federal courts (including the Supreme Court) • commander in chief of the military • implements and enforces congressional law	• via the role of president • has the power to veto (reject) laws passed by the legislature
Legislative Branch	

• power to approve or reject presidential appointments (via the Senate)
• power to indict, try, and determine the guilt of a president (indictment may only be for treason, bribery, and other "high crimes and misdemeanors"); crimes specific to office holders:
  • perjury
  • abuse of power
  • misuse of funds
  • dereliction of duty
	• can override the president's veto (with a two-thirds vote) and pass the law anyway

Judicial Branch	
• hears cases concerning laws and treaties, disputes between states, maritime law, and bankruptcy	• determines the constitutionality of laws (judicial review)

The separation of powers limited the powers within the federal government, but it did not address the power relationship between the federal government and the states. Under the Articles, the federal government was completely beholden to the states for its very existence. However, it was clear that complete state sovereignty did not work. Instead, the Constitution created a **federal** relationship between the two levels of government:

Federalism is a system in which both the state government and federal government retain sovereignty by dividing up the areas for which they are responsible.

Table 3.6. Federalism in the United States

Federal Government Sovereignty	State Government Sovereignty

• charged with matters that concern the population at large:
  • handling federal lands
  • coining money
  • maintaining an army and navy
• handles conflicts between the states (via the federal judiciary)
• regulates interstate trade
	• handles matters of regional or local concern
	• codified in the Tenth Amendment of the Constitution:
	  • Any powers not explicitly given to the federal government are reserved for the states.
	• The federal government's authority generally supersedes that of the states in cases of conflict between the states and the federal government:
	  • guided by the **supremacy clause** (Article 6, Clause 2) which states that the Constitution is the "supreme law of the land"

The division of power has shifted over time with more power going to the federal government as its scope has expanded. The federal government also can exert influence over state governments through **grant-in-aid**—money that is provided for a particular purpose—by attaching stipulations to this funding.

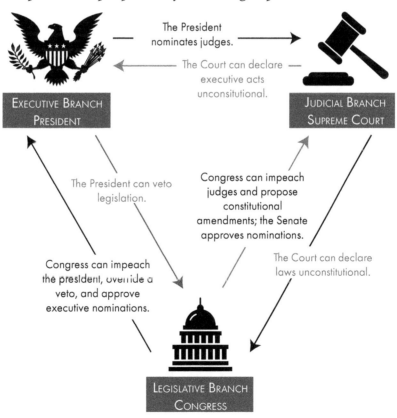

Figure 3.4. Checks and Balances

For example, grant-in-aid money was given to the states in the late 1970s for highway improvement.

▶ States who accepted the money were required to set the drinking age at twenty-one years old in their state.

▶ This way, the government influenced law that was technically beyond its purview.

PRACTICE QUESTIONS

15) **Where does the state governments' power derive from in the American federal system of government?**

   A. the Constitution

   B. the people of that state

   C. the state legislatures

   D. the people of the nation

16) **Which of the following best illustrates the system of checks and balances?**

   A. state and federal government power to levy taxes

   B. a governor's right to send the National Guard in a crisis

   C. the Senate's power to approve treaties signed by the president

   D. Congress's power to censure its members

TYPES OF GOVERNMENT POWERS

In its original form—as described in the Constitution—the federal government was made up of three branches. Almost immediately upon the ratification of the Constitution, it began to grow and now includes a massive bureaucracy made up of departments and agencies.

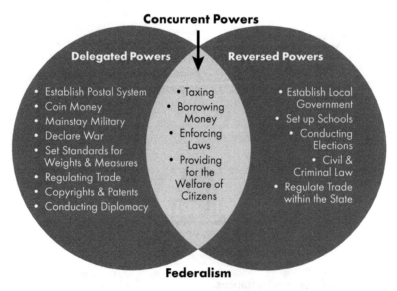

Figure 3.5. Enumerated, Concurrent, and Reserved Powers

Governmental powers in the Constitution can be divided into six types:

Table 3.7. Governmental Powers in the Constitution

Type of Power	Description
Expressed powers	• also known as enumerated powers • powers that are specifically granted to the federal government only • Example: The power to make treaties with foreign nations is an expressed power.
Implied powers	• powers the federal government has that are not in the Constitution • derived from the elastic clause of the Constitution, Article I, Section 8, which gives Congress the right to "make all laws necessary and proper" for carrying out other powers • Example: As new technologies emerged, such as radio and television, the commerce clause expanded to allow the federal government to regulate them.
Reserved powers	• powers that are held by the states through the Tenth Amendment • all powers not expressly given to the federal government belong to the states • Example: The management of public education is a reserved power.
Inherent powers	• powers that derive specifically from US sovereignty • powers that are inherent to its existence as a nation • Example: The powers to make treaties and wage war are both inherent.
Concurrent powers	• powers that are shared equally by both the national and state government • Example: The power to tax and establish courts are concurrent powers.
Prohibited powers	• powers that are denied to both the national and state governments • Example: Passing bills of attainder (laws that declare someone guilty without a trial) is a prohibited power.

The Supreme Court supported implied powers in *McCulloch v. Maryland* (1819). The state of Maryland tried to tax the Maryland branch of the Bank of the United States. The bank refused to pay, and the case landed in the Maryland Court of Appeals. The court ruled the Bank of the US unconstitutional, as the Constitution does not expressly give the federal government power to operate a bank. Later, the Supreme Court overturned the ruling, citing the elastic clause.

17) **Which of the following describes the power to coin money?**

   A.   inherent power

   B.   prohibited power

   C.   concurrent power

   D.   expressed power

18) **Which of the following describes the power to hold elections?**

   A.   inherent power

   B.   prohibited power

   C.   concurrent power

   D.   expressed power

THE LEGISLATIVE BRANCH

At the writing of the Constitution, the branch of the federal government endowed with the most power was the legislative branch. **Congress** was composed of a bicameral legislature (two houses) based on the British model.

Most colonies—and then states—had bicameral legislatures with an upper and lower house. This structure was not originally adopted under the Articles of Confederation, but rather chosen by the framers when reorganizing the government largely due to a dispute at the convention over the structure of the legislative body—specifically the voting power of each state.

Small states and more populous states would each advocate for plans that would determine their number of representatives:

Small states advocated for the **New Jersey Plan**:

▶   equal representation with each state having the same number of representatives, each with one vote

▶   distributed decision-making power equally between the states, regardless of land mass or population

More populous states found the New Jersey Plan to be unfair. They supported the **Virginia Plan:**

▶   based on **proportional representation**—each state assigned a number of representatives based on its population

▶   Enslaved people deprived of their rights would even be counted among the population, benefiting those states with large slave populations.

In the end, the **Great Compromise** was reached. There would be two houses, each with its own advantages:

1. The **House of Representatives** (the lower house) would have proportional representation.

   ▷ directly elected by the people

2. The **Senate** (the upper house) would have equal representation.

   ▷ elected by the state legislatures

This supported the federal structure of the government: one house would directly serve the needs of the people; the other would serve the needs of the states. It also curbed federal power by fragmenting it and slowing down the legislative process.

POWERS OF CONGRESS

The structure and powers of Congress are outlined in Article I of the Constitution. As the most representative branch of government, the legislative branch was also designed to be the most powerful. Hence, it has the most expressed powers in the Constitution. Section Eight contains eighteen clauses listing specific powers which can be divided into peacetime powers and war powers:

Table 3.8. Powers of Congress According to Section Eight

Clause	Peacetime Powers	Clause	War Powers
1	to establish and collect taxes, duties, and excises	11	to declare war; to make laws regarding people captured on land and water
2	to borrow money	12	to raise and support armies
3	to regulate foreign and interstate commerce	13	to provide and maintain a navy
4	to create naturalization laws; to create bankruptcy laws	14	to make laws governing land and naval forces
5	to coin money and regulate its value; regulate weights and measures	15	to provide for summoning the militia to execute federal laws, suppress uprisings, and repel invasions
6	to punish counterfeiters of federal money	16	to provide for organizing, arming, and disciplining the militia and governing it when in the service of the Union
7	to establish post offices and roads		
8	to grant patents and copyrights		

continued on next page

Table 3.8. Powers of Congress According to Section Eight (continued)

Clause	Peacetime Powers	Clause	War Powers
9	to create federal courts below the Supreme Court		
10	to define and punish crimes at sea; define violations of international law		

Clause	Peacetime Powers
17	to exercise exclusive jurisdiction over Washington, DC, and other federal properties
18	to make all laws necessary and proper to the execution of the other expressed powers (**elastic clause**)

PRACTICE QUESTIONS

19) **Congress was similar to the Congress of the Confederation in that**

   A.   both were designed to be slow-moving and deliberative.

   B.   both represented the states only.

   C.   both held very limited powers.

   D.   both were unicameral.

20) **Which of the following congressional powers was a direct response to the failings of the Articles of Confederation?**

   A.   the power to grant patents

   B.   the power to make laws governing land forces

   C.   the power to levy taxes

   D.   the power to declare war

HOUSE OF REPRESENTATIVES

The **House of Representatives** was designed to directly represent the people. The House of Representatives was:

► originally the only part of the federal government that was directly elected by the citizens

► the larger of the houses

The number of representatives from each state is based on the states' population (**proportional representation**):

▶ at least one representative guaranteed for every state

▶ apportionment of representatives based on the census

▶ seats reapportioned every ten years with the new census

At the convention, Southern states argued that their (nonvoting) enslaved population should count toward their overall population, therefore entitling them to more representatives. Northern states with few slaves disagreed.

DID YOU KNOW?

Women, who could not vote until the ratification of the Nineteenth Amendment, were also counted in the census.

This issue was settled with the **Three-Fifths Compromise**, which declared that each enslaved Black Americans would count as three-fifths of a person for the purpose of the census.

Figure 3.6. The House Chamber

The size of the House grew every ten years along with the population of the United States until 1929, when Congress set the number at 435 voting representatives. It has remained there since.

Today, each member of Congress represents approximately 700,000 people. Residents of Washington, DC, and territories held by the United States (Guam, American Samoa, and the US Virgin Islands) are represented by nonvoting observers. Puerto Rico is represented by a resident commissioner.

Each state legislature divides its state into essentially equally populated congressional districts. This process can often become quite political, with political parties attempting to draw the lines to ensure the maximum number of seats for their party. This is called **gerrymandering**. The Supreme Court has made several rulings to limit gerrymandering, including requiring each district to have equal population and contiguous or connected lines. It is also unconstitutional to draw lines based solely on race.

Members of the House of Representatives are elected for two-year terms in an effort to keep them beholden to the people. The Constitution lays out basic requirements for membership to the House:

- Candidates must be at least twenty-five years old.

- Candidates must be a US citizen for at least seven years.

- Candidates must live in the state they are representing at the time of the election.

The leader of the House is called the **Speaker of the House**—the leader of the majority party in the House.

Certain specific powers belong only to the House of Representatives:

- All revenue bills must start in the house.

  ▷ While the Senate may amend the bills, the framers wanted to keep the power of the purse in the hands of the house most beholden to the people.

- The House may bring charges of **impeachment** against the president or a Supreme Court justice.

  ▷ **Impeachment** is the process by which a federal official can be formally charged with a crime.

  ▷ If found guilty, the federal official is removed from office.

  ▷ Impeachment followed the British model in which the House of Commons (the lower house) had the power to impeach, and the House of Lords (upper house) heard arguments and decided.

To impeach a president or justice, a simple majority is required. Three presidents have been tried for impeachment:

- Andrew Johnson (1868)

- Bill Clinton (1998)

- Donald Trump (2019, 2021)

The House must choose the president if there is no majority in the Electoral College. This has only happened once, in 1824. Andrew Jackson, John Quincy

Adams, and Henry Clay split the electoral vote. Jackson had the plurality (the greatest percentage), but he did not win a majority. The vote went to the House, and, after some backroom politics, they voted for John Quincy Adams, much to Jackson's dismay.

THE SENATE

The **Senate** was designed to be the house of the states.

▶ representation is apportioned equally to signify that no one state is more important than any other

▶ two senators per state, for a total of 100 senators

▶ designed by the framers to have representatives chosen by the state legislatures

▶ originally, no direct connection between the Senate and the people

Figure 3.7. The Senate Chamber

However, as the power of the federal government grew, the people increasingly came to think of it as representing themselves rather than their states.

Corrupt state legislatures sold Senate seats to the highest bidder rather than electing the most qualified individual. As a result, the Senate seemed disconnected from the democratic process—a millionaire's club rife with corruption.

The tension between the people's perception of their relationship to the federal government and the mechanism of Senate elections came to a head during the

Progressive Era. Political machinations led to deadlocks in state legislatures over appointments, leaving Senate seats vacant for months at a time.

In 1913, the **Seventeenth Amendment** to the Constitution was ratified. It required the direct election of senators by the people of a state.

As the upper house, the Senate was designed to have greater autonomy with stricter qualifications.

Senators are elected for six-year terms (rather than the two-year terms of members of the House). These longer terms are to give senators time to make decisions that might not be popular but that are best for the nation.

They are staggered into three groups, with one group up for election every two years. This ensures that all senators do not face re-election at the same time, allowing for more consistent governance.

Qualifications for Senate include:

▶ Candidates must be at least thirty years old.

▶ Candidates must be a citizen of the United States for at least nine years.

▶ Candidates must live in the state they will represent at the time of the election.

The president of the Senate is the US vice president and only has the power to vote in case of a tie. The vice president is often absent from the Senate, in which case the **president pro tempore** presides. This person is generally the longest-serving member of the Senate.

Much like the House, the Senate has certain unique or specific powers:

▶ The Senate acts as the jury in the impeachment of a president and determines his or her guilt.

  ▷ In order to remove, or oust, a president from office, the Senate must vote two-thirds in favor.

  ▷ This has never happened in American history; Andrew Johnson's removal failed by one vote.

▶ The Senate approves executive appointments and appointments to federal positions in the judicial system:

  ▷ members of the Supreme Court and other federal courts

  ▷ the attorney general

    ▷   cabinet members

    ▷   ambassadors

► While the president may make appointments, no one may take one of these offices without the approval of the majority of the Senate.

► The Senate approves (ratifies) all treaties signed by the president.

    ▷   The president is in charge of foreign relations and is responsible for negotiating all treaties; however, as part of the system of checks and balances, the president requires the Senate's approval before any treaty becomes a permanent agreement.

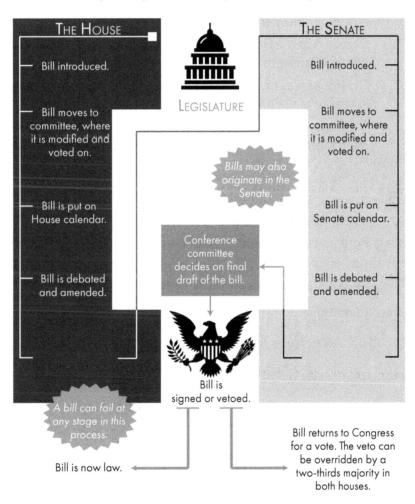

Figure 3.8. Bill to Law

PRACTICE QUESTIONS

21) **Which of the following is NOT an example of how the Senate represents the states?**

A.   the power to approve treaties

B.   equal representation of each state in the Senate

C.   vice president serves as president of the Senate

D.   selection of senators by state legislatures (before 1913)

22) **Why did the framers give the House of Representatives the power to start revenue bills?**

A.   Based on their qualifications, members of the House would have more economic knowledge.

B.   Members of the House would be less influenced by outside forces and political parties than members of the Senate.

C.   The House was more truly a national legislature; therefore, it should be in charge of the national budget.

D.   The frequency of elections for House of Representatives would make them more responsive to the will of the people in terms of spending.

LAWMAKING

The primary function of the legislature is to write and pass laws, and the process by which this is done is intentionally cumbersome and complicated. The framers of the Constitution believed that the longer the process took, the more deliberation there would be, decreasing the risk of abuse of power.

▶   Approximately 5,000 bills are introduced in Congress each year.

▷   Only 2.5 percent of these become laws.

▶   There are no restrictions on who can write a bill.

▷   Most are not written by Congress but begin either in the executive branch or are written by special interest groups.

▶   A member of Congress is required to introduce the bill.

▶   With the exception of revenue bills, bills can start in either house.

▶   Because the two houses have parallel processes, the same bill often starts in both houses at the same time.

▶   Once the bill is placed in the "hopper," it is assigned a number and sent to the appropriate committee.

▷   Committees and their subcommittees are where most of the hard work of lawmaking is actually done.

▷ Bills are read, debated, and revised.

▷ This is also where most bills die, by either being **tabled** (put aside) in subcommittee or committee, or voted down.

▶ If a bill does get voted out of committee, it goes to the floor for debate.

▷ In the House of Representatives, the powerful **Rules Committee** not only determines which bills make it to the floor for debate, but also sets time limits for debate on each bill.

Figure 3.9. Bill Hopper

▶ Debate in the Senate is unlimited.

▷ This allows for a unique tactic called the **filibuster**, in which a senator or group of senators continues to debate indefinitely to delay the passage of a bill.

▷ Sixty votes are needed to end a filibuster; therefore, senators often attempt to gather sixty or more votes for a bill before it comes to the floor to ensure it is not filibustered.

▶ After debate has ended, the members of each house vote on the bill.

▷ If it passes out of both houses, it moves to the **Conference Committee.**

▷ The **Conference Committee** must transform the two very different draft bills into one. (Different revisions and amendments are made as the bill makes its way through each house.)

▶ Once the draft bills are consolidated, the unified bill returns to both houses for a final vote.

    ▷ If it passes, it then proceeds to the president for signature or veto.

    ▷ If the president does veto the bill, it returns to Congress where both houses can vote again.

    ▷ If two-thirds of each house vote in favor of the bill, Congress will override the veto and the bill will become law anyway. This rarely happens.

AMENDING THE CONSTITUTION

Congress is responsible for another significant legislative process: amending the Constitution. The framers understood that they could not possibly foresee every threat to state sovereignty and personal liberty nor every need that would require government management.

They therefore added Article V to the Constitution:

▶ Article V lays out a procedure for amending the Constitution.

▶ Article V is one of the most significant aspects of the Constitution and makes it a "living document."

Amendments to the Constitution can either come from Congress or from the state legislatures:

▶ For Congress to propose an amendment to the Constitution, two-thirds of each house must vote in favor of the amendment.

▶ Alternatively, an amendment can be proposed if two-thirds of the states call for a national constitutional convention. To date, all amendments have been proposed by Congress.

▶ Either way, once the amendment has been officially proposed, it is not ratified until three-quarters of state legislatures (or special conventions convened by each state) approve it.

DID YOU KNOW?

Two-thirds is a magic number in American government. Two-thirds of Congress is needed to 1) override a veto; 2) propose an amendment to the Constitution; or 3) remove a president, judge, or other civil official after impeachment (Senate only)

There are twenty-seven amendments to the Constitution, the first ten of which were passed immediately in 1791.

These first ten amendments, now called **the Bill of Rights**, were a condition for ratification imposed by those who thought the new government wielded too much power. These **antifederalists** argued that individual liberty had to be explicitly protected from federal intervention.

The amendments outline what the government is not permitted to do:

▶ Amendment I: prohibit freedom of religion, speech, press, petition, and assembly

▶ Amendment II: prohibit the right to bear arms

▶ Amendment III: require citizens to quarter troops in their homes

▶ Amendment IV: conduct unlawful search and seizures

▶ Amendment V: force anyone to testify against themselves or be tried for the same crime twice

▶ Amendment VI: prohibit the right to a fair and speedy trial

▶ Amendment VII: prohibit the right to a jury trial in civil cases (The original Constitution only guaranteed a jury in criminal cases.)

▶ Amendment VIII: force citizens to undergo cruel and unusual punishment

▶ Amendment IX: violate rights that exist but are not explicitly mentioned in the Constitution

▶ Amendment X: usurp any powers from the states not given to them in the Constitution (In other words: all other powers not listed in the Constitution belong to the states.)

Unofficial Changes to the Constitution

While the only official way to change the Constitution is through the amendment process, other loopholes for change exist within its framework. These include:

▶ **Clarifying Legislation**: Using the **elastic clause**, much legislation has been passed whose purpose is to clarify or expand the powers of the federal government. For example, the Constitution only provides directly for the Supreme Court but empowers Congress to create other courts. The Judiciary Act of 1789 created the federal judiciary.

▶ **Executive Actions**: Although Congress holds most lawmaking power, the president is able to issue executive actions which have the force of law without having to involve Congress. The most famous of these is Abraham Lincoln's Emancipation Proclamation.

▶ **Judicial Decisions**: In *Marbury v. Madison* (1803) the Supreme Court established the precedent of **judicial review**, the power of the Supreme Court to determine the constitutionality of laws. *Marbury v. Madison* not only illustrated how judicial decisions can expand federal power in general, it also broadened the power of the Supreme Court in particular, laying the groundwork for future decisions that would have a similar impact.

▶ **Political Parties**: The rise of political parties changed the political landscape as well. Some aspects of American politics—like how the Speaker of the House is chosen and nomination conventions for presidential candidates—have come from political parties rather than through a formal legislative process.

PROHIBITED POWERS

Although Congress was made much more powerful by the Constitution, a real fear of tyranny existed among the framers. While Section VIII of the Constitution lists the powers of Congress, Section IX lists what Congress cannot do. Most notable are:

▶ **No suspension of habeas corpus**: A writ of habeas corpus is a legal demand prisoners can make to appear in court in order to profess their innocence. Essentially a means of preventing unreasonable imprisonment, this was viewed as an essential element of a just government. The Constitution forbids its suspension except in cases of rebellion or invasion.

DID YOU KNOW?

Abraham Lincoln was the first president to suspend habeas corpus (during the Civil War).

▶ No bills of attainder: A bill of attainder is a law that declares an individual or a group guilty of a crime without holding a trial. Much like with the writ of habeas corpus, this was seen as an essential protection in a fair society.

▶ No ex post facto laws: An ex post facto law punishes an individual or group for breaking a law that was not a law when the act was committed.

▷ Example: Slavery was abolished in 1865. If an ex post facto law was passed at that time, it would have punished anyone who had owned slaves before 1865.

▶ No titles of nobility: It was important to the framers to provide safeguards against a return to monarchy. Therefore, they prohibited an American nobility of any kind.

PRACTICE QUESTIONS

23) **Which of the following is an example of the "unwritten" Constitution?**

A. the Senate's confirmation of a Supreme Court justice

B. the nomination of a presidential candidate at a nominating convention

C. Congress writing a law regulating interstate commerce

D. the House of Representatives voting to impeach the president

24) **The clause of the Constitution that prohibits the suspension of writs of habeas corpus except in cases of rebellion or invasion demonstrates that the framers believed that**

    A.   the people of the nation were likely to rebel.

    B.   the president sometimes—like in cases of war—needs unlimited power.

    C.   it is important to balance individual liberty with the security of the nation.

    D.   the new laws would be resisted by most people.

THE EXECUTIVE BRANCH

The **executive branch** is defined by Article II of the Constitution. It enforces all federal law.

▶ Article II only provides for a president, vice president, and an unspecified number of executive departments.

▶ Out of the three executive roles mentioned, the president is the only one that is specifically defined in the Constitution.

The federal government, however, has expanded considerably over the past 225 years, in large part due to the expansion of the executive branch:

▶ Today, the executive branch is also responsible for administering a federal bureaucracy that spends $3 trillion a year and employs 2.7 million people.

The president serves a term of four years and may be re-elected up to two times:

▶ The term length was set in the original Constitution.

▶ The term limit was added in the Twenty-Second Amendment (1951).

Qualifications for the presidency include:

▶ Candidates must be natural-born American citizens.

▶ The minimum age requirement is thirty-five years old.

▶ Candidates must have resided in the US for at least fourteen years.

> **DID YOU KNOW?**
>
> The Twenty-Second Amendment was added in response to Franklin Delano Roosevelt's four elections to the presidency. (He was the first—and last—president to be elected to more than two terms.) Many felt that allowing unlimited terms threatened liberty and opened the door for a de facto dictator.

While the Constitution does not specifically list requirements for the vice presidency, it does state that the vice president becomes the president in case of death, resignation, or impeachment. As a result, the vice president must meet the same qualifications as the president.

The **cabinet** consists of the heads of the executive departments and may advise the president on a variety of matters.

The cabinet is not directly referred to at all in the Constitution; instead, it is derived from one line in Section 2: "he may require the opinion, in writing, of the principal officer in each of the executive departments, upon any subject relating to the duties of their respective offices."

The cabinet as we know it today was established immediately under George Washington. He established four executive departments, so the first cabinet consisted of four positions:

▶ the Secretary of State (Thomas Jefferson)

▶ the Secretary of the Treasury (Alexander Hamilton)

▶ the Secretary of War (Henry Knox)

DID YOU KNOW?

The Secretary of War is now known as the Secretary of Defense.

▶ the Attorney General, or head of the Justice Department (Edmund Randolph)

Over time, eleven new executive departments were added, for a total of fifteen cabinet positions. The additional eleven are:

▶ Department of the Interior

▶ Department of Agriculture

▶ Department of Commerce

▶ Department of Labor

▶ Department of Energy

▶ Department of Education

▶ Department of Housing and Urban Development

▶ Department of Transportation

▶ Department of Veterans Affairs

▶ Department of Health and Human Services

▶ Department of Homeland Security

These fifteen departments employ more than two-thirds of all federal employees.

In addition to managing their departments, the members of the cabinet are also all in the line of presidential succession as established by the Presidential Succession Act (first passed in 1792 but most recently amended in 1947).

The line of succession is as follows:

▶ vice president

▶ Speaker of the House

▶ president pro tempore of the Senate

▶ each cabinet member in the order of the department's creation (beginning with the Secretary of State and ending with the Secretary of Homeland Security)

PRACTICE QUESTIONS

25) **The cabinet is made up of**

    A.   the president's closest advisors.

    B.   the heads of each executive department.

    C.   the heads of each house of Congress and the chief justice of the Supreme Court.

    D.   the secretaries of state, defense, the treasury, and the attorney general.

26) **Which of the following criteria must a vice president meet according to the Constitution?**

    A.   must be a natural-born citizen of the United States

    B.   must be of the same party as the president

    C.   must have previously served in the legislature

    D.   no specified requirements

Article II is considerably shorter than Article I because the framers intended the role and powers of the president to be more limited than those of Congress. The president does, however, have several expressed powers:

APPOINTMENT POWER

▶ One of the most significant presidential powers is the power to appoint federal officials.

▶ The president's appointment power is far-ranging and includes cabinet members, heads of independent agencies, ambassadors, and federal judges.

- ▶ Through this power, the president controls the entirety of the executive branch, foreign policy, and significant and long-term influence over the judicial branch.

- ▶ This power is not unlimited.

  - ▷ Based on the advice and consent clause of the Constitution, the Senate must approve all presidential appointments.

  - ▷ US presidents have the power to remove their appointees from office—with the exception of judges—without Senate approval.

COMMANDER IN CHIEF

The first line of Section 2 of Article II declares the president **commander in chief** of the army and navy, making the president the supreme leader of US military forces. As commander in chief, the president can deploy troops and dictate military policy.

However, this power is checked: while the president controls the military, Congress retains the power to declare war.

Presidents have circumvented this check in the past by deploying troops without requesting a formal declaration of war. In the twentieth century, this happened most notably with the Vietnam War, which was never officially declared.

In 1964, Congress passed the **Gulf of Tonkin Resolution** in response to the perceived attack on an American ship in the Gulf of Tonkin. The resolution essentially gave the president a blank check for military action in Vietnam, which led to a rapid and massive escalation of US military spending and troops.

Consequently, in 1974 Congress passed the War Powers Resolution, which:

- ▶ requires the president to inform Congress within forty-eight hours of a troop deployment

- ▶ restricts deployment unsupported by congressional authorization to sixty days.

DIPLOMAT–IN–CHIEF

The president is also considered the **chief diplomat** of the United States:

- ▶ In this capacity, the president has the power to recognize other nations, receive ambassadors, and negotiate treaties.

  - ▷ Any treaties negotiated by the president must be approved by the Senate before taking effect.

▶ Many of the president's diplomatic powers are informal.

▷ In the twentieth century, the US became a superpower, transforming the role of the president into that of a world leader as well as the leader of the nation.

▷ As a result, the president is now expected to manage international crises, negotiate executive agreements with other countries, and monitor and maintain confidential information related to the security of the nation and to the rest of the world.

JUDICIAL POWERS

While the executive and judicial branches are quite separate, the president has powers intended to check the power of the judicial branch:

▶ the power to appoint federal judges

▶ the power to grant pardons and reprieves for individuals convicted of federal crimes

The purpose of pardon power is to provide a final option for those who have been unfairly convicted. This is one of the president's more controversial powers, as pardons are often seen to be politically motivated or a tool for those with political or personal connections.

> **DID YOU KNOW?**
>
> The number of pardons granted by presidents has fluctuated over time, with Woodrow Wilson granting the most: 2,480. In recent years, presidents have issued fewer than one hundred pardons per president.

LEGISLATIVE POWERS

Like the judicial branch, the president is constitutionally accorded some legislative powers in order to limit the powers of the legislative branch.

All laws that are passed end up on the desk of the president. The president has the choice to either sign the bill—in which case it becomes a law—or **veto** the bill. The president's **veto** prevents the bill from becoming law (unless Congress overrides the veto).

The president is required to either fully accept or fully reject a bill and cannot veto only sections of it. This is called a **line-item veto**, and the Supreme Court declared it unconstitutional in 1996.

If the president does not wish to take such a clear stand on a bill, the president can choose to simply ignore it. If the president does nothing for ten days, the bill automatically becomes law, even without a signature. If there are less than ten days left in Congress's session, and the president does not sign the bill, it automatically dies. This is called a **pocket veto**.

The president has the power to convene both houses of Congress to force them to consider matters requiring urgent attention.

While this is technically the extent of the president's legislative powers, in reality the position has a much greater legislative impact. First, the president sets the policy agenda both as the leader of his or her party and through the **State of the Union** address:

▶ Section 3 of Article II states, "He [or she] shall from time to time give to the Congress information of the state of the union, and recommend to their consideration such measures as he [or she] shall judge necessary and expedient."

▶ This has evolved into an annual formalized address to Congress in which the president lays out executive legislative priorities.

In addition, many bills originate in the executive branch, either from the president's office or from one of the executive departments. The president also often uses the power of the veto to influence legislation: by threatening to veto, the president can force changes to bills to align more with the president's agenda.

ELECTION OF THE PRESIDENT

Almost half of Article II is dedicated to describing the process of electing the president. The framers wanted to ensure that the president represents all of the states and is immune from the mob rule of democracy. As a result, they created the **Electoral College.** Over the years, the political parties have expanded the process into a nine-month series of elections by various groups of people.

The first step in choosing a president is selecting the candidates. Originally, this was done in smoke-filled back rooms; it then became the provenance of party caucuses and then conventions, eventually evolving into the current system of primaries and caucuses:

▶ In a **primary** election, members of a political party in a state vote at a polling place for the person they believe is the best candidate for their party.

▶ In ten states, a **caucus** system is used: members of a party in a state gather together at party meetings and vote for the candidate using raised hands or by gathering in groups.

In July of the election year, the party holds a **national nominating convention**. Historically, this is where the candidate was chosen after days of heated debate and dealings. But because of the primary and caucus systems, delegates at the convention arrive already knowing whom their state supports. At the convention:

▶ The delegates vote for the candidate who won their primary or caucus.

▶ The candidate with the most votes becomes the party's nominee.

Presidential elections are held nationwide every four years on the first Tuesday in November.

- Today, all American citizens over the age of eighteen are allowed to vote, but this was not always the case.

  - The framers viewed the electorate as a small, select segment of the population; however, no voter qualifications are written into the Constitution; those were left to the states.

  - In 1789, in every state, only propertied White men—one in fifteen White men—were allowed to vote.

  - Starting with the removal of property qualifications during the Jacksonian era (1830s), views of democracy began to change, and the electorate expanded.

- Aside from property requirements, each expansion resulted from a new amendment to the Constitution.

Table 3.9. Constitutional Amendments Expanding Voting Rights

Amendment	Year	Provision
Fifteenth	1870	All male citizens, regardless of race, are allowed to vote.
Nineteenth	1920	Women are allowed to vote.
Twenty-Third	1961	Residents of the District of Columbia are allowed to vote in presidential elections.
Twenty-Fourth	1964	Poll taxes, an indirect restriction of Black voting rights, are prohibited.
Twenty-Sixth	1971	All citizens over the age of eighteen are allowed to vote (in most states the voting age had previously been twenty-one years).

THE ELECTORAL COLLEGE

While the popular vote is tallied on Election Day, it does not determine the outcome of the presidential election. The **Electoral College** determines the president.

- The Electoral College is composed of electors from each state who vote for the president.

- Electors are apportioned based on population:

  - The number of a state's electors is the same as its number of representatives plus its number of senators.

  - Each state has at least three electors.

In its original conception, each state selected its electors by whatever means it chose. At first, most states allowed their state legislatures to choose their electors. By the end of the 1830s, almost every state allowed for the direct election of electors.

HELPFUL HINT

A state's number of electors is equal to its number of representatives plus its number of senators (which is two for every state). So, every state (and Washington, DC) has at least three electoral votes. There are a total of 538 votes available.

In the January following the election, electors gather in their states to cast their votes for president:

▶ Today, most states are winner-take-all: the electors are expected to all vote in line with the outcome of the state's popular vote.

▶ The president must win a majority of the Electoral College in order to win—at least 270 votes.

The Electoral College was designed to elect a president for a nation that was scattered and had greater loyalty regionally than nationally. It favors small states and minority groups, giving them greater influence on the election than they would have in a direct election system.

DID YOU KNOW?

Technically, electors are not bound to vote in line with their state's popular vote; however, rarely has an elector taken advantage of this, and it has never affected the outcome of an election.

Today many people feel that the Electoral College is outdated and ill-fitting.

▶ They argue that it is undemocratic, giving undue importance to certain states based on their number of electoral votes.

▶ They support a direct election system instead.

PRACTICE QUESTIONS

27) **Which of the following is an implied power of the president?**

A. granting pardons for federal crimes

B. seeking ratification of a treaty from the Senate

C. appointing a justice to the Supreme Court

D. holding a regularly scheduled cabinet meeting

28) **Which of the following earns the president the unofficial title of "Chief Legislator"?**

A. The president maintains US embassies abroad.

B. The president votes in Congress in case of a tie.

C. The president sets the agenda for much of what is debated in Congress.

D. The president chooses the Speaker of the House.

29) **What is the presidential action that best exemplifies this role as that of the Chief Executive?**

    A.   appointment of a new Secretary of the Interior

    B.   vetoing a bill

    C.   negotiating a treaty with Russia

    D.   receiving the ambassador from Finland

30) **The Electoral College represents which of the beliefs of the framers of the Constitution?**

    A.   Government derives its authority from the consent of the people.

    B.   Concentration of power can lead to tyranny.

    C.   The federal government derives its authority from the states.

    D.   The federal government needs greater power to provide stability to the nation.

THE JUDICIAL BRANCH

The Constitution's framework for the judicial branch is the least detailed of the three branches. It is also a passive branch. Where the legislative branch creates laws, and the executive branch takes actions to enforce those laws, the **judicial branch** can only weigh in when an actual case is presented to it. It may not rule or make decisions based on hypotheticals.

Still, this branch has grown to be at least as influential as the other two branches both in setting policy and molding the size and shape of the federal government.

DUAL COURT SYSTEM

The United States has a complex **dual court system**:

▶   Each state has its own multipart judicial system in addition to the federal one.

▶   Even though federal district courts handle over 300,000 cases a year, 97 percent of criminal cases are heard in state and local courts.

▶   While the federal courts hear more civil cases than criminal, the majority of these are still handled within the states.

Because of the federal system, state courts have **jurisdiction**—the authority to hear a case—over most cases.

Only cases that meet certain criteria (a dispute between two states, a case involving federal employees or agencies, or a violation of federal law, for example) are heard in federal courts.

Most cases also can only be **appealed**—reviewed by a higher court—up to the state supreme court.

For the federal Supreme Court to review a state supreme court's decision, there must be an issue involving the interpretation of the federal Constitution.

Article III, the article of the Constitution which discusses the judicial branch, only details the Supreme Court. It then empowers Congress to create the rest of the judiciary, which it did beginning with the Judiciary Act of 1789.

The federal court system is composed of three levels of courts:

1. the district courts

   ▷ ninety-four in the country, served by 700 judges

   ▷ handle eighty percent of all federal cases

2. the twelve circuit courts of appeal

   ▷ review the decisions of district courts and federal regulatory agencies

3. the **Supreme Court**

   ▷ highest-level court

   ▷ sometimes called the "court of last resort"

   ▷ reviews cases from the circuit court and estate supreme courts

   ▷ the final arbiter of constitutionality

   ▷ establishes **precedents**—rulings that guide future court decisions at all levels of the judicial system

THE SUPREME COURT

While the Constitution delineates which kinds of cases the Supreme Court may hear, its real power was established by the precedent of an early case, *Marbury v. Madison* (1803).

William Marbury—citing the Judiciary Act of 1789—sought relief from the court when James Madison, Secretary of State to the newly inaugurated Thomas Jefferson, did not deliver the federal appointment Marbury was given under the previous president, John Adams.

Under Chief Justice John Marshall, the court ruled that while Madison was in the wrong, the section of the Judiciary Act allowing Marbury to petition the Supreme Court was unconstitutional because it extended the jurisdiction of the court beyond the scope established in Article III.

▶ This established **judicial review**—the Supreme Court's power to determine the constitutionality of laws.

▶ Judicial review has become the most significant function of the court and has allowed it to shape public policy.

Figure 3.10. US Supreme Court Building

There are nine justices who serve on the Supreme Court:

▶ They are appointed by the president and approved by the Senate.

▶ Supreme Court justices serve for life.

▶ The Constitution does not provide any criteria for serving on the court, but unofficial requirements do exist:

▷ Justices must demonstrate competence through high-level credentials or prior experience.

Today, all of the justices on the Supreme Court hold law degrees from major universities and first served in federal district or appellate courts. They also generally share policy preferences with the president who appointed them, although judicial inclinations do not always neatly align with political ones.

HELPFUL HINT

Judicial activism is when judges expand the meaning of the Constitution or laws, rather than just interpret it. Under Earl Warren, the Supreme Court was accused of judicial activism, in part for expanding the rights of defendants.

It is very difficult to have a case heard by the Supreme Court. The court only has **original jurisdiction** (first court to hear the case) in three situations:

1. if a case involves two or more states

2. if a case involves the US government and state government

3. if a case involves the US government and foreign diplomats

> **DID YOU KNOW?**
>
> The court determines its own caseload. It receives approximately 9,000 requests for **writs of certioraris** each year but typically only accepts eighty cases.

All other cases come to the Supreme Court through the federal appellate courts or the state supreme courts:

▶ Appellants must request a **writ of certiorari**, an order to the lower court to send up their decision for review.

▶ Once a case is accepted, each party must file a brief arguing its side of the case, specifically referencing the constitutional issue in question.

▷ Other interested parties may also file **amicus briefs**, position papers supporting a particular side or argument.

▶ Once all briefs are read, both parties present **oral arguments** in the Supreme Court.

▷ Each lawyer presents an oral summary of his or her party's argument and then fields questions from the justices.

▷ Oral arguments are limited to thirty minutes per side.

▶ Next, the justices meet in private to discuss the case and vote.

▶ The chief justice then assigns a justice to write the **majority opinion**, a detailed explanation of the majority's decision and reasoning.

▷ Other justices who did not vote with the majority may write **dissenting opinions**.

▷ Dissenting opinions have no force of law but are a record of alternative reasoning which may be used in future cases.

▷ Sometimes justices also write **concurring opinions**, which agree with the majority's ruling, but provide different reasoning to support the decision.

SIGNIFICANT SUPREME COURT CASES

There are several significant Supreme Court cases to know, some of which are listed in Table 3.10.

Table 3.10. Supreme Court Cases

Case Name	Ruling
Marbury v. Madison (1803)	This case established judicial review.
McCulloch v. Maryland (1819)	The court ruled that states could not tax the Bank of the United States; this ruling supported the implied powers of Congress.
Dred Scott v. Sandford (1857)	The Supreme Court ruled that enslaved persons were not citizens; it also found the Missouri Compromise unconstitutional, meaning Congress could not forbid expanding slavery to US territories.
Plessy v. Ferguson (1896)	This case established the precedent of separate but equal (segregation).
Korematsu v. US (1945)	This case determined that the internment of Japanese Americans during WWII was lawful.
Brown v. Board of Education (1954)	The Supreme Court overturned *Plessy v. Ferguson* and ruled that separate but equal, or segregation, was unconstitutional.
Gideon v. Wainwright (1963)	The Supreme Court ruled that the court must provide legal counsel to poor defendants in felony cases.
Miranda v. Arizona (1966)	This ruling established that defendants must be read their due process rights before questioning.
Tinker v. Des Moines (1969)	This case established "symbolic speech" as a form of speech protected by the First Amendment.
Roe v. Wade (1973)	This case legalized abortion in the first trimester throughout the United States.
Bakke v. Regents of University of California (1978)	This case ruled that while affirmative action was constitutional, the university's quota system was not.
Citizens United v. Federal Elections Commission (2010)	The court ruled that restricting corporate donations to political campaigns was tantamount to restricting free speech; this ruling allowed the formation of influential super PACs, which can provide unlimited funding to candidates running for office.
Obergefell v. Hodges (2015)	The court ruled that same-sex marriage was legal throughout the United States.

PRACTICE QUESTIONS

31) **Where did the Supreme Court's power of judicial review come from?**

 A.   the Judiciary Act of 1789

 B.   an order by the president

 C.   an amendment to the Constitution

 D.   the court's own interpretation of the Constitution

32) **Why are justices appointed for life?**

 A.   to insulate them from political pressure

 B.   to prevent them from running for political office

 C.   to ensure continuity of decisions

 D.   to make the judicial branch the strongest branch of government

33) **The Warren Court in the 1960s was accused of judicial activism, or legislating through court decisions. Whose rights were expanded under the Warren Court?**

 A.   those of Black people

 B.   those of women

 C.   those of defendants

 D.   those of youth

34) **Which of the following would be written by a special interest to lobby the court?**

 A.   writ of certiorari

 B.   amicus brief

 C.   bill of attainder

 D.   writ of habeas corpus

CIVIL LIBERTIES AND RIGHTS

Fresh from revolution and influenced by the ideas of the Enlightenment, the framers of the Constitution valued **civil liberties. Civil liberties** are rights—provided for either directly by the Constitution or through its historical interpretations—that protect individuals from arbitrary acts of the government.

DID YOU KNOW?

The amendments restrict the actions of the federal government instead of granting a freedom to the people.

The framers protected some liberties explicitly in the Constitution via the prohibited powers and expanded on them in the **Bill of Rights** (listed earlier in this chapter under "Amending the Constitution.").

THE FIRST AMENDMENT

The liberties most central to the American identity are articulated in the **First Amendment**:

- speech

- press

- petition

- assembly

- religion

The first four are all closely related.

No liberty is truly unlimited, and the court has imposed restrictions on speech over time. It has upheld laws banning libel, slander, obscenity, and symbolic speech that intends to incite illegal actions.

The **freedom of religion** comes from two clauses in the First Amendment: the **establishment clause** and the **free exercise clause**:

- The **establishment clause** prohibits the government from establishing a state religion or favoring one religion over another.

- The **free exercise clause** prohibits the government from restricting religious belief or practice.

- Again, freedom of religion is not unlimited. For example:

  ▷ The court has found that religious practice can be banned if it requires engagement in otherwise illegal activity.

  ▷ There are continuing debates on allowing prayer in schools and granting vouchers to students to attend parochial schools.

RIGHTS OF THE ACCUSED

Most of the civil liberties written into the body of the Constitution address the rights of the accused, including prohibitions on bills of attainder, ex post facto laws, and denials of writs of habeas corpus. Three of the amendments in the Bill of Rights address this as well:

1. **The Fourth Amendment** restricts unlawful searches and seizures.

   ▷ In *Mapp v. Ohio* (1961), the Supreme Court ruled that evidence obtained illegally (in other words, in violation of the Fourth Amendment) could not be used in court.

    ▷   This **exclusionary rule** is very controversial, and the courts have struggled since to determine when and how to apply it.

2.   **The Fifth Amendment** protects the accused from self-incrimination.

    ▷   In *Miranda v. Arizona* (1966), the Supreme Court ruled that arrestees must be informed of their due process rights before interrogation in order to protect them from self-incrimination.

    ▷   These rights, along with those in the Sixth Amendment, are now colloquially known as **Miranda rights**.

3.   **The Sixth Amendment** guarantees the accused the right to a fair, speedy, and public trial and, in criminal cases, the right to counsel.

    ▷   While originally this only applied at the federal level, in *Gideon v. Wainwright* (1963) the Supreme Court ruled that states must provide counsel to those who cannot afford it.

THE FOURTEENTH AMENDMENT

The Fourteenth Amendment was ratified in 1868. Its original purpose was to ensure the equal treatment of Black Americans under the law after the abolition of slavery. Its use has been expanded far beyond that original purpose.

The Court's ruling in *Gideon v. Wainwright* was based on the Fourteenth Amendment's **equal protection clause**:

▸   This clause has been used to protect the **civil rights**—protections against discriminatory treatment by the government—of individuals of a variety of groups

Equality is a tricky concept for Americans. It is central to the American ideology, a guiding principle of the Declaration of Independence: "All men are created equal..."

The courts have regularly protected political and legal equality, as well as equality of opportunity (like the *Brown v. Board of Education* decision in 1954). The courts, however, do not recognize a right to economic equality.

The Supreme Court also recognizes the need for reasonable classifications of people and allows discrimination along those lines. For example, certain activities are constitutionally restricted to people of a certain age:

▸   alcohol consumption

▸   driving

▸   voting

The Supreme Court has also used the Fourteenth Amendment over time to extend federal civil liberties

CHECK YOUR UNDERSTANDING #3

List the freedoms protected by the First Amendment.

to the state level. Today, all states are held to the same standard as the federal government in terms of civil liberties.

The second part of the Fourteenth Amendment extends the Fifth Amendment's **due process guarantees** to the state level:

▶ "No person shall be deprived of life, liberty, or property without the due process of law...."

While this typically refers to the processes of the accused, as discussed above, it has also come to represent certain unnamed, or **implied rights**.

▶ At the heart of most of these **implied rights** is the right to privacy, which is not specifically protected in the Constitution.

▷ The court has ruled that it is implied by the Fourth, Fifth, and Fourteenth Amendments; this was the basis for its decision to legalize abortion in *Roe v. Wade* (1973).

PRACTICE QUESTIONS

35) **Which of the following is NOT considered protected speech?**

    A. burning the American flag

    B. writing an article criticizing the government

    C. publishing a false list of supposed KKK members

    D. protesting outside of an abortion clinic

36) **Which of the following does NOT address a due process issue?**

    A. a law prohibiting marriage between cousins

    B. a law establishing grounds for termination of parental rights

    C. a law prohibiting airplane travel by convicted felons

    D. a law prohibiting indecent exposure

37) **Which of the following is an absolute right?**

    A. freedom to hold any religious belief

    B. freedom of speech

    C. freedom from search and seizure

    D. freedom to bear arms

38) **If the police search a home without a warrant, any evidence found could not be used. What is this based on?**

    A. the equal protection clause

    B. the exclusionary rule

    C. the establishment clause

    D. Miranda rights

AMERICAN POLITICAL SYSTEMS

While the structure of the American government operates much as it is described in the original Constitution, a whole network of systems that support it has developed since it was written.

These systems operate within the framework of the government and greatly impact how it functions. As the federal government has expanded and grown in power, so have these systems:

> **DID YOU KNOW?**
>
> While faith in core political beliefs like liberty, equality, individualism, and democracy persists, Americans have become increasingly distrustful of government since the 1950s. As a result, there has been a steady decline in civic participation, leading to a decline in the efficacy of government and its political systems.

- ▶ **public opinion**
  - ▷ one of the biggest influences on the American political system
  - ▷ describes the public's attitude toward institutions, leaders, political issues, and events

- ▶ **political efficacy**
  - ▷ the extent to which individuals believe they can effect change in the political system; used by analysts
  - ▷ a measure of the health of a political system

POLITICAL PARTIES

Although the framers envisioned a political system without political parties, two official parties existed by the election of 1800.

A political party is a group of citizens who work together in order to:

- ▶ win elections
- ▶ hold public office
- ▶ operate the government
- ▶ determine public policy

Some countries have one-party systems; others have multiple parties.

Although party names and platforms have shifted over the years, the US has maintained a two-party system. Since 1854, our two major parties have been the **Democratic Party** and the **Republican Party**:

- ▶ Democrats generally follow a liberal political ideology.
- ▶ Republicans espouse a conservative ideology.

▶ The parties operate at every level of government in every state.

Although many members of a party serve in elected office, political parties have their own internal organization and are hierarchical:

▶ national leaders

▶ state chairpersons

▶ county chairpersons

▶ local activists

The parties serve an important role in the American political system and fulfill functions that aid government operations. These include:

▶ recruiting and nominating candidates for office

▶ running political campaigns

▶ articulating positions on various issues

▶ connecting individuals and the government

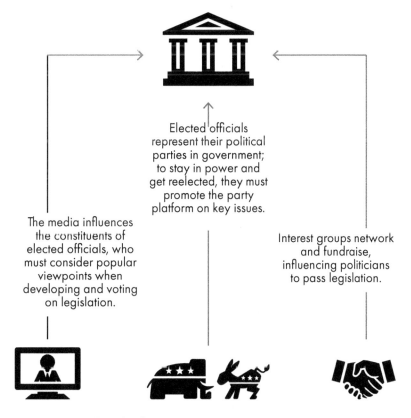

Elected officials represent their political parties in government; to stay in power and get reelected, they must promote the party platform on key issues.

The media influences the constituents of elected officials, who must consider popular viewpoints when developing and voting on legislation.

Interest groups network and fundraise, influencing politicians to pass legislation.

Figure 3.11. Political Influence

In Congress, parties have become integral to the organization of both houses:

▶ The leadership of each house is based on the leadership of whichever party has the majority.

▶ The majority party also holds all of the committee chairs, assigns bills to committees, holds a majority in each committee, controls the important Rules Committee, and sets the legislative agenda.

While still very important, the power of political parties has declined dramatically since the beginning of the twentieth century. In response to the dominance and corruption of political machines, many states implemented **direct primaries** to circumvent the parties. Individual politicians can now build power without the party machinery.

Although the United States has a two-party system, third parties still emerge periodically. These parties are always relatively small and come in three types:

1. **Charismatic leadership parties**

   ▷ parties that are dominated by an engaging and forceful leader

   ▷ examples include the Bull Moose Party (Teddy Roosevelt, 1912); the American Independent Party (George Wallace, 1972); and the Reform Party (Ross Perot, 1992 and 1996)

2. **Single-issue parties**

   ▷ parties organized around one defining issue

   ▷ examples include the Free Soil Party and the Know Nothing Party in the 1840s, and the Right to Life Party in the 1970s and 1980s

3. **Ideological parties**

   ▷ parties that are organized around a particular non-mainstream ideology

   ▷ examples include the Socialist Party and the Libertarian Party

Although they rarely succeed in gaining major political office, these third parties play an important role in American politics. The two main parties trend toward the middle in an attempt to garner the majority of votes. Third parties, on the other hand, target select populations and are thus able to express strong views on controversial issues.

Because their views are usually shared by the most extreme elements of one of the major parties, their stances often push the major parties into more radical or progressive (or sometimes regressive) positions.

HELPFUL HINT

Do not worry about learning the names of all of the past third parties. It is more important to understand what they do than who they are.

Third parties can also affect the outcome of an election, even without winning it. By siphoning off a segment of the vote from one of the dominant parties, they can "spoil" the election for that party.

For example, in the 2000 presidential election, Ralph Nader (Green Party candidate), did not win any electoral votes. He did, however, draw away votes that most likely would have otherwise gone to Al Gore (Democratic Party candidate), contributing to George W. Bush's (Republican Party candidate) election.

PRACTICE QUESTIONS

39) **All of the following result from the two-party system EXCEPT**

A. how the Speaker of the House is selected.

B. the lack of effective third parties.

C. the lifetime appointment of Supreme Court justices.

D. how members are assigned to committees.

40) **Third parties primarily impact presidential elections by**

A. increasing voter turnout.

B. preventing either party from winning a majority in the Electoral College.

C. encouraging more voters to officially join a political party.

D. bringing forward issues to be adopted by the major parties later.

INTEREST GROUPS

An **interest group** is a private organization made up of individuals who share policy views on one or more issues. Organized together, the group then tries to influence public opinion to its own benefit.

Interest groups play an important role in American politics:

▶ They connect citizens to the government.

▶ They bring their members' concerns and perspectives to government officials.

▶ They share information with their members about government policy.

    ▷ They wield more influence than the average citizen: they speak for many, and they raise money to influence policymakers, thereby influencing policy.

Interest groups play an increasingly dominant role in American political life, with the number of groups increasing from 6,000 in 1959 to 22,000 in 2010.

Most interest groups focus on one core issue or on a set of issues and draw their membership from people interested in those issues. For example, the National Rifle Association focuses on protecting the right to gun ownership.

Other organizations, however, focus on a specific group of people and then determine their interests based on the interests of that group. For example, the AARP (American Association of Retired Persons) determines which issues are most relevant to senior citizens (who make up their membership), and pursues those issues.

Large corporations, industry organizations, agricultural groups, professional associations, and unions also act as interest groups.

Interest groups **lobby** lawmakers to try to effect the change they wish to see.

▶ *To lobby* means to attempt to persuade policymakers to make a certain decision.

▶ There are about 30,000 lobbyists in Washington, DC, making a combined $2 billion a year.

▶ It is their full-time job to advance the agenda of their interest groups.

▶ They do this by testifying before congressional committees, meeting with aides, connecting influential constituents to lawmakers, drafting legislation, and providing relevant technical information to members of Congress.

When all else fails, interest groups will turn to the courts to help them achieve their goals.

▶ They write amicus briefs in Supreme Court cases or initiate court cases to challenge existing laws.

▶ They can also play a significant role in determining who is nominated to the federal courts, including the Supreme Court.

Another tool interest groups use to influence policymakers is the **political action committee**, also known as a PAC:

▶ These are committees that interest groups form with the purpose of raising money to support the campaigns of specific candidates who can further their interests.

▶ PACs are limited to contributions of $5,000 per candidate per election. (It is important to note that primary elections count as separate elections.)

▶ The Supreme Court ruled in *Citizens United v. Federal Elections Commission* (2010) that limiting corporate donations to candidates was tantamount to limiting free speech.

    ▷ This controversial decision resulted in the creation of **super PACs**, which have no limits on spending.

The role of lobbying, and most specifically PACs and super PACs, in American politics is a hotly debated one:

▶ Some political analysts are concerned that politics and money have become too closely tied together.

▶ Others argue that the sheer number of special interest groups is a benefit because they balance each other out.

In order to accomplish anything, politicians must bargain and compromise, creating solutions that are ultimately better for more people.

Others still argue that rather than creating solutions, the number of competing interests leaves politicians scared to take any action for fear that they will anger one interest group or another.

Mass Media

Any means of communication—newspapers, magazines, radio, television, or blogs—that reaches a broad and far-reaching audience is considered part of the **mass media**.

Although certainly not a formal part of the political process, the mass media has a significant impact on American politics:

▶ It connects people to the government by providing them with inside information on its people and processes, through reports, interviews, and exposés.

▶ The media also can help set the political agenda by drawing attention to issues through its coverage.

▷ Example: The medical treatment of veterans became a significant political issue after two lengthy exposés in the *Washington Post* on the conditions at Walter Reed Medical Center in 2007.

Mass media has also reshaped American campaigns:

▶ Campaigns have become more candidate-centered rather than issue-centered, as candidates now must consider their image on television and other video sources.

> CHECK YOUR UNDERSTANDING #4
>
> What common function do political parties, interest groups, and mass media all share?

▶ Candidates also have to be media savvy, making appearances on popular nightly shows and radio programs.

▶ The need for a strong media presence is largely responsible for the increase in campaign spending, as candidates work to maintain an up-to-date web presence and spend millions of dollars on television advertising space.

▶ Candidates' lives and pasts are also more visible to the public as journalists research their backgrounds to a further extent than ever before.

One example of the impact of mass media on American politics occurred during the 1960 presidential campaign.

John F. Kennedy and Richard Nixon engaged in the first televised presidential debate in American history. Those who listened to it on the radio declared Nixon—who was confident in speech but sweaty and uncomfortable on camera—the winner. Those who watched it on television saw the suave and image-savvy Kennedy as the victor.

Many credit this debate for Kennedy's eventual win. This demonstrated the new importance of crafting a public image for politicians.

PRACTICE QUESTIONS

41) **Which of the following is an example of an issues-driven organization?**

    A.   Americans for Tax Reform

    B.   the American Medical Association (AMA)

    C.   the AFL-CIO

    D.   the National Association for the Advancement of Colored People (NAACP)

42) **What is the most effective task for a lobbyist?**

    A.   organizing protests

    B.   giving expert information to legislators

    C.   mobilizing letter-writing campaigns

    D.   leading politicians' campaigns for election

43) **Throughout the twentieth and twenty-first centuries, changes in politics have coincided with the emergence of new media or a change in the organization of media. This shows that**

    A.   new media develops in response to political changes.

    B.   media has a greater impact on the functioning of government than other political systems.

    C.   there is no connection between the functioning of media and politics.

    D.   politics is responsive to changes in how people communicate.

COMPARATIVE POLITICS AND INTERNATIONAL RELATIONS

All nations have governments; however, those governments come in very different forms.

A government's structure is influenced by environmental factors:

▶ geography

▶ population size

▶ economic strength

▶ industrial development

▶ cultural diversity

Significant changes to any of these categories can lead to a restructuring of the government itself. Governments are either ruled by man or ruled by law, and categories of governments can be divided up in three different ways.

> **DID YOU KNOW?**
>
> In the fifth-century Roman Empire, the Twelve Tables and other laws were developed across the Eastern Roman Empire and in the sixth century were organized into the Justinian Code by the Byzantine emperor. These became the basis of many modern legal systems, including that of the United States.

Table 3.11. Type of Government Rule

Rule by Man: arbitrary and absolute decisions

- **autocracies:** rule by one person
- **dictatorship:** ruler's power derived from political control, military power, or a cult of personality
- **monarchy:** authority derived from a **divine right** to rule given by God
- **oligarchies:** ruled by a powerful group; based on wealth, social status, military position, or some level of achievement
- **aristocracies:** ruled by an elite class; based on wealth, social status, military position, or some level of achievement
- **theocracy:** authority held by a small group—the religious leadership—and is derived from divine right

Rule by Law: governance according to a code of law

- some form of republic or democracy

Most modern nations are—at least in theory—ruled by law.

GEOGRAPHIC DISTRIBUTION OF AUTHORITY

A second way to organize different types of governments is by how their authority is distributed across the territory of the state or nation:

- A **unitary government** vests all of its power in the central government.

  ▷ This is the kind of the government used by most nations.

  ▷ Example: Great Britain, France, and China all have unitary governments.

- A **confederate government** is decentralized with power distributed among regional governments.

  ▷ The first government of the United States under the Articles of Confederation is a prime example of this.

- In a **federal** system of government the power is shared between the central government and the regional governments.

  ▷ The current US government is an example of a federal government.

SEPARATION OF POWERS

Governments can be organized depending on the way power is divided within the government itself.

In an **authoritarian government**:

- There is no division of power.

- All aspects of government are controlled by the same body—a single ruler or a council of some kind.

  ▷ North Korea is an example of an authoritarian government.

In a **parliamentarian government**:

- The legislative and executive functions of government are combined, with the judicial acting as a separate body.

- The head executive—the **prime minister**—and that person's cabinet are chosen from the legislature.

- As long as the prime minister's party (or parties) maintain a majority in the legislature, the prime minister maintains power.

  ▷ Great Britain is an example of a parliamentary government.

The final type is the US-style, three-branch system which has been discussed at length in this text.

PRACTICE QUESTIONS

44) The British historian Lord Acton said, "Power corrupts; absolute power corrupts absolutely." Based on this, which of the following systems do you think he would have most likely supported?

A. a monarchy

B. a democratic republic

C. a unitary government

D. an aristocracy

45) In the Soviet Union, Joseph Stalin used secret police, purges, and censorship to rule. What is this type of government called?

A. monarchy

B. democratic republic

C. dictatorship

D. oligarchy

POLITICAL PARTY SYSTEMS

Almost all modern governments are run by political parties. However, party systems come in three different types: single-party, two-party, and multiparty.

The **one-party system** is the simplest party system:

▶ Only one party controls the entire government without opposition or challenge.

▶ Elections are still held, but their purpose is to allow citizens to show their support for the existing government.

▶ Autocratic governments are one-party systems.

▶ China, North Korea, and Cuba all have one-party systems.

In a **two-party system**, two major parties compete for control.

▶ Fewer differences divide the parties, and each party trends toward the middle in order to try to gain as much public support as possible.

▶ The parties generally split along the liberal-conservative line; neither one takes an extreme stance on an issue.

▶ The United States, Great Britain, and Australia all have two-party systems.

In **multiparty systems, s**everal different parties compete for government power.

▶ The parties in a multiparty system represent very different and often more radical ideologies (unlike those in two-party systems).

▶ Parties seek **pluralities**—the largest percentage of votes—rather than **majorities**—more than half of the votes.

- ▶ Consequently, the government is run by a coalition of different parties that form alliances.

- ▶ There must be some degree of consensus between at least some parties.

- ▶ France, Italy, and Israel all have multiparty systems.

In both two- and multiparty systems, citizens use their votes in elections to support certain policies or agendas.

The framers of the Constitution intentionally tried to avoid political parties, yet a party system emerged anyway. But why was it a two-party system? Several factors make a nation more receptive to a two-party or multiparty system.

A key structural factor affecting the development of a party system is the apportionment of power within the legislature.

In **single-member districts**, states are divided into districts.

- ▶ Each district elects one representative in a winner-take-all model.

- ▶ This discourages the growth of smaller parties, as they are unlikely to win a majority—the only way they can gain any power.

- ▶ Example: Power is distributed among single-member districts in the United States.

In **proportional representation,** the number of seats any one party gets is based on the percentage of the vote it wins overall.

- ▶ This encourages smaller parties as they can still win some seats with only a small percentage of votes.

- ▶ Example: Italy distributes power using proportional representation.

Party-based proportional representation should not be confused with the proportional representation of the House of Representatives. In that case, the "proportion" refers to how representatives are divided amongst the states. Even though a state like Texas may have a greater proportion of representatives than Delaware, in both cases the actual representatives are still chosen in a single-member district, winner-take-all style.

In the United States, these natural tendencies have been strengthened by legislation passed by the two major parties, which makes it more difficult for third parties to gain a foothold:

- ▶ Example: Only Democratic and Republican candidates automatically appear on the ballot; all other parties must petition to gain access.

- ▶ In spite of its diversity, the US generally has a high level of consensus on core issues. This is most likely a result of the fact that the nation was founded on a common ideology.

PRACTICE QUESTIONS

46) **Autocratic governments typically have which kind of party system?**

    A.   a single-party system

    B.   a two-party system

    C.   a multiparty system

    D.   no party system

47) **Which of the following is NOT true of multiparty systems?**

    A.   They lead to coalition governments.

    B.   They have parties with more radical views.

    C.   They result from single-member districts.

    D.   Parties seek to win a plurality of votes instead of a majority.

FOREIGN POLICY

Foreign policy describes how and why one nation interacts with the other nations of the world.

As new technologies emerge and the world becomes more interdependent, foreign policy has become an increasingly important part of any nation's governance. The goals for international engagement vary from country to country and even from moment to moment. These goals influence how policy is defined and communicated. Foreign policy goals include the following:

▶ protecting and increasing a nation's independence

▶ improving national security

▶ furthering economic advancement

▶ spreading political values to other nations

▶ gaining respect and prestige from other nations

▶ promoting stability and international peace

Nations use a variety of tools—military, economic, and political—to further their foreign policy goals:

▶ They may build up their military resources or position troops in strategic locations.

▶ At the most extreme, they can deploy troops to engage hostile nations or support allies.

▶ Economic tools can be used as either punishment or support.

    ▷ Example: A country may impose economic sanctions on another country to try to pressure it into changing an undesirable policy, or it may offer economic support in exchange for a favorable outcome.

▶ Countries may also use political pressure to influence the decisions of others by forming alliances or granting or withholding official recognition of another state.

While nations are the key players in foreign policy, the following also wield a great deal of influence:

▶ non-state ethnic minorities (Basque separatists in Spain, for example)

▶ world organizations

▶ multinational corporations

▷ While often indirect, these groups use many of the same tools to influence political leaders to form policy friendly to their own objectives.

American foreign policy has grown increasingly complex as the United States has undergone extensive changes in its relationship to the rest of the world since the eighteenth century.

In George Washington's Farewell Address, he warned against forming any "permanent alliances" with other nations. This call for **isolationism** set the tone for American foreign policy until the end of the nineteenth century. While not always successful—or even consistent—American political leaders maneuvered to keep the United States out of major foreign entanglements, especially European affairs. But as American economic interests and power increased, so did American engagement with the rest of the world.

The first half of the twentieth century saw divisions between groups favoring **internationalism** (more engagement in global affairs) and others favoring a return to isolationism.

After World War II, the United States became a global superpower, taking responsibility for affairs in and among countries around the world. With the end of the Cold War and the fall of the Soviet Union, the political landscape shifted again: there were no longer two major superpowers dictating the world's foreign policy.

As the world has become more globalized, the United States has responded with a shift in its foreign policy to one of **interdependence**—mutual reliance with and on other countries.

The president, as commander in chief and head diplomat, is the primary foreign policy leader and is supported from within the executive branch by the Secretary of State, the National Security Agency advisor, and the Secretary of Defense. Congress also plays a significant role as it controls the appropriation of money and declarations of war. The Senate also has the power to ratify treaties negotiated by the president and to control representation of the United States abroad by confirming diplomatic appointments.

48) The United States and the Cuban leader Fidel Castro were at odds following the Cuban Revolution. Which of the following is NOT an example of an attempt by the US to influence Cuba during the twentieth century?

    A.   encouraging emigration from Cuba to the United States

    B.   placing severe economic sanctions on Cuba

    C.   building a military base at Guantanamo Bay

    D.   supporting the failed Bay of Pigs invasion

49) What was US involvement in Europe after World War II an example of?

    A.   internationalism

    B.   isolationism

    C.   interdependence

    D.   none of the above

THEORIES OF INTERNATIONAL RELATIONS

The study of **international relations** is based around the idea that states always act in their own national interest. In deciding how to interact with other nations, they are always seeking to promote the foreign policy goals listed in the previous section. However, theorists disagree on which of those goals is of utmost importance. There are two main schools of thought: realism and liberalism.

First articulated by Hans J. Morgenthau, **realism** argues that a state's primary interest is self-preservation.

▶ Self-preservation can only be achieved by maximizing power.

▶ As a result, nations are always working to acquire more power relative to the power of other states.

▶ This theory is a direct continuation of Machiavelli's political theory: morality has no place in policy.

▶ Realists believe war is inevitable.

▶ Realists do not believe any kind of global policing (in the form of a supra-national law enforcement body) is truly possible:

    ▷ Its power would only extend as far as the world's nations allowed it.

    ▷ They would only allow it insofar as it did not diminish their own nation's individual power.

If all states are acting in their own self-interest, there is no room for global interest. Realism guided Cold War politics from both the US and Soviet perspectives.

Liberal theorists argue that realism is outdated. **Liberalism** emerged in the 1970s as the clear lines of the early Cold War became muddled and the consequences of military action—specifically in Vietnam—came to light.

▶ Globalization and international trade have created too many ties among nations to allow for each to truly have a national interest separate from that of other nations.

▶ Liberals argue that the world is now a system of complex interdependence, greatly decreasing the usefulness of military power.

    ▷ In fact, the consequences of military force usually outweigh the benefits, as it is impossible to strike another nation without serious repercussions in one's own.

    ▷ Instead, economic and social power are much more effective tools.

▶ Liberals acknowledge that different states will have different primary interests, but international cooperation is actually in the best interest of every state.

▶ Liberals also argue that international organizations and rules—policing and otherwise—help to foster that cooperation, build trust, and lead to prosperity for all.

▶ Idealists are a subgroup among liberals. **Idealism** moves even further away from realism.

▶ Idealists stand in direct opposition to Machiavelli, arguing that states must follow moral goals and act ethically in order to serve their best interest.

▶ Woodrow Wilson's Fourteen Points envisioned a world beyond war and conflict: peace and prosperity through moral foreign policy.

PRACTICE QUESTIONS

50) **Which of the following actions follows a realist approach?**

    A. creating the United Nations

    B. building the Berlin Wall

    C. imposing economic sanctions on Russia following conflict with Ukraine

    D. sending economic aid to Afghanistan

51) In 1994, over half a million people were killed in Rwanda during a genocide that lasted only a few weeks. An idealist response by the United States to this tragedy would have been to

  A. take no action.

  B. declare war on Rwanda.

  C. insist that the UN or other international organizations take action.

  D. impose economic sanctions on Rwanda.

CURRENT GLOBAL RELATIONS

Realism and liberalism describe how various theorists think nations should act; they have also dictated foreign policy over time:

- ▶ Realism guided policy in the eighteenth, nineteenth, and first half of the twentieth centuries.

  - ▷ It resulted in the rise of the nation-state in the eighteenth century, widespread nationalism throughout the nineteenth, the rise of global colonialism, and the development of imperialism among Western European countries, Russia, and the United States.

- ▶ Although liberalism was not articulated as a theory until the 1970s, its guiding principles began to emerge at the end of the nineteenth century.

  - ▷ Ideology and "isms" replaced the domineering policies of the previous centuries.

From the second half of the twentieth century to this day, another shift is occurring:

- ▶ Technological advancement and globalization have reshaped global politics, led to increased interdependence, and given greater influence to transnational organizations and nongovernment entities (terrorist groups, for example).

Today, **international organizations** are as important as individual nations to global politics. There are two types of international organizations: nongovernmental organizations (NGOs) and intergovernmental organizations (IGOs).

⟶
Go on

Table 3.12. IGOs and NGOs

Type of International Organization	Description
Nongovernmental Organizations (NGOs)	• funded primarily by individuals or foundations • provide services or advocate for certain policy positions within a particular nation or across national borders • vary widely in their missions, their ideologies, and their practices but all work outside of national governments • entirely private, and therefore operate under a loose definition • vary from highly religious or political in nature to intentional avoidance of all such associations • address issues such as health care, the environment, human rights, and development • approximately 1.5 million NGOs in the US alone; millions more worldwide
Intergovernmental Organizations (IGOs)	• comprised of individual sovereign nations (they can also be made up of other IGOs) • official governing bodies that must adhere to international legal guidelines • to be created, all participating members must sign (and ratify) a treaty establishing the organization's existence and outlining its mission and functioning; not all treaties create IGOs

The following are three examples of NGOs:

DID YOU KNOW?

The North American Free Trade Agreement (NAFTA) does not create an official organization, although the signatories may need to meet from time to time to ensure its proper implementation.

1. Doctors without Borders, an independent group that provides medical services on a global scale where it is most needed

2. World Wildlife Fund, an environmental organization with an international scope

3. Amnesty International, an independent group that works to address injustices throughout the world

Three examples of IGOs follow.

The North Atlantic Treaty Organization (NATO) is an organization of countries that pledged to come to each other's defense in case of external aggression, mainly in response to the threat posed by the Soviet Union.

▶ was created after World War II

▶ original members were ten Western European nations, the US, and Canada

▶ currently has thirty member states

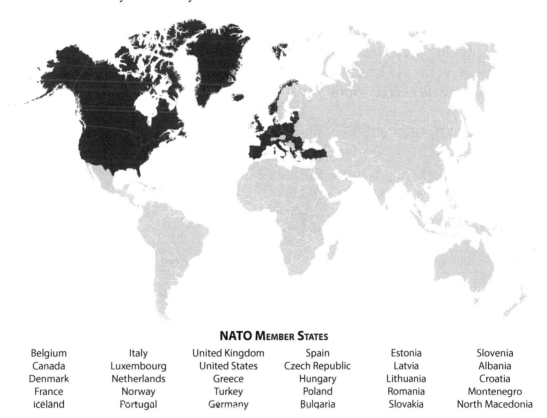

NATO MEMBER STATES

Belgium	Italy	United Kingdom	Spain	Estonia	Slovenia
Canada	Luxembourg	United States	Czech Republic	Latvia	Albania
Denmark	Netherlands	Greece	Hungary	Lithuania	Croatia
France	Norway	Turkey	Poland	Romania	Montenegro
Iceland	Portugal	Germany	Bulgaria	Slovakia	North Macedonia

Figure 3.12. NATO Member States

The United Nations (UN) was the second attempt at an international organization dedicated to promoting world peace. While it is a significant player in world politics, its effectiveness is often questioned as it has very limited military power and is subject to the consent of its members.

▶ created after World War II

- addresses economic, health, social, cultural, and humanitarian issues throughout the world

- currently has 193 member states

The United Nations is made up of several components, each dedicated to one of its focus areas. The most powerful is the **Security Council**, which is tasked with the maintenance of international security and peace.

- It must approve the application of any country seeking admission to the United Nations before it can be voted on by the General Assembly.

- The Security Council is composed of five permanent members—the United States, Great Britain, Russia, China, and France—and ten elected members who serve two-year terms.

- Each of the permanent members holds veto power and can single-handedly stop any Security Council resolution. The affirmative vote of each permanent member—as well as two-thirds of the General Assembly—is needed to amend the UN charter.

The primary purpose of **the World Bank** is to eliminate poverty in the world. However—a product of its time—it is also designed to support and encourage the growth of capitalism. The World Bank:

CHECK YOUR UNDERSTANDING #5

What is the key difference between an IGO and an NGO?

- was created after World War II

- provides loans to developing nations for capital projects

- works closely with the United Nations

Today, the World Bank has eight primary goals:

1. to eradicate extreme poverty and hunger

2. to achieve universal education

3. to promote gender equality

4. to reduce infant mortality

5. to improve maternal health

6. to combat highly infectious diseases like HIV/AIDS and malaria

7. to ensure environmental sustainability

8. to develop a global partnership for development

PRACTICE QUESTIONS

52) **Which of the following is NOT an example of an NGO?**

A. Greenpeace

B. Wikimedia Foundation

C. Oxfam

D. the World Trade Organization

53) **Which of the following issues would be addressed by the United Nations?**

A. the voting age in France

B. the election of the president of the United States

C. the national highway system in Canada

D. disarmament after civil war in Sierra Leone

PRACTICE QUESTIONS ANSWER KEY

1) **C.** In Little Rock, the governor of Arkansas, Orval Faubus, refused to enforce the Supreme Court-ordered integration of the public schools. President Eisenhower sent troops to Little Rock to enforce national authority over a noncompliant state. This was an internal matter, not a matter of state sovereignty.

2) **A.** Both former West and East German citizens recognized the newly unified German Federal Republic as the legal and political authority over both territories. Bringing the national capital back to Berlin legitimized the government in the eyes of the East, while maintaining the western currency and many western laws did so in the West.

3) **B.** Montesquieu believed that the separation of powers into three branches of government was essential to the success of a republic.

4) **A.** The inalienable rights described in the Declaration of Independence, "life, liberty, and the pursuit of happiness," are a direct reference to the natural rights described by John Locke. The only variation: "pursuit of happiness" rather than "property," is seen as an expansion by Thomas Jefferson on Locke's original theory.

5) **D.** Social contract theory argues that government is the natural consequence of individuals' attempts to protect their natural rights.

As a result, individuals agree to turn over some of their sovereignty to a governing body in order to best enjoy those rights. Central to social contract theory is the idea that the people ultimately hold the power and can either allow a government to exist or remove it if it does not serve its purpose.

6) **B.** Machiavelli was a pragmatist rather than a theorist. His writing focused on the best way for actual rulers to govern, rather than on determining the philosophical sources of their right to rule.

7) **C.** Protection of the environment is a central liberal goal. Because liberals view government as a vehicle for the improvement of society, they believe the government has a duty to actively protect nature for its citizens.

8) **D.** A libertarian would certainly support lower taxes. In fact, a libertarian would likely argue for a complete repeal of taxes. Taxes are collected in order to support government activity, most of which is opposed by libertarians. In their view, lowering taxes returns the money to the hands of the individual where it belongs. A liberal, however, would oppose lowering taxes. The money collected from taxes is used to support social programs which they believe are the responsibility of the government and are necessary for a stronger, more effective country.

9) **B.** The perceived tyranny of Britain's rule was fresh on the minds of the framers. Their primary goal was to prevent it from re-emerging.

10) **D.** Fear of an overpowering central government was the primary factor considered in writing the Articles of Confederation.

11) **B.** The inability of the federal government to suppress the rebellion showed a major weakness in the new government.

12) **D.** Merchants' income relied on trade, which disintegrated under the Articles of Confederation. They required strong trade relationships with other countries, as well as clear laws governing trade between the various states.

13) **D.** The Constitution provides for the direct election of representatives (to the House of Representatives) to establish the sovereignty of the people. By selecting their leaders, the people are endowing these individuals with the authority to make governing decisions.

14) **A.** In a government ruled by man, those who make and enforce the laws would be exempt from following them. However, in the United States, even those in authority are subject to punishment if they do not respect the rule of law.

15) **B.** Each state government is a democratic republic in which authority is derived from the consent of the governed.

16) **C.** With the authority to approve treaties, the Senate can review and even restrain presidential foreign policy. One example of this was the Senate's rejection of the Treaty of Versailles, which ended World War I in 1919. Although President Wilson signed the treaty and was even one of its chief architects, the Senate refused to ratify it. As a result, the United States was never a party to the treaty or part of the League of Nations.

17) **D.** Article I of the Constitution states that Congress has the power to coin money.

18) **C.** Federal, state, and local governments all have the authority to hold elections.

19) **A.** While Congress was designed to be more efficient and effective than the Congress of the Confederation, which was able to achieve very little, it was still divided into two houses with complicated structures in order to prevent a consolidation of power through quick legislation.

20) **C.** An inability to levy taxes crippled the first federal government, making it unable to pay off its debt or function in any legitimate way.

21) **C.** The vice president's role in the Senate has nothing to do with the influence of states on the national government; instead, it is a way for the executive branch to check the legislative branch.

22) **D.** The framers thought it was important that those who spent the money be held most accountable to the people to avoid corruption and misuse.

23) **B.** This process for selecting a presidential nominee was created by the political parties and is not addressed at all in the Constitution.

24) **C.** Under the Articles of Confederation, they had seen the danger of putting too high of a premium on individual liberty. While it was still

one of the highest priorities for them, the needs of the nation had to come first.

25) **B.** Based on Section 2 of Article II of the Constitution, the cabinet is the formalization of the president's right to seek advice from the heads of the executive departments.

26) **D.** There are no specific requirements for the vice president in the Constitution; however, because the person in that role must be able to step in for the president, it is implied that the vice president must meet the same criteria as the president.

27) **D.** While the Constitution does permit the president to seek the advice of executive department heads, it does not explicitly create a body like the cabinet which meets regularly with the president.

28) **C.** United States presidents lead public policy using legislation promoted through various executive departments, their presidential role as leader of their party, and the State of the Union address.

29) **A.** As Chief Executive, the president is responsible for the management of the federal bureaucracy and all of the federal departments.

30) **C.** The Electoral College is designed to balance the power of the states and best represent their interests without allowing a single state to dominate.

31) **D.** The court endowed itself with the power of judicial review in the case of *Marbury v. Madison*.

32) **A.** The framers were very concerned about judges making unfair decisions based on fears of job security or political allegiances.

33) **C.** Several cases during the 1960s expanded the rights of defendants in court. Two of the most notable were *Miranda v. Arizona* and *Gideon v. Wainwright*.

34) **B.** Amicus briefs are written by organizations, agencies, or other groups who hope to influence the court to take a particular decision.

35) **C.** Incorrectly alleging that someone is a member of a hate group is considered libel (if written) or slander (if spoken). This is not protected by the Constitution.

36) **D.** There is no fundamental right to public nudity. Nudity generally falls under the right to privacy; however, when it becomes a public act, the individual's rights only extend as far as those of others in society.

37) **A.** The government has no authority to restrict people's beliefs. They may, however, restrict religious activity if it violates other laws.

38) **B.** The exclusionary rule prohibits any evidence obtained illegally from being used at trial.

39) **C.** While the appointment of Supreme Court justices can certainly be very political, their lifetime terms are constitutionally mandated and unrelated to political parties.

40) **D.** This is by far the most significant role third parties play. They are able to discuss more controversial issues and espouse more radical positions. This often pushes the major parties to discuss the issues as well and take a stand.

41) **A.** This organization was formed around the issue of tax reform. People who are interested in this issue then join this group.

42) **B.** Lobbyists are a resource for legislators and their aides can influence their thinking on a particular topic.

43) **D.** Politicians are always trying to find the best way to connect to their constituencies; therefore, they must be adaptable to new media as it emerges. Also, new media changes the way in which politics is reported, which then changes the way it functions.

44) **B.** In a democratic republic, power is distributed across multiple branches of government.

45) **C.** An autocratic government in which power is maintained by force is a dictatorship.

46) **A.** Because autocratic governments are controlled by one person or a small group of people, challenges to their authority are unwelcome; however, party affiliation usually indicates members of the ruling group and gives a semblance of democracy.

47) **C.** Two-party systems result from single-member districts where there is a winner-takes-all race for each individual seat. In a multiparty system, seats are apportioned based on the percentage of the vote

received by each party.

48) **C.** The US military base at Guantanamo Bay was established before the Cuban Revolution.

49) **A.** Learning from worldwide depression and the rise of totalitarianism after World War I, the US took on the responsibility of aiding the quick rebuilding of Western Europe. This is a clear example of internationalist foreign policy.

50) **B.** East Germany built the Berlin Wall in order to prevent defections to the West. This is an example of self-preservation.

51) **C.** Idealists would insist on intervention as the only moral option. They would also believe in the enforcement power of an international organization like the UN to maintain peace.

52) **D.** The World Trade Organization is an IGO that governs the rules of trade between nations.

53) **D.** From 1999 to 2005, the UN stationed peacekeeping troops in Sierra Leone to disarm combatants after the country's civil war. Creating a stable and peaceful Sierra Leone was directly in line with the UN's mission to promote global peace. In this mission, the UN destroyed more than 42,000 weapons and 1.2 million rounds of ammunition.

CHECK YOUR UNDERSTANDING ANSWER KEY

Check Your Understanding #1

Liberals: Government effects positive change; government should regulate economy, implement social programs, and intervene economically to promote equality; government should not limit citizens' rights; implied rights are supported.

Conservatives: The individual and private sector effect positive change; government is ineffective at solving social problems; government should be limited; government interference only to facilitate operation of the individual or private entity; free market should solve economic problems.

Check Your Understanding #2

Government could not levy taxes or raise an army; there was no national judicial system or currency; it was nearly impossible to change the Articles.

Check Your Understanding #3

religion, assembly, petition, press, speech (RAPPS)

Check Your Understanding #4

Political parties, interest groups, and mass media all connect people to the government.

Check Your Understanding #5

Nongovernmental organizations (NGOs) are privately funded. They offer services or advocate for policy positions, with a wide variety of missions.

Intergovernmental organizations (IGOs) are composed of individual sovereign nations or other IGOs. They are official governing bodies and must follow international legal guidelines.

4

Principles of Geography

WHAT IS GEOGRAPHY?

In its most basic form, geography is the study of space; more specifically, it studies the physical space of the earth and the ways in which it interacts with, shapes, and is shaped by its habitants.

Geographers look at the world from a spatial perspective. This means that at the center of all geographic study is the question, *Where?* For geographers, the *where* of any interaction, event, or development is a crucial element to understanding it.

This question of *where* can be asked in a variety of fields of study, so there are many subdisciplines of geography. These can be organized into four main categories:

▶ regional studies, which examine the characteristics of a particular place

▶ topical studies, which look at a single physical or human feature that impacts the whole world

▶ physical studies, which focus on Earth's physical features

▶ human studies, which examine the relationship between human activity and the environment

THE FIVE THEMES OF GEOGRAPHY

Geographers ask three main questions:

1. Where? (a starting point question)

2. Why is it there?

3. What are the consequences of it being there?

DID YOU KNOW?

Chicago is an example of the human impact on the environment. In 1900, engineers successfully reversed the flow of the river so that it pulled water from Lake Michigan rather than feeding into it.

Asking these latter two questions helps geographers engage in real study.

To answer these questions, geographers have developed five themes of geography. Each of these addresses the basic geographic questions, and all of geography can be organized around these five themes.

Table 4.1. The Five Themes of Geography and the Questions They Ask

Theme	Question Asked	Example
Location	• Where is it specifically located?	• the address of someone's house or a description of where it is in the neighborhood
Place	• Why is it there? • What is it like there? • What are its qualities and characteristics?	• a description of the neighborhood where a house is found
Region	• Why is it there? • What do different areas have in common and why?	• comparing that neighborhood to others in the area
Human-environment interaction	• What are the consequences of it being there? • How do humans shape the environment and how does the environment shape them?	• the development of cities • steep streets in San Francisco as a result of the physical landscape on which it is built
Movement	• What are the consequences of it being there? • How do places connect to and interact with one another?	• blues music spreading from the South into the rest of the United States and beyond

PRACTICE QUESTIONS

1) **Which of the following is NOT an example of geographic study?**

   A. patterns of volcanic eruptions

   B. climate change and global warming

   C. settlement patterns in Southern Europe

   D. the rise and fall of the American dollar

2) **Migration patterns are an example of which geographic theme?**

   A. location

   B. place

   C. movement

   D. region

LOCATION

Location is the most specific and concrete of the themes. It simply describes where something can be found on Earth. A location can be **relative** or absolute.

In **relative location**, the object in question is positioned in relation to something else.

▶ Relative location is most often used in informal settings.

▶ Example: If a family says their house is located two blocks north of the school, they are providing a relative location for the house.

Absolute location is generally used in formal geographic settings.

▶ A location is absolute when it is described by its position on Earth, without reference to other landmarks.

▶ Example: The tallest building in the world—the Burj Khalifa—is located at 25.2°N and 55.3°E.

Something's location can also be described by either its site or situation.

Description by **site**:

▶ This is when a place is described by its internal physical and cultural characteristics.

▶ Example: The site of a football stadium could be described by the number of seats, the field, the JumboTron, the concession stands, and even the screaming fans.

Description by **situation**:

▶ When a place is described by its **situation**, its characteristics are described relative to those around it.

▶ Example: The football stadium might be described by its relative size as compared to the other buildings in the city, its accessibility, or the amount of foot traffic it receives.

▶ The more connected a location is to powerful places, the better its situation; therefore, the front row of seats in a stadium is better situated than the top row.

MAPS

Because of Earth's size, it is difficult to articulate and visualize the absolute location of a place or thing; instead, illustrations are used.

To make the information more manageable, the scale can be adjusted, allowing these illustrations to communicate more detailed and complete information quickly and effectively. Globes and maps are illustrations used to show location.

Globes are spherical representations, or models, of Earth:

▶ They show the correct size, shape, and location of land masses, and the accurate distance between places on Earth.

▶ Because globes are models for the entire Earth, it is impossible for them to provide much detail.

Maps are flat representations of Earth or its parts:

▶ Because they are flat, maps can range in what they illustrate, from a single park to the entire planet.

▶ The more specific the area of a map covers, the more detailed it can be.

▶ Maps do, however, have drawbacks which will be discussed later in this section.

Whether map or globe, both types of illustrations use the same system for identifying location. This is known as the **grid system**.

The earth is divided by imaginary, equidistant lines running vertically and horizontally to create a grid. Each line is measured as a **degree** (°), which can be subdivided into **minutes** (′) and **seconds** (″).

The lines that run horizontally around the earth, parallel to the equator, are called lines of **latitude**:

▶ Degrees of latitude are numbered 0° to 90° running north and south from the equator (the equator is 0°).

▶ In actuality, there are approximately 69 miles between each degree of latitude. This number shifts slightly because Earth is not a true sphere but rather slightly egg-shaped.

HELPFUL HINT

An easy way to distinguish between longitude and latitude is to remember that lines of longitude are "long," so they stretch from pole to pole. Lines of latitude lie "flat" (*flat-itude latitude*) and run horizontally.

The lines that run north and south from pole to pole are called lines of **longitude**, or **meridians**. Because there is no natural center of the earth when measuring this way (like the equator), a 0° line was established by international agreement. Called the **prime meridian**, it is the line that runs through the Royal Observatory in Greenwich, England. Meridians are then numbered up to 180° running east and west of this line.

The organization of time zones is loosely based on the meridians. Each time zone represents approximately 15°. Time is measured as an offset of Universal Coordinated Time (a system that measures time based on Earth's rotation).

This is a general rule, but there are many exceptions. For example, China uses one time zone for the entire country.

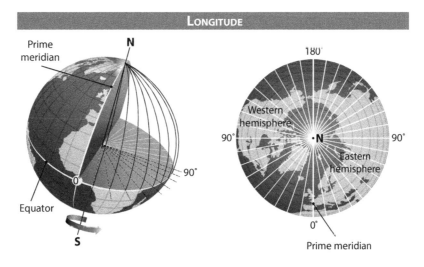

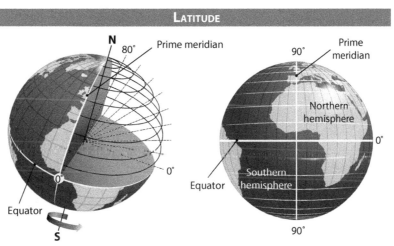

Figure 4.1. Longitude and Latitude

While the flat nature of maps provides greater flexibility in terms of focus and scale, representing something spherical—Earth—as flat inevitably leads to distortion.

Every map is a **projection**, a representation of Earth's features on a flat surface. There are different ways to do this, but every projection has four main properties:

▶ the size of areas

▶ the shape of areas

▶ consistency of scales

▶ straight line directions

HELPFUL HINT

At approximately 180° opposite the prime meridian is the International Date Line. This is where the date changes in order to allow the global time zone system to work.

No map is able to accurately depict all four of these properties: every projection must sacrifice accuracy in at least one.

In general, mapmakers choose to maintain the accuracy of one property and distort the others as needed. The perspective of the mapmaker and the purpose of the map determine which property is maintained:

On an equal area map, the accuracy of the size of areas is maintained. Each land mass is kept to scale in its size:

▶   Example: The **Gall-Peters** projection distorts the shape of land masses in order to preserve land mass size.

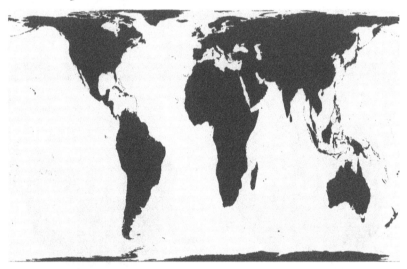

Figure 4.2. Gall-Peters Projection

Conformal maps maintain the shape of areas at the expense of accuracy in size. The most used conformal map is the **Mercator** projection:

▶   It uses straight lines for latitude and longitude, rather than curving them to indicate Earth's curve

▶   It is made by wrapping the paper into a cylinder around a globe, called a **cylindrical projection**.

▶   The scale is accurate only at the equator or at two parallels equidistant from the equator. The farther from the equator, the more enlarged land masses appear.

▶   It is used primarily for marine navigation.

The **azimuthal equidistant projection** maintains accuracy in scale for distances from one single point on the map to all other points on the map:

▶   It is most often used to show airplane routes from one city to multiple other cities.

Figure 4.3. Mercator Projection

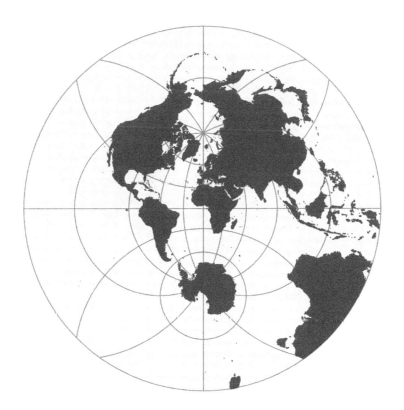

Figure 4.4. Azimuthal Equidistant Projection

A **gnomonic projection** preserves the property of accuracy of distance. Every straight line on a gnomonic projection is the arc of a **great circle**, which represents the shortest distance between any two points on the earth.

A **great circle** is any circle that bisects a sphere. In most projections, great circles are curved due to distortion resulting in the maintenance of one or more other properties; the gnomonic projection is the exception:

▶   This projection is particularly useful in navigation by sea or air where direction—for its own sake—is important.

▶   It is also often used to map the poles which are usually highly distorted in other map projections.

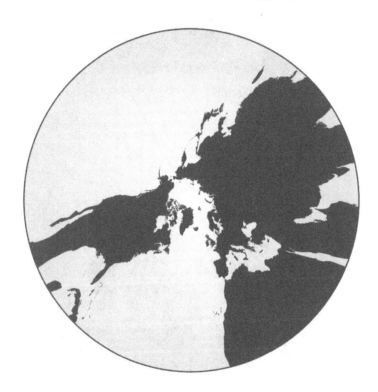

Figure 4.5. Gnomonic Projection

The most commonly used maps are some sort of **compromise map**, meaning they distort all four properties to some degree in order to minimize distortion overall. The most popular of these are the **Robinson projection** and the **Winkel Tripel projection**:

▶   From 1988 to 1998, the National Geographic Society used the Robinson projection for all of its world maps. It was then replaced with the Winkel Tripel projection, which has less area distortion at the poles.

▶ Both projections balance size and shape, with minor distortions in each.

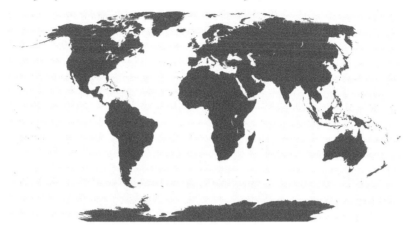

Figure 4.6. Robinson and Winkel Tripel Projection

Most maps have five main tools to aid in the reader's understanding.

Table 4.2. Map Tools

Title	• provides a description of the purpose of the map as well as the area of focus.
	• Without a title, the reader would not know what the map is depicting.
Scale	• tells the reader the relationship between the unit of measurement used on the map and real distances on the earth
	• important when using a map for distance or navigation
Grid	• consists of lines placed on the map to aid in finding locations
	• often based on lines of longitude and latitude
	• maps of smaller areas will use different, more effective grid systems for their size
Legend	• explains the meaning of any symbols used
	• For example, a dot map showing population would have a legend explaining how many people are represented by each dot.
Compass rose	• indicates the four directions: north, south, east, and west
	• allows the user to properly orient the map and accurately identify direction

Some maps are designed to illustrate information other than absolute location, direction, land mass, and shape. **Contour maps** illustrate varying levels of elevation in an area. Rather than having the standard markings of latitude and longitude

CHECK YOUR UNDERSTANDING #1

Use a map to determine which city is at N 41.9°, E 12.5°.

lines, the lines on the map connect points of equal elevation, with the provided scale indicating the distance between the lines. **Relief maps** also depict elevation, but through shading to create a three-dimensional effect, rather than the drawing of lines.

An **isothermal map** is used to illustrate ranges of temperature. Much like contour maps, the lines are used to show areas of equal or constant temperature.

PRACTICE QUESTIONS

3)   In a conformal map, areas are represented accurately in terms of which of the following?

   A.   shape

   B.   size

   C.   direction

   D.   all of the above

4)   Which of the following is an advantage of globes over maps?

   A.   Globes provide more detailed information.

   B.   Globes can be used to show a variety of sizes of areas.

   C.   Globes are accurate models of Earth without distortion.

   D.   Globes show elevation levels in addition to size, shape, and location of areas.

5)   To determine the distance between Tokyo and Shanghai on a map of Asia, which of the following parts of the map would be used?

   A.   compass rose

   B.   scale

   C.   legend

   D.   grid

6)   A scientist exploring Antarctica would most likely use which type of map?

   A.   equal Area projection

   B.   azimuthal equidistant projection

   C.   conformal projection

   D.   gnomonic projection

MENTAL MAPS

While most maps are illustrations, some maps exist inside an individual's mind. These are called **mental maps** and are an individual's internal representation of the physical and human aspects of the earth.

Some mental maps are very much localized, such as mental maps of someone's own bedroom or house, for example.

Others are regional or even global. For example, one's understanding of the location of oceans or the continents would constitute a mental map.

Mental maps are constructed from both direct experiences—actually being in a place—and indirect experiences—such as reading about a place in a magazine or looking at a friend's vacation pictures. As a result, they have elements that are both objective and subjective. Example:

▶ There is a four-story building in a residential neighborhood.

▶ Its presence is an objective fact.

▶ A local resident's perception of the distance between the building and that person's home, or the resident's understanding of how the building is accessed, could be subjective elements.

> **HELPFUL HINT**
>
> When examining mental maps, it is important to consider both what the map indicates and what the map does not indicate (in other words, what the individual or group does *NOT* account for).

Mental maps are gateways into understanding perspectives not only of individuals but of entire cultures.

PRACTICE QUESTIONS

7) **Which of the following is NOT an accurate description of a mental map?**

A. Mental maps always reflect a personal location.

B. Mental maps can be based in both fact and perception.

C. Mental maps are studied in order to understand different cultures.

D. Mental maps can be based on both direct and indirect understandings of a place.

8) **A teacher asks two students in her class to describe the school's gymnasium. Student A—a basketball player—describes it as being in the middle of the school, with bleachers, high ceilings, bright lights, two basketball hoops, and markings on the floor. Student B—a soccer player—describes it as down the hall from the main office, small, stuffy, and poorly lit. What conclusion may be drawn about the mental maps of these two students?**

A. Student A has a more accurate mental map of the gymnasium than Student B.

B. Student B's mental map is clouded by his or her dislike of basketball.

C. Neither Student A nor Student B has constructed a useful mental map of the gymnasium.

D. Both Students A and B have constructed mental maps influenced by their relationship to the gym and their respective sports.

PLACE

The second theme of geography—place—is directly related to location. If location answers the question, *Where?*, place answers the question, *What?*

To describe a geographic place is to describe all of the characteristics—both human and physical—of a location.

Physical attributes:

▶   climate

▶   terrain

▶   natural resources

Human attributes:

▶   language

▶   religion

▶   art

▶   political organization

▶   customs.

Different geographers focus on different aspects of place, but understanding place is at the core of any geographic study.

PHYSICAL CHARACTERISTICS OF PLACE

To describe a place physically, five main categories must be addressed: **land**, **water**, **climate**, **vegetation**, and **animal life**, with the latter two dependent on the first three.

Land forms categorize areas by elevation: **mountains**, **hills**, **foothills**, and **plateaus** on one hand; **plains** and **valleys** on the other. They also describe areas created by water:

▶   **deltas**—the flat plains created by deposits from diverging branches of a river

▶   **basins**—the bowl-like land that catches water and directs it toward a river

▶   **marshes**—wetlands that are frequently inundated with water

▶   **swamps**—any wetland primarily covered in woody plants

Geographers also look at **soil**: how fertile it is, the kind of life it can support, and how easily it is shaped by wind and water.

Bodies of water can be subdivided into several categories as well. The biggest bodies of water are Earth's five oceans:

- The **Atlantic Ocean** separates North and South America from Europe and Africa.

- The **Pacific Ocean**—covering almost one-third of the earth—separates North and South America from Asia and Australia.

- The **Indian Ocean** touches Africa, Asia, and Australia.

- The **Arctic Ocean** extends from the northern edge of North America and Europe to the North Pole and is composed primarily of ice for much of the year.

- The **Southern**, or **Antarctic Ocean** extends from the southern tips of South America and Africa to Antarctica.

In addition to these, there are other bodies of saline water called **seas**, which are smaller than oceans and surrounded—in part or wholly—by land:

- The largest sea is the **Mediterranean Sea**.

- The largest fully enclosed sea (or salted lake) is the **Caspian Sea**.

- Land-bound freshwater bodies of water are called lakes and can be found in varying sizes throughout the world.

DID YOU KNOW?

Canada has a particularly high concentration of lakes: more than 60 percent of Earth's lakes can be found there.

Finally, and most important for the development of civilization, are **rivers**, bodies of water that flow toward the ocean. The world's major river systems all gave birth to early and complex civilizations:

- Nile

- Tigris and Euphrates

- Indus

- Ganges

- Huang He (Yellow River)

- Yangtze

- Amazon

- Mississippi

HELPFUL HINT

While the majority of lakes are freshwater, there are some that are saltwater. The biggest example of these is the Great Salt Lake in Utah.

Climate is the average weather for a specific location or region.

▶ It is based on monthly and yearly temperatures as well as the length of the **growing season** (which then has a direct impact on human characteristics of a place).

▶ Climate is shaped by the latitude of a location, the amount of moisture it receives, and the temperatures of both land and water.

▶ Varying climates create different **ecosystems**, the communities of living organisms and nonliving elements of an area. These are discussed more in depth later in this chapter.

PRACTICE QUESTIONS

9) **Which of the following is NOT a physical characteristic of Switzerland?**

   A. mountain chains on both the northern and southern sides of the country

   B. three river valleys

   C. shared borders with Germany, France, Italy, Austria, and Liechtenstein

   D. over 1,400 lakes

10) **Which of the following statements best illustrates the geographic theme of place?**

   A. Northern Mali is primarily composed of desert.

   B. St. Louis is approximately 300 miles from Chicago.

   C. Beijing is located at approximately N 40°, E 116°.

   D. English is the dominant language in North America as well as Australia.

REGION

A **region** is a group of places that share common characteristics, whether human or physical. Regions can be large—incorporating multiple continents—or quite small.

Table 4.3. Types of Regions

Type of Region	Description
Formal region	• shared characteristics define the region • Example: The Middle East is a formal region, as the area has common physical and cultural traits.
Functional region	• an area defined by common movement or function • have a focal point (a node) around which they are organized, related to their function • Example: A school district is a functional region organized around a school (or set of schools).

Table 4.3. Types of Regions

Type of Region	Description
Perceptual region	• areas grouped not by actual commonalities but by perceived ones • Example: Africa is often addressed as a single region, even though the continent has a large number of differing cultural systems and physical characteristics.

To analyze global phenomena, geographers divide the world into **realms**, the largest logical regions possible. Realms are based on clusters of human population, economic, political, cultural, and physical traits.

There are twelve widely accepted realms:

1. Sub Saharan Africa
2. North Africa and Southwest Asia
3. Europe
4. Russia
5. South Asia
6. East Asia
7. Southeast Asia
8. North America
9. Middle America
10. South America
11. the Austral Realm
12. the Pacific Realms

DID YOU KNOW?

Asia and North America are so large that their interiors are not subject to the ocean winds.

Regions are not static and can change over time. The borders of regions are also often not sharply defined, but instead gradually shift from one region to the next. The areas between regions, then, are called **transition zones**. Transition zones are marked by a greater diversity of cultural traits. Furthermore, they more often experience conflict.

Human geographers study regions the way they study place, applying the same concepts on a larger scale. While regions are defined primarily by their commonalities, geographers often study them in order to create comparisons. For example, they might look at economic development, the growth of religions, or gender roles in different regions.

The various theories and models apply as well. Geographers can use the demographic transition model (DTM) to understand demographic growth in a region as a whole, not just a specific place.

In physical geography, one of the key ways regions are organized is by climate. These regions are called **biomes**. Earth's biomes, or ecosystems, can be divided by latitude, with different latitudes having different climates.

HELPFUL HINT

In the low and high latitudes, the farther north, the drier the climate. In the middle latitudes, distance from the ocean determines how wet or dry the climate is.

Table 4.4. Earth's Biomes

Climate	Description of Climate
Low latitudes (from the equator to latitudes 23.5° north and south)	
Tropical rainforests	• found in the equatorial lowlands • experience intense sun and rain every day • Temperatures rarely go above 90°F, but the combination of sun and rain creates high humidity levels, leading to extreme heat.
Savannah	• found north and south of the rainforest • dry in the winter; wet in the summer • experiences an average of ten to thirty inches of rain • Temperatures generally stay below 90°F with lower temperatures (under 80°F) in the winter.
Desert • Sahara Desert • Australian Outback • Arabian Desert	• lies beyond the savannah to the north and south • the hottest and driest parts of the earth • fewer than ten inches of rainfall a year • Temperatures swing widely from extreme heat during the day to extreme cold at night.
Middle latitudes (from latitudes 23.5° to 66.5° north and south)	
• a greater variety of climates determined more by proximity to water than by exact latitude • contain three climates that receive the most rain and are the most fertile	
Mediterranean climate • Mediterranean area • southwest Africa • southern and southwestern Australia • Black Sea area • Chile • southern California	• found in lands between latitudes 30° and 40° north and south that lie along the western coast • features hot summers and mild winters • rainy winters; generally dry summers • allows a year-round growing season

Table 4.4. Earth's Biomes

Climate	Description of Climate
Middle latitudes (from latitudes 23.5° to 66.5° north and south)	
• a greater variety of climates determined more by proximity to water than by exact latitude	
• contain three climates that receive the most rain and are the most fertile	

Humid subtropical climate

• Japan	• located on coastal areas north and south of the tropics
• southeastern China	• receives warm ocean currents and warm winds year round; warm and moist climate
• northeastern India	
• southeastern South Africa	• long, wet summers; short, mild winters
	• long growing season
• the southeastern United States	• supports the greatest percentage of the world's population
• parts of South America	

Marine climate

• Western Europe	
• the British Isles	
• the Pacific Northwest	• very temperate weather
• southern Chile	• winters rarely below freezing; summers below 70°F
• southern New Zealand	• warm and rainy, resulting in part from the warm ocean winds
• southeastern Australia	
• western coast of Canada	

Humid continental climate

• northern and central United States	• the true four-season climate
• south-central and south-eastern Canada	• varying average temperatures based on distance from the ocean
• northern China	• fertile land
• the western and south-eastern parts of the former Soviet bloc	• warm, hot, humid summers; cold to extremely cold winters
	• evenly distributed precipitation throughout the year

Steppe (grassland or prairie)	• dry flatlands with minimal rainfall (ten to twenty inches annually)
• interiors of North America and Asia	• can become deserts if rainfall consistently dips below ten inches per year
	• hot summers; very cold winters

continued on next page

Table 4.4. Earth's Biomes (continued)

Climate	Description of Climate
High latitudes (66.5° north and south to the poles)	
Tundra	• extremely cold and long winters • frozen ground for most of the year; mushy ground during short summer • low precipitation; less snow than the eastern United States • no arable land; home to few people • abundant plant life close to the ground; vibrant animal life
Taiga • Northern Russia • Sweden • Norway • Finland • Canada • Alaska	• south of the tundra • home to the world's largest forestlands • contains many swamps and marshes • farther from the ocean; more extreme temperatures • very short growing season; meaningful agriculture not possible • sparsely populated (due to lack of growing season) • distinctive and extreme mineral wealth

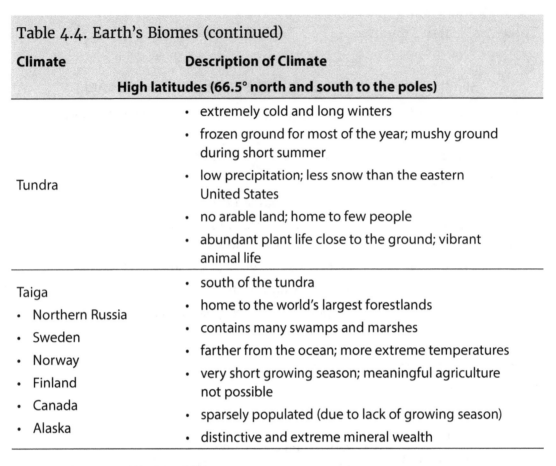

■ Tundra
▨ Taiga
▦ Temperate deciduous forest
▤ Grassland
▦ Tropical rainforest
☐ Desert

Figure 4.7. The World's Biomes

DID YOU KNOW?

Tundra means "marshy plain" in Russian; taiga means "northern forest."

PRACTICE QUESTIONS

11) Which ecosystem experiences extreme temperatures—both hot and cold—in a single day?

A.   tundra

B.   rainforest

C.   desert

D.   savannah

12) A congressional district is an example of which kind of region?

A.   a functional region

B.   a formal region

C.   a perceptual region

D.   a node region

13) According to the map below, if biome 1 is tundra, which type of ecosystem is represented by biome 2?

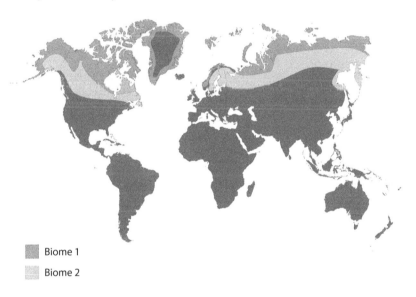

Biome 1

Biome 2

A.   marine

B.   taiga

C.   desert

D.   steppe

HUMAN CHARACTERISTICS OF PLACE

The human characteristics of a location or region make up its **culture**:

▶   shared values

▶   language

▶   religion

▶ the ways in which people feed, clothe, and shelter themselves

Cultures can be very specific or regional, like **folk cultures**, or they can be diffuse and widespread, like **popular culture**.

THE STUDY OF CULTURE

Cultural geographers study the ways in which each of these characteristics is shaped by the physical characteristics of a place:

The **material components** of a culture are a key area of study for cultural geographers. Material components include physical artifacts that can be left behind, like a bowl or a religious icon.

The **nonmaterial components** of a culture are the thoughts, ideas, and beliefs of a people, like their code of law or their religion.

The **cultural landscape** of a place is also known as a *built landscape. It includes* the impact a culture has on its environment, such as the kind of buildings or infrastructure created. (For example, the development of railroads is an important part of the cultural landscape of the American West.)

> **HELPFUL HINT**
>
> A folk culture is the sum of cultural traits of a localized, traditional group. Folk culture is often threatened by the spread of popular culture.

Cultural geographers (also known as **human geographers**) use a variety of tools to interpret and analyze geographic information. Tables and graphs help geographers organize information and reveal trends over time:

▶ A **histogram** is a specific type of graph that illustrates the distribution of data and shows how frequently various phenomena occur.

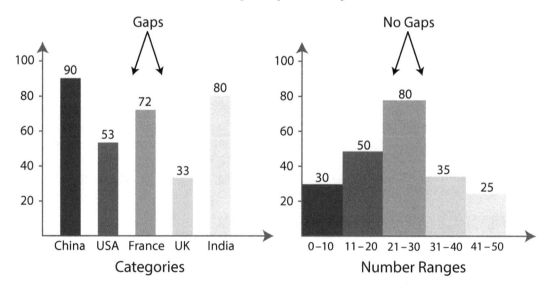

Bar Graph   **Histogram**

Figure 4.8. Bar Graph Versus Histogram

▶ **Scatter plots** show the relationship between two sets of data to allow for broader comparison.

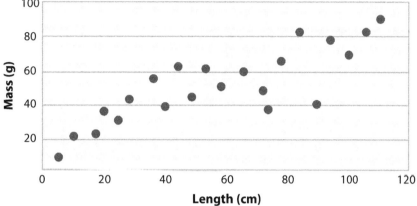

Figure 4.9. Scatterplots and Correlation

From tables and graphs, geographers can develop **descriptive statistics**—like the mean, mode, range, and average—which allow for more detailed understanding of the data.

Geographers use **geographic models** to recognize and understand spatial patterns. For example:

▶ A **concentric zone plot** shows urban social structures.

▶ The **demographic transition model** explains the population patterns. (This will be discussed later in this section.)

But where does the data come from that is used in these various graphs, tables, and models? Geographers use both **primary geographic data** and **secondary geographic data** to build models and interpret information:

▶ **Primary geographic data** comes from the researcher's own observations in the field.

> **HELPFUL HINT**
>
> The US Census Bureau, CIA World Factbook, the Population Reference Bureau, the National Institutes of Health, and the United Nations are all good sources for secondary data.

▶ **Secondary geographic data** is taken from sources that have already collected and aggregated useful data.

▶ Geographers also use **geographic information systems (GIS)**, which are any computer systems that store, manage, manipulate, or analyze spatial data.

PRACTICE QUESTIONS

14) **Which of the following is an example of a nonmaterial component of a culture?**

   A.   a statue of Buddha

   B.   the teachings of Aristotle

   C.   a newspaper from October 29, 1929

   D.   a medieval sword

15) **A geographer visits a village along the Amazon River and collects information about the role the river plays in the culture of the village. What is this an example of?**

   A.   a descriptive statistic

   B.   a geographic information system

   C.   primary geographic data

   D.   secondary geographic data

STRUCTURES OF CULTURES

Each culture is made up of countless, specific **culture traits. Culture traits** are single aspects of a culture, like shaking hands in greeting, or eating with a fork.

A culture trait is not necessarily unique to one culture, nor does it—in and of itself—define a culture. For example, Eastern Orthodox nuns and conservative Jewish women cover their hair, but these are clearly two distinct cultures. This is because while the two cultures might have this one distinct trait in common, the combination of all of their culture traits—their **culture complexes**—are quite different.

No two cultures have the exact same complex; therefore, wherever a difference in traits can be identified, two separate culture complexes exist.

If, though, two culture complexes have many overlapping traits, they will form a **culture system**. For example, after the fall of the Berlin Wall there were distinct differences between East and West Germany, based on physical characteristics and differing histories.

CHECK YOUR UNDERSTANDING #2

Using chopsticks is an example of what?

East Germans had a greater collective sense due to the socialist political and economic system they had experienced. West Germans were more individualistic, having lived in a more capitalist society. The West had more access to technology; therefore television, movies, popular music, and video games were all a bigger part of West German culture. There were also differences in language. Most West Germans spoke English as a second language, whereas most East Germans spoke Russian.

The East and the West made up distinct culture complexes. However, they also had enough traits in common—a common language, a common government after reunification, and a shared history—to be a single culture system.

That culture system had linguistic and historical connections with the Netherlands, Norway, Denmark, and Sweden. These countries all, in turn, share history and have similar music and arts with France, Italy, Spain, and other neighboring countries. As such, they all make up a common **culture region** (Western Europe).

That cultural region also has a shared history with Eastern Europe, as well as similarities in art and music. Together, they comprise a **culture realm**.

DEVELOPMENT OF CULTURES

While cultures exist today in a multitude of forms across the earth, there are eight locations where formal culture—meaning the development of agriculture, government, and urbanization—began. These locations are known as **culture hearths**:

▶ In the Americas, culture began in Andean America and Mesoamerica.

▶ In Africa, the culture hearths were in West Africa and the Nile River valley.

▶ In the Middle East, culture began in Mesopotamia.

▶ In Asia, hearths existed in the Indus River Valley, the Ganges River delta, and along the Wei and Huang Rivers in China.

In each of these hearths, similar innovations—the seeds of culture—developed completely independently of one another. Once the seeds sprouted, they spread across the earth in a process called **cultural diffusion**, moving outward from the hearths in a variety of ways.

Sometimes this occurred through inheritance, when one culture left an imprint on a place that was then used by the next culture to inhabit the same place. This is called **sequent occupancy**.

For example, New Orleans was founded by the French. It then switched between French and Spanish control several times, all the while attracting immigrants from Europe and importing slaves from West Africa and the Caribbean. The influence of each of these various cultures can be seen in the hybrid culture of New Orleans today.

Other times, cultures change by coming into contact with each other, which is known as **transculturation**. This can be symbiotic, as in **cultural convergence**, when two cultures adopt traits of each other and become increasingly similar.

For example, with the advent of national television programming, broadcasters and actors developed neutral accents and dialects which could be understood throughout the United States. These then diffused into the public, reducing regional language differences.

Cultural convergence can also be less balanced. A weaker culture may take on the qualities of a more powerful culture; this is called **acculturation**. Examples of acculturation throughout history abound, particularly in places subjected to colonization. In extreme cases, the weaker culture fully **assimilates**, losing all aspects of its own original culture.

Cultures can also **diverge**, or change from being one culture complex into two if they begin to develop differing traits. For instance, as American mainstream culture modernized, the Amish diverged into a separate culture maintaining traditional ways.

SETTLEMENT PATTERNS

For cultures to grow, an area must first be settled. **Settlements** are the cradles of culture. They allow for the development of political structures, the management of resources, and the transfer of information to future generations.

While settlements differed greatly, they did all share some commonalities:

▶ Settlements all began near natural resources that can support life, namely water and a reliable food source.

▶ A settlement's success was based on its proximity to these natural resources and its ability to collect and move raw materials.

▶ As each of these characteristics reached a new level of sophistication, population in that area began to concentrate near the point of resource allocation and production.

The spatial layout of these settlements, then, was determined by the environment and the primary function of the settlement. For instance, European villages were clustered on hillsides to protect against invaders. Flat areas were left for farming. Settlements that rose up around trade, like those on the outskirts of the Saharan desert, concentrated around access to the trade routes and were generally more dispersed.

Later in history, successful settlements also needed an ample work force and the ability to produce and deliver finished products elsewhere. Once transportation methods were developed, the populations of these settlements became mobile, allowing for a faster diffusion of culture, and—eventually—the development of industrial centers, which became cities.

A **city** is a major hub of human settlement with a high population density and a concentration of resource creation or allocation. Today, almost half of the world's population lives in cities; in more developed regions, the percentages are even higher.

With the development of cities, three types of areas emerged:

▶ **urban** (in the city itself)

▶ **suburban** (near the city)

> ▶ **rural** (away from the city).

In some cases today, urban and suburban areas or multiple urban areas merge into a **megalopolis**, or super-city.

PRACTICE QUESTIONS

16) **Which of the following statements is an example of cultural diffusion?**

    A.   Russia has the most lumber in the world.

    B.   There is a Starbucks at the Mall of the Emirates in Dubai.

    C.   Chopsticks are a key utensil in China.

    D.   Spanish is the official language of Spain.

17) **The adoption of French as an official language throughout most of West Africa is an example of which of the following?**

    A.   sequent occupancy

    B.   cultural convergence

    C.   cultural divergence

    D.   acculturation

18) **The majority of people in the world today live in**

    A.   urban areas.

    B.   suburban areas.

    C.   rural areas.

    D.   megalopolises.

19) **Settlements developed near rivers would most likely**

    A.   be designed in a circular fashion a few miles away from the river.

    B.   be built into nearby hills.

    C.   be long and narrow to follow the shape of the river.

    D.   have clear access to land trade routes.

DEMOGRAPHIC PATTERNS

Demography is the study of human population. It is a major branch of human geography since the distribution of people and population density are closely tied to other factors in both human and physical geography.

> ▶ The **distribution** of people describes how people are spread across the earth.

> ▶ The **density** describes the number of people in a particular area.

As mentioned, more than half of the world's population today lives in cities. While this is a relatively recent change, the population has always been unevenly distributed based on resources. As cities have become better at obtaining and allocating resources, they have attracted more people.

This uneven distribution can be seen in other ways as well:

▶ Seventy-five percent of all people live on only 5 percent of Earth's land.

▶ Much of the world's wealth is concentrated in North America and Western Europe.

▶ Eighty percent of people live in poor, developing countries in South America, Asia, and Africa.

▶ The most populated area in the world is East Asia, which is home to 25 percent of the world's population.

▶ In terms of population, East Asia is followed by Southeast Asia, and then Europe, from the Atlantic Ocean to the Ural Mountains.

Demographers use **population equations** to analyze changes in population.

▶ **Global equations** look at Earth's total population, including the number of births and deaths that occur.

▶ **Sub-global equations** look at total population in a given area and include immigration and emigration as factors.

Over the last 300 years, the population of Earth has exploded. Population has been growing at an exponential rate, meaning the more people are added to the population, the faster it grows:

▶ In 1765, the global population was 300 million people; today it is six billion.

▶ This increase has raised concerns for many demographers, particularly in the areas with a higher population concentration.

To determine if an area is at risk, demographers determine its **carrying capacity**, the number of people the area can support. The carrying capacity of various areas can differ greatly depending on technology, wealth, climate, available habitable space, access, and **infrastructure**—institutions that support the needs of the people.

When a country exceeds its carrying capacity, it suffers from **overpopulation**. Countries in danger of overpopulation may attempt to restrict their growth, like China did through its one-child policy. Conversely, they may attempt to increase their carrying capacity by increasing their resources using technology, such as irrigation or desalination, or increasing their access to trade.

For example, Japan greatly increased its carrying capacity by importing significant quantities of food. As a result, it is able to maintain a much larger population than it would otherwise be able to.

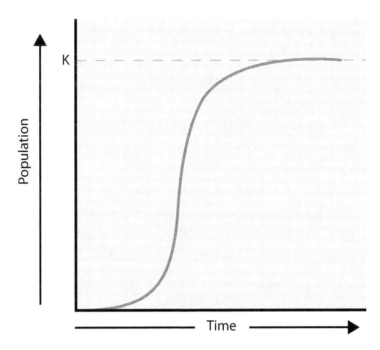

Figure 4.10. Carrying Capacity

Despite the population boom, some countries actually suffer from **underpopulation**. They have a much greater carrying capacity than their population uses. This is due to their high levels of production, amount of land, or abundance of natural resources.

Demographic Transition Model

In order to understand how populations will change, demographers use the **demographic transition model**. This is a geographic tool which predicts changes in population using the **crude birth rate (CBR)**, **crude death rate (CDR)**, and the **rate of natural increase (RNI)**—how much the population is increasing based on the first two factors.

The model ties the changes in population to economic development by making two major assumptions:

1. All population growth is based on economic status.

2. All countries pass through the same economic stages.

While both of these assumptions have been challenged, the demographic transition model is still the best indicator of population change.

The demographic transition model outlines four stages of economic and population growth, and one theoretical one.

Table 4.5. Economic and Population Growth According to the Demographic Transition Model

Stage One

- This is a low growth stage.
- Both CBR and CDR are high, resulting in low or stationary RNI.
- Fluctuation will occur based on disease, war, and famine, all of which are somewhat common in stage one economic development.
- Most of the population consists of subsistence farmers.
- Today, there are no countries that are still considered stage one because of advances in medical technology, which have eventually permeated down to every country.
- The prevention of disease—and death from it—decreases CDR, allowing RNI to increase.

Stage Two

- Because CDR has declined but CBR remains high, this is a high growth stage.
- Medical advances can have an immediate impact on CDR, but CBR tends to be a deeply-rooted cultural tradition and is much more difficult to change.
- In stage two countries, the majority of the population still engages in subsistence farming.
- Many developing countries today are stage two countries.

Stage Three

- As countries move from subsistence farming into industrialization, CBR begins to slow.
- Women have more choices in work; this, in conjunction with urbanization—and the reduced living space that goes along with it—leads to a decline in the birth rate.
- Most Latin American and Asian countries today are stage three countries.

Stage Four

- Industrialization leads to modernization.
- Once countries become fully industrialized and develop more complex service economies and advanced health care and education systems, CBR and CDR are once again equal but at a much lower rate, leading to a low RNI.
- This is a low growth stage.
- Stage four is considered to be the ideal stage for population growth as the country is stable and prosperous, and population growth is slow and steady.
- The United States, Argentina, and Singapore are all stage four countries.

Stage Five

- This last stage is a mostly theoretical one, although several countries are moving towards it.
- Medical advances not only succeed in limiting early deaths but also in extending the life of the elderly.
- The decline in CBR continues, leading eventually to a negative RNI.
- Many countries in Western Europe and Japan are facing such graying populations.

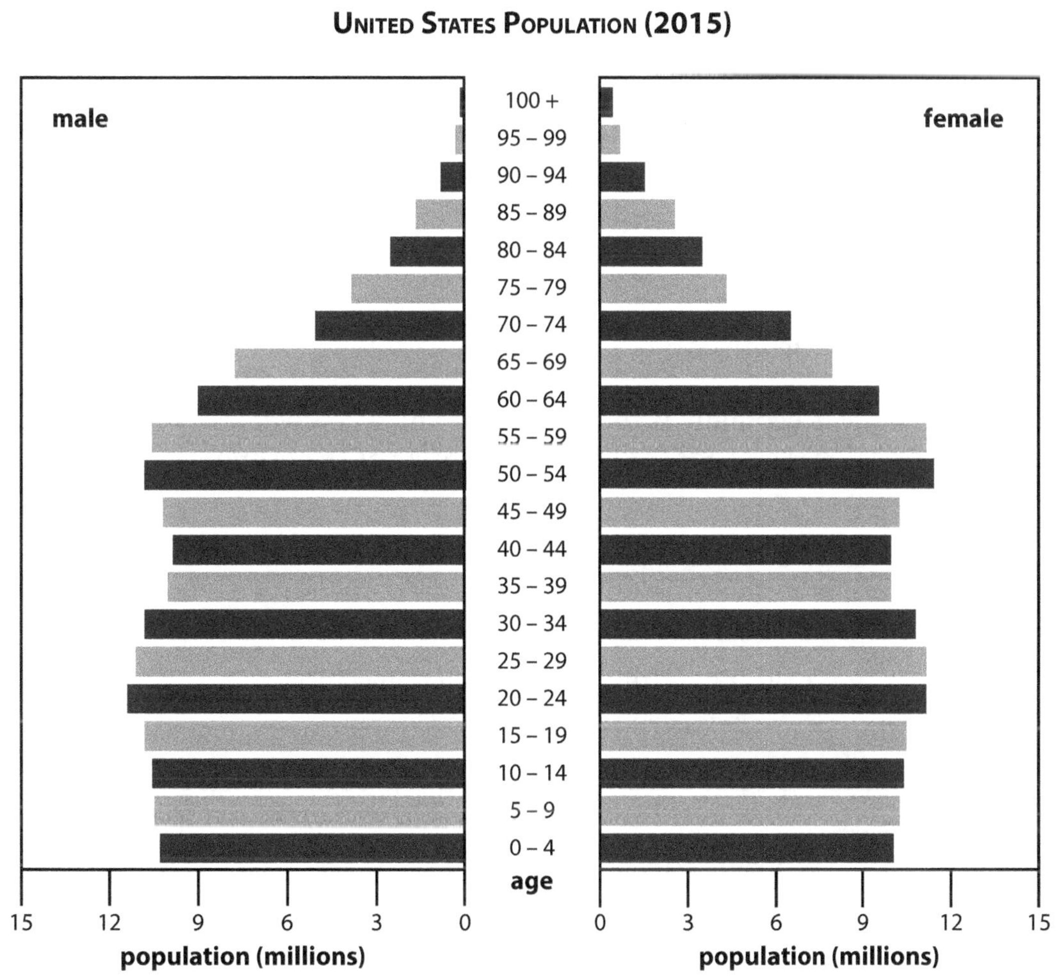

UNITED STATES POPULATION (2015)

Figure 4.11. Population Pyramid

PRACTICE QUESTIONS

20) Overpopulation is most likely to occur in which stage of the demographic transition model?

    A.   stage one

    B.   stage two

    C.   stage three

    D.   stage four

21) Which of the following areas has the highest population density?

    A.   India

    B.   United States

    C.   Germany

    D.   Belgium

22) **Canada produces more resources than its population can consume. What is this an example of?**

    A.   overpopulation

    B.   carrying capacity

    C.   underpopulation

    D.   graying population

ECONOMIC PATTERNS

A country or area's **economy** is the system by which it produces, consumes, and distributes resources and goods. The various parts of the economy are classified into five sectors:

Table 4.6. Sectors of the Economy

Sector	Description
Primary sector	• focuses on the extraction of raw materials • includes mining, farming, and fishing • the smallest part of an industrialized economy
Secondary sector	• processes the raw materials extracted by the first sector • made up primarily of factories • includes steel, canned tuna, and rubber
Tertiary sector	• moves, sells, and trades the products created by the secondary sector • known as the service economy • includes transportation companies, merchants, and stores
Quaternary sector	• does not deal in physical products, but instead creates and transfers information • includes university researchers, journalists, and information technology specialists • only exists in highly developed countries with well-established, complex industrial economies
Quinary sector	• involves those at the highest levels of decision-making • focuses on managing the overall functioning of the economy • made up almost exclusively of government agencies and officials

Most economies also have an informal sector which encompasses all business transactions that are not reported to the government. The range of this sector includes everything from unregistered street vendors to neighborhood babysitters to illegal sales of drugs.

INDUSTRIALIZATION

As areas develop and economies grow, manufacturing becomes increasingly important to the functioning of the economy. This is called **industrialization**.

Industrialization is a relatively recent phenomenon:

> ▶ The **Industrial Revolution** began in Great Britain in the 1760s.

> ▶ By 1825, it had diffused to Western Europe and North America.

> ▶ The discovery of new energy sources, like coal (which was later replaced by oil), and technological advancements which allowed machine labor to replace human labor led to the emergence of manufacturing centers and a shift in the functioning of the economy.

Industrialization had significant spatial implications:

> ▶ The extraction of resources and the construction of factories changed the physical landscape of places.

> ▶ As transportation infrastructure improved and labor was commodified, migration—from rural to urban areas—increased.

> ▶ Population settlements grew up around energy sources (like the coal deposits in Pennsylvania, Ukraine, and Ruhr Valley in Germany) and around factories (like Manchester and Liverpool in England).

> ▶ Related industries are often developed near each other in order to share resource costs. This is called **agglomeration**.

>> ▷ Modern examples of agglomeration are high-tech corridors or **technopoles**, areas of high-tech production, like Silicon Valley in California.

In some cases, an area can become over-agglomerated and pollution, traffic, restricted labor pools, and over-taxed resources can lead industries to spread out. This is known as **deglomeration**. Increasingly, industries also are moving their operations to places with lower labor costs, even though they may incur higher transportation costs.

PRACTICE QUESTIONS

23) **An owner of a grocery store is part of which sector of the economy?**

    A.   primary

    B.   secondary

    C.   tertiary

    D.   quaternary

24) **Which of the following is NOT a consequence of industrialization noted by geographers?**

    A.   significant changes to the physical characteristics of the area in which industrialization takes place

    B.   decrease in subsistence farming

    C.   migration to suburban areas

    D.   increased importance of energy sources like coal and oil

ECONOMIC DEVELOPMENT

The growth of economies is strongly connected to **development**, the use of technology, and knowledge to improve the living conditions of people in a country. While economic in its foundation, development focuses on a range of quality of life issues like access to basic goods and services, education, and health care.

Countries on the wealthier side of the spectrum are called **more developed countries (MDCs)**:

▶ MDCs are concentrated primarily in the Northern Hemisphere.

▶ Their primary economic concern is maintaining growth.

Countries on the poorer side of the spectrum are called **less developed countries (LDCs)**:

▶ LDCs are found mostly in the Southern Hemisphere.

▶ They face the challenge of improving their economic conditions by stimulating significant and sustainable economic growth.

There are several different measures used for development. The most common is a country's **gross domestic product (GDP)**, the value of the total output of goods and services produced in a country in a given period of time, typically a year.

▶ GDP is usually calculated per capita.

▶ In MDCs, the per capita GDP is more than $20,000.

▶ In LDCs, it is less than $1,000.

GDP should not be confused with another measure of development, the **gross national product (GNP)**. **Gross national product (GNP)** is the value of goods and services owned and produced by citizens of a country, regardless of where those goods and services are produced.

Neither of these, however, take into account the distribution of wealth in a country or nonmonetary factors in quality of life. They also exclude the informal sector. Therefore, both of these are considered ineffective measures of development. Instead, two other measures provide a better understanding: purchasing power parity (PPP) and the Human Development Index (HDI).

Purchasing power parity (PPP) is an exchange rate that determines how much currency it would take to buy the equal amounts of goods in two different countries. For example, a Big Mac in South Africa costs 19.45 rand, 9.50 real in Brazil, and $4.07 in the United States (as of 2011).

Which is actually the most expensive?

By looking only at the numbers, it appears significantly harder to buy a Big Mac in South Africa; therefore, quality of life seems lower in general for South Africans. However, once the PPP is determined (by dividing the numeric cost of each Big Mac) and then adjusted using the currency exchange rate, a Big Mac in South Africa actually costs US $2.87, and a Big Mac in Brazil costs US $6.17.

Therefore, Big Macs are significantly less expensive in South Africa and significantly more expensive in Brazil. The perceived disparity between South African development and American development is less than it originally seemed (when measured by a Big Mac!).

The **United Nations Human Development Index (HDI)** is based on the idea that development is actually best measured by the choices available to the population of a country.

▶ HDI focuses on quality-of-life measures like education, health care, and general welfare.

▶ GDP is only one measure among others, including life expectancy, level of education attainment, and literacy rates.

> **DID YOU KNOW?**
>
> As of 2019, Norway has the highest HDI ranking in the world (0.957). Ireland and Switzerland follow closely behind (0.955) and share second place.

HDI creates a ranking system of the world's countries with the highest score being 1.000 and the lowest 0.000.

ROSTOW MODERNIZATION MODEL

In the 1950s, sociologist Walt Rostow created a model to explain the economic development of countries. He argued that each country goes through five stages.

Table 4.7. Walt Rostow's Five Stages of Economic Development

Name	Description
	Stage One
Traditional Society	• An economy consists mostly of subsistence farming with little trade or industry. • comprised of LDCs
	Stage Two
Preconditions for Takeoff	• Small groups of individuals initiate "takeoff" economic activities. • They begin to develop small industries in certain pockets of a country. • comprised of LDCs
	Stage Three
Takeoff	• Those small industries begin to grow very quickly and become an increasingly significant part of the economy. • The shift from subsistence farming to industry begins. • comprised of LDCs
	Stage Four
Drive to Maturity	• Advanced technology and development spread beyond the takeoff areas to the rest of the country. • A skilled and educated workforce emerges and becomes sustainable. • Other industries begin to grow rapidly. • comprised of MDCs
	Stage Five
High Mass Consumption	• Most people are employed in service (rather than factory) jobs. • The level of education of the populace is higher overall as a result. • Economic development reaches new levels, leading to increased consumption. • comprised of MDCs

Critics of Rostow's model offer numerous arguments against his explanation of the economic development of countries:

▶ They argue that it is too Anglo-centric.

▶ They point out that it unrealistically assumes countries develop independently of one another, and so it does not take into account the impact of colonization (discussed in the next section).

Critics also take issue with Rostow's fifth stage, arguing that increased consumption is not a necessary consequence of economic growth. Instead, they argue that the surplus wealth could lead to increased social welfare programs or sustainable activities. Northern Europe more closely models this version of a fifth developmental stage.

DEVELOPMENT GAP

By any measure, the gap between MDCs and LDCs is widening.

In the last ten years, the GDP of MDCs has tripled, while the GDP of LDCs has only doubled. The RNI in MDCs has dropped by 85 percent in the same time period; it has only decreased by 5 percent in LDCs. Several theories attempt to explain this trend.

Dependency theory argues that the root of the problem can be traced back to colonization and imperialism. It is built on the idea that the decisions and actions of one country directly impact those of others.

Most MDCs today were colonizers, whereas most LDCs were colonized. The goal of the colonizing countries was to increase their wealth by using the colonized area as both a source of natural resources and as a market for the sale of their finished goods. Industrialization, therefore, was suppressed in the colonies.

Even after colonization, MDCs need LDCs to maintain their economic growth and dominance:

▶ LDCs rely on MDCs for aid and support.

▶ Therefore, LDCs are kept in a cycle of underdevelopment by the structure of the global economic system.

The **core-periphery model** presents a similar perspective and divides the countries of the world into three groups:

The *core* consists of industrialized countries—those with the highest per capita income and standard of living (e.g., United States, Canada, Australia, New Zealand, Japan, and Western Europe).

The *semi-periphery* is composed of newly industrialized countries that usually have significant inequities between the haves and have-nots in their population (e.g., India, Brazil, South Africa, and China).

> **HELPFUL HINT**
>
> The demographic transition model (DTM) is based off of Rostow's modernization model. The five stages of each model align. This can help with questions that ask you to analyze the relationship between population and development.

> **HELPFUL HINT**
>
> Most semi-periphery countries are spatially located between core and peripheral countries, and between two competing core areas. They typically also have larger land masses (like India, China, and Brazil); however there are exceptions to this (Poland, Greece, and Israel).

The *periphery* consists of countries with very low levels of industrialization, infrastructure, per capita income, and standards of living; these are essentially LDCs (e.g., most of Africa, parts of Asia, and parts of South America).

Sociologist Immanuel Wallerstein attempted to explain this structure. According to **world systems analysis theory**, the global system is capitalist and interlocked by competition, both political and economic.

This competition made for the inevitable exploitation of some countries by others. Those who did the exploiting became the core; those who were exploited became those on the periphery and semi-periphery (based on location and, to a degree, size).

IMPROVING ECONOMIC DEVELOPMENT

There are three main approaches for improving the economic development of LDCs:

- ▶ self sufficiency
- ▶ international trade approach
- ▶ structural adjustments

The **self-sufficiency approach** is based on the idea that a country can only develop if it provides for its people itself, rather than relying on outside aid and support. Countries cannot concentrate on just one industry (which is more typical for LDCs based on the colonization model) but must promote development across all sectors and all regions. A closed economic state with minimum imports and high tariffs to limit international trade is required.

Critics of the self-sufficiency approach argue that, while it may allow native industries to grow, it stifles competition, which will ultimately inhibit growth.

On the other hand, the **international trade approach** is an export-oriented approach. A country focuses on products that it can provide to the rest of the world. By doing this, a country develops a **comparative advantage** in that industry, meaning it becomes better than the rest of the world in that industry.

For instance, Japan chose to focus on developing a comparative advantage in high-tech products rather than food production. Instead, it imports much of its food.

Critics of the international trade approach argue it only works if a country can develop a comparative advantage. If a country invests in developing a comparative advantage in one industry but is unable to become the "best," it has wasted its resources and crippled the rest of its economy.

Even if a country does develop a comparative advantage, this approach can still leave the country open to exploitation, particularly if its chosen market is an export-based product.

This can best be seen in many African countries that export raw materials like gold, diamonds, rubber, and cocoa. While exportation levels might be high, development remains low, as the push to produce more leads to severe mistreatment of labor with limited opportunities for small business growth, market competition, or upward mobility.

Finally, intergovernmental organizations attempt to improve the development of LDCs through **structural adjustments**:

▶ Organizations like the **World Bank** or the **International Monetary Fund** offer loans in exchange for changes to a country's economic structure.

▶ These usually involve increasing privatization, which negatively impacts families reliant on resources previously provided by the government.

▶ Advocates argue that this is only a short-term negative impact that is necessary for longer-term gain.

PRACTICE QUESTIONS

25) The countries of West Africa remain LDCs because of their dependence on Western MDCs developed during French colonization of the area. This statement most reflects which of the following?

   A.   Rostow's modernization model

   B.   world systems analysis theory

   C.   international trade approach

   D.   dependency theory

26) Which of the following is true of MDCs?

   A.   They have GDP per capita in excess of $20,000.

   B.   They are concentrated in Western Europe and North America.

   C.   both A and B

   D.   neither A nor B

27) Purchasing power parity is a better measure of economic development than gross domestic product because

   A.   PPP allows for direct comparisons of what money can acquire in different countries.

   B.   it is based on more accurate numbers than GDP.

   C.   GDP is only calculated every ten years, whereas PPP is annual.

   D.   PPP takes into account class differences in quality of life.

28) **How does the UN Human Development Index differ from other measures of economic development?**

    A.   It focuses on the gap between the wealthy and the poor in a country.

    B.   It considers nonmonetary factors like health care, literacy rates, and education.

    C.   It only examines the top fifty and bottom fifty nations in the world.

    D.   It is the only measure focused on comparative economic growth.

GLOBALIZATION

Globalization is the trend of increasing interdependence and spatial interaction between disparate areas of the world economically, politically, and culturally. At its core, globalization is an economic trend. But it has significant cultural and political impacts as well.

For example, the exportation of American fast-food restaurants, like McDonald's, to other parts of the world reflects the capitalist drive to find new markets. Furthermore, the introduction of this type of food has a significant impact on one of the major distinguishing cultural traits of other countries—their cuisine.

The primary driving forces of globalization are **multinational corporations (MNCs)** or **transnational corporations (TNCs)**, which are:

▶ composed of several smaller companies that all contribute to the same production process

> **CHECK YOUR UNDERSTANDING #3**
>
> What are some examples of MNCs you interact with daily?

▶ companies whose headquarters are in one country (usually an MDC) and whose production is in one or more different countries (usually an LDC)

The process of moving production to a different country is called **outsourcing**, and it allows for several financial advantages for the MNC:

▶ reduced labor costs

▶ lower tax rates

▶ cheaper land prices

The new country also often has more relaxed safety and labor standards. Although outsourcing increases transportation costs, this increase is offset by a lower cost in labor. This is called the **substitution principle**.

Some countries create **special economic zones (SEZs)** to encourage outsourcing. In these zones, companies are held to lower environmental and labor standards and can receive special tax breaks and other incentives.

Special economic zones also encourage companies to invest directly in the economy of the hosting country to help maintain the government that is supporting their business.

Similar to SEZs are **export processing zones**, also known as free trade zones, in which duties and tariffs are waived and restrictions on labor practices are significantly loosened. Again, the goal is to attract the factories of MNCs.

The globalization of the manufacturing process has created a **new international division of labor.** This describes when different parts of a product are manufactured in different places of the world, then sent to yet another location to be assembled. Essentially, this is a globalization of the Ford assembly line.

The problem with this model is that LDCs become very dependent on MNCs. Multinational corporations may engage in **direct investment** in the country as part of their activities there, investing directly into its economy.

In the long run, local involvement allows MNCs to gain disproportionate influence over governmental affairs. Why? MNCs advocate for governmental policies favorable to their own financial goals, especially **free trade**, or no regulations, on outsourcing. **Free trade** allows the global market to run its course because the market always maximizes efficiency (sometimes to the detriment of workers and the environment).

Advocates argue that outsourcing allows for economic growth in otherwise struggling economies. They point to the Four Asian Tigers—Singapore, Hong Kong, South Korea, and Taiwan—as examples of countries that began as sources of production for MNCs and then became **newly industrialized countries (NICs)**, experiencing unprecedented economic growth.

As a result, today many argue that these countries should now be considered MDCs.

Critics argue that free trade only benefits MNCs because it does not protect local workers, local environments, or ensure an appropriate quality of life in the countries that provide the labor.

They argue that the Asian Tigers succeeded not because of outsourcing, but because they shifted their focus from production

HELPFUL HINT

NICs are countries that are not yet developed but are doing so faster than other less developed countries. They have strong manufacturing export economies, a great deal of foreign investment, strong political leadership, and increasing rights for citizens.

for MNCs to developing a comparative advantage in service industries, namely high-end technology and financial management.

These critics argue for **fair trade**—governments oversee and regulate outsourcing to ensure all workers receive a living wage.

PRACTICE QUESTIONS

29) **Special economic zones attract multinational corporations by doing all of the following EXCEPT**

   A.   offering them tax breaks.

   B.   providing them space for their headquarters.

   C.   lessening environmental standards.

   D.   loosening labor laws.

30) **What does the substitution principle state?**

   A.   Corporations headquarter their company in one country and produce their goods in another.

   B.   Companies can invest money directly into a country's economy.

   C.   Companies will accept increased transportation costs in exchange for decreased labor costs.

   D.   NICs switch from hosting production to focusing on new, cutting-edge industries.

POLITICAL GEOGRAPHY

The study of political organization—another human characteristic of place—is called **political geography**.

Political structures emerged over time in response to ongoing competition for control over territory, resources, trade routes, and people. To strengthen their positions, groups often cooperate with each other through alliances and agreements. For example, today the world is mostly divided into various state sovereignties as different groups came together to access different resources, solidify their power, or control strategic positions.

> **DID YOU KNOW?**
>
> The only unorganized area left in the world is Antarctica.

Cooperation exists on the **supranational scale** as well in the form of multinational organizations like the United Nations. More often, however, competition between groups leads to conflict. Those same agreements and alliances that allow for cooperation may also determine the sides of a conflict. These sides are often based on culture traits—religion, political ideology, national origin, language, or race. They can be local, regional, national, or global. Within a state, different regions might compete for a greater share of government funds, or two towns might fight over access to roads or rivers.

Humans desire to establish ownership of their own specific, personal space. This is referred to as **human territoriality** and has manifested differently over time from tribes, clans, and villages to kingdoms and empires.

In Europe, city-states emerged in Greece and Rome, followed by the rise of feudal society after the fall of these empires. Feudal society led to monarchy, which eventually transformed into nation-states (which have become the global organizing political principle since World War II).

At the center of each of these political forms is the concept of **sovereignty**—the public recognition of an individual or group's control over a place, its people, and its institutions.

STATES

In political geography, there is a distinction between the physical area and the people of a place.

A **state** refers to the physical place: it is any area with defined borders, a permanent population, and a relatively effective government and economy.

The borders, or **political boundaries**, of a state can be drawn in three different ways:

1. **Physical boundaries** are based on natural features, like rivers or mountains.

2. **Cultural-political boundaries** are based on religion or language (or, rarely, another cultural trait).

    ▷ Pakistan and India were separated into two countries based on religion: Pakistan became home to more Muslims; India primarily became home to Hindus.

3. **Geometric political boundaries** are drawn as straight lines without regard to natural or cultural features.

    ▷ When Korea was divided after World War II, a geometric political boundary was drawn between North and South at the thirty-eighth parallel.

Most modern boundaries are the result of negotiation between states or human settlement or interaction. These are called **subsequent boundaries**.

Other boundaries either predate human cultures—**antecedent boundaries**—or were imposed by an outside force—**superimposed boundaries**. For example, after World War I and the collapse of the Ottoman Empire, the Middle East was organized into states by Britain and France using superimposed boundaries.

Relict boundaries are boundaries that are no longer functioning but serve as a reminder that the boundary used to exist. The Great Wall of China is a relict boundary.

To create a legal political boundary, four steps must be followed:

1. The boundary must be legally described (**definition**). This is where most of the negotiation between states takes place.

2. The boundary must be drawn onto a map (**delimitation**).

3. The boundary must be marked, in some way, on the physical landscape (**demarcation**).

4. The boundary must be policed and enforced (**administration**).

In this process, there are many opportunities for disagreement and conflict. Disputes over borders can arise over their actual location, how that location is defined, how the border is administered, and how resources are distributed near and across the border. Disputes also arise in **frontiers**, areas where boundaries are either not well established or not well maintained.

On land, boundary negotiations can be tricky, but they become significantly more complicated in the oceans. States have agreed that each state has an **exclusive economic zone** up to 200 miles from its shore. If there are less than 200 miles between two countries, the ocean area is divided equally in half. This is called the **median line principle**.

Boundaries determine the outer edges of a state. From the inside, states are organized around a **core**, the location of the concentration of power.

The core is essential in determining the functionality of a state. If the core is well-integrated into the rest of the state, development is more likely to spread evenly. In this case, **centripetal forces** pull the state and the people together to create a unified identity.

If a state has several cores—a **multicore state**—development can occur unevenly and in pockets. South Africa has divided its political core into three different cities: the executive capital is Pretoria, the legislative capital is Cape Town, and the judicial capital is in Bloemfontein.

Centrifugal forces can divide the state and its people. Infrastructure is often underdeveloped and inefficient, and internal conflict is likely. This can lead to **balkanization**, the disintegration of a state into smaller pieces.

In some countries, there may be a single core, but it is not well-integrated, and development is not evenly distributed. Instead, the core is located in a **primate city**, where all of the resources are concentrated. Smaller cities serve as support for the primate city. The primate city serves as the political center for the country and holds greater economic power than any other city in the state.

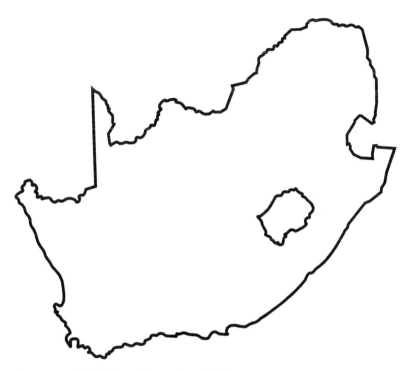

Figure 4.12. Multicore State: South Africa

Primate cities are common in less developed countries. Lagos, with a population of 13.4 million, is a primate city in Nigeria. The second biggest city in the country, Kano, has a population of only 3.6 million.

Primate cities can also be found in very old nation-states, like Hungary (Budapest) and Great Britain (London). In these cases, the primate city not only has a concentration of political and economic power but is the cultural center of the country, too.

Figure 4.13. Budapest

To disperse the concentration of power and resources, some states attempt to remove political power from the primate city by creating a **forward capital** which better serves national goals. For example, Abuja is the capital of Nigeria even though Lagos is Nigeria's primate city. Abuja was built in the 1980s specifically to reduce the power of Lagos and shift political power to a neutral location that would neither help nor hinder any of Nigeria's various religious and ethnic groups.

TERRITORIAL MORPHOLOGY

Different boundaries lead to states with different shapes, which then create different political situations for each country. This is known as **territorial morphology**—the relationship between a state's size, shape, location, and political situation.

Territorial morphology is critical to political geography.

Table 4.8. Territorial Morphology

Type of State	Description	Examples
Compact state	• relatively small and nearly square or circular in shape • center of power always close, no matter where a group or individual is within the state	Switzerland, Uganda
Fragmented state	exists in several pieces	Indonesia, the Philippines
Elongated state	states that are long and thin	Vietnam, Chile
Prorupted state	states with a piece that protrudes	Thailand

States that are **landlocked** face economic challenges because they have no direct access to the ocean for trade. They have a greater potential for boundary disputes since they have more borders to administer. These states must rely more on their neighbors, which can lead to political problems.

Many small, landlocked states end up serving as **buffer states**, independent states that are sandwiched between two (usually larger) conflicting countries. Jordan is a buffer state between Israel and Iraq.

Most landlocked countries are simply surrounded by multiple other countries (e.g., Switzerland). But others are **perforated states,** which make a hole in the middle of another country. Lesotho is a perforated state within South Africa.

While sovereignty is a defining character of a state, not all states enjoy the same level of sovereignty:

▶ **Satellite states** are technically independent but heavily controlled by another, more powerful state.

▶ Belarus is a satellite state of the Russian Federation.

Sometimes, states are divided:

▶ A **political enclave** is a state—or part of a state—that is surrounded by another.

▶ A **political exclave** is part of a state that is separated from the rest of the state.

▶ During the Cold War, West Berlin was a political exclave of West Germany and a political enclave within East Germany.

PRACTICE QUESTIONS

31) **The country of Panama is an example of which of the following kinds of states?**

   A. landlocked state

   B. compact state

   C. fragmented state

   D. elongated state

32) **The mountains surrounding Switzerland create which kind of boundaries?**

   A. physical boundaries

   B. relict boundaries

   C. geometric political boundaries

   D. superimposed boundaries

33) **What is a disadvantage that results from a primate city?**

   A. The primate city has limited access to political power.

   B. A primate city creates a multi-core state.

   C. A primate city has a disproportionate share of a state's resources.

   D. A primate city is particularly vulnerable to invasion and conflict.

34) **Why is Poland is considered a buffer state?**

    A. It shares a border with seven other states.

    B. It was between Germany and the Soviet Union during World War II.

    C. It sits on the Baltic Sea.

    D. It is in Eastern Europe.

NATIONS

A **nation** is a group of people who identify as a group and share a culture:

▶ In most cases, a state is composed of one nation (and so called a nation-state).

▶ Sometimes states are multinational (e.g., the former Soviet Union).

Stateless nations exist as a nation but do not have their own territory. The Romani people throughout Europe exist as a nation but do not have their own territory.

DID YOU KNOW?

Today, the Kurds are primarily based in northern Iraq. However, Kurdish people are dispersed throughout Turkey, Syria, Iran, and Azerbaijan.

Conflict can often arise between stateless nations and the states in which they reside. For instance, the stateless nation may be a minority within a state and at odds with that state in terms of cultural traits or political beliefs. In these cases, members of a stateless nation become **ethno-nationalistic**, maintaining allegiance for their nation over the state.

If a nation is dispersed across multiple states—as is often the case—that nation may strive to reunite its various parts. This is called **irredentism** and was Hitler's goal in occupying Czechoslovakia in 1939. Hitler believed German people needed to be brought together under one administration.

GEOPOLITICS

The study of the interaction between states—politically and territorially—is called **geopolitics**. Geopolitical theory has been very important in shaping the major global conflicts in history.

Table 4.9. Geopolitical Theories

Theory	Description	Example
Organic theory (Friedrich Ratzel)	• States are essentially living organisms that feed on land. • They must obtain more land to grow. • Ratzel argued this process was the root of all state decision-making and conflict.	Adolf Hitler used organic theory to justify his aggressive actions toward neighboring countries.
Heartland theory (John Mackinder)	• This theory was first published in 1904. • Mackinder stated that the world was made up of the World-Island (Europe, Asia, and Africa), outlying islands (Great Britain and Japan) and offshore islands (North America, South America, and Australia). • To control the world, one needed to control Eurasia (the World-Island). • In order to do that, a country needed to control Eastern Europe—the heartland of Eurasia.	• The Soviet Union's foreign policy was based on heartland theory. • Heartland theory not only motivated Soviet aggression in Eastern Europe, but US attempts to curb it as well. • This theory was the basis for the American concept of **domino theory**—the idea that if one country fell to communism, the whole region would fall.
Rimland theory (Nicholas Spykman)	• This theory argued for a balance of power in the periphery of Eurasia in order to prevent the emergence of a global power there (namely, a Soviet or Chinese global power). • As a result, the US developed containment—a policy to keep communism contained to the areas where it already existed.	This policy, rooted in domino theory, drove both the Korean and Vietnam Wars.

PRACTICE QUESTIONS

35) Which of the following BEST describes the Basque people in Spain?

    A.   a nation-state

    B.   a stateless nation

    C.   a multinational state

    D.   a divided nation

36) **The United States became involved in what was essentially a Korean civil war (resulting in the Korean War), primarily because of which geopolitical theory?**

    A.   organic theory

    B.   heartland theory

    C.   domino theory

    D.   irredentism

HUMAN–ENVIRONMENT INTERACTION

The relationship between humans and their environment—the ways in which cultural traits impact physical traits and vice versa—is of utmost importance to geographers.

Humans have always modified the environment to suit their needs. With the advent of agriculture, humans began loosening the topsoil to make planting easier. A looser topsoil is more susceptible to erosion from wind and rain, allowing greater changes to the physical landscape. Cities significantly reduce the amount of exposed ground in an area and lead to a concentration of fuel and resource consumption.

The environment has also shaped human activity. The main economic activities of a place—farming, fishing, trade—have historically been determined, in large part, by the physical characteristics of the place. People living in deserts have traditionally been nomadic because the restricted access to food and water sources requires them to continually move around.

Climate impacts clothing, housing, and work and leisure patterns. For instance, a period of rest in the middle of the day is common in cultures in hot climates.

Theorists continually debate the cause-and-effect nature of the relationship between humans and their environment. There are four main schools of thought.

Table 4.10. Theories of Human–Environment Interaction

Theory	Description	Example
Environmental determinism	Human behavior is controlled by the physical environment.	• When Europeans first arrived in Hawaii, they concluded that the natives were "lazy" because they did not see them toiling over crops. • They believed that the ideal climate and abundant natural food sources had created a slothful people, even though the Hawaiians used systems of resource management not based on plantation agriculture.

Table 4.10. Theories of Human–Environment Interaction

Theory	Description	Example
Possibilism	The environment does replace restrictions on the options available to a group of people, but it is still ultimately the people who make the choice.	Possibilists would point to Europeans and Americans who settled in Hawaii and built large and productive plantations, rather than becoming "lazy." (Hawaiians actually were engaged in their own agricultural endeavors, despite the European perspective.)
Cultural determinism	The environment places no restrictions on the development of culture; the only restrictions come from human limitations.	Despite their island locations, Japan and the United Kingdom colonized other areas and created trade agreements to gain access to other resources.
Political ecology	The government of a region affects the environment, which in turn affects the choices available to the people.	US government allowed railroad companies to construct the transcontinental railroad using dynamite.

THE FIRST AGRICULTURAL REVOLUTION

The primary way humans have affected the earth is through the development of agriculture. With the domestication of plants and animals, humans transitioned from a nomadic existence to a sedentary one. They learned not just to locate food, but to cultivate it themselves.

Early domestication consisted of cutting a stem off of a plant and planting that stem or dividing a plant by the roots. This process diffused from multiple hearths: Southeast Asia, northwestern South America, and West Africa.

Approximately 12,000 years ago, humans began to collect and plant seeds and raise animals for their own use. This was the start of the **First Agricultural Revolution**.

Like the advent of agriculture itself, this revolution diffused from several hearths:

▶ Western India

▶ Southwest Asia

▶ Northern China

▶ Ethiopia

▶ Southern Mexico

▶ Northern Peru

Humans became stationary and self-supporting. Large communities—a hindrance for nomads—became an asset for farmers.

As communities grew, civilization emerged. Of course, not all people became farmers; many still continued to live a nomadic existence. However, those numbers dropped dramatically with each wave of agricultural innovation.

Not only did the advent of seed agriculture and animal domestication change the way people lived, but it also increased the carrying capacity of the earth. Attempts to increase yield led to the development of more advanced tools. (The plow emerged in Mesopotamia around 6,000 years ago.)

With specialized tools came specialized skills which added even more value. People began to use their skills to benefit the larger community rather than just themselves.

Increased agricultural efficiency eventually led to surplus that could be traded for other goods. As a result, markets and trade systems developed as did the notion of **wealth** as the accumulation of goods.

Figure 4.14. Early Plow

The revolution did not bring about only positive change, however:

▶ Farmers were vulnerable to the weather in ways nomads were not and had to depend on specific planting and harvesting times.

▶ Those who had acquired goods were vulnerable to theft of their wealth; consequently, humans developed secure storage methods (as they no longer carried everything around with them) and began to construct fortifications to protect their communities.

Success in seed agriculture led to **subsistence farming** in which farmers grow only enough food to feed their own family. This type of farming is still very common today, especially in less developed countries. Subsistence farming takes three main forms.

Extensive subsistence farming uses a large amount of land to farm food for a family:

▶ It is found mostly in areas with low populations but a great deal of land.

▶ The land, however, tends to have a thin topsoil, and is therefore limited in its production capacity.

Large amounts of land are needed because farmers practice **shifting cultivation**, meaning they rotate which types of crops are grown in each field in order to maintain healthy soil. Once the soil becomes too worn out, fields are left fallow for several years to rebuild nutrients.

In some cases, the farmers will use **slash-and-burn** to clear the land. They will cut down the plants then burn the remaining stalks, stumps, and roots to create new farmland (called making it **swidden**). Most farmers who use this technique also practice **intertillage**, planting different crops in the same area to reduce the risk of crop failure and promote a healthier diet.

Today, extensive subsistence farming can be found mostly in tropical areas, especially in the rainforests of Africa, near the Amazon, and throughout Southeast Asia. Extensive subsistence farming has serious environmental ramifications:

▶ As populations have grown and the land available for agriculture has decreased, farmers need to replant fields too soon, leading to permanent soil damage.

▶ The desire for more land has led to the destruction of other types of areas—like rainforests—to allow for the creation of new farmland.

Intensive subsistence farming uses a small amount of land as efficiently as possible to feed a family:

▶ This type of farming can be found in areas with high populations and very fertile soil.

▶ Intensive subsistence farming is marked by innovative farming techniques like terrace-farming pyramids, which make use of vertical *and* horizontal space for farming.

▶ Another technique used is **double-cropping**, when farmers plant two subsequent crops in the same field in a single year.

▶ For thousands of years, this type of farming has been most dominant in Asia, especially in China, India, and Southeast Asia.

▶ Rice is commonly grown using intensive subsistence farming; however, wheat, corn, and millet are also grown using this method in areas that are too cold for rice.

Pastoralism is a type of farming that emerged with the domestication of animals. Rather than raising crops, pastoralists breed and herd animals (primarily goats, camels, sheep, and cattle) for food, clothing, and shelter.

Pastoralism is dominant in areas with very limited growing capabilities, such as grasslands, deserts, and steppes like North Africa, central and southern Africa, the Middle East, and Central Asia. Pastoralists can be sedentary or nomadic, moving their herds in search of new food sources or improved climate depending on the season.

The land used by pastoralists is shrinking as governments take control of it to use for other economic purposes, like drilling and mining.

PRACTICE QUESTIONS

37) **Which of the following is NOT an accurate descriptor of the First Agricultural Revolution?**

    A.   Humans began to settle in stationary communities.

    B.   Humans began to use technology to increase food production.

    C.   It led to the development of a more stable food supply.

    D.   It allowed for significant population growth.

38) **Which of the following farming techniques would most likely be used in a Vietnamese rice field?**

    A.   intertillage

    B.   slash-and-burn

    C.   double-cropping

    D.   shifting cultivation

THE SECOND AGRICULTURAL REVOLUTION

The **Second Agricultural Revolution** began around 500 CE, was centered in Europe, and was marked by an increase in agricultural technology. This revolution occurred in two major bursts.

The first was right after the fall of Rome, when the feudal village structure emerged:

▶ Agricultural production was organized by the **open-lot system** in which there was one plot of land for the community, and all members worked in it to provide for themselves and their families.

▶ Refinement of tools like the plow and the introduction of other, more complex tools like water mills increased production.

The second burst came about 1,200 years later:

▶ The growth of capitalism shifted the way people farmed, and individuals began fencing off their land in what was called the enclosure movement.

▶ This coincided with the Industrial Revolution and the decline of the feudal system.

▶ As people began to migrate in increasing numbers to the cities, the demand for food to be shipped to these areas of population concentration skyrocketed.

▶ New innovations in farming, like the steel plow and the mechanical reaper, led to higher outputs and an eventual population boom that kept the entire cycle continuing.

As the demand for food increased—and has continued to increase—subsistence farming was replaced in industrialized countries by **commercial farming:**

▶ In commercial farming, food is grown to be sold on the market rather than to feed one's own family.

▶ There are several forms of commercial farming; however, they all have one thing in common—they are designed to maximize profit.

Mixed crop and livestock farming is commercial farming that involves both crops and animals. This was the first type of commercial farming to emerge in the Second Industrial Revolution and evolved from subsistence farming. It differs from subsistence farming in two notable exceptions:

▶ These farms are generally much bigger than the average subsistence farm.

▶ Most crops are raised not for human consumption but to feed the animals. The income from the farm, then, comes from the sale of animal products—wool, eggs, and meat; thus, these types of farms are not as dependent on the seasons as crop-only farms.

Other types of commercial agriculture focus on one animal byproduct. For example, **ranching**, the commercial grazing of animals, became a profitable form of farming:

▶ The textile mills of Europe's Industrial Revolution demanded high quantities of wool, greatly increasing the value of sheep worldwide.

▶ In the US, the advent of refrigerated railcars allowed for the transport of meat over long distances.

▶ The demand from the burgeoning cities led to a ranching boom— mostly cattle—in the second half of the nineteenth century.

Ranching was, and remains, especially popular in areas where the climate is too dry to support crops but where land is abundant: the western United States, northern Mexico, Argentina, southern Brazil, Uruguay, the west coast of Latin America, and some areas of Spain and Portugal. At the same time, ranching has had a significant negative impact on the environment, destroying grasslands through overgrazing.

Figure 4.15. Ranching

Overall, ranching is on the decline. Government standards for beef show a preference for fattier meat rather than the tough, stringier meat from cattle that roam far to graze. Instead, more and more cattle are raised on "fattening farms," where they are kept in a closed lot and fed large amounts to fatten them for slaughter. Furthermore, low grain prices make it unnecessary to allow the animals to roam in order to feed them.

Another type of specialized commercial farming is **dairying**, farming which focuses solely on bringing milk-based products to market. Because milk is so perishable, the distance from the market became very important for determining what a farm could produce.

Originally, farms within the **milkshed**—the area surrounding the market in which fresh milk could be safely transported—usually focused their efforts on milk and other fluid products because these are more perishable. Those outside of the milkshed focused mostly on more sustainable products, like butter and cheese. Over time, the milkshed has grown as a result of technological advances in transportation and refrigeration.

Dairy farms differ from other farms in that they are particularly **capital intensive**, meaning they require a great deal of machinery over manual labor. Dairy farmers must invest a great deal of money into their equipment, so these farms tend to be small.

The most common type of commercial farm is the **large-scale grain production farm**. These farms:

▶   focus solely on the production of one to two key grain crops

▶   increase the food supply by providing grain for people AND food for animals raised for consumption

▶ are found primarily in humid continental climates (e.g., Canada, the United States, Argentina, Australia, France, England, and Ukraine)

▶ mainly grow wheat

Figure 4.16. Large-Scale Grain Production Farm

Like dairy farming, large-scale grain production is capital-intensive; however, the farms tend to be much bigger to allow for the growth of a profitable quantity of grain. In addition, more large-scale grain production is dedicated to animal feed than to food for humans to eat.

DID YOU KNOW?

The United States and Canada are responsible for over half of the world's wheat.

Similar to large-scale grain production are **plantation farms**, which focus on producing only one or two crops. These farms are also large-scale. But unlike grain farms, they are labor-intensive rather than capital-intensive. Plantation farms:

▶ rely on large numbers of seasonal workers

▶ mainly grow crops that cannot be easily mechanized (e.g., bananas, cotton, tea)

▶ must be located near ports to allow for easy export of crops

The location of plantation farms reflects the global power structure. They are located primarily in less developed countries—mostly low-latitude Africa, Asia, and Latin America—but are owned by and produce crops primarily for export to more developed countries. They monopolize the high-quality land in these areas, leaving little for local farmers and impeding development within the host country.

Figure 4.17. Plantation Farm

Both the development of new technology and the growth of factories led to a globalization and industrialization of agriculture. It became increasingly cost effective to grow food in one place and process it in another. For example, Great Britain and the northeastern United States dominated the textile industry; however, the cotton they used was grown primarily in the American South, India, and Egypt.

CHECK YOUR UNDERSTANDING #4

Which theory of human-environment interaction states that the type of farming that develops in a location depends on the climate?

The methods being used to improve the efficiency and profit of industry were applied to agriculture as well. Developing seeds, fertilizing fields, farming, processing, packaging, distributing, and advertising all became part of a larger **agribusiness**. As a result, the number of people involved in agribusiness has increased, while the number of actual farmers has steadily declined. In 1950, farmers comprised 12 percent of the American workforce; today they compose less than 1 percent.

In the 1820s, Johann Heinrich von Thünen developed the first spatial economic theory. Called **agricultural location theory**, it was a theoretical model he created before the Industrial Revolution was in full swing to determine how distance impacted human location decisions.

In order to do this, he had to treat all other factors as constants in order to isolate distance. He assumed there was one city with one market in which all farmers sold their goods, and that there was only one type of transportation. Therefore the only factor impacting price of transportation was distance. He also assumed that all land was equally farmable; therefore, the only thing affecting rent was distance from the market.

Based on this model, he predicted that the city would be surrounded by rings of agricultural activity moving from the most intensive, like dairy—which requires less land and carries a higher risk of spoilage—to the most extensive, like large-scale grain production or ranching—which requires much more land and can be transported farther without reducing quality. This was the first model to look at economics through a geographic lens.

PRACTICE QUESTIONS

39) In which of the following ways did the Industrial Revolution NOT impact agriculture?

A. The emergence of the feudal system created more labor-intensive farming.

B. Increased technological innovations led to more efficient farming and greater production.

C. The rise of capitalism led to the individualization of farmland.

D. The demand for food made growing crops for the market more profitable.

40) Which of the following types of commercial farming are most capital-intensive?

A. dairy and ranching

B. ranching and plantation farms

C. large-scale grain production and dairy

D. plantation farms and large-scale grain production

41) According to agricultural location theory, what is the relative location to the city of a dairy farm and a mixed crop-livestock farm that specializes in cheese and butter?

A. The dairy farm will be closer to the city.

B. The mixed crop-livestock farm will be closer to the city.

C. They will be equidistant from the city.

D. Their distance from the city cannot be determined with the information given.

THE THIRD AGRICULTURAL REVOLUTION

The **Third Agricultural Revolution** is also known as the **Green Revolution** and centered on a dramatic increase in crop yields based on **biotechnology**, scientific modifications to seeds and fertilizers.

In response to the burgeoning global population, scientists looked to find ways to improve grain production capabilities. As a result of their efforts, from 1945 – 1990, grain production increased by 45 percent in Mexico, where this work began. In Asia, rice production increased by 66 percent by 1985. By the 1980s, India no longer needed to import rice and wheat to feed its growing population; the country was self-sufficient in production of these crops.

Norman Borlaug, seen as the father of the Green Revolution, won a Nobel Prize for his work in 1970. The world's food supply was no longer an issue in terms of quantity.

Unfortunately, however, this does not mean that hunger no longer exists. The world's food supply, while large, is unevenly distributed, and hunger persists as a global problem due to social and transportation issues. Yield was increased for many crops—but not all—and most Green Revolution crops are not arable in Africa. The base crops of Africa—sorghum and millet—have received very little attention. As a result, less than 5 percent of African farmers use Green Revolution seeds for farming.

Other problems emerged as a result of the Green Revolution:

▶ Farming jobs decreased dramatically as less labor was required to produce the same amount—or even more—food.

▶ The higher yield crops are more susceptible to disease and pests, making crop failure more common.

Green Revolution technology had a significant environmental impact as well:

▶ Overall, farming high-yield crops requires more technology and machinery, which requires more fuel, thereby increasing pollution and consumption.

▶ These crops also require more water, straining water supplies.

▶ The pesticides which were developed to protect the crops cause pollution and soil contamination; they have even led to health problems in those workers who experience prolonged exposure to the chemicals.

▶ Global genetic diversity in plant life has been reduced as local strains of various crops are phased out to make room for high-yield crops. While this has led to a growth of the food supply, it has also greatly increased its vulnerability.

RENEWABLE AND NONRENEWABLE RESOURCES

One of the most significant ways humans impact their environment is through the use of natural resources. Some resources are **renewable resources**, meaning they are virtually unlimited or can be grown and regrown. Examples of renewable resources include:

▶ wind

▶ sun

▶ plants

Other resources are **nonrenewable resources** because they cannot be replaced once they are consumed. Examples of nonrenewable resources include:

▶ iron ore

▶ coal

▶ petroleum

Trees can be considered both renewable and nonrenewable, depending on how they are used. If managed properly, they can be replanted and grown again; however, the rapid consumption of old-growth forests uses up a resource that essentially cannot be replaced. Also, the land trees are on is often repurposed for farm land, urbanization, or mining once the trees are removed, resulting in a permanent loss of the resource.

Consuming nonrenewable resources—and consuming renewable resources too quickly—is a growing concern as industrialization has greatly increased overall consumption. Many countries are searching for ways to promote **sustainable development**, the use of natural resources and the growth of new ones at a rate that can be maintained from one generation to the next.

The **United Nations Commission on Sustainable Development** defines several criteria for global sustainable development:

▶ caring for the soil

▶ avoiding overfishing

▶ preserving the forest

▶ protecting species from extinction

▶ reducing air pollution

Other sustainability efforts focus on indirect factors impacting Earth's natural resources. For example, efforts to reduce fuel consumption are motivated by both the finite quantity of oil in the world and the **greenhouse effect** caused by industrialization:

▶ Industrial production unleashes carbon dioxide, methane, and other gases.

▶ These create a vapor that transforms radiation into heat, which leads to **global warming**, an overall rise in Earth's temperature.

▶ As a result, the ice caps are melting prematurely, leading to rising sea levels and changes in oceanic patterns.

PRACTICE QUESTIONS

42) **In Asia, the Green Revolution resulted in**

A. the introduction of new crops, like wheat and barley.

B. new farming techniques, such as terrace farming.

C. an increase in the importation of grain.

D. a dramatic increase in rice production.

43) **Which region of the world shared least in the benefits of the Green Revolution?**

A. Southeast Asia

B. Africa

C. Central America

D. Europe

44) **Which of the following statements is true about sustainable development?**

A. Sustainable development requires a prohibition on the use of nonrenewable resources.

B. Sustainable development only applies to energy resources like wind, sun, oil, and coal.

C. Sustainable development requires the proper management of renewable resources like trees and fish.

D. Sustainable development contributes to the greenhouse effect and increases global warming.

MOVEMENT

Geography is the study of spatial patterns, and movement includes many important spatial patterns. All types of movement—of people, of things, of phenomena—are important to the study of geography.

Geographers examine **spatial interaction**, the ways in which different places interact with one another through the flow of people, goods, or ideas. The ways in which farmers move their goods to market, the movement of labor from rural areas to urban areas, and the diffusion of culture are all examples of spatial interaction.

Distance is an important factor in the study of movement:

▶ Geographers examine the **friction of distance** in movement, or the extent to which distance interferes with the spatial interaction.

▶ The level of energy—and money—required to overcome distance increases with the distance itself.

There is less friction of distance—and greater spatial interaction—between Boston and New York than between Boston and Shanghai.

Distance also impacts the intensity of phenomena that travel between places. This **distance decay** can be seen in the impact of an earthquake:

▶ Those who are closest to the earthquake will see the biggest changes to the physical characteristics of their place, as well as the most cultural, political, and economic ramifications.

▶ Those who are hundreds or thousands of miles away may feel little to no impact at all.

The impact of distance decay has been decreasing over time. **Time-space compression** is the feeling that the world is getting smaller, resulting from globalization. For instance, the 2011 earthquake and tsunami in Japan had significant consequences as far away as Chicago. Markets were affected, trips were canceled to and from Japan, and sadly, people around the world lost family and friends in the disaster.

DIFFUSION

The type of movement most commonly studied in geography is **spatial diffusion**, the spread, or movement, of people, things, and ideas across space. Cultural diffusion (discussed earlier in this chapter) is a major subset of spatial diffusion. There are two main types of spatial diffusion.

The first, **expansion diffusion**, describes the process of a phenomenon remaining strong at its hearth while expanding outward to new places. As it spreads to a new place, the new adopters may modify the idea; this is called **stimulus expansion diffusion**. For example, the sport of tennis began in the royal courts of France and England and was played on grass. As the game diffused to new areas—and new groups of people—different playing surfaces (clay and hardcourts) were adopted.

Hierarchical diffusion describes when the phenomenon starts with a person or place in a position of power or influence and then spreads to others in a leveled pattern. For example, sushi arrived in the United States from Japan as a result of stimulus expansion diffusion. It began in New York City, a city of significant cultural power, and then followed a hierarchical diffusion pattern by spreading to other large cities, then midsize and smaller cities, and finally suburbs and some towns.

The final method of expansion diffusion is **contagious diffusion**, which describes when multiple places near the hearth become adopters, rather than the phenomenon spreading in a sequential manner.

As the name implies, the classic example of contagious diffusion is a disease. When people in one town became ill during the flu pandemic of 1918, the disease then spread to all the surrounding towns, and so on. This is the most widespread type of diffusion.

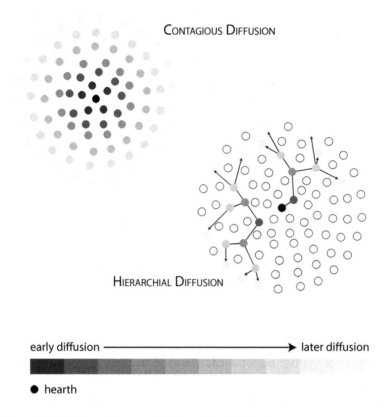

early diffusion ⟶ later diffusion

● hearth

Figure 4.18. Contagious and Hierarchical Diffusion

Diffusion does not always occur in an expansive manner. Sometimes, the original adopters move from the hearth to a new place, taking their ideas with them. This is called **relocation diffusion**. For instance, in the 1850s, Mormons moved west from New York State to Illinois and then to what would become Utah. As they moved, the hearth of Mormonism moved with them as well.

A variant on this is **migration diffusion**—when the original adopters move but the idea or trait lasts only a short while in the new place. This is called migration diffusion because it occurs most often among immigrants, who move to a new place originally carrying the traits of their home culture. However, in a relatively short time (a generation or two) they shed their original cultural traits and adopt the traits of the new culture. This is a common story among immigrants to the United States who begin in ethnic enclaves and then, over time, diffuse into the general population. In this type of diffusion it is often hard to pinpoint the epicenter because the phenomenon fades so quickly.

CHECK YOUR UNDERSTANDING #5

Which type of diffusion is most closely associated with the spread of disease?

Most diffusions follow more than one of these patterns. However, all diffusions follow an *S*-curve pattern when the number of users over time are plotted on a graph.

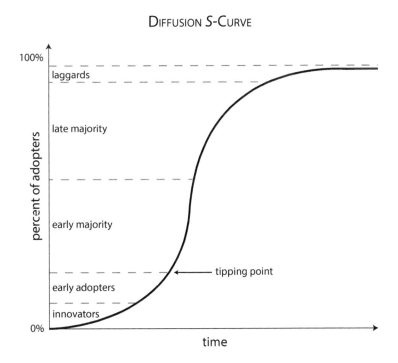

Figure 4.19. Diffusion S-Curve

For example, when the MP3 player was first introduced, only a small group of early adopters used it. As time passed, those early adopters introduced it to more people, advertising became more effective, and an early majority were downloading music on these devices. The more people who bought and used MP3 players, the more common they became, and the more they seemed like a cultural norm, prompting other adopters to join.

During this time, the adoption rate was high and continued until the majority of people abandoned their CD players for an MP3 player. Then, adoption tapered off, and then only the last few stragglers were left.

PRACTICE QUESTIONS

45) **The diffusion of smartphones within the United States is an example of which kind of diffusion?**

A.   stimulus diffusion

B.   relocation diffusion

C.   hierarchical diffusion

D.   contagious diffusion

46) Based on the *S*-curve graph, the LEAST number of new users occurs at which point in the diffusion process?

    A.   the very beginning only

    B.   the middle only

    C.   the end only

    D.   both the beginning and end

MIGRATION PATTERNS

Migration is the permanent relocation of an individual or group from one home region to another region. As globalization and space-time compression have increased, global mobility has increased as well, both in frequency and length of migrations.

Some migration is internal—people moving from one place to another within the same region—like urbanization. Other migration involves people moving from one region of the world to another. Many immigrants have migrated to the United States from other countries around the world.

Geographers study migration to understand *how* people move through space as well as *why* they move through space. To answer the question of *how*—the manner and numbers of people moving—geographers examine **migration streams**:

> ▶ Migration streams are the specific spatial movement from the starting location to the destination.

> ▶ These are mapped using arrows of differing thickness to indicate the number of migrants.

> ▶ Migration streams are usually paired with **migration counter-streams** of people returning home.

HELPFUL HINT

Migrants who cross international borders fleeing persecution, governmental abuse, war, or natural disaster are called **refugees**. People who migrate intranationally by moving from one part of a country to another are called **internally displaced persons**.

To answer the question *why?* geographers look at both push factors and pull factors.

▶ **Push factors** describe the negative aspects of the home region that make someone want to leave it.

    ▷   Push factors include high taxes, high crime rates, resource depletion, and corrupt governments.

▶ **Pull factors** describe positive aspects of the new region that make someone want to move there.

    ▷   Pull factors include new, better-paying jobs, schools, abundant resources, and greater protection of individual rights.

Migration rate per
1,000 people in 2011

< –10

–9.9 to –5

–4.9 to –0.1

0 to 5

5.1 to 10

> 10.1

Figure 4.20. Migration Streams

A common pull factor for new immigrants are previous immigrants to a place. This is called **chain migration**:

▶ Example: In the late 1990s Eritreans began to immigrate to the United States as the result of the Eritrean-Ethiopian War (a push factor). They settled primarily in Washington, DC, and Los Angeles, prompting other Eritreans to move to these two cities as well (a pull factor).

If a location attracts more **immigrants** (people moving into a place) than it has **emigrants** (people moving out of a place), it has **net in-migration**, and is considered to have **high place desirability**. Western Europe, the United States, and Canada all have net in-migration.

On the other hand, if a place has more emigrants than immigrants, it has **net out-migration**. Today that includes most of Asia, Africa, and Latin America.

Geographers determine how likely someone is to migrate using **migration selectivity**. While personal, social, and economic factors all play a role, age is actually the most important factor in migration. Many Americans, for example, typically migrate to a new town, city, or state between eighteen and thirty years of age. Research has also shown that greater education leads to greater mobility.

Not all migration is voluntary. History has many examples of **forced migration**, when a group of people is forcibly removed from their home and brought to a new region. The African slave trade and the removal of Native American tribes from the Southeastern United States are both examples of forced migration.

Migration patterns tend to be predictable and can be determined using three key theories: Ravenstein's laws of migration, the gravitational model, and Zelinsky's model of migration transition.

In the 1880s, geographer Ernst Georg Ravenstein developed his laws of migration, known as **Ravenstein's laws of migration,** which remain the basis for migration theory today and include the following ideas:

▶ Most migrants travel only short distances. Even when they do travel longer distances, they often use **step migration**, traveling in short steps to ultimately achieve a longer distance.

▶ People living in rural areas are more likely to migrate, especially in areas that are industrializing.

▶ Migrants who do travel farther tend to choose big cities as their destination.

▶ Large towns grow by migration instead of by natural growth.

▶ Mostly adults migrate.

▶ Young adults are more likely to cross borders than families who tend to migrate internally.

▶ Every migration stream has a counter-stream.

HELPFUL HINT

The DTM, Rostow's modernization model, and Zelinsky's model of migration transition are all closely related. If you master one—probably Rostow's—you can use it as a tool to help you recall the others.

The **gravitational model** of migration estimates the size and direction of migration between two places:

▶ It is based on the assumption that the migrational "gravity" of a place is determined by its size and distance.

▶ Places that are larger and/or closer attract more migrants.

The limitation of this model is that it only considers location and does not include migration selectivity factors.

Using the DTM, Geographer Wilbur Zelinsky developed a model of migration, known as **Zelinsky's model of migration transition**, based on the development stage of a country.

▶ Countries in stage one of the DTM migrate locally to search for food and shelter materials.

▶ In stage two, the high RNI overstresses resources resulting in emigration out of the country; there is also a high rate of rural-to-urban migration.

▶ In stage three, rural-to-urban migration is surpassed by urban-to-urban migration, and immigration exceeds emigration.

▶ In stage four, urban-to-suburban migration (and vice versa) emerges as the dominant form of migration, stabilizing in stage five.

PRACTICE QUESTIONS

47) Which of the following events would be considered a pull factor for migration?

    A.   the opening of a new factory in a different town

    B.   a drought in the home region

    C.   an increase in terrorist activity in the home region

    D.   the construction of a high-speed train between the hometown and the nearest city

48) During the late 1990s, Ireland had such a strong economy that it was known as the "Celtic Tiger," attracting migration and investment. Recent Irish immigrants to the United States and even some Irish Americans began returning to their homeland with their families. This phenomenon is best explained by which of the following?

    A.   the US's stage of development (stage four) based on Zelinsky's model of migration transition

    B.   the size of Ireland, based on the gravitational model of migration

    C.   Ravenstein's law that young adults are more likely to cross borders than families

    D.   Ravenstein's law that for every migration stream, there is a counter-stream

Practice Questions Answer Key

1) **D.** A study of the rise and fall of the American dollar does not address the question of *Where?* It is solely an economic question, not a geographic one.

2) **C.** Migration patterns show how people—or animals—move in and out of different areas. This is a clear example of the theme of *movement*. It describes how places are interconnected.

3) **A.** Conformal maps are designed to ensure the shape of all land masses are correct. In order to do this, they distort the other properties of the map, specifically, size.

4) **C.** A globe is a model replica of Earth. It is precisely scaled to reflect the dimensions of the planet, accurately preserving size, shape, direction, and distance.

5) **B.** The scale shows the ratio between distance on the map and true distance.

6) **D.** The gnomonic projection map allows for great circles and accurate straight-line directions. It is often used for mapping the poles and would be an excellent choice for an explorer of Antarctica.

7) **A.** Mental maps can reflect locations personal to the individual, but people also develop mental maps of entire cities, regions, and the world.

8) **D.** The two mental maps are very different, but not necessarily contradictory. Instead, both are possible descriptions of the same place. Each student, however, has a different relationship to the gym. We can assume, as a basketball player, Student A spends more time in the gym than Student B. The stuffiness and poor lighting noted by Student B could simply be a reflection of the fact that, as a soccer player, Student B is used to playing sports outside in an open field. Student A may have located the gymnasium at the center of the school because of the central importance it plays in that student's school experience.

9) **C.** Political borders are man-made; therefore, they are considered human characteristics of a place.

10) **A.** *Place* answers the questions: *What is an area like? What are its defining features?* This identifies the primary physical characteristic of a specific area.

11) **C.** The desert has extreme heat during the day and extreme cold at night.

12) **A.** A congressional district is a region with a common purpose—representation in Congress.

13) **B.** Taiga is found just south of the tundra, primarily in Sweden, Norway, Finland, northern Russia, Canada, and Alaska.

14) **B.** While Aristotle's physical writings would be material components, his actual teachings—what he believed and said—are nonmaterial.

15) **C.** Because the geographer is alone while collecting the data on the river, this is primary geographic data.

16) **B.** Starbucks began in the United States and is distinctly American. Its existence and popularity in Dubai is an example of cultural diffusion.

17) **B.** The adoption of French in West Africa as an official language is a classic example of a local culture overcome by a powerful force and taking on the traits of what would thus become the dominant culture. This occurred wherever colonization took place.

18) **A.** More than half of the world's population lives in cities.

19) **C.** In order to maximize the residents' access to the water, the settlement would grow along the bank of the river.

20) **B.** In stage two, the crude death rate (CDR) declines (as a result of medical advancements), but the crude birth rate (CBR) remains high. This leads to high population growth, putting the country at risk of overpopulation.

21) **A.** The second biggest population center in the world is Southeast Asia (the first is East Asia).

22) **C.** When a country does not have enough people to utilize its resources, it is underpopulated.

23) **C.** The tertiary sector sells and trades processed goods. Any store is part of the tertiary sector.

24) **C.** With industrialization, geographers note a rise in the migration of people from rural to urban areas, not suburban.

25) **C.** Dependency theory argues that colonization created a dependent relationship between less developed countries (LDCs) and more developed countries (MDCs) that cannot be broken due to the global economic structure.

26) **C.** Both statements about more developed countries (MDCs) are accurate descriptors.

27) **A.** By looking at the ratio of the cost of certain items (or groups of items) in different countries, purchasing power parity (PPP) gives a more accurate comparative measure of development.

28) **B.** The United Nations Human Development Index (HDI) defines development as the expansion of choices for the people. As a result, it looks at many factors, many of which are nonmonetary.

29) **B.** Most multinational corporations (MNCs) headquarter their companies in more developed countries (MDCs) and only use the less developed country's (LDC's) special economic zones (SEZs) for production purposes.

30) **C.** Although outsourcing leads to higher transportation costs since companies have to pay to get finished goods back to their markets, the reduced cost of labor is enough to offset it. This is called the substitution principle.

31) **D.** Panama is an elongated state because it is long and thin.

32) **A.** Mountains are an example of physical boundaries because they are part of the landscape.

33) **C.** Because of their concentration of power, primate cities also have a much greater share of a country's resources.

34) **B.** A buffer state lies between two states in conflict. A great deal of fighting took place in Poland during World War II as a result of the conflict between Germany and the Soviet Union.

35) **B.** Having a distinct culture complex from the rest of Spain, the Basque people make up a separate nation; however, as they do not have their own state, they are considered a stateless nation.

36) **C.** The domino theory states that if one country falls to communism, the rest around it will as well. Once communist forces began to gain power in the north, US officials became concerned that all of the peninsula—and then the rest of Asia—would become communist.

37) **B.** The First Agricultural Revolution resulted from humans learning how to gather and replant seeds to grow crops. Technology did not play a significant role.

38) **C.** Double-cropping is the intensive subsistence farming practice of planting subsequent crops within the same year. Vietnam's climate is ideal for this type of farming.

39) **A.** The feudal system was ending as the Industrial Revolution got underway, and farming actually became less labor-intensive with the introduction of new machinery.

40) **C.** Both large-scale grain production and dairy are highly mechanized, requiring significant capital investment.

41) **A.** Because the dairy farm is a more intensive farming practice that requires less land, it will be located closer to the city. It also carries a greater risk of spoilage (milk versus butter and cheese), so it requires a shorter distance to market.

42) **C.** As a result of high-yield rice developed during the Green Revolution, rice production increased by 66 percent in the 1980s.

43) **B.** Most Green Revolution crops cannot be grown in Africa, and little research was done on millet and sorghum, the most common grains used in African countries.

44) **C.** The goal of sustainable development is to ensure resources are available for the next generation; therefore, renewable resources must be managed to make sure consumption does not outpace the rate of replacement.

45) **C.** Smartphones were first adopted by those who could afford them (because the price point was prohibitive for others) and who were in a

position of power. They then diffused through economic levels as the prices changed and companies provided opportunities to make them more affordable.

46)   **C.** Early adopters and laggards are the two smallest groups of adopters.

47)   **A.** A new factory would provide jobs and encourage migration into the area.

48)   **C.** Historically, the Irish fled poverty and oppression in Ireland, with many settling in North America. The migration of Irish to Ireland from the United States constitutes a counter-stream to the migration stream of the Irish diaspora.

CHECK YOUR UNDERSTANDING ANSWER KEY

Check Your Understanding #1

Rome, Italy

Check Your Understanding #2

culture trait

Check Your Understanding #3

Some common examples of multinational corporations (MNCs) include McDonald's, Exxon, Starbucks, Facebook, Microsoft, Apple, and many more!

Check Your Understanding #4

environmental determinism

Check Your Understanding #5

contagious diffusion

5

Principles of Economics

Fundamental Economic Concepts

Scarcity

There are some basic concepts that are part of all branches of economics. Scarcity, choice, and opportunity costs all figure in everyone's day-to-day living.

In economics, there is an assumption that all people have unlimited wants; however, there are limited resources to satisfy those wants. This concept is called **scarcity**. Scarcity forces individuals to make a **choice**—to select one want over another.

In making choices, people seek to maximize their **utility**, the point of greatest happiness. A student wants to go to the movies with friends but also wants to do well on exams the next day. The resource—in this case, time—is limited, so the student must choose between the options.

The student will weigh the cost—value lost—of not studying for her exam, against the benefit—value attained—of seeing the movie, and vice versa. The value of the option not selected is called the **opportunity cost.** So, the opportunity cost of staying home to study is the lost fun of seeing the movie and strengthening bonds with friends.

Resources, also called **factors of production**, fall into four basic categories:

1. labor

2. land or natural resources

3. physical capacity

4. entrepreneurial ability, or know-how

Each of the four factors of production is necessary to the process of producing anything in the marketplace, and they are considered some of the most basic parts of the business equation.

Law of Diminishing Marginal Utility

Total utility is the sum of an individual's happiness or the extent to which an individual's needs are met.

Marginal utility is the increase in happiness one gains from a product. A child desires a treat, and receives an ice cream cone, thereby increasing her utility. The child then receives a cupcake, which further increases her utility. That increase is her marginal utility.

While needs are unlimited, an individual's need for a specific product can be met. In fact, the **law of diminishing marginal utility** states that the more units of a product one has, the less one needs. Think of a very hungry person: his need for food seems unlimited; however, with each bite he takes, his need—and the amount of additional utility a bite brings—is shrinking or diminishing, until he is finally satiated.

Marginal Analysis

People tend to make decisions **at the margin,** meaning as an addition to the status quo.

Recall the student who wants to see a movie. The student has already studied for an hour (and already spent time with friends and seen movies on previous days), so the choice is a marginal one.

The student is considering the **marginal benefit** (the additional benefit) and **marginal cost** (the additional cost) of studying for another hour or the marginal benefit and cost of going to the movies.

Marginal analysis is used in many economic decisions, including production, consumption, and hiring: When a company looks at the extra costs of producing a good or service regarding the benefit of producing that good, it uses marginal analysis.

Marginal analysis is most helpful in company decision-making regarding production. Changes in marginal costs and benefits can also affect decision-making in both the short and long term. If consumers are happy with an item and they buy it in quantity, then businesses flourish.

A company would use marginal analysis to determine if the benefit of offering more of the item outweighs the cost of increasing production. Similarly, a new company would use marginal analysis to decide if the benefit of selling a popular item outweighs the cost of heavy competition from many similar companies on the market, or if the cost of a lower price is overshadowed by the benefit of potentially selling more units than the competitor.

PRACTICE QUESTIONS

1) Which of the following is NOT an example of the principle of scarcity?

   A. overfishing in key coastal waters

   B. a pharmaceutical company lowers the price of a commonly used generic drug

   C. drought reduces the amount of pumpkins sold in fall farmer's markets

   D. flu season ramps up and flu vaccines are hard to find

2) A company is looking to hire a new website designer to refresh its website. This would be the first job for the first candidate, who is fresh out of college. The second candidate has worked as a website designer for ten years; however, the company would have to pay that candidate twice as much as the first candidate. Which of the following illustrates how the company uses marginal analysis to decide which candidate to hire?

   A. weigh the cost of hiring a web designer against the benefit of having customers

   B. weigh the cost of increased pay for the second candidate against the benefit of more experience

   C. weigh the cost of the first candidate's lack of experience against the cost of the second candidate's high price

   D. weigh the benefit of the first candidate's price against the benefit of the second candidate's experience

3) At an amusement park, two children take their first rollercoaster ride. They love it so much that they want to ride again. According to the law of diminishing marginal utility, which of the following is most likely to happen after the children take their tenth ride?

   A. The children will have a greater desire to ride the rollercoaster than on their first ride.

   B. The children will never want to ride any rollercoaster again.

   C. The children will experience the same level of excitement as after their first ride.

   D. The children will be less interested—or uninterested entirely—in riding the rollercoaster again that day.

PRODUCTION POSSIBILITIES CURVE

A **production possibilities curve** determines if an individual, company, or nation is producing at its most efficient level and which product will likely make the highest profit. The curve assumes that there are two choices for production.

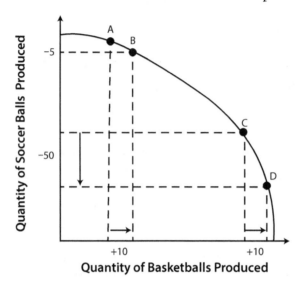

Figure 5.1. Production Possibilities Curve

A production possibilities curve demonstrates:

▶   opportunity costs

▶   economic efficiency

▶   economic growth

▶   scarcity

A company that produces soccer balls is looking to diversify and produce basketballs as well. For each basketball the company produces, there is an opportunity cost in soccer balls. Perhaps it takes a worker twice as long and costs twice as much money to make a basketball as a soccer ball.

The opportunity cost of making a basketball is two soccer balls. The production possibility curve plots the relationship between the number of soccer balls and basketballs produced to help the company find the most efficient combination of production.

This curve is also called the **production possibility frontier** because it represents the maximum level of production. It is not possible for a company to produce soccer balls and basketballs beyond the curve. The scarcity of resources (materials for soccer balls and labor) creates this upper bound. At the points under the curve, the company's resources are not being used to their maximum potential.

Economists believe that the frontier expands over time, a process called **economic growth.** This results from one or more of the following:

▶ an increase in the quantity of resources

▶ an increase in the quality of existing resources

▶ technological advancements in production

The reflection in the production possibility curve, however, is not proportional. An increase in resources or new technology does not impact all sectors of the economy in the same way.

A classic historical example is the invention of the cotton gin. The cotton gin was a technological advancement allowing cotton seeds to be separated from harvested cotton by machine rather than by hand. This dramatically expanded the production possibility of cotton, shifting the curve. But it had no impact on the actual production of cotton plants.

Opportunity cost can be determined by calculating the slope of the curve:

▶ The slope represents the opportunity cost on the x-axis.

▶ The inverse of the slope represents the opportunity cost on the y-axis.

The production possibility frontier is curved because opportunity costs increase as the quantity produced increases. This is called the **law of increasing costs.**

Economic efficiency is as necessary for consumers as it is for business entities. For consumers, setting a budget for monthly expenses is part of running a household. At the same time, businesses must continually analyze production possibilities curves to determine more efficient production processes, cost-cutting measures, and ways to boost profits.

MARKET EFFICIENCY

As discussed, an economy is working inefficiently if it is producing below the production possibility curve. This is called **productive inefficiency.**

An economy's efficiency is not only measured by its use of resources but by the benefit it provides to society, called its **allocative efficiency.**

For example, a country could direct all its resources to the production of hats. This economy might have high productive efficiency, maximizing its output, but it is providing little benefit to its citizens, and so has low allocative efficiency.

DID YOU KNOW?

Equatorial Guinea is rich in petroleum. But only a few have profited; the standard of living for most of the country remains extremely low. Equatorial Guinea therefore exhibits low allocative efficiency.

Absolute and Comparative Advantage

When deciding between producing two different products, a company must also consider its production capabilities for each item relative to the rest of the market.

If a company (or nation) can produce a good more efficiently than all competitors, it has an **absolute advantage** in that market. Looking back at the soccer ball company: if that company can produce soccer balls more efficiently than all other soccer ball companies, it has an absolute advantage in soccer ball production.

A company can have an absolute advantage in more than one product (if the company also produced basketballs most efficiently, for example). It may then seem that the company should produce both products; however, that is not necessarily the case.

The ball company may be able to produce both soccer balls and basketballs more efficiently than its competitor, but, if the company has workers specifically trained to quickly stitch high-quality soccer balls, the opportunity cost of producing basketballs instead will be high.

The company's competitor, on the other hand, may have workers who can stitch quality soccer balls at a much slower rate, leading to a lower opportunity cost for producing basketballs. (But the first company's opportunity cost for producing soccer balls will be lower.)

In this case, the competitor actually has a **comparative advantage** in producing basketballs, and the original company has one in producing soccer balls. Comparative advantage compares the opportunity cost of producing an item between companies.

It would, therefore, be in the best interest of the original company to specialize in soccer balls and the competitor to specialize in basketballs, even though the original company can produce both more efficiently.

Specialization and Interdependence

Specialization occurs when an individual, company, or nation focuses on producing one thing, typically because it has a comparative advantage.

> **HELPFUL HINT**
>
> Specialization leads to increased profits for companies and lower prices for consumers.

A doctor is also the fastest wood chopper in a town. However, the doctor does not both chop the town's wood and tend to its patients; the opportunity cost of chopping wood is too high. This individual therefore specializes in being a doctor, leaving the wood chopping to someone else (even though that person is not as fast).

Interdependence is part of a larger global or regional economy. When countries or businesses are interdependent, goods from one are necessary to the economy of another and both must function together for both to work.

Colonization is a classic example of interdependence. The mother country relied on the colony both for raw materials and as a market for its finished goods. On the other hand, the colony relied on the mother country as a market for its raw materials, and as a source for finished goods.

Both globalization and specialization lead to increased interdependence. Countries depend on treaties and business partnerships to provide goods necessary for production. One country provides lithium to another for cell phone battery production while the lithium-providing country is permitted to buy stockpiles of seed corn for its agricultural concerns. Both sides gain from this trading equation.

PRACTICE QUESTIONS

4) At point A on the production possibilities curve below, which of the following is true about the economy?

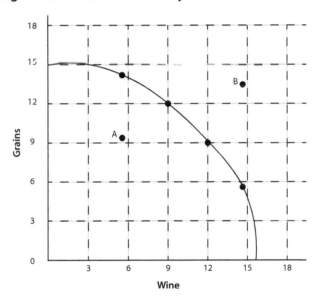

A. The economy should increase wine production and decrease grain production.

B. New resources are required before production can increase.

C. Some resources are being underutilized or wasted.

D. The economy is producing at its greatest efficiency.

5) Which of the following is NOT a consequence of specialization?

A. lower wages

B. higher quality goods

C. higher profits

D. lower prices

6) Company A can produce 900 pencils at the cost of producing 300 pens. For the same cost, Company B can produce either 200 pens or 1000 pencils. Which company has the comparative advantage and which company has the absolute advantage in producing pencils?

A. Company A has the comparative advantage; Company B has the absolute advantage.

B. Company A has both the comparative and absolute advantages.

C. Company A has the absolute advantage; Company B has the comparative advantage.

D. Company B has both the comparative and absolute advantages.

Types of Economic Systems

There are four kinds of economic systems: a traditional economy, a pure command economy, a pure market economy, and a mixed economy.

Table 5.1. Economic Systems

Type of System	Description
Traditional economy	a pre-industrialized economy, guided by tradition and often using bartering rather than currency
Pure command economy	• usually found in communist societies • The government—rather than the market—determines all aspects of production. • Today, they are very rare (e.g., North Korea).
Pure market economy	• also known as capitalism • governed by the laws of supply and demand with no outside interference
Mixed economy	• governed by both the market and the government • The people may decide what is produced by what they are willing to buy, but the government regulates different aspects of the economy regarding the safety of the population. • Most modern economies are mixed economies.

Functions of the Market

There are several defining principles of a market economy.

A pure market economy is a self-running entity; its internal forces govern its functioning, and it does not require outside intervention. Therefore, government has no place in a pure market economy. This leads to two key principles: private property and freedom of choice.

Table 5.2. Key Principles of a Market Economy

Private Property

- The market favors private ownership of most economic resources.
- Private ownership leads to innovation and investment, which in turn lead to growth.
- Private ownership allows for the trade of services and goods.

Freedom of Choice

- All individuals are free to acquire, use, and sell resources without restriction or regulation.
- This allows market forces to function properly.
- Two important elements in the market are supply and demand.
- For example, a restriction on buying large cars would artificially alter demand and throw off the functioning of the automobile market.

Private property and freedom of choice create the two primary driving forces of the market: self-interest and competition.

Table 5.3. Primary Driving Forces of a Market Economy

Self-Interest

- Market theory assumes that people are motivated by self-interest in their use of their own resources.
- The seller in the market wants to maximize resources (or profit); the buyer wants to maximize utility (or happiness).
- The seller offers goods that will maximize the happiness of buyers in order to attract sales.
- Self-interest, then, leads to innovation and quality, as it creates a market where the best products are available to buyers.
- Example: Apple has noted that technological integration brings buyers a great deal of happiness, so the company works to continually innovate new ways of integrating technology (like the Apple watch) in its quest for profit.

Competition

- All individuals are motivated by self-interest, so new sellers will enter the market when they determine that there is a possibility for profit.
- All individuals have freedom of choice, so buyers will buy from the sellers whose products maximize their happiness (usually either through prices or quality).
- Sellers therefore compete to attract buyers by appealing to their maximum happiness.
- Competition leads to lower prices and higher quality.

Consequently, the primary communication tool of the market is **price.** Because of competition, prices are set by the market rather than by individuals. As a result, price signals buyers and sellers who, in turn, use it to make decisions about how to use their resources.

Prices communicate the relative value of products in the market and deliver to both sellers and buyers what they seek through their own self-interest: profit and happiness, respectively.

PRACTICE QUESTIONS

7) In the 1870s in the United States, Americans favored laissez-faire economics, minimizing government regulations and controls on business. This most closely resembles which type of economy?

   A.   traditional

   B.   command

   C.   market

   D.   mixed

8) A buyer decides to switch to a new brand of detergent that promises to leave clothes cleaner. Which of the following market principles is NOT involved in this decision?

   A.   self-interest

   B.   freedom of choice

   C.   competition

   D.   price

SUPPLY AND DEMAND

If price is the communication tool of the economy—determining the allocation of resources by both buyers and sellers—then what determines price?

Price is the result of the interplay between two important economic forces: demand and supply.

LAW OF DEMAND

The **law of demand** is simple: as the price for a good or service increases, the demand for it will decrease, if all other factors are held constant. In other words, if the price goes up, purchases usually go down.

For example, a coffee shop sells coffee for $1 a cup, and sales skyrocket. The coffee shop then quadruples the price to $4 a cup; sales plummet.

Only **relative (real) price** affects demand. The relative price of a good is its value in relation to other items of similar value. Looking back at the coffee example, one might wonder what else could $4 purchase.

Perhaps the same coffee shop sells doughnuts for $2. Yesterday, the buyer could have gotten two cups of coffee for the price of one doughnut. Now two donuts are equivalent to the price of one cup of coffee. This is called the **substitution effect.**

Relative price is also determined by the percentage of one's income the price demands. If the buyer makes $16 an hour, the cup of coffee is 25% of that buyer's hourly income versus the 6.25% that the $1 price was.

This is called the **income effect.** The actual number of $4—the **absolute** price—does not impact demand.

DEMAND CURVE

A **demand curve** shows how demand changes as prices increase. The curve actually measures **quantity demanded** in relation to price. In economics, this is different from simple demand.

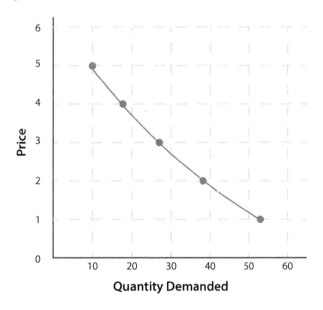

Figure 5.2. Demand Curve

Once again, a demand curve assumes all other factors remain constant, an assumption often made in economics to allow for the creation of models.

If multiple factors were taken into consideration (price, weather, and income, for example), it would be impossible to determine causation. These other factors are called **determinants of demand** and include the following:

- ▶ consumer income (buyer's ability to pay)

- ▶ price of a substitute good (in the example above, tea)

- ▶ price of a complementary good (in the example above, doughnuts)

- ▶ consumer preferences

- ▶ consumer expectations about future pricing (Do consumers anticipate the price will go down in the future?)

- ▶ number of buyers in the market

While changes in price affect the quantity demanded, changes in determinants of demand lead to changes in demand overall—regardless of price—which are shown by a shift in the entire demand curve:

Consider a fruit stand that sells raspberries. As the end of the season approaches, buyers anticipate that prices will increase when less fruit is available. Fruit buyers therefore increase their demand for raspberries. This is translated into a rightward shift in the demand curve. (Conversely, a decrease in demand is shown by a leftward shift in the curve.) This shift is unrelated to the current price; in fact, it would be seen regardless of the price of raspberries.

So, whether raspberries are $2 per pint or $4 per pint, there will be an increase in demand a week or two before the end of the season.

Law of Supply

Whereas demand addresses the behavior of buyers, supply deals with the behavior of sellers. The **law of supply** states that as the price of a good increases, suppliers will increase the quantity of the good they supply, if all other factors are held constant. This is because of **increasing marginal costs**: as suppliers increase the amount they are supplying, the marginal costs of production increase as well.

Suppliers will therefore only increase supply if price is high enough to offset that cost. For example, during the holidays, a toy company decides to double its supply of its most popular toy. To do so, the company must hire more workers, keep the factory open longer, run the machines longer, pay more in electricity, and pay more in packing materials and shipping costs to get the toys to the stores. If they decided to triple the supply, these costs would only increase. The price of the toy would therefore need to be at a point that it could generate enough revenue to offset these additional costs.

Supply Curve

A **supply curve** shows the relationship between what something costs and how much a business is willing to supply for sale.

In Figure 5.3., the vertical line on the left indicates price while the horizontal line shows quantity produced for sale: the higher the price, the higher the supply (holding all other factors constant).

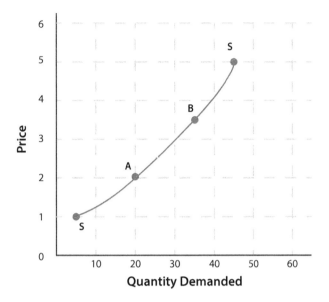

Figure 5.3. Supply Curve

Just like with the demand curve, points on the supply curve represent the **quantity supplied** rather than the overall supply.

Changes in the overall supply result from **determinants of supply,** which shift the curve either rightward or leftward. These include the following:

▶ the cost of an input

▶ technology and productivity

▶ taxes or subsidies

▶ producer expectations about future prices

▶ the price of alternative goods that could be produced

▶ the number of similar companies in the industry

For example, the price of flour drops. Because it now costs less to make baked goods, bakeries across the industry will increase their production of muffins and cakes. This is an overall increase in supply, shifting the curve rightward. In the same way, if flour suddenly became more expensive, bakeries would produce less (as cost of production increased), and the curve would shift leftward.

SUPPLY AND DEMAND

The interplay of supply, demand, and price is used to describe the state of the market. When the quantity demanded equals the quantity supplied at a given price, the market is in a state of **equilibrium**. Essentially, this means that both suppliers and buyers are satisfied with the price:

▶   In a graph, equilibrium is located where the supply and demand curves intersect.

▶   The other areas of the graph, where the supply and demand curves do not meet, are states of **disequilibrium**.

When the quantity demanded exceeds the quantity supplied, a **shortage**, or **excess demand**, exists. Shortages occur when prices are low because low prices lead to high demand but low supply.

For example, if the market price of a television is $20, demand for these inexpensive TVs will be high. However, the marginal cost of increasing supply at that price would quickly outweigh the revenue from sales, keeping the supply low.

When the quantity supplied exceeds the quantity demanded, a **surplus**, or **excess supply**, exists. Again, this is caused by the opposing relationships of supply and demand to price. If the TVs are now $2,000 each, fewer buyers will be willing to purchase one. However, the high price allows the supplier to clearly outstrip the marginal costs.

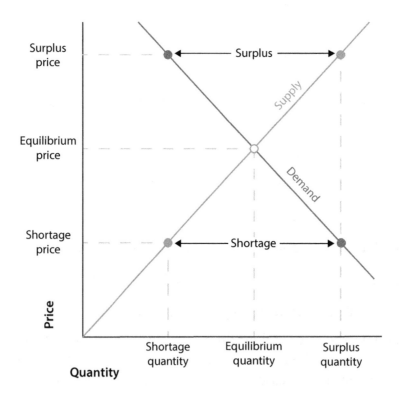

Figure 5.4. Equilibrium Price

The market always tends toward equilibrium. So, in the case of a shortage, buyers will offer to pay more—say $50—for the television— and suppliers will begin to increase supply. This trend will continue until they reach equilibrium.

On the flip side, when a surplus exists, suppliers will lower prices to attract buyers, thereby increasing demand until equilibrium is reached.

Changes in overall supply and demand impact equilibrium as well. The ability to stream television shows on a tablet or phone created an equivalent product. If the cost of a tablet dropped below the cost of a television, there would be a decreased overall demand for TVs, shifting the demand curve to the left. This would, in turn, shift the equilibrium price, also called **market clearing**.

If both supply and demand are changed (for example, the price of tablets drop and a tornado destroys half of the television factories), the relative degree of each change must be gauged before a new equilibrium can be determined.

PRACTICE QUESTIONS

9)   At the price of $15, a pottery manufacturer expects to sell 10,000 bowls. If the bowls are instead offered at a price of $20 per bowl, how many can the manufacturer anticipate selling?

   A.   fewer than 10,000 bowls

   B.   exactly 10,000 bowls

   C.   more than 10,000 bowls

   D.   More information is needed to make the prediction.

10)   Which of the points below is the original equilibrium?

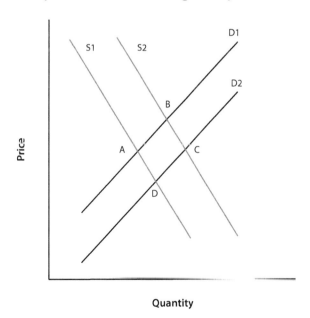

   A.   A

   B.   B

   C.   C

   D.   D

11) **Workers at pen factories earn minimum wage. When the state raises the minimum wage, what impact will that have on the market supply of pens?**

    A.   The supply curve will shift to the right.

    B.   The supply curve will remain unchanged, but the quantity supplied will increase.

    C.   The supply curve will shift to the left.

    D.   The supply curve will remain unchanged, but the quantity supplied will decrease.

Elasticity

Price Elasticity of Demand

The law of demand states that demand increases when price decreases. It does not, however, provide a means for determining the magnitude of decrease. **Elasticity,** in general, is the measure of sensitivity to change.

Price elasticity of demand measures the extent to which changes in price alter demand. For example, if the price of bread were to increase, price elasticity of demand would indicate the extent to which people would stop buying bread.

In a perfect world, the elasticity of the price will find equilibrium between price and demand. Price elasticity of demand is calculated using this mathematical equation:

$$E_d = \frac{\text{(\% of change in quantity demanded)}}{\text{(\% of change in price)}}$$

The greater this ratio, the more responsive buyers are to the change in price.

When the change in demand is greater than the change in price ($E_d > 1$), demand is called **price elastic**. For example, the price of a car increases by 5% and there is a 20% decrease in quantity demanded:

$$E_d = \frac{20}{5} = 4$$

$$4 > 1$$

This shows that the change in price greatly affected the quantity demanded.

When the change in price is greater than the change in demand ($E_d < 1$), demand is called **price inelastic**. Reversing the previous example, if the price of a car increases by 20% and there is a 5% increase in quantity demanded, it is clear the change in price had only a small effect on consumer demand.

$$E_d = \frac{5}{20} = 0.25$$

$$0.25 < 1$$

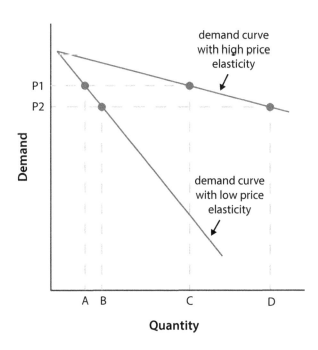

Figure 5.5. Price Elasticity of Demand

If any change in price will lead to unlimited demand, demand is **perfectly elastic**. This usually occurs in cases where there are many substitutes of the product. For example, a coffee shop surrounded by other coffee shops might have perfectly elastic demand.

If there is no change in quantity demanded based on a change in price, demand for that good is considered **perfectly inelastic**. A life-saving drug for a rare disease might have perfectly inelastic demand—it does not change regardless of how expensive the drug becomes.

CHECK YOUR UNDERSTANDING #1

What are some examples of elastic and inelastic goods?

A perfectly elastic demand curve is horizontal, whereas a perfectly inelastic curve is vertical.

Finally, if the change in price equals the change in demand ($E_d = 1$), demand is **unit elastic**. The price for chewing gum decreased by 7% and the quantity of chewing gum demanded increased by 7%.

Several factors impact elasticity:

▶ proportion of income

▶ number of good substitutes

▶ time

HELPFUL HINT

The steeper a demand curve, the less elasticity it has.

PRACTICE QUESTIONS

12) **The price elasticity of demand measures which of the following?**

    A.   the extent to which changes in demand impact price

    B.   the extent to which changes in price impact demand

    C.   whether demand will decrease based on price

    D.   whether demand will increase based on price

13) **If the supply curve for a product shifts to the right, creating a 5% decrease in price and a 4% increase in demand, the price elasticity of demand would be which of the following?**

    A.   1.25%

    B)   1%

    C)   0.8%

    D)   The demand would be perfectly inelastic.

FACTORS OF PRODUCTION

LABOR

Just like production, labor is also subject to the market forces of supply and demand. A **supply curve of labor** shows the number of hours laborers are willing to work at a given wage rate.

Because engaging in labor is an individual economic decision, opportunity cost plays a role: as wages increase, workers are willing to forgo leisure activities to increase their labor and thereby increase their earnings. This is called the **substitution effect.**

HELPFUL HINT

Generally speaking, whereas labor supply curves are upward sloping overall, labor demand curves are downward sloping.

However, as income increases, so does the demand for leisure activities. Therefore, when wages reach a certain amount, the number of hours people are willing to work decreases as they increasingly choose leisure over labor. This is called the **income effect.** As a result, labor supply curves that extend to these high wages can take a backward-bending shape.

The labor supply curve can shift overall based on the following factors:

▶   population growth or increased immigration

▶   changing worker attitudes

▶   changes in alternative opportunities

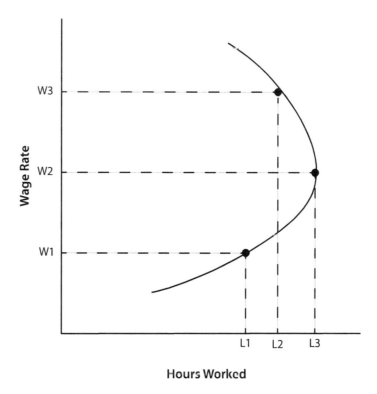

Figure 5.6. Supply Curve of Labor

Labor demand is more complicated to calculate as it is a function of wage, desired quantity of production, and price of unit sold.

The **equilibrium wage rate** and quantity occurs where the quantity of demanded labor equals the quantity supply of labor.

THE BASIC CATEGORIES OF FINANCIAL ASSETS

Stocks and bonds are securities, monetary units that can be exchanged. Public and private interests as well as individuals may invest in stocks as stockholders, or in bonds as lenders.

Stocks and bonds are traded on the stock market, a venue where private individuals, businesses, government agencies, and even foreign investors and countries can invest. Stocks are essentially shares of any given company or corporation that has "gone public," or offered its stock for sale to the highest bidder, whomever that may be.

In the last century, the value of the stock market has come to reflect the state of the American economy as never before.

In 1929, the stock market was the precursor to an economic downturn that history has called the Great Depression. It was not just an American economic downturn. There were few nations unaffected by the stock market crash in 1929 and the decade of Depression that followed. Figure 5.7. shows the pitfalls of more than a decade of questionable buying practices by investors of all economic demographics.

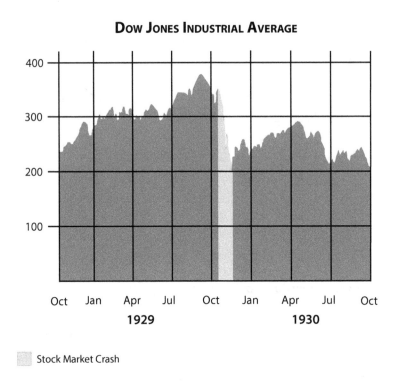

Figure 5.7. Stock Market Crash and Consequences

The American economy is still more or less a mirror reflection of the American stock market, and its movement—both up and down—is the fodder of presidential campaigns and Congressional debate.

For smaller investors, it's often boom or bust, bear or bull markets. There are fortunes to be made (and lost) for anyone who wants to take the risk. Figure 5.8. explores the three different stock measures over a period of several years.

Money market funds invest in short-term investments, like treasury bonds. These are considered safe and solid investments, much like bank deposits, but encompass a broader scope for large-scale investors.

STOCK MARKET TRENDS

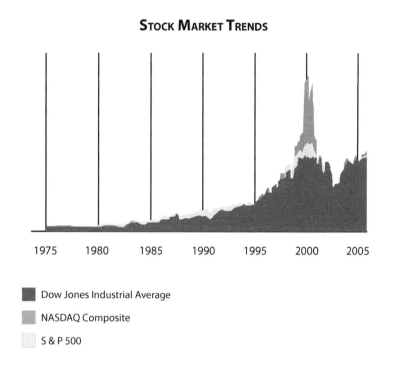

Figure 5.8. Stock Measures

THE ALLOCATION OF RESOURCES

Allocation of resources, or how resources are distributed across an economy, can fall to either the government or the market, depending on the type of economy.

Within a specific firm, the allocation of resources is determined by profit maximization: how can the resources be used most efficiently?

One of the best ways to explain government control of the allocation of resources is to look at rationing during the Second World War in the United States: rather than allow the public to hoard goods and create shortages, the federal government decided to control the flow of goods to civilians by allocating only a small amount of goods to the public on a weekly and monthly basis.

Most resources are limited. In this case, economists determine the best way to allocate resources that does the least harm to all parties.

Public goods are products that individuals can consume without reducing their availability to other individuals; they are equally available to all:

- ▶ basic television

- ▶ plumbing infrastructure

- ▶ sewage systems

DID YOU KNOW?

Some people now argue that internet access should be a public good.

In a pure market economy, the market would provide for all public goods; however, in reality, private markets often fail to provide the allocatively efficient level of public goods, and providing then falls to the government.

PRACTICE QUESTIONS

14) **When a new factory paying higher wages opens two towns over from Smallville, what will happen to Smallville's labor supply curve?**

   A.   It will begin to slope upwards.

   B.   It will begin to bend backwards.

   C.   It will shift to the right.

   D.   It will shift to the left.

15) **Which of the following is NOT an example of a public good?**

   A.   air travel

   B.   streetlights

   C.   public parks

   D.   radio broadcasts

BEHAVIOR OF FIRMS

In economics, any organization that uses factors of production to produce a good or service which it intends to sell for profit is called a **firm**. Firms can range from a child's lemonade stand to a multinational corporation, like Walmart.

While individuals make economic decisions to maximize their utility, firms make economic decisions to maximize their profit.

Economic profit is different from simple accounting profit (subtracting costs from revenue). Economic profit takes into consideration nonpriced, or **implicit costs**.

Imagine a young entrepreneur starts a bicycle sandwich delivery business and charges $4 per sandwich plus a $1 delivery fee. In the first month, 200 sandwiches are sold, which equals revenue of $1,000. The entrepreneur spent $400 in **explicit costs**:

> ▶ $300 on bread, meat, and fixings

> ▶ $50 on packaging

> ▶ $50 for the bike and basket

The entrepreneur's accounting profit for the month was $600 ($1000 − $400 = $600).

DID YOU KNOW?

The availability of credit meant that the financial risk of the corporation was spread out among a larger pool of business leaders and therefore even more attractive than before.

However, economic profit takes into account other nonpriced factors. These include opportunity costs, such as wages not earned from another job or interest not earned on money that has been liquidated.

In this case, the entrepreneur passed up a job working at a coffee shop for $700 a month. Taking that into account, the entrepreneur's economic loss would actually be $100.

TYPES OF FIRMS

Firms can be categorized into three types: **sole proprietorship, partnership, and corporation.**

Table 5.4. Types of Firms

Type	Description
Sole proprietorship	• a business belonging to a single individual, either as the sole owner or the inventor • depends on the skills and income of a single individual
Partnership	• a joint venture between two individuals or two business entities • the next step in business ownership according to some • allows a sole proprietor with too much business or inventory to hire more help or bring in a partner to share both the risk and the profits
Corporation	• a group of individuals or businesses working together to share the business risk and its profit • the newest of the economic terms listed here • originated during the nineteenth century in the second phase of the Industrial Revolution • took off with the availability of credit in the beginning of the twentieth century

PRACTICE QUESTION

16) **Which of the following is an example of an implicit cost?**

A. the money an entrepreneur anticipates spending in the next six months to grow a business

B. ad space purchased in a local newspaper to advertise an entrepreneur's new business

C. money spent on certification courses to achieve a license in a field

D. the time an entrepreneur spent researching information to launch a new business

SHORT-RUN LOSS AND LONG-RUN EQUILIBRIUM

Firms make decisions in both the short and long term:

In economics, the **short run** is a period in which at least one production input is fixed and cannot be changed. For example, a store experiences a major increase in foot traffic and sales during the holiday season. It can respond by increasing staff and extending hours; it may even be able to order more merchandise. It cannot, however, increase the size of the store during that time.

The **long run** refers to a period of time in which all production inputs are changeable. While that same store could not change its size for the few months of the holiday season, it could do so over the course of a year or two if high foot traffic continued.

Firms operating at a loss will continue to produce in the short run if money coming in—revenue—exceeds variable costs.

Loss of profit in the short run is unimportant as long as there is a long-term profit. If there is no long-term profit, then the item will likely be discontinued and replaced with more cost-effective, profitable merchandise.

Of course, loss is not sustainable beyond the short run. If an industry is perfectly competitive, it will reach equilibrium (or **long-run equilibrium**) when price is the same as the average total costs. This point is called **zero economic profit**—the amount of income that a business needs to break even in the marketplace.

FIXED AND VARIABLE INPUTS

Fixed inputs are any production inputs that cannot be changed in the short run. These are the costs that do not change and must be paid monthly or bimonthly:

▶   wages

▶   rent

▶   materials costs

CHECK YOUR UNDERSTANDING #2

What are some variable costs a firm might have?

Variable inputs are production inputs that can be changed in the short term:

▶   the cost of labor (if the number of employees is increased or decreased)

In Figure 5.9., fixed inputs, or fixed costs, appear as the stable bottom of the graph, while variable inputs, or variable costs, appear as an ever-changing line going up in terms of price.

Marginal costs are the costs of producing one more unit.

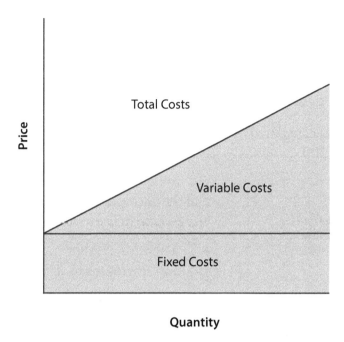

Figure 5.9. Fixed and Variable Inputs

Changes in any of the above costs can affect the final cost of production. Of all the costs in the productivity of a business, the ones most likely to change would be variable costs (VC).

PRACTICE QUESTION

17) **Which of the following is an example of a variable input?**

   A.   a contractor's work crew

   B.   money obtained from a bank loan

   C.   a caterer's kitchen

   D.   a magazine's printing press

LABOR ANALYSIS OF PRODUCTION AND TYPES OF COSTS

Economic analysis of production is based on production measures: total product of labor (TPL), marginal product of labor (MPL), average product of labor (APL).

Table 5.5. Production Measures

Measure	Description
Total product of labor (TPL)	the total amount of product at each quantity of labor
Marginal product of labor (MPL)	the change in amount of product resulting from a change of labor
Average product of labor (APL)	the total product divided by the amount of labor, which gives the average productivity of a market's labor

For example, the sandwich entrepreneur's total product of labor is based on the variable inputs of the labor involved in the sandwich-making and the time spent on the bike.

▶ In the first month, the entrepreneur used 1 unit of labor, creating a TPL of 200 sandwiches.

▶ The APL is calculated by dividing the TPL by the units of labor: $200 \div 1 = 200$.

Imagine the sandwich business takes off and the entrepreneur decides to hire someone else to help deliver sandwiches.

▶ The unit of labor increases to 2 and the TPL increases to 275.

▶ The MPL is the change in TPL for the additional unit of labor.

▶ In this case, then, the MPL would be 75, and the new APL will be 137.5.

There are several types of costs, discussed in Table 5.6.

Table 5.6. Types of Costs

Type	Description
Fixed costs	• business costs that remain stable (rent, wages, or insurance)
Variable costs	• business costs that change with the markets (items needed for production or the cost of utilities)
Total costs	• all of the costs to reach a certain level of production • the bottom line in a new business; will include both fixed and variable costs with a hope of profit at the end of the fiscal year
Average costs	• all of the costs to produce items divided by the number of items produced • the cost per item that a business must consider and hope to lower
Marginal cost	• the difference in price when production is increased by one unit • can either increase or decrease the overall price of the item produced • depends on a whole variety of different factors, including the market at the time

PRACTICE QUESTION

18) If a firm wants to know the impact that hiring 100 new workers would have on production, which of the following would it examine?

    A.   total product of labor (TPL)

    B.   variable costs

    C.   marginal product of labor (MPL)

    D.   fixed costs

LONG–RUN AVERAGE COSTS

How do firms determine how and when to expand? By examining long-run average cost (LRAC). A firm can calculate its LRAC by combining snapshots of its short-run average costs (SRAC) at various production points.

For example, the sandwich entrepreneur could calculate the SRAC based on selling 0 – 100 sandwiches, then calculate costs at 75 – 250, and so on. The entrepreneur's LRAC would combine these graphs to indicate when the business can prepare to expand.

An LRAC graph would show a decrease in price with increasing quantity, followed by a leveling out, and then an increase in price with increasing quantity.

The first section of the graph, in which price decreases, is called **economies of scale**. This shows the advantages (in decreased costs) of greater production and expansion. Labor and management are able to specialize. As an example, the sandwich entrepreneur now focuses on assembling the prettiest sandwiches and hires others—who are faster and more efficient—to organize supplies, wrap the sandwiches, and make deliveries.

However, the entrepreneur will eventually reach a point where adding more workers will bring fewer and fewer advantages. This is called the **law of diminishing returns**.

If the entrepreneur hires more riders than needed at one time, the same benefit will not be seen as it was when each new rider allowed deliveries to happen faster. This stage is called **constant returns to scale**.

Finally, a firm reaches a point where expansion hurts profit rather than helps. This is called **diseconomies of scale**. In our sandwich example, the increase in production becomes more costly. The entrepreneur now has hired too many people to help in the sandwich preparation process. They are bumping into each other and working inefficiently.

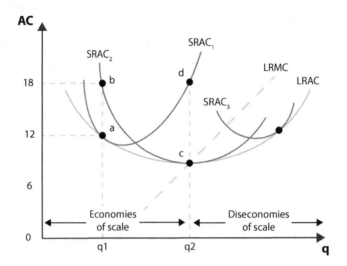

Figure 5.10. Long-Run Average Costs

19) If an LRAC curve is falling left to right, this indicates that a firm should do which of the following in that price and quantity range?

A.   expand its operation

B.   maintain its operation at its current size

C.   decrease the size of its operation

D.   There is insufficient information to make a determination.

TYPES OF MARKETS

PERFECT COMPETITION

There are four main characteristics of **perfect competition**:

1.   There are many small and independent buyers and sellers.

2.   Everybody produces the same product.

3.   There are no barriers to the entry of new—or exit of old—firms.

4.   All firms must accept the price where it is and produce as much as they want at that price (because they cannot change it).

Put simply, perfect, or pure, competition occurs when there is no one business that controls the entire marketplace because no one business is big enough to do so.

As an example, imagine three pizza restaurants competing against each other in a small college town. Price wars and showmanship may establish one of the restaurants as a leader for a time, but none of the three restaurants dominates the market because they all produce the same product for roughly the same price.

PRACTICE QUESTION

20) If a market has perfect competition, which of the following is true?

  A.   There are many buyers, but only a few sellers.

  B.   There are many sellers, but only a few buyers.

  C.   There are many sellers and buyers.

  D.   There is an equal number of buyers and sellers.

MONOPOLIES AND OLIGOPOLIES

Not all markets are perfectly competitive. When one corporation or business controls one entire area or product of a given market, it is called a **monopoly**. In addition, monopolies are marked by a lack of close substitutes for the product, barriers to entry for new firms, and market power.

Barriers can be legal, such as licensing restrictions or copyright laws.

The advantages of producing large quantities (discussed later in this chapter) can also edge newcomers out of the market. For example, big-box stores like Walmart can purchase or produce products on a large scale. This allows them to decrease their costs and lower their prices.

On the other hand, a small family-owned store in the same town—buying a fraction of the same products—cannot compete.

> **CHECK YOUR UNDERSTANDING #3**
>
> Can you think of any modern examples of monopolies?

Finally, if a firm controls all of the resources needed in production, it can prevent others from entering the market. Andrew Carnegie used this technique at the end of the nineteenth century with his company, US Steel: he purchased every layer of production, allowing him to streamline costs and prevent competitors from accessing the resources.

Monopolies function best in a new market where competition is either too expensive or not possible because of legal roadblocks like patents.

An **oligopoly** occurs when a few businesses control one market. As a result, they become interdependent—the action of one affects the others. For example, when one airline started to require payment for checked luggage, the others quickly followed suit.

> **DID YOU KNOW?**
>
> In response to Carnegie and others like him, the US government legislated the breakup of monopolies across the country and even inspired a board game of the same name during the Great Depression.

In an oligopoly, the product can be standardized, as in a perfectly competitive market, or it may be differentiated. Telephone service is essentially a standardized product, whereas the car industry is an oligopoly with differentiated products.

Like monopolies, oligopolies have entry barriers.

PRACTICE QUESTION

21) Which of the following types of markets have barriers to entry for new firms?

    A.   monopolies and perfect competition markets

    B.   oligopolies and perfect competition markets

    C.   monopolies only

    D.   monopolies and oligopolies

GOVERNMENT INTERVENTION

PRICE FLOORS AND PRICE CEILINGS

A **price floor** is the lowest price established by the government. Governments use price floors to aid producers in unfair markets with depressed prices.

If the price floor instituted by the government is lower than the price the market will support, the price floor is ineffective. This is demonstrated by Figure 5.11., where line *F* is the price floor set by the government.

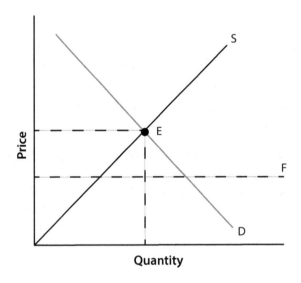

Figure 5.11. Ineffective Price Floor

When set above the market price, a price floor can lead to a surplus. Price floors lead to overall inefficiency in the market because neither producers nor consumers are maximizing the available resources. They also can price people out of the market.

A **price ceiling** is the highest price allowed by government. Often the price ceiling dictated by the government is higher than the market actually allows. See Figure 5.12., where the government's set price ceiling is indicated by line F.

If the price ceiling is set below the market price, then demand will outstrip supply, leading to a shortage.

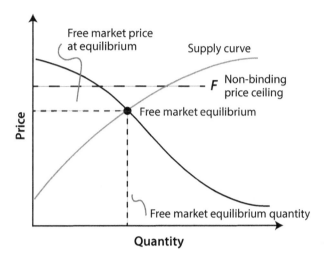

Figure 5.12. Price Ceiling

ANTITRUST LAWS

Antitrust laws promote a competitive market environment. They protect consumers from illegal mergers and other unfair business practices.

Antitrust laws emerged out of the Progressive movement of the nineteenth century in response to the monopolies and trusts dominated by banking and heavy industry during the Second Industrial Revolution. The richest businessmen of the nineteenth century were called **robber barons** because they controlled vast amounts of money and property.

For the robber barons, controlling all aspects of one given industry was simply good business practice. A steel magnate might control the steel industry of a given region of the United States, including:

▶ the mines where raw ingredients are extracted from the earth

▶ the miners (providing company houses and a company store)

▶ the railroad that hauls the raw ingredients to the steel foundries (which the magnate owns)

▶ the railroads that carry the finished product to its destination.

Competition is key to a market economy and a capitalist system. Establishing a **trust**—control over the entire industrial process—defeats that purpose. It was for that reason that the US government set out to break the trusts of the late nineteenth and early twentieth centuries.

Figure 5.13. Homestead Steel Works

Types of Taxes

Progressive taxes tax the income of the wealthy more than other groups in society, or so the theory goes. Progressive taxes increase gradually as income rises for an individual. But in a free market economy, taxes are adjusted to account for income losses in business, charitable contributions, and other circumstances. In reality, tax rates may vary considerably across income levels.

CHECK YOUR UNDERSTANDING #4

What type of tax is a sales tax?

Other forms of taxation include proportional and regressive taxes:

▶ **Proportional taxes** are similar to flat rate taxes in that all taxpayers are taxed at the same rate or at the same proportion of their incomes.

▶ **Regressive taxes** affect everyone at the same rate without a sliding proportional scale, making life more expensive for the lower classes.

PRACTICE QUESTION

22) **Which of the following statements is true of antitrust laws?**

   A. They are designed to modify perfect competition markets.

   B. They are designed to protect controlling firms in oligopolies.

   C. They are designed to shift perfect competition markets toward monopolies.

   D. They are designed to decrease the power of monopolists.

MACROECONOMICS

CIRCULAR FLOW MODELS

A **circular flow model** shows where money goes in any given economy. It follows money as it enters the marketplace to be spent by consumers and invested by businesses. The model also reveals places in the economy where money is being wasted.

In a **closed economy** model (as in Figure 5.14.), households provide factors of production to firms, which the firms then transform into goods and services. The firms pay the households competitive compensation for those factors of production, providing income for the household. The household then uses that income to buy the goods and services created by the firms.

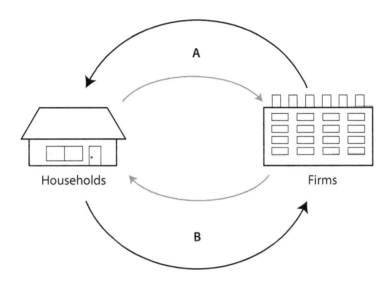

Figure 5.14. Circular Flow Model

Governments also play a role in the circular flow, acting as both recipients of factors of production (in the form of tax collection) and creators of goods and services.

The study of macroeconomics focuses on how to keep this flow moving at a strong and steady pace, primarily through the use of measurement tools.

GROSS DOMESTIC PRODUCT (GDP)

The **GDP, (gross domestic product),** is the total value of domestic production—the market value of all the final goods and services produced within a nation in one year.

▶ **Final goods** are those that are ready for consumption.

▶ **Intermediate goods**, goods that still require more processing, are not counted.

▶ For example, tomatoes are intermediate goods, but jarred tomato sauce is a final good.

▶ To avoid **double counting**, the count takes place at the final sale.

GDP focuses on what was actually produced within a country, regardless of where it is headquartered. So if a shoe company has its headquarters in California, but all of its production takes place in Vietnam, the total production of shoes would contribute to Vietnam's GDP, not that of the United States.

Secondhand sales, nonmarket transactions, and underground economies are all excluded from GDP. Countries in which these play a stronger role—usually developing countries—have relatively weak GDPs.

NOMINAL GDP IN BILLION U.S. DOLLARS IN 2014

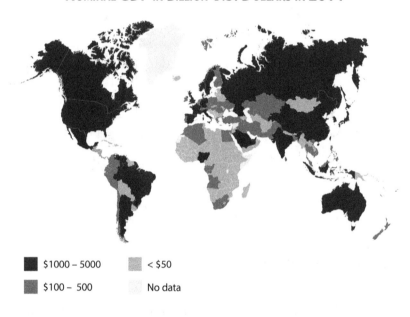

$1000 – 5000   < $50

$100 – 500   No data

Figure 5.15. 2014 World Economies Map

PRACTICE QUESTION

23) Which of the following transactions would be used in a calculation of GDP?

　A.　compensation a teenager receives for raking a neighbor's leaves

　B.　the resale of a coffee table on eBay

　C.　the sale of strawberries to a jam manufacturer

　D.　the sale of five pounds of carrots at a grocery store

INFLATION AND THE CONSUMER PRICE INDEX

To measure the health of an economy based on consumer spending, economists use the **consumer price index (CPI)**.

The **CPI** measures prices of goods and services as they change over time. It does this by selecting a base year and compiling a market "basket" of 400 consumer goods and services that year, ranging from gas to candy to refrigerators.

A price index is created for subsequent years by measuring the change in prices.

Table 5.7. CPI Example

Items in the basket	Quantity Purchased (2010)	2010 Price	2010 Spending	2015 Price	2015 Spending (based on 2010 quantities)
Candy Bar	12	1.50	18	1.75	21
Books	10	12	120	14	140
Movie Tickets	6	10	60	12	72
Total Spending			= 198		= 233

Use the equation:

$$\text{current year price index} = 100 \, \frac{\text{(spending current year)}}{\text{(spending base year)}}$$

$$\text{2015 price index} = 100 \times \frac{233}{198} = 117.68$$

This shows a 17.68% increase in price. To calculate the official CPI, the average price level of consumer goods is taken for the base year and the current year.

The percent change from year to year is called **inflation**. Sudden or unexpected inflation—particularly inflation that does not keep up with wages—causes problems within an economy.

The graph shows a sample of the CPI for the United States between 1913 and 2014—just over a century. The dark line shows the average CPI for each year with 1982 – 1984 as the "base year" (when CPI = 100).

The graph shows that there has been an overall increase in CPI over time. The light line shows the percent change in average CPI from year to year. This is the measure that shows inflation within the economy.

DID YOU KNOW?

Inflation peaked in the 1970s and reached an all-time high; economists struggled to figure out how to bring it back down. Eventually, the Federal Reserve stopped issuing new money, leading to a sharp rise in unemployment but eventually curbing inflation.

Figure 5.16. US Consumer Price Index

PRACTICE QUESTION

24) **When is inflation an economic problem?**

    A.   when it continues over a long period of time

    B.   when it occurs unexpectedly

    C.   when it is lower than wage increases

    D.   It is always a problem.

ECONOMIC GROWTH

In its simplest form, economic growth is the outward movement of the production possibility frontier over time, which in turn results from an increase in **productivity**.

HELPFUL HINT

On a macroeconomics level, it is in a government's favor to craft policies that encourage investment in capital, innovation, and protection of natural resources; these drive growth.

In economics, productivity is defined as the quantity of output that can be produced per worker in a prescribed amount of time. There are four main **determinants of productivity:** physical capital, human capital, natural resources, and technology.

Table 5.8. Determinants of Productivity

Determinant	Description	Example
Physical capital	When the physical capital, or tools of production, are increased, productivity increases.	• A bottle maker has a machine that can produce 100 bottles an hour. • The company upgrades to a more efficient machine and can now produce 200 bottles an hour.
Human capital	The knowledge and skills of the labor force: the more skilled its labor, the more productive the economy.	• The Four Asian Tigers: South Korea, Singapore, Hong Kong, and Taiwan, began to grow thanks to factory jobs requiring unskilled workers. • Economic growth really took off when their skilled labor forces allowed them to dominate international banking and the manufacturing of information technology.
Natural resources	Government policies that provide for sustainable consumption of renewable resources and protection of nonrenewable resources can foster economic growth.	• minerals • soil • timber • waterways
Technology	Technology does not just include computers and machines; it refers to a nation's knowledge and ability to efficiently produce goods.	Discovering how to make fire was a technological advancement on par with smartphones.

Social and cultural changes can impact economic growth as well. For instance, significant economic reforms introduced market principles to the Chinese economy beginning in the early 1980s. Since then, China has experienced rapid economic growth fueled by government policies that capitalize on the country's huge labor pool.

The graph looks at economic growth between the years of 1990 and 2006 in the United States and different countries. It gives a glimpse of the economic highs and lows of the last two decades. It also reveals the peaks and valleys that accompany not only the economic, but social, cultural, and historic events as well.

HELPFUL HINT

Increasing human capital does not simply mean encouraging education (although that is part of it). Health initiatives, such as vaccination drives that create a healthier workforce, also increase human capital and productivity.

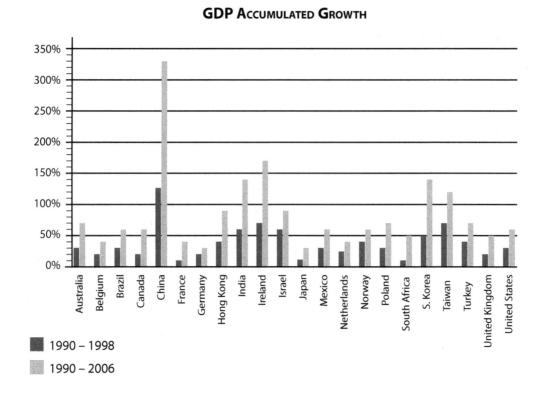

Figure 5.17. Global Economic Growth (1990 – 2006)

PRACTICE QUESTION

25) **Which of the following policies would be LEAST likely to increase a nation's productivity?**

   A.   a law providing free post-secondary education

   B.   a national immunization campaign against malaria

   C.   government funding for research into high-yield crops

   D.   a government-mandated minimum wage

MACROECONOMIC EQUILIBRIUM, INFLATIONARY AND RECESSIONARY GAPS

Aggregate supply (AS) is the relationship between the total of all domestic output produced and the average price level. Essentially, AS is the sum of all of the micro-economic supply curves in an economy.

The **long-run aggregate supply (LRAS)** assumes that input prices have had enough time to adjust to changes in the various product markets. All markets—product and input—are at equilibrium, and there is full employment. This means that output does not change, regardless of price, creating a vertical curve.

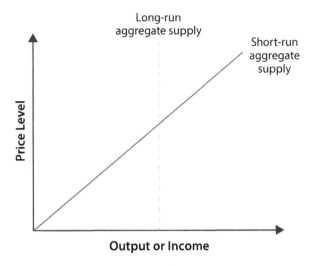

Figure 5.18. Aggregate Supply

Short-run aggregate supply (SRAS) curves fluctuate without impacting employment. However, if the LRAS curve shifts, there must be a change in the output level at full employment.

These shifts result from a change in technology, productivity, and the availability of resources, both of which could alter a nation's output when working at full employment. In this way LRAS can be used as a measure of economic growth.

An economy is in **macroeconomic equilibrium** when the quantity of output demanded in an economy (as shown by **aggregate demand**—the sum of all demand curves in an economy), is equal to the quantity of output supplied.

This equilibrium does not always occur at full employment, though. If it does not, the economy is either experiencing inflation or recession—an aggregate supply and demand graph will reveal this information.

An **inflationary gap** occurs when the intersection point between **aggregate demand (AD)** and SRAS is at a higher output level than the LRAS curve.

The LRAS curve represents the output level of full employment, so if the SRAS curve and the aggregate demand curve intersect at an output level beyond the LRAS curve, the economy is producing at an output level that is higher than full employment.

This usually happens when quantity demanded is suddenly increased through foreign or government spending, or even just very active consumers. When demand increases like this, factories stay open longer and pay their workers more overtime, thus exceeding full employment output.

On the other hand, if the equilibrium point is lower than LRAS, a **recessionary gap** exists. This indicates that the nation is experiencing high levels of unemployment.

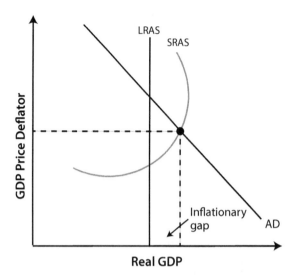

Figure 5.19. Inflationary Gap

PRACTICE QUESTION

26) In the New Deal, the government created jobs for people to counteract the recession (the Great Depression). Which of the following BEST describes the economic theory guiding that policy?

   A.   Government-created jobs increase aggregate demand, which shifts the equilibrium point closer to the LRAS curve.

   B.   Government-created jobs shift the LRAS curve to the left to bring it closer to the equilibrium point between short-run aggregate supply and aggregate demand.

   C.   Government-created jobs increase the nation's productivity, which eliminates recession.

   D.   Government-created jobs increase aggregate supply, which shifts the intersection between SRAS and long-run aggregate supply.

THE FEDERAL RESERVE

The Federal Reserve (the Fed) behaves as a central bank of the United States and ensures the safety of the American monetary system.

In the century since its inception, the role of the Fed has expanded tremendously:

▶   Its primary role is to maximize employment and stabilize prices in the United States.

Figure 5.20. The Federal Reserve

▶ It was created in 1913 to thwart the economic "panics" that seized the nation every few years.

▶ The Fed is meant to stabilize the US money supply and moderate interest rates.

▶ Its duties have expanded to include monitoring and maintaining reserves for US banks.

▶ The Federal Reserve is among the most important components of the US federal government; it has its own seal and flag.

The Federal Reserve is the arbiter of interest rates for mortgages, the stock market, and any other monetary policy involving interest (such as money markets).

In recent years, interest rates established by the Federal Reserve are at all-time lows, which can be a boon for borrowers.

The interest rate set by the Federal Reserve is established by a number of factors, including the federal funds rate, which is the interest that the Federal Reserve charges banks.

The graph shows the fluctuating interest rates that banks have paid in recent decades and how they ultimately trickled down to consumers.

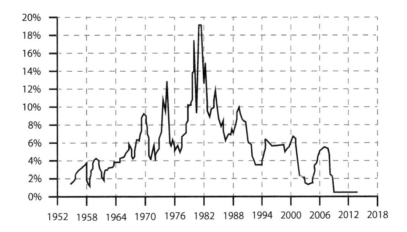

Figure 5.21. Federal Funds Rate

The Federal Reserve also monitors **monetary stabilization**. Monetary stabilization includes efforts to keep prices, unemployment, and the money supply—

CHECK YOUR UNDERSTANDING #5

How do the decisions of the Federal Reserve impact individual Americans?

among other fiscal indicators—relatively stable.

Monetary stabilization also helps prevent the economy from oscillating between inflation and recession.

PRACTICE QUESTION

27) **Which of the following is NOT a responsibility of the Federal Reserve?**
   A.   to set interest rates
   B.   to determine government spending
   C.   to maximize employment
   D.   to stabilize prices

FISCAL POLICY

Fiscal policy is an approach to economic management in which the government is deeply involved in managing the economy.

When an individual or firm spends or saves money, those choices impact that individual's or firm's own finances. When the government makes similar choices, the government's decisions impact the economy as a whole. These economic decisions are called **multipliers**.

In **expansionary fiscal policy**, the government either increases spending or decreases taxes in order to increase the AD curve to counteract a recession.

When the economy experiences inflation, the government uses **contractionary fiscal policy**: reducing government spending or increasing taxes.

A **tariff** is a tax or duty paid on anything imported or exported into or from a given country. Low tariffs encourage foreign goods to enter the market. Countries may do this to stimulate trade or in exchange for other trade agreements. For example, the North American Free Trade Agreement (NAFTA) essentially eliminated tariffs among Canada, the United States, and Mexico.

High tariffs protect domestic industry by making foreign goods more expensive. However, they also risk slowing trade. Between World War I and World War II, the United States passed a very high protectionist tariff. In response, other countries instituted retaliatory tariffs to block American trade as Americans had blocked foreign trade. Consequently, world trade ground to a halt.

When governments make changes to spending and taxes, it affects their budget.

▶   When revenue (primarily money from taxes) exceeds spending, the government has a **surplus**.

▶   When spending exceeds revenues, the government has a **deficit**.

A deficit is not the same thing as a debt. A deficit is the gap between what the government has spent and what it has earned. To cover that deficit, the government must borrow money, which generates government debt.

Changes in **currency** are caused by and impact the strength of a nation's economy.

▶ **Currency appreciation** occurs when a country's money gains value in national and international markets.

This increases foreign investment, as other countries gain more value for their money. However, a strong currency makes that nation's exports more expensive, which can affect trade.

▶ **Currency depreciation** occurs when a country's money loses value in national and international markets.

It may point to instabilities in the nation's economy (such as high rates of inflation). However, when carried out in an intentional and orderly manner, it can increase a nation's global competitiveness by lowering the cost of its exports. For example, China has used intentional currency depreciation to build a strong export-based economy and foster economic growth.

PRACTICE QUESTION

28) Which of the following would NOT be an example of contractionary fiscal policy?

    A.   freezing annual cost of living increases on the salaries of government employees

    B.   reducing the operating hours of national parks

    C.   increasing property taxes

    D.   financing a new dam

PRACTICE QUESTIONS ANSWER KEY

1) **B.** The lowered price in and of itself does not create scarcity since the supply of the drug is not impacted.

2) **B.** Here, the additional cost of the second candidate's higher salary is weighed against the extra ten years of experience that candidate brings.

3) **D.** The law of diminishing marginal utility states that the additional utility gained for acquiring new units of a product (rollercoaster rides) decreases with each new acquisition. In this case, each subsequent rollercoaster ride offers less marginal utility, until it no longer exists.

4) **C.** Point A is below the production possibility frontier, indicating that the use of resources is not being maximized.

5) **A.** Specialization does not cause low wages. Sometimes, specialization in the workforce, or the division of labor, can lead to lower wages because the skills required of a worker are reduced; however, specialization can also lead to higher wages because it may require a higher level of skill from a worker.

6) **D.** Company B can produce 100 more pencils than Company A at the same cost, giving it an absolute advantage. Its opportunity cost for producing pencils is .2 (200/1,000), whereas Company A's is .33 (300/900), giving Company B a comparative advantage as well.

7) **C.** Laissez-faire economics essentially means to leave the market alone to function. The United States came close to having a pure market economy in the 1870s.

8) **D.** The buyer makes this decision based on the effectiveness of the product rather than its price. Price does not come into play.

9) **A.** The law of demand states that when price increases, demand drops. This means the manufacturer will make fewer sales.

10) **A.** The original equilibrium can be found at the intersection between the original demand curve (D1) and the original supply curve (S1).

11)   **C.** An increase in the minimum wage raises the cost of producing pens, which in turn reduces supply, since pen manufacturers do not want to invest when their margins of profit are reduced.

12)   **B.** Price elasticity of demand measures how much demand will change based on changes in price.

13)   **C.** When the change in demand (4) is divided by the change in price (5), the elasticity is .8.

14)   **D.** Smallville's labor pool will shrink as workers leave the town to work higher-paying jobs at the new factory. A reduction of the labor pool results in a leftward shift of the graph.

15)   **A.** Air travel is not available to everyone; it is restricted by price. Also, once one person "consumes" air travel by taking up a seat on a plane, the passenger prevents someone else from "consuming" that good.

16)   **D.** Time spent researching information is a nonpriced cost. There are many other things the entrepreneur could have been doing but did not; therefore, this is an implicit cost.

17)   **A.** A contractor can hire or cut employees in response to changes in the short term. That makes the contractor's crew a variable input.

18)   **C.** In economics, the term *marginal* always means "additional." In this case, the marginal product of labor (MPL) is a measurement tool used to determine the additional output resulting from an increase in labor.

19)   **A.** A long-run average cost (LRAC) curve that falls left to right shows decreasing cost with increasing quantity, or economies of scale. In this situation, it is beneficial for a company to expand.

20)   **C.** A perfectly competitive market has a large number of small buyers and sellers, which prevents any one (or two) entities from controlling price.

21)   **D.** Both monopolies and oligopolies are markets in which a very small number of firms—one or a few, respectively—control the market. In order to maintain control, they must stifle competition from new firms. This is done by maximizing the benefits of large-scale operations or controlling relevant resources.

22)   **D.** With the rise of the robber barons and the consolidation of market power in several industries (including steel, railroads, and oil), the government took action to reduce that power and restore balance in the market.

23)   **D.** Because the carrots are going directly to a consumer and not being used to create another item for sale, they are considered a final good.

24)   **B.** Unexpected and sudden inflation causes problems because people do not have time to prepare for it, and wages do not have time to catch up. This kind of inflation leads to the sudden loss of value of money, investments, and capital.

25)   **D.** Mandating a minimum wage does not affect productivity; it improves wages for labor and impacts the cost of production.

26)   **A.** The jobs generated by the New Deal created new demand for labor, increasing aggregate demand and shifting the equilibrium point closer to long-run aggregate supply (LRAS), which is at full employment. The danger is in going too far the other way and creating an inflationary gap.

27)   **B.** Although the Federal Reserve plays an important role in fiscal policy, it has no control over government spending.

28)   **D.** If the government builds a new dam, it injects new spending into the economy, thereby expanding the economy.

CHECK YOUR UNDERSTANDING ANSWER KEY

Check Your Understanding #1

possible inelastic goods: medications, gasoline, health care treatments

possible elastic goods: luxury cars, vacations, soft drinks

Check Your Understanding #2

certain labor costs (especially in seasonal work); raw materials (oil, for example); production supplies

Check Your Understanding #3

Modern companies with few competitors include Facebook (Meta), Amazon, Google, Microsoft, and more.

Check Your Understanding #4

A sales tax is a regressive tax: it doesn't change depending on who is paying it.

Check Your Understanding #5

The Federal Reserve determines interest rates, which affect mortgages, loans, and other segments of the economy. It also has tools to curb inflation or unemployment; depending on the actions of the Fed, Americans could be affected by higher or lower prices, or have more or fewer job opportunities.

6

California History

CALIFORNIA GEOGRAPHY

California is a large state with a diverse geography. It encompasses 163, 696 square miles, eclipsed in size only by Alaska and Texas.

Originally one unified region under Spanish control, today's state of California is actually **Alta California**, or upper California. **Baja California**, or lower California—the southern peninsula—was once part of Spanish California and is now part of Mexico. Many still refer to the modern state of California as having two parts: Northern California (NorCal), which has a wetter, colder climate, and Southern California (SoCal), which has a warmer, desert climate.

North and south are not the only regional distinctions that can be made. The Central Valley, also known as the **Great Valley**, runs through the center of the state for approximately 450 miles. This rich flatland, the heart of California agriculture, is bound on both sides by mountains: the eastern **Coast Ranges** (including both the Northern Coast Ranges and the Southern Coast Ranges) and the western **Sierra Nevada**. The Sierra Nevada mountain range is fifty to eighty miles wide and stretches four hundred miles from north to south. The largest peak is over fourteen thousand feet. Within the Sierra Nevada mountains is **Yosemite National Park**, which spans nearly 1,200 square miles and features hundreds of thousands of acres of wilderness, including its famous giant sequoia trees. Established in 1890, in part due to the efforts of environmentalist John Muir, the park continues to be one of the state's top tourist destinations.

Though it is the largest and perhaps most famous mountain range, the Sierra Nevada is only one of the state's ranges. The **Transverse Ranges** span three hundred miles in Southern California, and the **Peninsular Ranges** span 930 miles from Southern California into Baja California. In the north of the state and stretching into Oregon are the **Klamath Mountains**, which extend over 150 miles. Also running through part of Northern California is the **Cascade Range**, or the Cascades, which run nearly seven-hundred miles through Canada, Washington, and Oregon.

California also boasts part of the **Great Basin**, a desert region that spans 190,000 square miles. This large valley extends into many other states as well as Mexico's Baja California region. The Great Basin is distinct because water that it takes in from rainfall never reaches the sea. This water retainment is what makes the Great Basin known as an endorheic watershed.

South of the Great Basin desert region is the **Mojave Desert**, a popular tourist destination with many attractions, such as Joshua Tree National Park and Death Valley National Park. **Death Valley** is famous for being the lowest elevation in North America (282 feet below sea level). It is also considered to be one of the hottest locations on the planet, with recorded temperatures well into the 120s and perhaps even 130s.

Second only to Death Valley in feet below sea level is the area known as the **Salton Sink**, located within the larger **Salton Trough**. The Salton Trough, a pull-apart basin created by tectonic plates, is a large region in southeastern California that extends into Baja California. Within the Salton Trough and its Salton Sink is the **Salton Sea**, which, at 210 feet below sea level, is the lowest lake in North America.

The **Colorado River**, one of the most important river systems in the country and a vital water source for Californians, also flows through the state and makes its boundary with Arizona. Of course, much of California also borders the **Pacific Ocean**, and its 840 miles of coastline include numerous beaches and bays that draw tourists from all over the world.

PRACTICE QUESTION

1) Which geographic feature of California is the lowest elevation in North America?
   A.   Salton Sea
   B.   Great Basin
   C.   Great Valley
   D.   Death Valley

Pre–Columbian Period
Through the End of Mexican Rule

This section describes and analyzes the early history of California up to statehood.

PRE-COLUMBIAN PEOPLES

The earliest people of California were the descendants of those humans who first crossed the Bering Strait from Asia into North America. Due to the particular geography of the state, the Native Peoples of California had a different existence than did many other Native Peoples of North America, such as those who lived in the Great Plains region of what is now the United States. Because of the myriad landforms in the state, including deserts and mountain ranges that prevented easy travel, the Native Peoples of present-day California often settled in smaller, isolated units.

Unlike the history of the Native Peoples of the Great Plains, large confederacies and alliances are largely absent from the story of California before European colonization. The state's abundant resources often prevented conflict over real or perceived scarcity, so Indigenous groups of California, who lived apart from one another in regions with distinct geographical barriers, had little incentive to engage in warfare.

Several distinct cultural groups inhabited the land that would become California. Most groups lacked a central political structure and instead were organized into smaller tribal groups (sometimes referred to as **tribelets**). Depending on the size of this group, which could range from the hundreds to the thousands, people lived in a single village or a group of villages organized around one central or capital village. The type of structures and daily life of these groups varied based on the region and its natural resources. Where trees were plentiful, such as in the North, homes were built of wood; where trees were scarce, homes were built of mud, brush, or palm—some were even built underground. Similarly, the climate and ecology of the region dictated daily life:

- ▶ Tribes in the Northwest constructed canoes out of the redwoods to fish for salmon.
- ▶ Centrally located tribes in the rich valley engaged in agriculture and hunting.
- ▶ Tribes that lived along the coast fished and traded with other tribes.

Some tribes had advanced techniques of food preservation, including leaching and hermetic sealing, which allowed for food to be stored for longer periods. Families traded food and other goods within the tribelet, but many communities also had a group of merchant traders who bought and sold goods from other regions.

Most tribelets had a chief who managed domestic affairs. Shamans, who organized religious rituals, were also important members of many communities. Religious beliefs varied among tribelets, but scholars note that some religious traditions were more common than others. The **Kuksu** faith, which dominated in the northern region, and the **Toloache** faith, more common in the southern part of what would become California, were two such belief systems.

The Kuksu and Toloache were religious traditions that spanned tribal affiliation and involved a formal initiation of devotees through ritual. In the Northwest, many tribes also practiced a similar religion dominated by myths and renewal rituals.

Many tribelets had highly developed cultural systems. Members composed and performed oral prose and poetry and created visual arts of many sorts. Rock paintings, pottery, and elaborate costumes, often used in religious rituals and ceremonies, were common in many tribelets in the region.

Basket weaving is the art that the Indigenous Peoples of California are perhaps best known for. These baskets are remarkable for their watertightness, strength, and durability. The Central Valley region inhabitants are believed to have made the most elaborate and varied baskets. This long tradition of artistry and skill has survived to this day, and fine baskets made by expert Native American craftspeople are displayed in museums and highly coveted among collectors.

Table 6.1. Major Tribes of California

Northeast	Modoc, Atsugewi, Achumawi
Northwest	Wiyot, Chilula, Chimarike, Karok, Shasta, Tolowa, Yurok, Hupa, Whilikut
South	Kitanemuk, Serrano, Gabrielino, Luiseno, Cahuilla, Kumeyaay, Chumash, Alliklik, Mojave
Central	Pomo, Miwok, Wappo, Yuki, Kato, Maidu, Yahi, Yokut, Yana, and many others

Though many Native groups of California were destroyed in the process of conquest and colonization (and the diseases brought to the Americas via these processes), the state today has more Native Americans than any other, which includes some 360,000 people with over one hundred tribal affiliations. Some of California's Native Peoples currently live on small reservations or trust allotments throughout the state; these areas make up less than 1 percent of the state's total land area. The Native Peoples of California have contributed much to the state's culture and fabric.

DID YOU KNOW?

The Yoruk tribe, with five thousand members, is believed to be the largest of California's Indigenous communities.

PRACTICE QUESTION

2) Which statement BEST describes the distribution of California's Native American population before European arrival?

    A.   densest in the Great Valley, where Native Peoples lived in large villages

    B.   spread all over the state, where Native Peoples lived in small tribelets

    C.   spread all over the state, where Native Peoples lived in large villages

    D.   densest in the coastal regions, where Native Peoples lived in small tribelets

SPANISH COLONIZATION AND MEXICAN CALIFORNIA

The Spanish arrived in Baja, California, in the 1530s and made their way to Alta California in the 1540s. Early conquistadors claimed the land for the Spanish Crown and brought diseases that quickly spread and ravaged Indigenous populations. Still, there were few attempts to colonize this remote part of the new empire. The wealth of Mexico and Peru occupied Spaniards eager to exploit the gold and silver found there, and California was far removed from the center of the Spanish colonial empire. Thus, most Native Californians had few, if any, direct interactions with Europeans during the early colonial period.

Things began to change, however, after the **Seven Years' War**, or the **French and Indian War** (1754 – 1763), as it was called in North America. The war pitted French and British colonies against their Indigenous allies, which resulted in a British victory. The end of the war and the resulting Treaty of Paris of 1763 made Great Britain the dominant concern in North America, which tipped the uneasy balance of European power and incited the Spanish to action.

The fear of British expansion meant that Spain had to secure the land it had already claimed, including more remote areas like California. In 1769, the first permanent Spanish settlement, a **presidio**, or military fort, accompanied by a church formed by **Father Junípero Serra**, was established in San Diego. More presidios were established in

▶ Monterey (1770),

▶ San Francisco (1776),

▶ Santa Barbara (1782).

Presidios offered some military protection and thus attracted Spanish settlers in communities known as **pueblos**. Pueblos not directly tied to presidios were established in the late eighteenth and early nineteenth centuries at

▶ San Jose,

▶ Los Angeles,

▶ Branciforte,

▶ Sonoma.

Presidios and pueblos were important for bringing in settlers, but the center of Spanish interaction with the Native Peoples of California was the **mission**. By 1823, there were twenty-one of these religious settlements.

Franciscan priests operated Spanish missions to bring Native Peoples into the fold of Catholicism and convert them to a European way of life. In theory, the missions were to be temporary establishments, and Native Peoples who lived in missions were to become sufficiently Europeanized so they could then establish their own communities and live as the White settlers did. In reality, few Native Peoples were converted to the European way of life to the degree the Spanish missionaries would have liked. Thus, missions often became more permanent living and working arrangements.

Conditions in missions were often very poor, and missionaries were known to use force to achieve conversion and extract labor from their flock. Disease flourished in crowded missions, and Indigenous Peoples with no immunity to European pathogens became ill at alarming rates. In response to these conditions, Native Peoples tried different ways to resist forced assimilation, including continuing to worship their deities, escaping, and even directly rebelling against missionaries and other colonial authorities. Nevertheless, the labor of Native Peoples was central to the economy of Spanish California. Missions often produced the agricultural products that supplied the neighboring presidios and pueblos and formed the bedrock of the colonial economy.

> **DID YOU KNOW?**
>
> Scholars now believe that the knowledge of California's Native Peoples and their ability to live off the rich resources of the land influenced the success of Spanish colonialism in California.

Spanish California also included nonmilitary and nonreligious settlements in the form of ranchos. **Ranchos** were large tracts of land given to Spanish Californians, often in exchange for prior military service. These ranchos were not outright land grants during the Spanish period but rather the extension of grazing rights in a large area. Under the Spanish rancho system, the land would return to the Crown after the grantee's death. After Mexican independence from Spain in 1821, the rancho system was changed, and the rancheros—those living and working at ranchos—received legal titles to the land. After Mexico won independence from Spain, California came under a new political authority:

▶   The Franciscan mission system was quickly dismantled.

▶   Land grants increased, and the rancho system expanded.

▶   Cattle ranching became a central economic activity.

Rancheros traded beef and hides with American merchants via the Pacific Coast for the manufactured goods they needed. These wealthy, landed elite stood atop the social hierarchy and came to be known as **Californios**.

The economy of California was no longer self-sufficient as it had been during the Spanish colonial period. There was a tremendous reliance on trade to obtain certain goods; however, consistency in the labor force endured. Native Californians often worked on the ranchos as agricultural laborers or raising and tending cattle.

Settlement of California was opened to foreigners during the Mexican national period, and Europeans and Americans began to arrive throughout the 1830s and 1840s to avail themselves of the land's richness.

The first American in California was believed to be adventurer **Jedediah Smith**, who led a group of trappers on an expedition in 1826. He was soon followed by other American settlers. By 1846, California was likely home to fourteen thousand non-Native Peoples, two thousand of which were Americans.

However, California was not only the frontier of New Spain; it was also the frontier of Mexico. Far-removed from the seat of government, Mexico struggled to rule California effectively, and by the mid-1840s, California had established a degree of political independence.

PRACTICE QUESTION

3) **Why did Spain begin to take more of an interest in the settlement of California in the eighteenth century?**
   A. a desire to exploit the natural resources of the region
   B. a fear that it was losing political control over the Native Peoples
   C. a need to solidify colonial possessions after the British victory in the French and Indian War
   D. a desire to better ally itself with the French following the outbreak of the French and Indian War

THE MEXICAN–AMERICAN WAR AND STATEHOOD

Americans moved not only to California in the nineteenth century but also to remote Mexican territories. One of these was Texas. The Mexican government initially welcomed Americans to Texas; few Mexicans had an interest in settling there because the Comanche and Apache peoples who inhabited the land were seen as a threat.

To encourage settlement in light of this perceived barrier, the Mexican government passed the **Imperial Colonization Law** in 1823, which permitted slavery in Texas and provided exemptions for settlers on various tariffs and taxes.

The relationship between settlers and the Mexican government quickly soured, however. As settlers poured in, the Mexican government feared a loss of control and passed new laws to curb settlement and reimpose taxes. A new dictator-like figure, **Antonio López de Santa Anna**, became the Mexican president in 1833 and quickly repealed the existing constitution. This prompted further concerns in Texas, where many American settlers saw Santa Anna as a threat to their rights and freedoms.

In 1836, Texas declared independence from Mexico. After seven months of fighting, the Texans declared victory and became an independent republic. Though many, including Texas president Sam Houston, supported joining the United States, the existence of slavery in Texas posed a problem for the US government. Debates over the expansion of slavery into new territories were central to the political landscape of the time. In 1845, Texas joined the Union as a slave state.

President James K. Polk also looked to California, at this time still part of Mexico, as another possible way to expand the United States. In 1845, he sent **John Charles Frémont** and a group of army engineers to survey the Sierra Nevada.

For reasons debated, and perhaps at the direct instruction of Polk, Frémont and his men entered California in 1846 and told settlers there that he would support their rebellion against Mexico. On June 10, Frémont's men and a group of settlers attacked a lieutenant in the Mexican army. The Mexicans quickly surrendered, and the California Republic, or the **Bear Flag Republic**, as it was known because of its flag depicting a bear, existed for twenty-five days.

Figure 6.1. California Republic Flag

The **Mexican–American War**, or Mexican War (1846 – 1848), broke out largely over the annexation of Texas and disputed Texas–Mexico borders.

While US general **Zachary Taylor** focused on the border region, Colonel **Stephen Kearny** and his troops moved into California and New Mexico. In July of 1846, American marines arrived in California and claimed the land for the United States. Frémont and his troops joined American forces in their fight against Mexico, and the Bear Flag Republic ended.

The Mexican governor of California, Don Pío de Jesús Pico, known as **Pío Pico**, fled the state in August of 1846 after Americans took control of Los Angeles. However, Mexican Californio troops eventually regained the city, only to have it retaken in January of 1847. The surrender of the remaining Californio troops quickly followed, and the **Treaty of Cahuenga** was signed on January 13, 1847, ending Mexican Californio and American fighting in California. In September of 1847, Mexico City was captured by American troops under General Winfield Scott, and the war was largely won by the United States.

In 1848, the United States and Mexico negotiated the **Treaty of Guadalupe Hidalgo**. As a result, the United States gained territory—New Mexico, Arizona, Colorado, Utah, Nevada, and California—in exchange for fifteen million dollars. Mexico abandoned any claims to Texas.

Mexican citizens living in the ceded territories had the choice of moving back to Mexico, staying in their homes and becoming American citizens, or staying in their homes and retaining their Mexican citizenship. They had one year to make the choice. The majority, likely some one hundred thousand or more, chose to stay and accept American citizenship, though it is estimated that around three thousand people did return to land that was still part of Mexico.

Zachary Taylor, who had gained fame as a war hero, became the US president in 1848. The issue of California's formal entry into the Union was of particular importance to his government because gold had been discovered in the territory that same year.

The newly acquired territory, however, brought further debates over the expansion of slavery into new American territories. The proposed **Wilmot Proviso** would prohibit slavery in any of the areas acquired by the Treaty of Guadalupe Hidalgo. Though it was never enacted, it was vigorously debated by both abolitionists and proponents of slavery.

The American government was fiercely divided over whether to permit slavery in the enormous new territory obtained following the Mexican–American War. However, the desire to exploit the resources of these lands and open them to settlement drove leaders to compromise.

In the **Compromise of 1850**, Congress strengthened the **Fugitive Slave Act**, which provided for the return to bondage of enslaved persons of African descent found in free states. However, it also abolished the slave trade in Washington, DC. This compromise established the borders of Texas as they stand today.

Most important for California, the Compromise of 1850 admitted California as a free state, with slavery to be decided by popular sovereignty, or the will of the people in the state, in the Utah and New Mexico Territories.

PRACTICE QUESTION

4) Why did the American government want to quickly decide the issue of California becoming a state?

A. Gold was discovered in California.

B. The Mexican War began.

C. A future California revolt was feared.

D. The border with Mexico was disputed.

FROM THE GOLD RUSH TO THE PRESENT

This section describes and analyzes the history of California from the Gold Rush to the present.

THE DISCOVERY OF GOLD

On January 24, 1848, **James Marshall**, who was contracted to build a sawmill along the American River in California Territory, saw a glint of something in the stream. News of his discovery quickly spread, and a rush to the state began. California's population grew rapidly with the **Gold Rush** as people from all over the world descended on the region in search of riches.

Nearly one hundred thousand people moved to California in 1849. Known as "**forty-niners**," these men and women came from the United States, Europe, China, Australia, and beyond. Those who came from the United States had two choices: a long sea route or an even longer overland route. Immigrants with families often chose the overland path, bringing entire households with them. Many Americans also came to California to sell goods and services to these gold seekers.

With little guidance from the US government, the people of California drafted and approved their own state constitution in 1849, even before official statehood. However, finding gold—not establishing governmental bureaucracy—was the most pressing matter, and it largely fell to small mining camps to govern themselves. They did so fairly effectively, though vigilante justice was not unheard of.

After California became a state in 1850, it elected **Peter Hardeman Burnett** as its governor. His first order of business was eliminating the Native Californians he saw as standing in the way of the state's settlement and prosperity. He spread anti–Native American rhetoric and collected a cache of weapons, which he subsequently distributed to local militias to wage war on Native Peoples.

Local militias then began a process of extermination. The US Army and even civilian settlers joined in this mass slaughter of Native Peoples. Some White people formed official paramilitary groups, whose sole purpose was to find and kill Native Peoples.

As a result, the largely peaceful Native population of California was diminished by two-thirds in the first two years of the Gold Rush, a loss of some one hundred thousand men, women, and children. This period of violence and slaughter is now called the **California genocide**. Fortune was the ultimate goal of many who participated in the California genocide. They saw Native Peoples as "uncivilized" and standing in their way of mining for gold.

Despite the miners' goal of riches, California gold mining began very primitively. The earliest techniques often centered around a simple gravity method known as **panning**, whereby heavier gold could be separated from lighter water and silt. A system of panning multiple buckets at once with a device known as a **rocker box**, by which a screen identified gold in alluvial or water deposits, followed simple panning as a newer technique.

Once surface-level gold was exhausted, miners used picks and shovels to look for gold under the earth's surface. As mining became more complicated and less gold was available, miners banded together in large and small companies for a greater chance of success.

The Gold Rush brought fortune to the lucky few, but it also had broader impacts on California and the United States. Transportation and communication grew to meet the needs of prospectors. New roads, bridges, ferries, and ships were constructed to transport people and goods. The **Pony Express** was founded during this period to deliver packages and correspondence from California to the Midwest. Retail and wholesale businesses of many sorts, from lumber to textiles, also sprang up.

Though gold brought people to California, the rich land and favorable climate are what led many to stay, and several of California's vineyards and farms emerged during this era. Additionally, the Gold Rush led to an international economic boom of sorts. Nations far and wide began to trade more with both Californians and other Americans. New banks and financial service industries sprang up to take advantage of this boom.

However, not every result of the Gold Rush and its aftermath was positive, as the genocide of Native Peoples clearly shows. Additionally, the Gold Rush also created environmental concerns because the landscape was ravaged to extract gold as quickly as possible with no consideration for long-term impacts. In many places, there were also rampant labor shortages since many Americans left their farms and workplaces to flock to California. And, of course, one of the impacts of the Gold Rush was more gold in circulation, which led to inflation in the gold-backed currency system and thus higher prices for many consumer goods.

> **DID YOU KNOW?**
>
> The Gold Rush netted an estimated $216 million.

PRACTICE QUESTION

5) Which was NOT a result of the California Gold Rush?
   A. new transportation networks
   B. labor shortages in other parts of the country
   C. environmental degradation
   D. lower prices for consumer goods

NINETEENTH-CENTURY MIGRATION

Though people immigrating to California from Europe or Asia had no choice but to use sea travel, many Americans came overland. The **California Trail** system, spanning some 5,665 miles and ten states, was the most-used route. The remnants of this trail system can still be seen in many places.

Families using the trail from its beginnings in Missouri had a roughly 2,400-mile journey to California that could take up to six months. Along the way, they had to navigate deserts and mountains. Few towns existed along the route, forcing these settlers to depend on their resourcefulness to meet basic needs. An estimated two hundred thousand people traveled this route in the 1840s and 1850s. Some of them made it to their destination, but others perished from disease, starvation, or accidents along the way.

Americans were not the only people to feel the lure of the Gold Rush or other broader opportunities in the American West. Immigrants from Chile and Mexico in search of gold and a better life also came to California, where they joined Spanish-speaking Californios already living there.

During this era, Californios who had lived in the region under Mexico lost their land and were denied many of the rights that White people enjoyed—even though they had been promised US citizenship and equal rights under the Treaty of Guadalupe Hidalgo. They also suffered from racial and ethnic discrimination and were often wrongly portrayed as foreigners, though they were not immigrants.

Europeans also came to California, fleeing the wave of anti-monarchy revolutions of 1848 in Europe that left some nations in chaos. These immigrant groups, though often non-English-speaking, were generally accepted by White American Californians to a greater degree than were immigrants from Asia and Latin America. They were also more widely accepted than Californios. There was an irony to this: unlike the Californios who were in fact American citizens, these men and women were true American immigrants.

Tens of thousands of **Chinese migrants** came to California hoping to secure a future for their families as well; these migrants also became the target of xenophobia. White Americans in California feared and sometimes even outright despised these immigrants, whom they saw as having less right to the spoils of the American West than they did. As a result, a law passed in 1850 required non-Americans to hold a foreign mining license, which cost $20 per month, a hefty sum for the time. White Europeans—even immigrants like those fleeing the revolutions of 1848—could be exempted from the tax by becoming American citizens. This same option was not extended to Chinese Californians.

Unable to pay this tax, many Chinese migrants gave up mining and became businesspeople, establishing a thriving business sector in San Francisco dubbed "**Chinatown**." Eventually, the tax was lowered significantly, but anti-Chinese sentiment continued in California.

California was the land of opportunity because of its gold and other plentiful resources, but it remained largely removed from the rest of the United States throughout its earliest years of statehood. The California Trail provided a way to reach the American West, but it was far less efficient and more treacherous than rail travel. Things changed in 1863 with the construction of a transcontinental railroad. The Central Pacific Railroad would build 690 miles of track from Sacramento to connect at Promontory Summit, Utah, with the 1,085 miles being constructed by the Union Pacific from Omaha/Council Bluffs, Iowa. The Union Pacific employed a labor force that included Irish immigrants and Civil War veterans, but the Central Pacific relied largely on the labor of Chinese immigrants.

These Chinese American rail workers, who eventually made up 90 percent of the workforce laying the line, had a challenging job: they had to lay track through the Sierra Nevada mountains, which required the use of explosives. Historians estimate that at least one thousand employees died doing this dangerous work. Chinese rail workers were also paid less than half of what White workers made.

These conditions led to the largest organized labor movement of its time when a group of Chinese rail workers went on strike in June 1867, demanding safer and better working conditions and pay equal to that of White workers. The strike lasted eight days but was eventually squashed when the Central Pacific Railroad director diverted supplies like food to the demonstrating workers.

Despite these labor conditions, tens of thousands of Chinese workers helped complete the transcontinental railroad on May 10, 1869. The newly "connected" California continued to grow and change. With a transportation network by which to ship their produce and new and improved methods by which to irrigate land, large farms began to dot the state. Chinese laborers were now drawn to these large commercial farms, and many shifted from rail work to agricultural work.

However, an economic downturn and drought hit California in the 1870s. As unemployment swept the state, White Californians viewed Chinese Californians as competition for scarce jobs and began to stage numerous anti-Chinese campaigns. Mounting pressure from these groups led to the **Chinese Exclusion Act** of 1882, which prohibited emigration from China for ten years and dictated that Chinese-Americans, largely concentrated in California, could not become naturalized American citizens. This was quickly followed by the **Geary Act** of 1892, which prohibited Chinese immigration for another ten years and required Chinese Americans to obtain and carry documents known as "certificates of residence" at all times or face imprisonment or deportation. As a result, Chinese immigration to California declined sharply.

PRACTICE QUESTION

6) **Which development led to the growth of large farms in California?**
   A. European immigration
   B. the transcontinental railroad
   C. the Geary Act
   D. the growth of "Chinatown"

CONSTITUTIONAL AND POLITICAL DEVELOPMENT

Californians wrote their first state constitution in 1849 at the **Constitutional Convention of Monterey**. It was the basis for the subsequent constitution, drafted at the

Sacramento Convention of 1878 – 1879. The resulting state constitution, adopted in 1879 and revised many times since, has become well known for two reasons:

▶   its extreme length

▶   its specific provisions for individual rights that many interpret as going even beyond the Bill of Rights

The constitution was the result of many forces, most notably a desire for progressive reform. The California state legislature was dominated by the private interests of railroad and industry barons in the 1870s. The "everyday working people" of California resented this. In fact, many of the delegates at the Sacramento Convention were members of the **Workingmen's Party of California**, founded by **Denis Kearney**, a labor organizer. Though Kearney and his supporters often used a virulent anti-Chinese rhetoric, they were initially also concerned with the rights of labor and the need to hold politicians accountable for their actions.

> **DID YOU KNOW?**
>
> The first state constitution was written in both English and Spanish.

The resulting document was criticized. Some felt the constitution was too detailed and issues would have been better sorted out through subsequent legislation. Others protested its blatant disregard of the Fourteenth Amendment; the document stripped Chinese Californians of the basic rights guaranteed to all Americans, a notable result of Kearney's influence.

Further changes were made to the constitution in 1911. Unlike the US Constitution, California's Constitution, after these amendments, empowers voters with initiative, referendum, and recall:

1.   **Initiative** refers to the voters' rights to begin legislative action by petition. If the petition has a certain number of signatures, the proposed law can be brought before voters, and, if passed, it can become law. This process completely bypasses the legislature.

2.   **Referendum** is similar to initiative in that the public votes on a law either before it has been enacted (legislative referendum) or after it has been enacted and has been challenged (popular referendum).

3.   **Recall** is a process by which the public can, by petition, call for an election to remove a public official.

These provisions in the California Constitution were a direct attempt to limit the power of state government and were part of broader American **Progressive Era** reforms aimed at promoting growth and prosperity while keeping corruption and private interests in check.

The Progressive movement in California was largely led by Governor **Hiram Johnson**, who served from 1911 to 1917. Under his government, California passed the **Workman's Compensation, Insurance, and Safety Act** in 1913, which solidified the role of state government in protecting workers. He also created a state kindergarten program and teacher pension fund.

Despite progressive reform, Chinese Californians, Black Californians, and Native and Hispanic Californians still experienced marginalization and discrimination. However, women of California had some rights beyond other American women. The 1849 constitution had established the rights of women to control property. In 1911, California women earned the right to vote.

HELPFUL HINT:

One of the most famous California recalls was the 2003 recall of Governor Gray Davis, which resulted in Arnold Schwarzenegger being elected governor of California.

PRACTICE QUESTION

7) Which statement BEST describes the recall provision in the constitution of California?

   A. Citizens can begin legislative action by petition.

   B. Citizens can vote on a law after it has been enacted.

   C. Citizens can force the removal of an elected official.

   D. Citizens can enact a new law by popular vote.

TWENTIETH CENTURY

As California moved into the twentieth century, much had been accomplished, but more work remained. The state was no longer the frontier: by 1900, California was one of many growing western states. San Francisco was a particularly thriving city, but that peace and prosperity abruptly ended on April 18, 1906, with one of the most significant earthquakes in American history:

▶ The **San Francisco earthquake** formed a rupture of 296 miles along the Pacific coast and had a magnitude of 7.9 on the Richter scale.

▶ The quake was quickly followed by a four-day fire that consumed an estimated twenty-eight thousand buildings, or five hundred blocks of the city.

▶ The earthquake killed an estimated three thousand people and left another quarter of a million people without homes.

▶ Though destruction was severe and widespread, the city was rebuilt quickly, largely with earthquake-resistant construction methods.

Despite the threat of earthquakes, California continued to be a land of opportunity for many. Since California was a large state, land was cheaper there than elsewhere. Though larger agricultural operations were the norm, people also immigrated to the state to start small farms.

Large farms often relied on migrant workers. In California, many of these laborers came from the Philippines during the early twentieth century. The Filipino workers would work for less than White workers, which made them an attractive workforce to many landowners. This also made them a threat to White farm laborers who feared lowered wages. Tensions came to a head periodically: during the **Salinas Lettuce strike of 1934**, violence broke out between Filipino and White workers.

Mexican migrants fleeing the **Mexican Revolution** (1910 – 1920) also came to California in the early twentieth century, drawn by the prospect of work in the agricultural sector. Though the **Immigration Act** of 1924 sought to limit immigration, agricultural magnates in California and other states had a strong lobby and were able to ensure that Mexican migrants were exempted from these restrictions.

Many of these migrants settled in California permanently. Others returned to Mexico throughout the early decades of the twentieth century, having earned what they had hoped to or responding to changing economic conditions.

Oil was discovered in California in the nineteenth century, and production increased rapidly as new pockets were found throughout the 1920s. By 1923, this oil boom made California America's leading oil producer and brought more migrants to the state. Many settled in Los Angeles, which grew and expanded with roads, highways, and suburban communities. This growth was due in large part to the new, lower cost of automobiles resulting from Henry Ford's assembly line manufacturing process. The state highways were built largely via bond issues throughout the early twentieth century.

Unfortunately, the boom was not to last. Wages had been stagnant or decreasing for too long, and many workers could not even afford products they made or crops they harvested. Coupled with the stock market crash of 1929, these conditions led to the **Great Depression**.

HELPFUL HINT:

State highways and the national highway system brought tourists to California. Known for its beautiful weather and picturesque beaches, the state became a popular vacation destination for those with means throughout the 1920s.

Many lost their jobs and livelihoods; some became homeless. Forced to live in camps with whatever shelter they could find, some Californians took up residence in large concrete pipes in Oakland in what would become known as "Pipe City." Others lived in tents and shanties throughout the state. Such misery exacerbated the anti-immigrant sentiment that was already present:

▶ The 1935 Filipino **Repatriation Act** sought to encourage Filipino laborers to return to the Philippines via government subsidies for transportation.

▶ Resentment toward Mexican Californians, often the result of xenophobia and fear over competition for scarce jobs, led to mass deportations, known as **repatriations**, throughout the 1930s.

> The number of people forcibly deported during this period is debated, but some sources put the numbers at more than a million.

> Many of these deportees, perhaps up to 60 percent, were American citizens.

Anger and outrage toward those viewed as "outsiders" extended to migrants to California from other states. Drought and unsustainable farming practices led to extreme erosion and dust storms in Nebraska, Kansas, Oklahoma, New Mexico, Colorado, and the Texas Panhandle in the 1930s. Seeking to escape the widespread environmental and economic degradation known as the **Dust Bowl** that was exacerbated by the Great Depression, some three hundred thousand people migrated to California, the largest mass movement to the state since the Gold Rush. These migrants, derogatorily referred to as **"Okies"** because many came from Oklahoma, chose California for several reasons:

- Family members who had already migrated to the state in previous decades encouraged them.

- Agricultural work and farm labor jobs were left vacant by the deportation and repatriation policies of the era.

  > These jobs often paid more in California than in other states, as large farms required a large labor force.

- Direct government unemployment aid, a hallmark of Depression-era policy, was higher in California than in other places.

Many Dust Bowl migrants, who frequently traveled via the iconic **Route 66**, sought employment on the farms of California's **San Joaquin Valley**. Here, they often found poor conditions, either in employer-run labor camps or on their own in tents or makeshift shelters. Communicable diseases spread in such conditions, and many became sick. As the population in valley communities swelled by as much as 50 percent, conditions for everyone, migrant and Californian alike, worsened.

The influx of labor depressed wages and overwhelmed public services, like schools and hospitals. As California's agricultural labor force grew exponentially, the once-abundant agricultural job market dried up. This led to intense competition for scarce employment. Desperate, many Dust Bowl migrants worked for lower wages than existing California residents and were often willing to cross picket lines. Some historians argue that the Dust Bowl migrants held back existing efforts at labor organization, particularly among the Filipino and Mexican workforce. Such a situation resulted in widespread hatred of "Okies," whom many Californians from all walks of life saw as threatening their communities and livelihood.

Though some of the Dust Bowl migrants returned to their homes after the Depression ended, many stayed in California and made new lives. Some even achieved significant economic success and eventually owned farms or businesses. They also contributed to the state's culture, particularly in the San Joaquin Valley, where their descendants today make up nearly half of the population.

World War II brought widespread changes to California. The economy recovered, thanks in large part to mobilization for the war effort. Though agriculture was still important to feed Americans at home and serving abroad, California experienced rapid urbanization and industrialization. As migrants moved to the state to staff airplane- and ship-building factories, the cities' populations expanded. Some historians have dubbed this period the state's **second gold rush**.

While families migrated to California for work, many young men were fighting the war and could not fill the need for industrial labor. This meant that women moved into jobs in new industries. In fact, the number of California women working in the manufacturing sector quadrupled in just two years. As a result, federally funded childcare centers were built throughout the state; these facilities helped women overcome a potential barrier to working outside the home.

DID YOU KNOW?

Not all Dust Bowl migrants sought agricultural work. About one-third chased opportunity in Los Angeles, where skilled laborers could find work building planes and automobiles. However, most Dust Bowl migrants lacked such skills and struggled to find employment.

Though California experienced tremendous economic growth during the war, it was also the site of continued discrimination against Americans based on their ethnic origin. **Executive Order 9066**, signed by President Franklin Roosevelt in 1942, authorized the federal government to remove people with ancestry from the nations the United States was fighting in the war from certain areas deemed military zones.

With its strategic coastal location, California was deemed to have important military significance. Subsequent state and federal orders required the forced relocation of people of Japanese descent since Japan was one of the United States' enemies during the war.

Between 1942 and 1944, more than 110,000 people of Japanese ancestry, most of whom were US citizens, were forced into one of the nation's ten **internment camps**. Two of these camps, Tule Lake—a "special" facility for those who resisted internment—and Manzanar, were located in California.

Conditions in internment camps were harsh:

▶ Detainees were allowed to bring only what they could carry with them.

▶ They were forced to live in multifamily apartments with few modern conveniences, such as appliances or plumbing.

▶ The camps were monitored by armed guards and run largely like prisons.

Despite this, detainees used their own agency to keep hope alive through various community-building activities, such as recreation and sports.

In 1944, the Supreme Court ruled in *Korematsu v. US* that the US government did have the authority to remove people from a given location for military reasons and that Japanese internment was based on military necessity and not race. However, in **Ex parte Mitsuye Endo**, the Court subsequently ruled that loyal American citizens, regardless of ancestry, could not be forcibly interned.

The internment camps closed in 1945, though few reparations were made in the immediate aftermath. It was not until the **Civil Liberties Act** of 1988 that official governmental wrongdoing was recognized. A $20,000 payment was given to each former prisoner.

PRACTICE QUESTION

8) **Which of the following was a change in California resulting from World War II?**
   A. immigration of Dust Bowl refugees
   B. urbanization due to industrialization
   C. expanded rights for farmworkers
   D. new constitutional amendments

ENVIRONMENTAL ISSUES IN CALIFORNIA TODAY

Though World War II brought an economic boom to California, it also dramatically increased the state's population, from 6.95 million in 1940 to roughly 9.34 million in 1945. Subsequent decades have seen even more phenomenal growth:

- By 1950, there were 10.58 million people in California.
- By 1960, there were 15.71 million people in the state.
- By 1970, California had a population of 19.95 million.

Today, the population is a whopping 39.51 million. Inevitably, such a large population leads to concerns over the state's resources and their responsible uses.

California is a state rich in natural resources, but these resources are not infinite. One concern centers around the **water supply**. Most of California's fresh water in lakes and rivers is located in the northernmost part of the state, but the bulk of the demand for this water is in the southern region. To accommodate this, California devised an advanced and extensive system to transport water via aqueducts, dams, and reservoirs.

Still, water is not always plentiful, especially during droughts. There is competition surrounding water resources: large farms, urban residents, and environmental groups often have competing interests and priorities.

The vast network of dams and reservoirs brings water to the citizens of California, but it also brings broader environmental changes. Such changes have been criticized, particularly those affecting fish and other wildlife habitats and the plants that grow in these areas. Especially controversial is the **Sacramento–San Joaquin**

Delta, the state's central water source. This estuary provides much of the state's drinking water and irrigates many acres of farmland; however, human-made structures and activities to remove water from the estuary have put local wildlife in peril, resulting in multiple lawsuits and countersuits on behalf of those seeking to use the water without restriction. While access to water is a serious concern, **water quality** is another problem, fueled by the large amount of land in California under agricultural cultivation:

- Pesticides and fertilizers help increase agricultural output, but they are washed away in irrigation and stormwater runoff.

- These pollutants often make their way to lakes and rivers and, ultimately, into the drinking water system.

- Nitrates from fertilizer are of particular concern and are being carefully monitored by the California State Water Resources Control Board's Nitrate Project.

Widespread agriculture has also caused concerns over **soil quality**. Certain farming practices can deplete the soil of key nutrients and decrease plant health and crop yield. Further, exhausted soil leads to dust and erosion, and the possibility of a new Dust Bowl disaster is ever-present.

On the other hand, healthy soils can make a tremendous impact on biodiversity and help manage climate change via the sequestration of carbon. To promote healthy soil, the California Department of Food and Agriculture designed a **Healthy Soils Initiative** to encourage farmers and ranchers to implement best practices in promoting soil health.

Another environmental concern centers around air quality. Though air pollution is a problem in many cities with large numbers of cars and factories, it is particularly troubling in parts of California, like Los Angeles. This city is known to have **smog**, a type of air pollution that impacts visibility as pollutants react with sunlight. Because the city is in a lowland surrounded by mountains, smog cannot be as easily moved away by wind as it can in other places with different geography.

The first sighting of smog in Los Angeles was in 1943. Once its cause was discovered, the state took action to combat it, and by 1966, the state of California had established the nation's first automobile emissions standards. The California Air Resources Board, formed in 1967, is still tasked with maintaining California's air quality. Though its work has lowered emissions from vehicles significantly, air quality remains low, particularly in the San Joaquin Valley and Los Angeles.

Climate change exacerbates problems with air quality as well as with another concern: **wildfires**. Though naturally occurring wildfires are expected in the state annually beginning in late summer, these events have been growing bigger and more problematic in recent years.

More severe droughts and higher temperatures make conditions ideal for wildfires. Efforts to prevent dangerous wildfires are underway, led by the California

Wildfire and Forest Resilience Task Force. This organization works to increase the health of forests and protect communities from the potential impacts of wildfires.

As California has grown, its **transportation infrastructure** has been strained. The sheer number of cars on roadways, especially in large cities like Los Angeles, means traffic is a constant problem. These cars also contribute to growing greenhouse gas emissions. Though public transportation systems, like buses and trains, are already present, much of the existing commuter rail and bus infrastructure needs replacing.

A new high-speed rail system, which will eventually span eight hundred miles from San Diego to Sacramento and many places in between, is currently under construction. The new rail line is projected to reduce the emissions of greenhouse gases and lessen dangerous pollutants, such as smog. The first phase is planned to open in 2023.

California produces much of its own energy and ranks fourth in **energy** production in the United States; however, it ranks second (behind Texas) in energy production from renewable resources, such as geothermal and solar energies. The state ranks seventh in the production of crude oil, much of which comes from the San Joaquin Basin. Because it is such a populous state, it also consumes more energy than any other state aside from Texas. Much of this consumption is gas for cars and jet fuel for its many busy air travelers. The California Energy Commission regulates energy and encourages the shift to sustainable energy use via policy recommendations, regulations, and enforcement.

PRACTICE QUESTION

9) Which conditions are exacerbating wildfires in California?
   A. smog and other types of air pollution
   B. nitrates leaking into the groundwater
   C. droughts and higher temperatures
   D. high-speed rail construction efforts

Notable Places

California is admired for its scenic beauty and thriving tourist industry. It is also strongly associated with **Hollywood** and the **motion picture industry**. Interestingly, the center of the industry was once New Jersey, but certain situations made California more conducive to filmmaking.

Thomas Edison, the first to patent a movie camera called the "Kinetograph," was the film industry's most important early figure. Recognizing the power he had to control the industry, he created a licensing trust with others, including Kodak, which held the patent on film. This licensing trust vigorously enforced its patents, which meant that independent filmmakers in the Northeast had few options other than to pay the high prices for the products owned by Edison's trust.

But because travel and communications were more limited in the early twentieth century, California was literally at the other end of the country, far from Edison's group and their enforcers. Throughout the early 1910s, movie studios moved to the city of Hollywood in droves.

The first complete film shot in the city was *In Old California* (1910). It was quickly followed by many others. Producers found the lower production costs a draw, as well as the mild climate and varied terrain, which allowed for multiple shots with wide-ranging backdrops.

Though films were initially shot in black and white without sound, advances in the industry were swift. The first "talkie" was made in 1927, and though filming in color had been done, the 1939 color production of *The Wizard of Oz* brought the new type of film to the masses.

The 1920s and 1930s are considered the "Golden Age" of Hollywood. Studios, which typically owned the theaters that played their films, profited tremendously. However, changes brought about by World War II and a Supreme Court ruling that prohibited studios from owning theaters that showed only their productions marked the end of this "Golden Age." Nevertheless, Hollywood is still the undisputed center of the film industry and a major part of the state's economy.

California, America's largest economy, is also associated with **Silicon Valley**, the unofficial technology capital of the nation. The growth of this region—the cities around the southern portion of San Francisco Bay—can be traced back to Stanford University professor **Frederick E. Terman**.

Terman encouraged his students to start their own companies and even invested in them himself. In 1951, he led the establishment of **Stanford Research Park** (then called Stanford Industrial Park), a project that allowed technology companies to rent space at Stanford where they had access to the expertise of Stanford professors.

In 1956, **William Shockley** developed the transistor and opened a company in Stanford Research Park. His company fractured, and various others sprang up throughout Silicon Valley, which firmly established the region as a technology hub. However, these semiconductors were primarily for military use until the 1960s and 1970s, when other nonmilitary applications for this technology were developed. This led private investors eager to capitalize on the semiconductor boom to fund technology start-ups in Silicon Valley. As personal computing and the internet developed throughout the 1980s and 1990s, Silicon Valley continued to be a center of innovation. Companies like Apple and Google existed alongside countless other start-up firms.

Unfortunately, the year 2000 brought the bursting of what many have dubbed the "internet bubble," and many Silicon Valley ventures struggled or closed. The region eventually recovered, however, and continues to be a hub for entrepreneurship and innovation. Several major tech and nontech companies have headquarters in the region, including

- Apple,
- Google (Alphabet),
- Facebook (Meta),
- Visa,
- Wells Fargo,
- Chevron.

PRACTICE QUESTION

10) **Why did independent moviemakers relocate from the Northeast to Hollywood?**

   A.   They could show their films to a broader audience.

   B.   They could own theaters in California that showed only their own films.

   C.   They could capitalize on new technologies available in California.

   D.   They could make films without having to pay licensing fees to others.

ANSWER KEY

1) **D.** Death Valley, located in the Mojave Desert region, is 282 feet below sea level.

2) **B.** Geographic barriers often kept small tribelets isolated from each other and spread throughout what would become the state of California.

3) **C.** After the British won the French and Indian War, Spain became concerned about that country's increasing power in North America and sought to solidify its colonial possessions.

4) **A.** Gold was discovered in California in 1848, prompting interest in quickly making California a state.

5) **D.** More gold in circulation led to inflation, which increased the price of many consumer goods.

6) **B.** The transcontinental railroad gave California farmers a transportation system by which to ship their goods to new markets.

7) **C.** Recall allows California citizens to remove an elected official from office.

8) **B.** Mobilization for the war effort led to widespread industrialization, which brought people to cities in ever-growing numbers.

9) **C.** Droughts and higher temperatures caused by climate change are creating conditions that lead to more wildfires.

10) **D.** Thomas Edison's licensing trust required people using movie cameras and film to pay high fees. The trust's power to enforce its patents was limited because of California's remoteness.

CSET Practice Test 1

SUBTEST I

1

Which of the following best describes an ideal society according to Confucianism?

A. It is based on respect for authority and wisdom, making harmonious interaction a priority.

B. It allows respectful debate and discussion to encourage learning and the development of wisdom.

C. It encompasses a diverse group of people, to gather wisdom from different cultures.

D. It values hierarchy and enforces a caste system.

2

Islam originated in which of the following areas?

A. the Middle East

B. the Arabian Peninsula

C. Egypt

D. Iran

3

Which of the following best describes Buddhism?

A. It places value on monotheism, the belief in one god—the Buddha.

B. It places value on harmony with nature and the development of wisdom.

C. It places value on transcendence of the ego and desire for material things to relieve suffering and achieve nirvana.

D. It places value on filial piety in order to achieve a harmonious society.

4

Based on the core-periphery model, where are the majority of periphery countries located?

A. Africa, parts of Asia, and parts of South America

B. Asia, parts of Eastern Europe, and parts of South America

C. North America, Africa, and parts of Asia

D. South America, parts of North America, and parts of Eastern Europe

5

Which of the following statements best explains the relevance of bronze metallurgy in early human civilizations?

A. Bronze technology allowed early societies in the Fertile Crescent to develop improved irrigation.

B. The Bronze Age gave rise to the Neolithic Era.

C. The development of bronze allowed humans to create copper.

D. Early civilizations like the Sumerians were able to use bronze for tools and weapons; geographic expansion and technological innovation (including in weaponry) resulted.

6

Which of the following best describes humans during the Paleolithic Era?

A. *Homo sapiens* was the only species of human in existence.

B. Multiple species of humans existed.

C. *Homo sapiens* likely eliminated all competition for resources.

D. Humans had not yet evolved.

7

What concept did early Chinese imperial civilization and early Fertile Crescent civilizations share?

A. centralized government structure

B. written language

C. monotheism

D. A and B only

8

Which of the following best describes serfs in feudal Europe?

A. They were enslaved by the lords and knights.

B. They were bonded to the land but under the protection of the lords.

C. They were forced to fight for the lords.

D. They were able to eventually purchase their freedom from the knights in exchange for support fighting.

9

How did the Crusades enrich Europe?

A. All Crusaders returned home and increased the population.

B. European Crusaders enjoyed lasting land gains.

C. International trade and cultural exchange between Europe and the Levant increased.

D. European monarchies grew weaker and were replaced by parliaments.

10

How was Russia affected by the schism between Byzantine (Greek Orthodox) Christianity and the Roman Catholic Church?

A. Russia was unaffected.

B. Strong papal influences within Europe extended into Kiev and Russia, and Vladimir I converted to Catholicism, encouraging his subjects to do the same.

C. Byzantine missionaries moved north into Kiev and Russian territories; as a result, Vladimir I converted to Greek Orthodox Christianity and had his subjects do the same.

D. Disagreeing with the Catholic Church, Russia developed Eastern Orthodox Christianity and a separate Russian church.

11

Which of the following describes major influences on the European Renaissance?

A. cultural discoveries in North America

B. African music and culture

C. Greek Orthodox Christianity and learning brought by Byzantine missionaries

D. scientific knowledge from the Islamic empires and Greco-Roman philosophy and art

12

Which of the following would be considered a push factor for migration?

A. the discovery of oil in a new region

B. the outbreak of civil war in a new region

C. a new law in the home country requiring the practice of Catholicism

D. the relocation of a major company to the home region

Go on →

13

Which of the following led to the French Revolution?

A. food shortages, heavy taxation of the peasants and bourgeoisie, and Enlightenment thought

B. the rise of Napoleon and the militarization of French culture

C. the Congress of Vienna and shifting diplomatic alliances in Europe

D. the reign of Louis XIV

14

Choose the answer that presents events in the correct chronology:

A. the French Revolution, the American Revolution, the Industrial Revolution, World War I

B. the American Revolution, the French Revolution, Napoleon's conquests, World War I

C. the French Revolution, the Industrial Revolution, the American Revolution, World War I

D. the Rape of Nanjing, World War I, the Great Depression, World War II

15

Which of the following helped lead to the development of the Kingdom of Mali?

A. its control over the trans-Saharan trade routes, enabling it to tax traders transporting goods between Morocco and the Atlantic coast

B. its ability to repel Islamic influences from the north

C. its control over gold and salt resources, generating tremendous wealth for the kingdom

D. its control over the trans-Saharan slave trade

16

European imperialism in the nineteenth century was a function of which of the following?

I. an effort to gain natural resources to power industrialization in the Americas

II. a way of shouldering the "white man's burden," or helping to improve "backward" societies

III. a competition between European countries to control territory, leading to phenomena like the "scramble for Africa"

A. I and II

B. II and III

C. I, II, and III

D. I and III

17

What resulted from the 1884 Berlin Conference?

A.   It established extraterritoriality within important Chinese cities to support their nationals who were participating in trade in opium, silk, and other Chinese goods.

B.   It agreed upon spheres of influence whereby each European country would dominate different parts of China.

C.   It determined which parts of Africa would be controlled by which European powers, a process also called the "scramble for Africa."

D.   It established the Triple Alliance and the Triple Entente, setting the stage for the system of alliances that would eventually spark the First World War.

18

While the beginning of the Second World War is usually understood to be Hitler's invasion of Poland, some scholars date it even earlier. Which of the following events do some scholars identify as the beginning of World War II?

A.   the Rape of Nanjing

B.   the Japanese takeover of Korea

C.   the Japanese invasion of Manchuria

D.   the Chinese Civil War

19

Why was decolonization important?

A.   European colonies in Africa, Asia, and the Pacific became independent countries.

B.   Colonies gained a stronger position in trade negotiations.

C.   It helped implement the industrialization of sugar cane to other countries.

D.   It prevented independence among the states in America.

20

What happened to Afghanistan following the Soviet invasion of that country and subsequent withdrawal?

A.   It came under Indian influence, making it vulnerable to extremist movements like the Taliban.

B.   It descended into a period of instability and civil war, making it vulnerable to extremist movements like the Taliban.

C.   It temporarily joined Pakistan in an effort to regain stability.

D.   It temporarily came under NATO administration in an effort to regain stability and prevent the development of extremist groups.

21

During Partition on the Subcontinent, which states were created?

A. India and Pakistan

B. India, Pakistan, and Bangladesh

C. India, Pakistan, and Afghanistan

D. India, Pakistan, Afghanistan, and Bangladesh

22

The Robinson map (which slightly distorts shape, size, and straight-line direction) is an example of which kind of map?

A. gnomonic projection

B. azimuthal equidistant projection

C. equal area projection

D. compromise projection

23

In South America, how was the Inca Empire able to consolidate its rule?

A. The Inca used strong military technology and tactics to subdue conquered peoples and expand their empire.

B. Driven by the belief in conversion, the Inca were able to convert Andean peoples to their own religion, gaining followers and, therefore, loyal subjects.

C. The Inca civilization grew thanks to a surplus of maize and mastery of high altitude agriculture; their domestication of llamas and alpacas allowed them to sustain their military with supplies to travel through the mountains.

D. Due to the mountainous terrain of the Andes, the Inca were unable to expand their empire far.

24

The Qin dynasty was able to consolidate its power in China due to which of the following?

A. The Qin enforced Confucianism throughout China as a means to consolidate its power.

B. The Qin developed a common written language, allowing them to unite the disparate Chinese-speaking groups of people throughout China.

C. Emerging dominant following the Warring States period, the Qin developed standardized weights and measures and a unified bureaucracy.

D. The Qin dynasty established a democracy where everyone was unified and equal.

25

Enslaved African people were originally brought to the Americas as part of the triangular trade to do what?

A. work in factories and on assembly lines

B. own sugar plantations

C. work in Africans' homes

D. work in agriculture, mining, and domestic service

26

What was the Meiji Restoration?

A. a Japanese attempt to restore and reinvigorate the country and its culture as it had been before Western incursions into the country

B. a period of modernization and westernization in Japan

C. the early stage of Japanese imperialism in Asia when it invaded Korea

D. a cultural movement in Japan to restore Shintoism and traditional poetry

27

Why did the Silk Road eventually fall out of use?

A. The length of time it took for caravans to reach Europe from Asia interrupted trade within Europe, and demand for Asian goods there declined as a result.

B. Continuing attacks on caravans along the Silk Road eventually made it too dangerous to use and not worth the potential profit.

C. Thanks to new technology developed in the Umayyad Empire, better and safer roads were being used for transcontinental trade.

D. Sea travel was faster and more practical; improvements in navigation and ship construction had made it a more feasible alternative.

28

Which of the following was a consequence of nationalism in nineteenth-century Europe?

A. Italian unification

B. the Congress of Vienna

C. American unification

D. the French Revolution

29

Which of the following BEST describes the Mediterranean region during the Pax Romana?

A. It was a period of anxiety and civil unrest under Roman rule.

B. It was the center of farming activity.

C. It was a time of stability under Augustus Caesar.

D. It was a time of artistic advancement.

30

Which of the following is true about the Neolithic Era?

A. *Homo sapiens* was the only species of human in existence.

B. Multiple species of human existed.

C. *Homo sapiens* likely eliminated all competition for resources.

D. Humans had not yet evolved.

31

The Babylonians are known for having developed an early form of

A. irrigation, increasing agricultural production in the fertile areas near the Tigris and Euphrates Rivers.

B. cuneiform, the first known example of writing in which characters were connected to form words.

C. rule of law: the Code of Hammurabi.

D. iron weaponry and chariots, enabling them to control large areas of land.

32

Following the collapse of the Western Roman Empire and the subsequent, disorganized "Dark Ages" in Europe,

A. The Catholic Church based in Rome lost power in Western Europe to the rising Greek Orthodox Church based in Constantinople.

B. The Byzantine Empire was able to conquer unorganized European land in what is today Germany.

C. Charlemagne united parts of Western and Central Europe—what would become the Holy Roman Empire—leading to a period of stability.

D. Charlemagne united parts of Western and Central Europe (including what would become France) under his rule, leading to a period of stability.

33

In the nineteenth century, Britain occupied parts of Somalia, Kenya, and Egypt, and negotiated boundaries and treaties with other colonial powers and local governments. Which of the following best explains why the British prioritized organizing this area?

A. Britain wished to safeguard shipping routes through the Red Sea and into the Indian Ocean.

B. Britain wished to control the valuable and popular routes in the Red Sea to Mecca and Medina.

C. Britain was concerned about instability in Somalia.

D. Britain was unable to consolidate control further inland into Africa.

34

Which of the following statements is true about the political geography of Antarctica?

A. Antarctica is governed by the United Nations.

B. Antarctica is governed jointly by the United States, Great Britain, and Russia.

C. Antarctica is the only unorganized territory left in the world.

D. Antarctica is governed jointly by its four nearest neighbors: Argentina, Chile, South Africa, and Australia.

35

Which of the following is the main reason for the development of the Sunni-Shi'a schism in early Islam?

A. Sunnis believed that early Muslims should conquer lands west of the Arabian Peninsula, while Shi'ites thought it would make more sense strategically to invade the Mesopotamian regions and Persia.

B. Sunnis prioritized military conquest over Muhammad's religious and philosophical teachings, a development with which Shi'ites vehemently disagreed.

C. Sunnis were more willing to accept Jews and Christians as "People of the Book," but Shi'ites felt that they should be converted to Islam, or forced out of communities controlled by Muslims.

D. Sunnis and Shi'ites disagreed over the appropriate line of succession following the death of the Prophet Muhammad.

36

The Sino-Soviet Split was due in part to

A. the Chinese alliance with the United States.

B. the Soviet alliance with the United States.

C. the absence of the People's Republic of China from the United Nations.

D. division between the communist philosophies of Maoist China and the Marxist-Leninist U.S.S.R.

37

One reason Charlemagne was able to retain legitimacy and hold power in an unstable Europe was because

A. he was crowned by the Pope and had the support of the Catholic Church.

B. he had the support of the serfs, having pledged to end the feudal system.

C. he encouraged knights to travel to the Middle East to fight the Crusades.

D. he was seen as a counter to the tremendous power of the Catholic Church.

38

The collapse of the Mongol Empire was due in part to which of the following developments?

    I.   the rise of Islam and the growing power of the Abbasid Caliphate

    II. Ivan the Great's consolidation of power and conquest of Moscow

    III. the overthrow of the Yuan dynasty by the Ming dynasty in China

A.   I, II, and III

B.   I and II only

C.   II and III only

D.   I and III only

39

While the Crusades enriched Europe in many ways, they did NOT do what?

A.   provide new learning to the west

B.   result in lasting land gains

C.   provide religious indulgences

D.   offer the opportunity to gain personal wealth

CONSTRUCTED RESPONSE QUESTIONS

World History #1

The collapse of the Roman Empire led to a period of instability in Western Europe as well as a loss of the learning and infrastructure that had characterized Rome. However, in the Middle East and Eastern Mediterranean, under the Byzantine Empire and, later, under the Arab-Islamic and Ottoman Empires, imperial organization, brisk trade with partners in Asia, and philosophical and scientific learning continued.

Using your knowledge of world history, explain how the knowledge and organization sustained in the Middle East and Eastern Mediterranean eventually impacted the European Renaissance.

World History #2

Following the Second World War, the United States and the Soviet Union emerged as dominant world powers, ushering in the Cold War and a "bipolar world." Only a few years earlier, European powers, like England and France, controlled colonial empires around the world, dominating global affairs. In fact, the Soviet Union itself was only a few decades old.

Using your knowledge of world history, explain how the two superpowers were able to rapidly dominate global affairs following the Second World War.

World Geography

The global map is ever-changing as nation-states emerge, splinter, and form. At times, this process may seem unpredictable, but scholars have identified certain forces that may impact the health of a nation-state. These forces are sometimes divided into two categories: centrifugal forces and centripetal forces. Identifying the presence or absence of centrifugal or centripetal forces is part of analyzing the overall health of a nation-state.

Using your knowledge of geography, analyze centrifugal forces and centripetal forces and describe how they may impact a nation-state.

SUBTEST II

1

Which of the following is a safeguard against federal overreach built into the US Constitution?

A. a system of checks and balances, in which a president can only be elected to two consecutive terms

B. a system of checks and balances, in which the House, Senate, and president are able to limit each other

C. a system of checks and balances, in which the president—a civilian leader—controls the military

D. a system of checks and balances, in which the three branches of government—executive, legislative, and judicial—are able to limit each other

2

In the first half of the nineteenth century, social change in the US was driven by religious and social organizations that helped foster political interest in women's rights, abolitionism, and utopianism. What was this movement called?

A. the Industrial Revolution

B. the Second Great Awakening

C. the Enlightenment

D. the Glorious Revolution

3

What did President Monroe attempt to accomplish with the Monroe Doctrine?

A. keep the US involved in European conflicts

B. isolate the US from European intervention in its affairs

C. assert US hegemony in the Western Hemisphere by isolating it from Europe to prevent European powers from expanding there

D. increase US involvement in international affairs

4

Which of the following is one reason the framers called for the Constitutional Convention?

A.   to empower the local government to levy taxes

B.   fear that individual liberties were in jeopardy

C.   fear that the national government was unable to maintain order

D.   a desire to decrease trade

5

How did the Fugitive Slave Act empower slave states under federal law?

A.   Slave states had the right to take escaped slaves to court under the Fugitive Slave Act.

B.   Many states' rights advocates approved of the federal Fugitive Slave Act; it allowed them to pursue and capture slaves who had escaped to free states.

C.   Slave states were able to send police and military authorities into free states to capture escaped slaves.

D.   Slave states were able to prosecute free states in federal court for offering safe haven to escaped slaves.

6

What assets did the Confederacy have during the Civil War?

A.   The Confederacy had superior weaponry and production resources.

B.   The Confederacy maintained brisk trade with Europe, enabling it to fund the war.

C.   The Confederacy benefitted from strong military leadership and high morale among the population.

D.   The Confederacy's strong infrastructure allowed it to transport supplies and people efficiently throughout the South.

7

How did the *Dred Scott* decision affect the Fugitive Slave Act?

A.   It weakened the Act.

B.   It strengthened the Act.

C.   It had no effect on the Act.

D.   It abolished the Act.

8

What was a result of the Reconstruction Acts?

A.   They immediately improved conditions for African Americans in the South.

B.   They immediately benefitted the Southern economy.

C.   They were widely considered fair in Congress and by Southerners.

D.   They imposed Northern military control over the South.

9

What was the main reason behind the Sioux War?

A.   the flooding of the Rosebud River

B.   Native American exhaustion of prior battles which made it an opportune time for others to attack

C.   the resource-rich Black Hills, which contained gold and oil that the US president wanted

D.   lack of livestock that the Native Americans needed to survive

10

Which of the following best describes the Ten Percent Plan created by President Lincoln?

A.   It called for the rebel states to pay ten percent of the costs of the war in restitution to the North as a condition of readmission to the Union.

B.   It ensured that African Americans would be represented by at least ten percent of Congress following the Civil War.

C.   It readmitted any rebel state to the Union once at least ten percent of its citizens swore allegiance to the Union.

D.   It required ten percent of the population of a rebel state to move to the North before it would be readmitted to the Union.

11

What did the Homestead Act accomplish?

A.   The Lakota Sioux would be granted a homeland in the Black Hills of South Dakota.

B.   White immigrants would be allotted free land in the Plains states.

C.   The US government would provide land in the West for free to White settlers willing to farm it for at least two years.

D.   The Cheyenne and Arapaho would agree to remain on reservations so that settlers could establish homesteads in Colorado, Nebraska, and Wyoming.

12

Which of the following best describes the Interstate Commerce Act and the Sherman Antitrust Act?

A.   They immediately went into effect to regulate the railroad industry and break up monopolies.

B.   They remained largely toothless until the First World War.

C.   They remained largely toothless until the administration of Theodore Roosevelt.

D.   They immediately went into effect to promote congressional efforts to regulate interstate commerce.

13

The US entered WWI largely because of which of the following?

A.   the Zimmerman Telegram

B.   the rise of Nazi Germany

C.   the assassination of Franz Ferdinand

D.   the attack on the *Lusitania*

14

Which of the following is a core principle of the United States Constitution?

A.   Political parties are essential to the functioning of the government.

B.   The national government should be beholden to the people, not the states.

C.   The central government should hold the majority of power.

D.   The powers of the federal government should be limited.

15

SALT I and SALT II were indicative of what in the US – USSR relationship?

A.   a stalemate

B.   a period of conflict

C.   glasnost

D.   a period of diplomatic détente

16

What was a consequence of US support for Israel in the Six-Day and Yom Kippur Wars?

A.   OPEC's oil embargo, which was economically harmful for the Middle East

B.   OPEC's oil embargo, which was economically harmful for many working Americans

C.   increased Arab support for the United States in international forums like the United Nations

D.   improved relations between the United States, Saudi Arabia, and Iran

17

Which event caused the United States to enter the Second World War?

A.   Britain's need for assistance as it came under attack from Germany

B.   Nazi atrocities and genocide in Europe

C.   the Japanese attack on Pearl Harbor

D.   Japanese expansion and atrocities in Asia

18

Segregation was found unconstitutional by which of the following Supreme Court decisions?

A.   *Brown v. Board of Education*

B.   *Plessy v. Ferguson*

C.   *Scott v. Sandford*

D.   *Korematsu v. US*

19

What did the Voting Rights Act of 1965 accomplish?

A.   It gave African Americans the right to vote in the segregated states.

B.   It gave Americans under the age of twenty-one the right to vote.

C.   It ended segregation in voting.

D.   It ended restrictions that prevented African Americans from voting in many states with histories of institutionalized racism.

20

The Civil Rights Movement made use of which of the following to effect social change?

A.   nonviolent civil disobedience

B.   bombings of churches

C.   dismantling of economic barriers

D.   outreach to journalists

21

Even though the United States had supported Iraq during the Iran-Iraq War in the 1980s, it went to war with Iraq in 1991 following that country's invasion of Kuwait. Which of the following best explains why?

A.   The US wanted to secure access to oil in Kuwait and elsewhere in the Persian Gulf, especially Saudi Arabia.

B.   The US wanted to secure the region to prevent a resurgence of war with Iran.

C.   The US wanted to stabilize the region to prevent terrorism.

D.   The US wanted to effect regime change in Iraq.

22

What was the ultimate result of the Cuban Missile Crisis?

A.   the installation of the Castro regime

B.   the fall of the Castro regime

C.   a new opening of dialogue between the United States and the Soviet Union

D.   the end of a period of détente between the United States and the Soviet Union

23

Which of the following actions of the United States contributed to the fall of the Soviet Union?

    I.   the "arms race"—high extensive military spending and weapons development in the 1980s

    II. arming anti-Soviet proxies in Afghanistan—the mujahideen

    III. supporting Boris Yeltsin in the coup against Mikhail Gorbachev

A.   I and II

B.   I and III

C.   II and III

D.   I, II, and III

24

Initially, colonists were frustrated with the British government and insisted on which of the following?

A.   independence

B.   immediate self-government

C.   the overthrow of King George III

D.   repeal of unfair taxes and restrictions

25

Which of the following best explains the strategy behind the Anaconda Plan?

A.   The North would "squeeze" the South by taking control of the Mississippi River and establishing a naval blockade on the Atlantic coast; given the South's reliance on cotton export for revenue, this would be a devastating economic blow.

B.   "Squeezing" the South by taking control of the Mississippi River and establishing a naval blockade on the Atlantic coast would prevent raw materials from reaching the Confederacy to power its industrial growth.

C.   The North would crush Southern resistance by fighting primarily in Virginia; by "squeezing" the seat of Confederate government in Richmond, it hoped to cause the entire Confederacy to collapse.

D.   The North would surround the South with troops in Kentucky, West Virginia, Missouri, and elsewhere, hoping to outnumber their forces.

26

President Theodore Roosevelt, a Progressive, was known for which major action?

A. prosecuting the Northern Securities company under the Interstate Commerce Act, breaking up this large monopoly and earning his reputation as a "trust-buster"

B. developing the Works Progress Administration to assist working people in finding jobs and to support mistreated factory workers

C. ensuring the ratification of the Sixteenth Amendment

D. limiting the use of the Sherman Anti-Trust Act only to a few situations, earning his reputation as a "trust-buster"

27

The United States remained relatively neutral in international conflicts for much of its early history; its first major assertion of international power and foreign intervention overseas is considered to be which of the following?

A. the Spanish-American War

B. the First World War

C. the Texan Revolution

D. the War of 1812

28

Which Enlightenment concepts were included in the Constitution?

A. absolutism and consent of the governed

B. limited monarchy and absolutism

C. absolutism and the rule of law

D. consent of the governed and the rule of law

29

What was the US combat strategy during WWII?

A. Because Japan had attacked the United States, FDR believed it necessary to contain Japan using the tactic of island-hopping before addressing Europe.

B. The United States invaded Europe to defeat Nazi Germany first; after major combat in Western Europe and the defeat of the Nazis, it addressed Japan.

C. Due to the threat of kamikaze attacks from German U-boats, the United States was forced to lead a ground war in Europe, which it had tried to avoid.

D. The failure of island hopping forced a US invasion of Japan; the United States was then better prepared for ground combat in Europe.

30

How did the addition of the Bill of Rights to the Constitution come about?

A.   in response to the Supreme Court's ruling in *Marbury v. Madison*

B.   by the first Congress immediately after ratification

C.   by Congress slowly over the first twenty years of the nation's existence

D.   through George Washington's signature before he left office

31

Why was the Patriot Act controversial?

A.   It permitted the U.S. to search for weapons of mass destruction in Iraq, following the 9/11 terrorist attacks, but many believed that Iraq had not been involved in planning these attacks.

B.   It expanded the NSA's ability to spy on foreign heads of state, a violation of international law.

C.   It established Guantanamo Bay as a detention center for suspected terrorists captured in the War on Terror but without allowing them visits from the International Committee of the Red Cross, a violation of the Geneva Conventions.

D.   It broadened the government's powers of surveillance over the activities of American citizens, interpreted as a violation of Americans' rights under the Fourth Amendment and other rights to privacy.

32

Which of the following is an example of social liberalism?

A.   the passage of an Equal Rights Amendment to the Constitution guaranteeing equal rights to women and transgender people

B.   increased social acceptance of homosexuality and eventual legalization of same-sex marriage throughout the United States

C.   reduction in rates of imprisonment and emphasis on rehabilitation over punishment, particularly for nonviolent offenders

D.   a more equitable, progressive income tax

33

What was so controversial about the prison opened at the US naval base at Guantanamo Bay, Cuba, following the terrorist attacks of September 11, 2001?

A.   Surveillance programs secretly run from the prison at Guantanamo were found to have violated privacy laws in the United States.

B.   Both Democrats and Republicans argued that prisoners at Guantanamo Bay should be moved to prisons within the United States to save money, as the facility at Guantanamo was enormously expensive.

C.   Prisoners at Guantanamo Bay were denied the rights normally granted to prisoners of war under the Geneva Conventions, to which the United States is a party.

D.   A number of US and European citizens were found to have been mistakenly imprisoned in Guantanamo for crimes they did not commit.

34

Which of the following best explains why the temperance movement became popular?

A.   Because women were discouraged from public consumption of alcohol, women activists in the Progressive movement felt that prohibition of consumption of alcoholic beverages would encourage social equality.

B.   High prices for alcohol were an increasing problem for working class families, for whom this product was one of few affordable luxuries.

C.   Alcohol consumption by working men, generally the breadwinners in impoverished urban households, affected their wives and female partners, who were forced to cope with the resulting strain on household budgets and domestic violence.

D.   Since most alcohol was imported from overseas, a movement to decrease trade with European powers was popular with nationalists.

35

What did the framers recognize about the development of an efficient national government?

A.   National government should be temporary.

B.   As commander in chief, the president decides whether to declare war.

C.   A national government has both benefits and drawbacks.

D.   Power should be centralized in the federal government.

36

Why did the United States invade and occupy Iraq during Operation Iraqi Freedom in 2003?

A.   under the faulty premise that Saddam Hussein held weapons of mass destruction and was linked to al Qaeda, which had recently attacked the United States

B.   in order to capture Osama bin Laden, who was under the protection of Saddam Hussein

C.   after it was proven that Iraq provided al Qaeda with weapons it used to attack the United States on 9/11

D.   because Iraq attacked the United States on September 11, 2001

37

Which of the following reduced the ability of railroads to create monopolies and set prices without market interference?

A.   Sherman Antitrust Act

B.   Interstate Commerce Act

C.   International Commerce Act

D.   the Sixteenth Amendment

38

Which Enlightenment theorist most influenced the framers when they structured the national government?

A.   John Locke

B.   Jean Jacques Rousseau

C.   Alexis de Tocqueville

D.   Baron de Montesquieu

39

Which of the following tribes was Tecumseh able to unite in his confederacy?

A.   Shawnee, Lenape, Miami, Kickapoo, and others

B.   Algonquin, Shawnee, Iroquois, Miami, and others

C.   Shawnee, Cherokee, Miami, Apache, and others

D.   Shawnee, Lenape, Chickasaw, Choctaw, and others

CONSTRUCTED RESPONSE QUESTIONS

United States History #1

"Every nation, in every region, now has a decision to make. Either you are with us, or you are with the terrorists. From this day forward, any nation that continues to harbor or support terrorism will be regarded by the United States as a hostile regime." (President George W. Bush, "Address to a Joint Session of Congress and the American People," September 20, 2001)

Using your knowledge of US history, explain how President George W. Bush set the agenda for US foreign policy in this speech, made shortly after the terrorist attacks on September 11, 2001. Then compare US foreign policy between the twentieth and early twenty-first centuries.

United States History #2

"I shall see, this day, and its popular characteristics, from the slave's point of view. Standing, there, identified with the American bondman, making his wrongs mine, I do not hesitate to declare, with all my soul, that the character and conduct of this nation never looked blacker to me than on this Fourth of July! Whether we turn to the declarations of the past, or to the professions of the present, the conduct of the nation seems equally hideous and revolting. America is false to the past, false to the present, and solemnly binds herself to be false to the future. Standing with God and the crushed and bleeding slave on this occasion, I will, in the name of humanity which is outraged, in the name of liberty which is fettered, in the name of the Constitution and the Bible, which are disregarded and trampled upon, dare to call in question and to denounce, with all the emphasis I can command, everything that serves to perpetuate slavery—the great sin and shame of America!"

(Frederick Douglass, "Oration Delivered in Corinthian Hall, Rochester"; also known as "What to the Slave is the Fourth of July?," July 5, 1852)

Frederick Douglass condemned United States policy on and society's attitude toward slavery. Using your knowledge of US history, cite at least two examples of legislation that Douglass likely would have criticized, and explain how those laws reinforced slavery in the years preceding the Civil War.

United States Geography

Human experience is, in part, determined by the physical environment. However, nation-states do not always share one homogenous physical environment. The United States is one such example: it is a large nation with diverse physical features. Some Americans live in deserts, others in coastal regions, and still others in mountainous areas or on prairies. These diverse environments help shape the social, political, and economic realities of the people living in each region.

Using your knowledge of geography, analyze ways that the diverse physical environment has shaped life in the United States.

SUBTEST III

1

What are Supreme Court interpretations an example of?

A. the flexibility of the Constitution

B. the need to continually amend the Constitution

C. the growth of power of the judiciary over time

D. the federal government's supremacy over state governments

2

What does the location of the long-run aggregate supply curve (LRAS) indicate?

A. the full employment level of output

B. maximum consumer utility

C. maximum labor supply

D. the average price over a period of time

3

In American political culture, which of the following is a fundamental ideal?

A. wide-reaching government

B. natural, inalienable rights

C. no two people are truly equal

D. economic equality

4

What is the role of the Federal Reserve?

A.   to coin money

B.   to control government spending

C.   to determine tax policy

D.   to stabilize prices

5

Which mountain range had to be blasted through as part of the construction of the transcontinental railroad?

A.   Cascade Range

B.   Transverse Ranges

C.   Klamath Mountains

D.   Sierra Nevada

6

Media coverage has led to the rise of candidate-centered campaigns because of which of the following?

A.   coverage of candidate backstories and gaffes

B.   reporting on party platforms

C.   the variety of issues presented

D.   party labels

7

Which of the following actions aims to decrease the money supply?

A.   increase the federal tax rate

B.   lower interest rates

C.   create a new federal social welfare program

D.   fund military research for a new bomber

8

Inherent powers of government are most associated with which political concept?

A.   sovereignty

B.   legitimacy

C.   federalism

D.   republicanism

9

Mark buys five new shirts; when he looks to buy a sixth, he finds that the satisfaction he felt from buying the first five has greatly decreased. This is an example of which of the following?

A. the law of diminishing returns

B. the law of diminishing marginal utility

C. the law of demand

D. the income effect

10

Which describes a practice common to many Native American groups in California before European arrival?

A. a carefully planned central government

B. a rigid social hierarchy

C. alliances with other groups

D. adaptiveness to the local environment

11

Which of the following best describes implied powers?

A. They are specifically listed in the Constitution.

B. They belong to the states.

C. They are not specifically listed but are needed to perform other listed duties.

D. They exist because the United States is a sovereign nation.

12

A nation decides to concentrate its economy on the extraction and export of oil, at the expense of providing sufficient food, infrastructure, and healthcare. Production levels fall along the production possibility frontier. Which of the following statements is true about this country?

A. This nation is productively efficient, but allocatively inefficient.

B. This nation is allocatively efficient, but productively inefficient.

C. This nation is both productively and allocatively efficient.

D. This nation is both productively and allocatively inefficient.

13

What does the free exercise clause of the First Amendment protect?

A. the right to practice a religion of one's choosing

B. an individual's right to join a group

C. all citizens from the imposition of a national tax on behalf of the church

D. an individual's right to burn the American flag

14

Ed and Simon run a coffee shop. While both know how to make coffee and run the cash register, Ed makes better coffee and Simon is faster at the cash register. So, in their business, Ed only makes the coffee, and Simon only runs the cash register. This is an example of which economic concept?

A.   absolute advantage

B.   comparative advantage

C.   specialization

D.   interdependence

15

Who operated the system that sought to bring California's Native Peoples to the White European way of life?

A.   Franciscan priests

B.   Spanish officials

C.   wealthy Californios

D.   early conquistadors

16

How are interest groups and political parties similar in their contributions to American democracy?

A.   They centralize public authority.

B.   They articulate clear positions on issues.

C.   They influence members of Congress.

D.   They connect citizens to the government.

17

Which of the following is a principle of the pure market?

A.   government control of property

B.   self-interest and capitalism

C.   the real economic system

D.   government safety net

18

Which of the following presidential actions does not require the consent of the Senate or House?

A.   deploying troops

B.   appointing a federal judge

C.   appointing a cabinet member

D.   signing a treaty

19

A stationery store sells note cards for one dollar each and pens for three dollars each. When it raises the price of note cards to three dollars, sales plummet. Which of the following best explains this?

A.   The absolute price increased.

B.   The real price increased as a result of the substitution effect.

C.   The real price increased as a result of the income effect.

D.   The real price of pens decreased.

20

Which statement BEST describes the options Mexican citizens living in California had as described in the Treaty of Guadalupe Hidalgo?

A.   They could stay in California but could not become citizens.

B.   They had to relocate to territory that was still considered Mexico.

C.   They could stay in California and choose whether or not to become citizens.

D.   They could stay in California for one year but then had to return to what was still considered Mexico.

21

If appointed Secretary of State, a senator must resign from the Senate. What is this an example of?

A.   federalism

B.   judicial review

C.   term limits

D.   separation of powers

22

Which of the following statements is true about the equilibrium price?

A.   Buyers spend all of their money.

B.   Sellers sell all merchandise.

C.   Excess demand is less than excess supply.

D.   Quantity demanded equals quantity supplied.

23

What does it mean when the president vetoes a bill?

A.   The president is sending it back to the conference committee.

B.   The president is rejecting one part of the bill.

C.   The president is rejecting the whole bill.

D.   The president is declaring the bill unconstitutional.

24

Which of the following cannot shift a demand curve?

A.   changes in income

B.   price of related goods

C.   production costs

D.   consumer tastes

25

Which of the following was a result of the California Gold Rush?

A.   the founding of the Pony Express

B.   the construction of the transcontinental railroad

C.   widespread unemployment

D.   growing labor movements

26

After the president proposes the budget, where must it go next?

A.   to the cabinet

B.   to the Senate

C.   to the House of Representatives

D.   to the Department of the Treasury

27

If the price of razor blades increases, what will happen to the demand for shaving cream, a complementary good?

A.   Demand will increase.

B.   Demand will decrease.

C.   Demand will stay the same.

D.   Demand for shaving cream is unrelated to demand for razor blades.

28

What was the Supreme Court's decision in _Roe v. Wade_ based on?

A.   the equal protection clause of the Fourteenth Amendment

B.   the establishment clause of the First Amendment

C.   the right to privacy derived from the Fourth, Fifth, and Ninth Amendments

D.   the guarantee to due process of law in the Fifth and Sixth Amendments

29

Which of the following statements is true about a mixed economy?

A. The "invisible hand" of the market alone determines allocation.

B. Government departments determine decisions related to production.

C. The private sector and the free market work together to determine economic decisions.

D. Government and the market both solve economic problems.

30

What drew Dust Bowl migrants to California?

A. job vacancies in agriculture from repatriation policies

B. more modern farming practices

C. employment in ship and airplane manufacturing

D. fewer governmental restrictions on farming

31

What impact did the *Citizens United* case (which upheld the constitutionality of Super PACs) have on political parties?

A. It decreased their Influence.

B. It affected parties at the national level but not at the state level.

C. It solidified their role in American politics.

D. It did not affect them since it only applied to corporations and unions.

32

What is the primary difference between economic profit and accounting profit?

A. Land values are calculated at a higher value in accounting costs.

B. Accounting costs overestimate labor costs, whereas economics costs underestimate them.

C. Economic costs include more variable costs, whereas accounting costs consider more costs as fixed.

D. Economic costs include the opportunity cost of the owner's time, while accounting costs do not.

33

Constitutional amendments have been proposed to make abortion illegal, to ban same-sex marriage, and to prohibit flag burning. What can be deduced from these movements?

A. It is easy to amend the Constitution.

B. People sometimes disagree with Supreme Court decisions.

C. Some people believe that the Constitution is outdated.

D. Americans tend to avoid complicated social issues.

34

Several third parties have arisen in American history. Which of the following is a reason they are short-lived?

A.   They are guaranteed to lose.

B.   They often focus on a single issue and so did not have a broad enough appeal.

C.   They are legally prevented from participating in presidential elections.

D.   They aren't allowed to fundraise.

35

If the intersection point between aggregate demand and short run aggregate supply (SRAS) is at a lower output level than the long run aggregate supply (LRAS) curve, which of the following is true?

A.   A recessionary gap will occur.

B.   An inflationary gap will occur.

C.   The economy is functioning at full employment.

D.   The economy is under-utilizing all of its resources.

36

Where is most of the surface fresh water of California located?

A.   along the coast

B.   in the south

C.   in the north

D.   under the desert

37

Under which amendment are the activities of interest groups protected?

A.   First Amendment

B.   Fourth Amendment

C.   Sixth Amendment

D.   Ninth Amendment

38

What would the federal government have to do if it wants states to pass laws prohibiting guns in municipal parks?

A.   pass a federal law mandating it

B.   provide grant-in-aid for parks with the stated stipulation

C.   pass a constitutional amendment

D.   unable to do it

39

Price ceilings most directly affect the increase of _____, while price floors most directly affect the increase of _____.

A.   production, demand

B.   supply, demand

C.   demand, supply

D.   production, supply

CONSTRUCTED RESPONSE QUESTIONS

Civics

Civil society is often defined as the collective group of nongovernmental entities and organizations that seek to express the societal interests of public life as part of American democracy. Institutions that are part of civil society may promote various interests. In some cases, this reality has led to conflict because the interests promoted by civil society may not be in agreement with those of the broader public.

Using your knowledge of American democracy, analyze how civil society successfully advances the interests of broader American society, and analyze how civil society may work against some broader public interests in favor of the interests of individuals.

Economics

The American economic system operates with minimal governmental regulation, but this does not mean it is free of naturally regulating forces. The American market economy is often described in terms of neoclassical economic theory, which emphasizes the natural forces of supply and demand. Per subscribers to this theory, these two forces dictate much of what producers, consumers, and workers experience.

Using your knowledge of economics, analyze the forces of supply and demand and how they impact other facets of the economy, such as pricing, wages, and consumer demand.

California History

The Mexican-American War reflects a turning point in both the history of the United States and the history of California. Though the immediate cause of the war is often cited as the US's annexation of Texas and disputes with Mexico over borders, the roots of the conflict are far deeper.

Using your knowledge of California history, analyze one cause of the Mexican-American War beyond the annexation of Texas, and analyze one way that the Mexican-American War impacted the state of California.

Answer Key

SUBTEST I

1)

A Confucius taught others to respect authority—filial piety—and encouraged group harmony.

2)

B Muhammad was from Mecca, which is located in the Arabian Peninsula; Islam developed in Mecca, Medina, and that area (the Hijaz).

3)

C A core belief of Buddhism is that desire is the root of all suffering. Buddhists believe that nirvana, or a state of peace and joy, is achieved by transcending the ego.

4)

A Periphery countries are essentially less developed countries (LDCs), all of which can be found in Africa (with the exception of South Africa, parts of Asia, and parts of South America).

5)

D Bronze improved weapons and tools; improved weaponry meant expanded control over territory and more secure societies that could continue to develop.

6)

B Hominids like *Australopithecus* and later, *Homo habilis, Homo erectus,* and *Homo neanderthalensis* lived during the Paleolithic Era.

7)

D China and the Fertile Crescent civilizations, like the Sumerians, Assyrians, Babylonians, Egyptians, and Akkadians, had imperial or monarchical governments; they also developed written languages.

8)

B Serfs were bonded to the land—they had to work it for the lord—however, the lord was obligated to protect them.

9)

C Not all Crusaders returned home. European powers controlled some areas in the Levant, but only temporarily. There was a large increase in trade and cultural exchange. European monarchies remained strong.

10)

C Byzantine missionaries spread Orthodox Christianity north; Vladimir I converted and a tradition of Orthodox Christianity took root in Russia and Ukraine.

11)

D The Renaissance was inspired by science and technology imported from the Middle East during the Crusades, coupled with a resurgence of classical philosophy, art, and scholarship imported by Byzantine refugees.

12)

C This new law would push out any individuals who do not wish to practice Catholicism.

13)

A The peasants and bourgeoisie were dissatisfied with bearing the brunt of the heavy tax burden; meanwhile, poor harvests led to food shortages and panic in rural areas. These factors, along with Enlightenment thought and recent revolutions elsewhere, spurred the French Revolution.

14)

B The American Revolution preceded the French Revolution; resulting instability in France eventually led to the rise of Napoleon. Shifting European alliances triggered the First World War in the early twentieth century.

15)

C Mali became wealthy due to gold and salt, valuable natural resources.

16)

B The philosophy of taking on the "white man's burden" and the competition for global control of territory between European powers (among other factors) drove imperialism.

17)

C The 1884 Berlin Conference determined the division of Africa into colonies between the European imperial powers. This was done without regard for or consultation with Africans.

18)

C Given Japan's role as an Axis power and the conflict in East Asia, some historians believe that WWII began with Japan's invasion of Manchuria in 1931, earlier than Hitler's invasion of Poland in 1939.

19)

A Decolonization is the transition of power from a country in power to an independent colony.

20)

B   Afghanistan became unstable and entered into a period of civil war that ended only with the rise of the extremist Taliban, who brought stability to much of the country—along with an ideology embracing tribalism and extremely traditional Islamic values.

21)

A   Immediately following Partition, India and Pakistan were created. Pakistan was divided into two portions: East and West Pakistan.

22)

D   The Robinson map distorts all map characteristics in order to minimize overall distortion.

23)

C   Agricultural surplus and advanced transportation in high altitude terrain enabled the Inca military to range widely throughout the Andes.

24)

C   Under the Qin Dynasty, the emperor centralized Chinese bureaucracy and standardized weights and measures in order to centralize and consolidate imperial power.

25)

D   Enslaved people were forced to do work on cotton and sugar plantations; they did not run or own them independently. The transatlantic slave trade began long before industrialization.

26)

B   The Meiji Restoration was a period of industrialization and westernization in Japan.

27)

D   Improvements in navigation and shipping allowed speedier transport of goods from Asia to Europe.

28)

A   The Congress of Vienna followed the Napoleonic Wars; it was a meeting of European powers to determine how to manage Europe. American unification is unrelated. The French Revolution happened in 1789. Italy wanted unification.

29)

C   Augustus Caesar was the ruler during this time of stability.

30)

A   By the Neolithic Era, other hominids had died out.

31)

C   King Hammurabi's code meted out justice on an equal basis ("an eye for an eye, a tooth for a tooth").

32)

D   Charlemagne was Frankish and stabilized parts of Western and Central Europe; most of the Carolingian Empire eventually became France.

33)

A   The valuable routes into and through the Red Sea were essential for the British economy and Britain's connections to its colonies in India, East Africa, South Africa, and Australia. The security of those routes was of paramount importance.

34)

C   In 1961, a treaty was signed banning any individual claims on Antarctica and preserving it for scientific research. It is the only land in the world not claimed by a state.

35)

D   Sunnis believed that the Meccan elites should take over leadership of Muslims, while Shi'ites believed that Muhammad's cousin Ali was Muhammad's rightful successor.

36)

D   The Soviet establishment became increasingly alarmed at Maoist interpretations of communism, which differed from Marxism-Leninism.

37)

A   Papal endorsement of Charlemagne gave his rule legitimacy.

38)

C   Ivan the Great had weakened Mongol power in Northwest Asia, while the Ming had taken control of China from the Mongols.

39)

B   European powers controlled some areas in the Levant, but only temporarily.

WORLD HISTORY #1: SAMPLE RESPONSE

The Eastern Roman Empire was transformed into the Byzantine Empire, largely due to Justinian II's strong organization, rule of law, and successful military conquests. The strength and organization of the Greek Orthodox Church fostered intellectual development while Byzantine missionaries spread Christianity throughout the region. Scholarship and art in Greece and the Eastern Mediterranean were safeguarded from chaos as Western Europe became unstable and unsafe. Constantinople became a trading hub as international trade remained strong within the Mediterranean and into Asia thanks to relative political stability.

Christian Byzantium eventually fell into decline and became isolated from Anatolia as Damascus, the Levant, and eventually the whole of the Middle East and North Africa fell to Muslims from the Arabian Peninsula. Practitioners of Islam valued art, science, and scholarship. Arab-Islamic civilization boasted achievements in navigation, astronomy, medicine, and mathematics. European Crusaders returned to Western Europe with this knowledge, which later helped spark the Scientific Revolution in the sixteenth century. Christians in Constantinople, who had cooperated with the Catholic Church in Rome, began leaving Greece and Anatolia as Muslim

Ottomans gained power in Anatolia. When the Ottomans took Constantinople in 1453, the Byzantine Empire fully collapsed, and Christians fled westward, bringing ancient classical learning with them. Centuries after the collapse of the Roman Empire, the remnants of classical civilization enjoyed a resurgence. This Renaissance, which began in Italy, inspired a generation of artists and thinkers who developed new forms of human expression and scholarship.

This is a strong response because it cites the specific examples of the Byzantine Empire under Justinian II, the impact of the Greek Orthodox Church and Byzantine missionaries on scholarship and art, the contributions and stability of the Arab-Islamic caliphates, and the impact of the Crusades. It also cites the post-Ottoman migration of Byzantine Christians to Western Europe.

WORLD HISTORY #2: SAMPLE RESPONSE

Although they were victorious allies in the Second World War, the United States (US) and the Soviet Union (Union of Soviet Socialist Republics, or USSR) were not able to maintain a strong relationship for long. Despite losses of human life in the millions, the Soviet Union still had an enormous and powerful military. In violation of the agreements made at Yalta, Soviet leader Joseph Stalin occupied several Eastern European countries, preventing free elections. As a result, the US-led Western Hemisphere formed the North Atlantic Treaty Organization (NATO). In response, the USSR organized the Warsaw Pact.

The Soviet Union's Five-Year Plans of the 1920s sped up industrialization throughout the region. In the US, the New Deal and mobilization for the war strengthened its national economy. Both countries were rich in resources—developed substantially in heavy industry—and held strong, industrial militaries and advanced technological capabilities. By the end of the Second World War, the US had proven its weapons capacity by using the nuclear bomb. This technology, on the heels of its military domination of Europe and the Pacific, made it an undisputed global superpower. At the same time, the Soviet Union dominated land throughout Europe, Central, and East Asia, including vast mineral, petroleum, timber, and other natural resources. It, too, developed nuclear weapons and a military with a global reach. Furthermore, both countries extended their global reach diplomatically and militarily to spread their respective ideologies of communism (USSR) and democratic capitalism (US) in order to ensure global security.

By promulgating the Marshall Plan and supporting the establishment of the Bretton Woods Institutions (the World Bank and the International Monetary Fund), the US found ways to promote global capitalism. Meanwhile, the USSR supported Marxist independence and resistance movements in former colonies. Many Cold War battles were fought as proxy wars between the two superpowers in Africa, Asia, and Latin America. Each country had a global presence with bases, officers, diplomats, and military personnel in nearly every country in the world. As European empires collapsed in the wake of the Second World War, the Soviet Union and the United States dominated the global stage in ways no other countries could match.

This is a strong response because it specifically explains the rupture between the United States and the Soviet Union (the occupation of Eastern Europe). It provides specific examples of the industrial strength of both countries (New Deal and Five-Year Plans), as well as explanations of the tremendous military capacities of each country compared to those of the former global imperial powers of Europe. Both the US and USSR had an interest in spreading their respective economic and political philosophies, which are discussed here, along with specific institutions. Finally, specific instances of proxy wars and reasons for the global reach of each superpower are presented.

WORLD GEOGRAPHY: SAMPLE RESPONSE

Centrifugal forces are forces that tend to divide a nation-state, which may lead to its eventual failure. Centripetal forces, on the other hand, are forces that tend to keep a nation-state together.

Centrifugal forces are those that divide people. For example, regionalism, wherein people of a certain region feel an identity in opposition to that of others in the state, may lead to feelings of "otherness," which could eventually lead to separation. Beyond regional identity, people in a state may have different ethnicities, religions, and languages. These differences may serve as divisive forces if people begin to align themselves more with a subgroup within the state than with the broader nation. Poverty, totalitarianism, and lack of social justice may also be centrifugal forces as they cause people to lose confidence in their nation and possibly seek an alternative for governance.

Centripetal forces unite people and help prevent the dissolution of a nation. These forces include a shared history, ethnicity, religion, and language. However, other centripetal forces, like tolerance and acceptance of differences, can also work to hold a state together, even when there are multiple groups with distinct identities. Economic prosperity and economic opportunity for people of various social strata often serve as centripetal forces since people living in such conditions tend to feel more positively about their own futures as well as the future of their nation.

Nationalism, which is a sense of loyalty and devotion to a nation, can be either a centripetal force that holds disparate groups together, or a centrifugal force that excludes certain groups in the prevailing construct of national identity.

This is a strong response because it describes specific centrifugal forces, such as regionalism and different religions, ethnicities, and languages that may divide a nation. It also describes centripetal forces, like shared identity, acceptance of differences, and economic prosperity that may hold a nation together. The response also appropriately concedes that nationalism may be either a centrifugal or a centripetal force, depending on its degree of exclusion.

SUBTEST II

1)

D The Constitutional system of checks and balances is comprised of the three branches of government, which limit each other and thereby limit federal power.

2)

B The Second Great Awakening is characterized by religious movements like utopianism; interest in romanticism in the arts and humanism led to abolitionism and early progressive ideals.

3)

C The Monroe Doctrine was a US policy designed to insulate Latin America from European influence, increasing US dominance in the region.

4)

C Individual liberties were protected by state constitutions, and the central government was too weak to be any threat to them. The framers wanted to increase trade, not decrease it.

5)

B The Fugitive Slave Act—a federal law—actually benefitted those states' rights advocates who also favored slavery.

6)

C The Confederacy had excellent military leaders; many Confederate leaders and much of the population strongly believed in the right of states to make decisions without federal interference, not only about slavery but also about trade and other issues.

7)

B The ruling reinforced the Fugitive Slave Act by forcing Scott to return to a life of slavery.

8)

D The Reconstruction Acts effectively placed the South under martial law.

9)

C President Ulysses S. Grant ordered the government to retract a previous promise of leaving the territory alone in order to gain access to gold and oil.

10)

C   The Ten Percent Plan reunited the country by allowing states to rejoin the Union with only ten percent of their populations swearing allegiance to it.

11)

C   White settlers who were willing to farm land for at least two years in the West would be given that property for free by the US government.

12)

C   It was not until Theodore Roosevelt came into office that these acts were effectively used for their intended purpose: to create a fair market in the United States by eliminating trusts and monopolies.

13)

A   The Zimmerman Telegram, a German offer to assist Mexico in attacking the US, forced the United States to enter WWI, following a series of other German provocations.

14)

D   Through the separation of powers, checks and balances, specific prohibited powers, and the reserved powers of the state, limitations on the federal government are featured throughout the entire Constitution.

15)

D   The Strategic Arms Limitation Treaties (SALT I and SALT II) were reached during periods of diplomatic détente when productive dialogue between the Cold War powers was possible.

16)

B   In retaliation for its support for Israel, the Organization of Petroleum Exporting Countries (OPEC) placed an oil embargo on the United States. OPEC's embargo strongly harmed the US economy, which was very dependent on Middle Eastern oil at the time.

17)

C   The direct attack against the United States at Pearl Harbor in 1941 compelled the United States to enter WWII as a combatant.

18)

A   *Brown v. Board of Education* found that keeping races separate (in this case, in segregated schools) could not ensure that all people would receive equal treatment, and that segregation was therefore unconstitutional.

19)

D   The Voting Rights Act abolished discriminatory restrictions that prevented African Americans from exercising their right to vote.

20)

A   The Civil Rights Movement is considered a perfect example of nonviolent civil disobedience where those involved refused to comply with unjust laws.

21)

A   Iraq posed a threat to the biggest oil producers in the Persian Gulf; the United States needed to secure its energy interests there.

22)

C   Following the extreme tensions between the two countries, the United States and the Soviet Union improved dialogue in the early 1960s, leading to a period of détente.

23)

A   The United States outspent the Soviet Union in military and weapons, helping precipitate its fall. U.S. support for anti-Soviet fighters in Afghanistan also weakened the Soviet Union.

24)

D   Colonists were upset by what they perceived to be unfair taxes and restrictions on trade.

25)

A   By blocking the South's access to strategic waterways, the Union was able to prevent cotton exports and other vital trade, "strangling" the Confederacy economically.

26)

A   Roosevelt actually used the Interstate Commerce Act to carry out its original purpose: to break up trusts. By prosecuting the powerful Northern Securities railroad company, he became known as a "trust buster."

27)

A   The United States was the aggressor in the Spanish-American War—it was never definitively proven that the *Maine* was actually attacked by Spain. Furthermore, the war was fought in several different theaters worldwide.

28)

D   The Constitution and the government it created are based on these two concepts. Basing the nation on a governing document rather than on the authority of an individual supports the rule of law. The electoral system at almost every level supports consent of the governed.

29)

B   The United States helped ensure the defeat of Nazi Germany before defeating Japan.

30)

B   Including the Bill of Rights in the Constitution was a condition of ratification for several states.

Go on →

31)

D   The Patriot Act gave the federal government unprecedented surveillance powers over Americans within the United States.

32)

B   Same-sex marriage became legal in the United States in 2015 and the LGBTQ community is more accepted than ever before in many parts of the country.

33)

C   Lack of clarity over the status of prisoners at Guantanamo Bay and their treatment was—and remains—controversial.

34)

C   Temperance activists feared the negative impact of alcohol on poor and working-class families.

35)

C   The Framers recognized the benefits and drawbacks of a national government. They tried to mitigate federal power with checks and balances, the Bill of Rights, and ensuring the states hold certain

powers. The president is commander in chief of the military, but Congress has the power to declare war.

36)

A   The invasion and occupation of Iraq was part of the War on Terror and in accordance with President Bush's doctrine of preemption—that the US should preempt terrorist attacks by attacking threats first. Erroneous beliefs that Saddam Hussein had weapons of mass destruction and was linked to al Qaeda were reasons for the invasion.

37)

B   The Interstate Commerce Act specifically targeted railroads.

38)

D   Baron de Montesquieu wrote about the strength of the three-branch government, which inspired the framers to structure the government in the same way.

39)

A   Tecumseh, a Shawnee leader, united these tribes in the Northwest Confederacy.

US History #1: Sample Response

President George W. Bush responded to the September 11, 2001 (9/11), terrorist attacks with an ultimatum: the world is "either with us or you are with the terrorists." This statement was the precursor to the US approach of unilateralism. Under the Bush administration, the US withdrew from multilateral agreements, such as the Kyoto Protocol, and instituted a doctrine of preemption—the idea that the US should attack a country if it is confident that the country supported terrorism. Preemption was used to justify the 2003 invasion of Iraq, which was later proved to be based on faulty intelligence. This doctrine dominated US foreign policy following the 9/11 attacks and into the early twenty-first century. Bush's unilateral approach and aggressive foreign policy of preemption were reminiscent of the Truman doctrine. In the spirit of containing communism, the Truman doctrine asserted that the United States should prop up friendly governments worldwide through economic and military aid in order to stave off the communist threat. Domino theory postulated that if one country in a region "fell" to communism, others would soon follow. Domino theory, an extension of the Truman doctrine, pushed the US into both direct and proxy conflicts worldwide in an effort to halt communist movements. Both preemption and domino theory led the US into active military conflict overseas, including in Vietnam in the 1960s and 70s, and in Afghanistan and Iraq in the early 2000s. These foreign policies also encouraged ongoing conflicts overseas, such as in Afghanistan and Central America in the 1980s, and ongoing drone strikes in Pakistan and Yemen under the Bush and Obama administrations, fostering global US military engagement.

This is a strong response because it cites and explains specific US foreign policies, such as the Bush doctrine of preemption and the Bush administration's unilateral approach. It illustrates these philosophies with specific examples, including the invasion of Iraq and the US withdrawal from the Kyoto Protocol. The essay also reviews Cold War foreign policy, including the Truman doctrine, containment, and domino theory. It provides concrete examples of how those policies were put into action, citing the Vietnam War and military engagement in Central America and the Middle East.

US HISTORY #2: SAMPLE RESPONSE

The writer, abolitionist, activist, and formerly enslaved Frederick Douglass vehemently condemned slavery in the years preceding the Civil War. Indeed, the nineteenth century reflects division over the ethics and legality of slavery in the United States. Debate ensued over permitting the expansion of slavery as the US gained more territory. The Missouri Compromise of 1820 admitted Missouri as a slave state and Maine as a free state, in exchange for legislation that prohibited slavery for all western territories north of Missouri's southern border. However, pro-slavery activists continued to press for expansion of the practice and protection of the powers of enslavers.

The Compromise of 1850 was another attempt to resolve disputes over slavery in new territories added to the United States. California was admitted as a free state, while Utah and New Mexico were allowed to decide for themselves whether to be free or slave states. The Compromise of 1850 also strengthened the Fugitive Slave Act, which made federal marshals and other officials in any state responsible for capturing alleged escaped slaves and made it illegal for anyone to help an alleged fugitive slave.

Enslaved people were also denied the right for a jury trial and were not permitted to testify on their own behalf. In the case of *Dred Scott v. Sandford*, an enslaved man, Dred Scott, sued for his freedom on the grounds that his enslavers had held him in bondage for extended periods of time in a free territory before returning him to a slave state. His case made its way to the US Supreme Court, which ultimately decided that enslaved people were not citizens of the United States, and could therefore not expect any protection from the federal government or the courts.

The Kansas-Nebraska Act of 1854 repealed the Missouri Compromise by allowing states and territories to decide whether or not to make slavery legal by popular sovereignty. This permitted the expansion of slavery. Activists like Douglass who participated in the Underground Railroad, helping escaped slaves to safety in the north US and Canada, were at even more risk. Douglass would likely have considered this series of legislative compromises, federal acts, and judicial cases as part of the "hideous and revolting" conduct described in his speech above.

This is a strong response because it cites specific pieces of legislation (the Missouri Compromise, the Compromise of 1850, the Fugitive Slave Act, and the Kansas-Nebraska Act). It also explains the impact of each in historical context. Furthermore, it cites the Supreme Court case of *Dred Scott v. Sandford* in historical context. It invokes the Underground Railroad to bring social context and a personal perspective that Douglass may have had on the tumultuous period.

US Geography: Sample Response

Earth's physical features dictate what sort of economic activities people in a given region of the United States will most likely participate in. Fertile grasslands in the Midwest and rich valleys in California, for example, have led to the development of farms. Similarly, areas with access to rivers and seaports, like Houston, Texas, and Charleston, South Carolina, have lively shipping industries. Other regions that are rich in natural resources, such as the oil fields of Alaska and Oklahoma, have developed a thriving oil industry. The physical features present or absent in a given locale directly impact the industries that develop there.

Americans also experience differences in their daily lives based on their physical environments. For example, people living in coastal New England are more likely to eat seafood because of its accessibility. People in the desert region of the Southwest are far less likely to eat seafood because it will cost more since it is not available locally and must be shipped in.

Similarly, recreation varies in different regions of the United States. People who live in mountainous regions, like parts of Colorado or Utah, may enjoy snow skiing—an activity that is not possible in warmer regions, like Mississippi or Florida. People living near a lake or a beach may enjoy water recreation, a pastime largely not possible in landlocked regions.

Additionally, the physical landscape may impact the type of transportation available to people. For example, a subway system is possible in New

York City because of the integrity of the earth below. Such a system would be impossible in another region, such as Houston, where the earth is too moist to allow for subterranean tunnels.

This is a strong response because it describes the specific interconnections between the physical environment and life in certain regions of the United States. Examples include different types of economic development based on landforms and access to waterways, different foods people eat, different recreational activities people participate in, and different transportation systems people are able to access.

SUBTEST III

1)

A   The interpretation of different aspects of the Constitution has changed over time without significant changes to the document. For example, the equal protection clause was first used to establish the precedent of "separate but equal" in *Plessy v. Ferguson,* and then later to declare it unconstitutional in *Brown v. Board of Education.*

2)

A   Long-run aggregate supply (LRAS) indicates what the supply would be at full employment.

3)

B   While equality of opportunity is an important ideal, Americans do not in general believe that everyone has a right to the same economic success. Limited government and equality under the law are ideals. Everyone is granted natural, inalienable rights.

4)

D   The Federal Reserve's job is to stabilize prices in order to prevent inflation and keep the economy strong.

5)

D   The Sierra Nevada mountain range had to be blasted through with dynamite; Chinese Californians did much of this dangerous work.

6)

A   Media coverage tends to focus on candidates' personalities and the mistakes they make, emphasizing both the positive and negative attributes of a candidate. The media rarely looks at party platforms separately from the candidates; if they did, the result would be more issues-based campaigns.

7)

A   Increasing taxes requires people to send more of their money to the government, thereby taking it out of circulation and decreasing the money supply.

8)

A   Inherent powers are powers a government has by nature of being a sovereign state. For example, the power to defend the border is an inherent power.

9)

B The law of diminishing marginal utility states that the utility one receives from an acquisition decreases with each additional unit of the product, like a sixth shirt.

10)

D Native American groups in California adapted to the resources in the surrounding environment and used them to build homes, find food, and make tools.

11)

C Powers that are not listed but are necessary for the functioning of the government are called implied powers. They are made possible by the elastic clause.

12)

A This nation has maximized its production (because it is on the production possibility frontier); however, it has not allocated its resources to best benefit the people.

13)

A The free exercise clause is one of two clauses addressing freedom of religion. It provides all individuals with the right to practice their religion however they choose, as long as it does not violate preexisting, neutral laws.

14)

C Because of their respective comparative advantages, Ed and Simon each specialize in one area of the business to increase overall efficiency.

15)

A The mission system, operated by Franciscan priests, sought not only to convert Native Peoples to Catholicism but also bring them to the Spanish European way of life.

16)

D By connecting people to the government, interest groups and political parties give the people a greater voice and make the government more accountable to the people.

17)

B The principle of the pure market is an ideal, but it is not a real economic system. Market theory states that the market self-corrects, tending toward equilibrium. In this case, any government interaction acts only to impede the functioning of the market.

18)

A As commander in chief, the president may send troops without consulting Congress. Under the War Powers Act of 1973, though, the president must inform Congress within seventy-two hours and may only commit them for sixty days without a formal declaration of war.

19)

B Before the price increase, one note card was worth one-third of a pen. Now, a note card is worth one whole pen. In this way, the increase in price is understood in relation to the value of the pen.

20)

D Mexican nationals living in what was once Mexico that then became part of the United States territory could return to what was still Mexico or stay in California. If they stayed, they had one year to decide whether or not to become American citizens.

21)

D An official cannot serve in two branches of government at once; in order to prevent the concentration of power in any one branch, the framers assigned different powers to different individuals and groups.

22)

D A market is considered to be in equilibrium when it is at the price where quantity demanded and quantity supplied are equal.

23)

C A veto is a formal rejection of a bill by the president. The only way for a vetoed bill to become a law is through a two-thirds vote in both houses of Congress.

24)

C Production costs can impact the supply curve but not the demand curve.

25)

A The Pony Express was developed to carry mail and packages from California to the Midwest. It was needed because of the larger number of people living in California due to the Gold Rush.

26)

C Financial matters must begin deliberation in the House of Representatives.

27)

B If the price of razor blades increases, the demand for razor blades will decrease. Because shaving cream is a complementary good, the demand for each product is linked. As a result, the demand for shaving cream will decrease as well.

28)

C *Roe v. Wade* addressed a woman's right to an abortion. The Supreme Court ruled that a woman's body was a zone of privacy free from government interference.

29)

D A mixed economy utilizes both market forces and government intervention to ensure the economy benefits the greatest number of people.

30)

A Repatriation policies to remove Mexican and Filipino nationals left vacancies in agriculture.

31)

A Because individuals and private groups may now raise and contribute unlimited funds to candidates and campaigns, political parties are no longer the primary source of campaign funds. Thus, their support is less important for candidates; furthermore, parties have less control over policy.

32)

D Economic profit considers time lost as a legitimate cost of doing business, whereas accounting profit calculations only use explicit calculations.

33)

B Each of these amendments was proposed either after a Supreme Court decision or in anticipation of one. For example, in 1973 the Supreme Court determined in *Roe v. Wade* that abortions are legal. Now, the only way to change that would be through a new decision or constitutional amendment.

34)

B While it is more challenging for third parties to participate in presidential elections, they have never been legally prohibited from doing so; in fact, several third-party candidates have run for president. Third parties may fundraise; however, they often do not appeal to a broad range of Americans, so they generally cannot compete financially with bigger parties.

35)

A The long-run aggregate supply (LRAS) assumes full employment. If the intersection point is at a lower output level, then the economy is functioning at less than full employment, leading to a recession.

36)

C Most of California's surface fresh water is located in the north, which presents a problem because most of the population is in the southern half of the state.

37)

A Lobbying performed by interest groups is protected by both the freedom to petition and the freedom of speech. Both of these are protected in the First Amendment.

38)

B Grant-in-aid is money designated for a specific purpose. It is used by the federal government to control how money is used and to influence policy at the state level.

39)

B Because supply increases as price increases, price ceilings limit how high supply can increase. Demand increases as price decreases; therefore, price floors limit the rise of demand.

Civics: Sample Response

Civil society advances the interests of all Americans when its institutions advocate for the broader public good. For example, many nonprofit organizations are aimed at driving awareness of environmental degradation and action to combat it. Such organizations, like the Sierra Club or the Environmental Defense Fund, advance the interests of all of American society because the quality of the environment, and the benefits of cleaner air and water, can be experienced by all Americans. Advocacy on behalf of the environment is a way that civil society can manage finite resources for the common good, which is an important role that civil society plays in the fabric of America.

On the other hand, not all elements operating within the broader construct of civil society advance the interests of all Americans. Some advocacy groups are formed to protect the interests of some Americans at the expense of others, and promote resource management that benefits only certain individuals. For example, an advocacy group representing the interests of the oil industry, such as the Independent Petroleum Association of America, may promote policies that are an irresponsible use of resources. Its goal is to serve the interests of its individual members—not the interests of society at large. This type of group may work *against* the nonprofit environmental organizations previously mentioned. In this example, the interests of the individuals—to make as much profit as possible—may be in direct conflict with the interests of the broader societal good, which is responsible resource management to protect the environment.

This is a strong response because it includes a specific example of how civil society may work for the broader public good in advocating for a better environment to benefit all Americans. It is also used to explain how certain subsets of civil society may advocate solely for the interests of its members and not the broader environmental and public good.

Economics: Sample Response

Supply and demand are critical components of the market economy of the United States. *Supply* refers to how much of a good is available; *demand* refers to how much consumer demand there is for a product. Typically, the higher the price, the less consumers will demand the good. Inversely, the lower the price, the more consumers will want to buy. However, the higher the price of the good, the more it will be produced because the producer is motivated by potential profit.

Generally, these forces operate until there is equilibrium and prices stabilize. For example, a new product is introduced that is reasonably priced and useful to consumers. Consumers buy a lot of the product, which creates a shortage. The producer of that product will raise the price due to scarcity and will increase production to supply the market. An increase in price then lowers the demand consumers have for the product. It is only when the forces of supply and demand intersect that prices stabilize because the supply and demand are roughly equal.

Supply and demand also impact wages, though in this case, *supply* refers to the availability of workers in a given field and *demand* refers to the need for their labor. As certain fields or industries begin to require more workers (often as demand for the company's product or service increases) and there are few workers with the required expertise and training, wages will often increase. Similarly, as demand for workers decreases, due to a large, available labor pool and limited need, wages will often decrease. Just as the forces of supply and demand impact the prices of consumer goods, they also impact workers' wages.

This is a strong response because it shows the clear connection between supply and demand and how these impact prices and consumer demand. It also analyzes the forces of supply and demand on the labor force and explains the way these forces set wages.

California History: Sample Response

The United States annexed Texas in 1845, which set off an armed conflict that would come to be known as the Mexican-American War. However, this conflict has deeper roots. One of these underlying causes was the cultural belief of the US in its Manifest Destiny. The idea of Manifest Destiny was rooted in the notion that God himself desired the US to expand its scope and spread its democratic ideals throughout the continent. Because this doctrine appealed to American patriotism and highlighted beliefs about the uniqueness and exceptionalism of American political institutions and the American way of life, it united many citizens against Mexico. At one point, then-President James K. Polk actively attempted to purchase California and New Mexico from Mexico. Mexico refused and strengthened its stance against Americans. Ultimately, Polk and the US Congress declared war in response to battles between Mexican and American troops in Texas and Mexico.

The war significantly impacted California as American settlers in the region were already unhappy. Mexico had issued a proclamation that unnaturalized foreigners were no longer permitted to have land in California. In summer of 1846, a group of settlers staged the Bear Flag Revolt by declaring independence from Mexico and establishing a short-lived republic. The settlers were met by US troops, who were in the region as part of American operations in the Mexican-American War, and readily ceded to the US government. Thus, the war sealed the fate of California as settlers there allied themselves with the United States. This laid the groundwork for the Treaty of Guadalupe Hidalgo in 1848, which ended the war and gave ownership of California to the United States.

This is a strong response because it cites Manifest Destiny as one specific cause of the outbreak of the Mexican-American War. It describes how this belief was held not only by the American populace but by American President James K. Polk. It also explains that the Mexican-American War impacted the California independence movement by changing its course when American settlers in California allied themselves with the US in the conflict.